LITTLE BRAZIL

LITTLE BRAZIL

An Ethnography
of Brazilian
Immigrants in
New York City

Maxine L. Margolis

PRINCETON UNIVERSITY PRESS

PRINCETON, NEW JERSEY

Library of Congress Cataloging-in-Publication Data

Margolis, Maxine L., 1942–
Little Brazil : an ethnography of Brazilian immigrants
in New York City / Maxine L. Margolis.
p.   cm.
Includes bibliographical references and index.
ISBN 0–691–03348–X (cl.)
ISBN 0–691–00056–5 (pbk.)
1. Brazilian Americans—New York (N.Y.)—Social life and
customs.   2. New York (N.Y.)—Social life and customs.
I. Title.
F128.9.B68M37   1993
974.7′1004698—dc20   93–13699   CIP

This book has been composed in Adobe Sabon

Printed in the United States of America

10 9 8 7 6 5 4 3 2 1

10 9 8 7 6 5 4 3 2 1
(Pbk.)

IN MEMORY OF CHARLES WAGLEY

Student of Brazilian culture,

mentor extraordinaire,

and dear friend

Não saiam do Brasil, fiquem aqui, me ajudem.

Don't leave Brazil, stay here and help me.

—FERNANDO COLLOR DE MELLO,

in a televised address three days before being sworn in

as President of Brazil, March 1990

CONTENTS

■ ILLUSTRATIONS

Maps

Photographs

▌ TABLES

Migration has a dual economic function: from the standpoint of capital,
it is the means to fulfill labor demand at different points of the system; from
the standpoint of labor, it is the means to take advantage of opportunities
distributed unequally in space.

—ALEJANDRO PORTES AND ROBERT BACH, *Latin Journey*

BRAZILIAN immigration to New York City and elsewhere abroad is not
an isolated phenomenon. It is part of a global process in which emigrants
from newly industrializing and less industrialized nations become
"strangers at the gate"[1] of the industrialized countries, seeking employment. With the globalization of international migration, Poles, Czechs,
Albanians, and other Eastern Europeans are joining Turks and North
Africans in the trek to Western Europe. Brazilians and Peruvians of Japanese descent are flocking to the land of their ancestors for jobs. Citizens
of nearly every nation in South and Central America and the Caribbean
are heading for the United States in search of work. There they encounter
thousands more from India, Pakistan, Nigeria, Senegal, the Philippines,
China, Korea, and coming full circle, Eastern Europe, all travelers pursuing a bit of the American economic dream.

The traditional "push-pull" explanations of international migration
have proved inadequate in accounting for a worldwide phenomenon of
such magnitude. Push-pull theorists assert that the catalyst for international migration is the imbalance in labor supply and labor demand in
migrant-sending and migrant-receiving countries. But they tend to ignore
macrostructural factors that enmesh these global movements, such as rising expectations in sending countries brought on by increased levels of
education and media exposure to consumer patterns in advanced industrial states. Such macrostructural factors help explain why, as in the case
of Brazil, international migrants are not generally from the most impoverished countries or from the poorest sections of sending nations, as push-
pull theories would predict.

Proponents of push-pull scenarios for international migration generally emphasize individualistic responses, while structural analysts look to
macroeconomic trade and investment flows between countries. To be

sure, these approaches are not mutually exclusive, and both are useful, albeit at different levels of analysis. Structural factors shed light on the direction of large-scale migratory flows between nations and between different parts of the world, while push-pull factors and social network analyses are useful in explaining which individuals actually migrate, the distance they travel, and their specific destinations.

The movement of peoples from newly industrializing to industrialized states is in part fomented by what Alejandro Portes and Robert Bach call an "invidious comparison between [industrialized countries'] lifestyles and consumption patterns and those of sending countries."[2] But more significant yet is the safety valve feature of international migration: its role in diffusing extremely difficult internal problems of migrant-sending nations. For example, capital-intensive industrial and agricultural development have created labor surpluses in many Latin American and other newly industrializing economies. These labor surpluses and structural adjustment measures—currency devaluation, for example, and cuts in government services—spur migration from these countries because they increase unemployment and depress wages and living standards, including those of the middle class.

Contrary to the stereotype of international migrants as people driven from their homes by poverty and despair, in recent years middle-class migrants from the industrializing world also have become major players in these global movements. One reason is that international migration helps ameliorate the problem of the "overqualified" in many sending nations. This problem arises when large numbers of professionals are trained and educated, but although their skills may be sorely needed at home, insufficent jobs are available in their fields at wages they deem adequate compensation for their many years of schooling. Brazil, once again, is an apt example. Given the realities of the labor markets in many developing nations, higher education and professional training have led to shattered expectations for social mobility. International migration takes some of the heat off the problem by siphoning off many of the disgruntled over-qualified.

But the global movement of these migrants—we might call them the educated surplus—serves another purpose as well. Granted the low wages and underemployment that plague many newly industrializing nations, the remittance money that migrants send home from their jobs abroad helps subsidize the lifestyle of the middle class back home. Moreover, through the buttress of overseas migrants' remittances, the state is relieved of some of the political pressure that it would inevitably face from a populace dissatisfied with low wages and limited economic opportunities. Just how important remittances are to the economies of some industrializing nations is evident from the figures for the Dominican Republic. An estimated $300 to $600 million a year is sent there by Dominican migrants living in New York City, a sum that makes remittances the country's second largest industry.[3]

International migration, however, is always a two-way street, and however much the powers that be in industrial countries loudly protest the waves of immigrants flooding their shores, their complaints serve to obfuscate an underlying reality: receiving nations also stand to benefit from these global currents.[4] The industrial states, the primary destination of international migrant flows, are, after all, in the enviable position of having a nearly limitless supply of inexpensive labor clamoring at their gates. And in recent years advanced industrial countries such as the United States have been attracting skilled, highly motivated immigrants for even the most menial jobs. Moreover, through legislation and selective enforcement of immigration law, the state can not only create a profitable supply of cheap but powerless labor, but can partially regulate who passes through its portals.

These global voyagers are valuable to industrialized nations not only because of the relatively low cost of their labor but because of the temporary nature of their migration. At least initially, most international migrants view their stay in the host country as transitory. And it is this ready-made impermanence that meshes so neatly with the kinds of jobs that migrants fill. International migrants are overwhelmingly employed in the secondary sector of the labor market of industrialized nations, a market niche characterized by jobs with low wages, no job security, few or no benefits, low prestige, and little or no opportunity for advancement. Moreover, because of the low pay and other disadvantages of secondary sector jobs, finding native-born workers to fill them can be a problem. Enter international migrants, a fortuitous solution to this knotty labor dilemma. Seeing themselves as "here today and gone tomorrow," global migrants are less disheartened by the lack of career prospects and other drawbacks of the secondary job market.

The benefit of transnational migration to the industrialized world is substantial: it channels in a mass of low-cost, often well educated workers, who are willing, even eager, to take a variety of jobs that otherwise might go unfilled.[5] And at the same time, it relieves some of the economic and political pressures that might otherwise threaten the stability of numerous newly industrializing nations. It is well to keep these global issues in mind when looking at particular migrant flows to particular countries.

• • •

By the year 2000, New York will be one of only six metropolitan areas in the world with populations of 15 million or more.[6] New York's population is not only large but extraordinarily diverse. It is, after all, the quintessential city of immigrants, a complex ethnic mélange, whose precise components are duplicated nowhere else in the world. Especially within the last two decades, the streets of New York have been transformed by the sights, sounds, and smells of myriad newcomers. In Queens neighborhoods, Indian women in brightly colored saris push strollers past Arab butcher shops featuring mysterious cuts of meat. The recesses of upper Manhattan throb with the salsa of the large Dominican community that lives there, and parts of Brooklyn are redolent with spicy barbecued goat from Jamaican take-outs. Even the Bronx has its exotic newcomers: Albanians fleeing the political turmoil in their homeland.

Now a new ingredient has been added to this kaleidoscopic ethnic mix: Brazilians. The growing presence of Brazilians in New York City first became apparent to me sometime during the mid-1980s. A word about my own background by way of explanation: I am a native Manhattanite, an inveterate New Yorker—despite having taught at the University of Florida for over two decades—and an anthropologist who speaks Portuguese and specializes in Brazilian culture. During periodic visits to the city—for what I call my "New York fix"—I began noticing that more and more people on Manhattan streets were speaking Portuguese. I heard it not only in the midtown areas usually frequented by tourists, but also on city subways—a form of transportation that non–English speaking tourists generally avoid.

To be sure, there has always been a small Brazilian community in New York City. Composed of people who work for Brazilian companies, banks, airlines, and government agencies, plus a smattering of expatriate artists, writers, students, and Brazilian tourists, it is centered around Little Brazil. Little Brazil, or Brazil Street, as it is sometimes called, is a block-long stretch of West 46th Street between Fifth Avenue and the Avenue of the Americas, in the heart of midtown Manhattan. A distinctly Brazilian clustering of restaurants, travel agencies, and stores that cater to Brazilian residents and tourists alike has been present on West 46th Street at least since the late 1960s, when I used to frequent a restaurant there to eat *feijoada*, the Brazilian national dish, with my friends, fellow "Brazilianist" graduate students at Columbia University.

While the soft nasal sounds of Brazilian Portuguese were long familiar on West 46th Street, by the mid-1980s, I slowly began to realize that the location and scale of the Brazilian presence in the city was of a different order than it had been in the past. A chance conversation then became the final catalyst that inspired my research on New York's Brazilians and led to this book. During one of my trips to New York, I saw a cousin of mine who lives in Boston. Knowing of my interest in Brazil, she mentioned that she was very pleased with the Brazilian woman she had just hired as a housekeeper. "*A Brazilian,?*" I asked. *Was she certain that she was Bra-*

zilian? Despite my long acquaintance with Brazil and Brazilians, I had never heard of Brazilians' being employed as domestic servants in the United States. "Yes," she replied, "a lot of my friends employ Brazilian women as maids and nannies." Now, I thought, I must be on to something.

When I returned to Gainesville, I went through the holdings of the University of Florida library, with its extensive Latin American collection, to see if anything had been published on Brazilians anywhere in the United States. I came up dry.[7] As it turned out, despite the growing number of Brazilians in New York City—and elsewhere in this country—no research had been done on this newest addition to the city's "gorgeous mosaic," as New York Mayor David Dinkins calls it. Despite the plethora of studies on many recent immigrant groups, there are none on Brazilians. Yet there are entire monographs on far smaller immigrant communities in the city—Yemenis, for example—not to mention extensive research on other newcomers, including Koreans, Israelis, Indians, Chinese, Haitians, Peruvians, Dominicans, and Jamaicans.[8] At this point I decided to fill in the Brazilian lacuna.

Over time, this turned into more than simply a "need to know" book, one written for the sole purpose of recounting the experiences of an ethnic group that had not been studied before. Early in my research, I discovered that a significant proportion of Brazilian immigrants in New York City were undocumented aliens, that they were, in the parlance of U.S. immigration authorities, "visa overstayers," who had come to this country on tourist visas, taken jobs, and then stayed on after their visas had expired. Thus, while this is a study of Brazilian immigrants, it is also an ethnographic account of an undocumented immigration stream. I gathered data on visa acquisition and use, entry into the United States through different routes, and personal accounts of the trials and tribulations of living "out of status." But *nothing* in the pages that follow is unique to Brazilians. Nothing that Brazilians do to obtain tourist visas, green cards, or any other document that allows entry to or residence in the United States is associated only with Brazilians, nor are the machinations involved in qualifying for amnesty or other means of regularizing their status. Brazilians merely serve as vivid illustrations of undocumented immigrants, as surrogates for myriad other immigrant groups with powerful economic motives for living in this country despite their problematic status.

This is also a story that belies the American stereotype of the "illegal alien" as a young, uneducated male whose home is an impoverished village in rural Mexico. Almost from the moment I began my research, I knew that Brazilian immigrants in New York City bore little resemblance to this archetypical illegal. They were middle and lower-middle class, and many had university educations. Hence this also became a tale of a new kind of immigrant, of an immigrant who was not escaping extreme poverty or political repression. Brazilians are economic refuges fleeing from a chaotic economy back home. They view themselves as sojourners in this country, as temporary visitors here to work for a sliver of the American economic pie to take back with them to Brazil.

How the Study Was Done

The research on which this book is based was carried out in two phases. During the first phase, a nine-week period spread over the summers of 1988 and 1989, I informally surveyed and conducted open-ended interviews with fifty-three Brazilians, including both recent immigrants and long-term residents of New York City. Among them were such presumably "well-informed informants" as Brazilian consular officers, the editor of the local Brazilian newspaper, and the owners of stores, restaurants, travel and remittance agencies, and other businesses frequented by Brazilians.

The second phase of the research, also done in New York City, lasted from January 1990 to January 1991, while I was on sabbatical leave from the University of Florida. Part of my time was devoted to locating informants and filling out one hundred questionaires on a sample of them. The questionaires covered most aspects of Brazilian immigrant life, from the decision to come to New York, entry, and settlement, to subsequent experiences working and living in the city. There were also questions on who the immigrants are, not just their vital statistics, but their social and educational backgrounds and their prior work histories.

Choosing the subjects presented a major methodological problem because, for obvious reasons, it is notoriously difficult to estimate the size of populations that are partly composed of undocumented individuals. This is certainly true of Brazilians. Because many Brazilians are undocumented, there are no reliable data on the total number of Brazilians residing in New York City or on their residential distribution in the metropolitan area. As a result, there is no sampling frame for selecting individuals from this population, making a random sample of Brazilian immigrants in New York virtually impossible to obtain. Instead, snowball sampling, a nonrandom sampling technique, was used because it is a well-recognized means of contacting "hidden" populations, such as undocumented immigrants.[9] The drawback of snowball sampling is that the data gathered cannot be generalized beyond the sample at hand. In other words, the statistical data presented in this book should be seen only as a useful guideline because the sample on which they are based was not drawn randomly. However, with these caveats in mind, this means of sampling can be very credible when combined with qualitative ethnographic techniques.

Snowball sampling uses informants' own networks of friends and relatives in creating a sample. I used it as follows. After making initial contacts with a few informants through the monthly Brazilian newspaper published in New York City, I asked each informer for the names of one or two other Brazilians who might agree to be interviewed. These, in turn, were asked for additional names; the process continued, and a network of informants was created.

Aside from the subjects of the questionaires, I talked informally to dozens and dozens of other Brazilians—over 250 in all—while doing what anthropologists call participant observation. During both phases of the research, I visited peoples' homes and attended musical and sporting events. I went to church services and street fairs, and spent time at stores, restaurants, and nightclubs frequented by Brazilians. In short, I tried to immerse myself within the life of the city's Brazilian community.

During the summer of 1990, I visited Brazil. Over a three-week period, I interviewed officials of the U.S. consulate in Rio de Janeiro, as well as a handful of returned migrants. I then traveled to the city of Governador Valadares in Minas Gerais state, a major exporter of *brazucas*, as Brazilians living in the United States are called. There, I talked to a few dozen people—local officials, travel agents, families with relatives in the United States—and collected information on the history and impact of the emigrant flow. Insights and data from my stay in Brazil appear throughout this volume.

This, then, is an ethnographic rather than a sociological account of a new immigrant stream. I have not sought to present an insentient statistical portrait of the Brazilian immigrant population writ large. Rather, my account paints with fine brush strokes what it is like to be a recent immigrant to this most cosmopolitan of cities.

Brief sketches of some of the Brazilian immigrants whom I met or accounts of their experiences are interspersed with the text as vignettes to enliven impersonal descriptions of arrival and settlement in New York, employment, leisure, immigrant institutions, and so on. This very abbreviated life story approach is based on narratives given to me by informants, and I have used them because I believe that personal accounts of this sort lend a synthetic power to the narrative.[10] But a caveat is in order: these vignettes are used to illustrate the experiences of particular individuals, and they are not meant to be typical of the experience of all or even most Brazilian immigrants in New York City.

Another important point about this research is that the primary focus of the study is the immigrant segment of the Brazilian population in New York City. As such, it treats only tangentially the employees of large

Brazilian companies—whether temporary or permanent—and the diplomats and personnel of the Brazilian consulate and Brazilian mission to the
United Nations. I am interested in this latter nonimmigrant sector of the
Brazilian community in New York City only as it affects or interacts with
the main focus of the work: recent Brazilian immigrants.

Finally, I want to make it clear what this study is and is not about. As
previously noted, since the parameters of the Brazilian population cannot
be specified, my research is partly based on a nonrandom sample of Brazilians in New York City. I have tried not to—and I caution the reader not
to—overgeneralize the results. While I believe that the portrait I paint of
the Brazilian community in the city is an accurate one, it is a case study of
a specific migration flow, and its findings say nothing about the Brazilian
communities of White Plains, New York, Newark, New Jersey, Boston,
Danbury, Connecticut, Washington, D.C., Miami, San Francisco, or any
other place in the United States that has a sizable Brazilian population.
Simply put, this is a study of Brazilians in New York City, not a study of
Brazilian immigration to the United States.

● ● ●

Many Brazilians made this research relatively easy, and they certainly
made it pleasant. They were extraordinarily accessible despite the undocumented status of so many and the fear and suspicion that that status
necessarily entails. Over twenty months, I had contact with well over 250
Brazilians, of whom only two refused to cooperate in my research. I
thank all of the members of New York City's Brazilian community for
their help and kindness. I hope I can repay them by painting a sympathetic portrait of their lives in the Big Apple.

I want to single out specific individuals for special mention. Claudia
Ehrlich, my research assistant, a Brazilian and student of anthropology,
was an excellent sounding board and faithful companion. I am also
deeply grateful to Francisco Rego, a remarkably insightful informant,
whose own experiences as an immigrant and observations about his
compatriots have contributed immeasurably to this book. And there are
many others: Marcelo Viana, whose youthful political exuberance was so
dear; Edilberto Mendes, managing editor of *The Brasilians*, José Afonso
Fonseca, Roberto de Azevedo, Maria Luisa Penna Moreira, Luis Guerra,
and Margaret Kowarick for initial contacts; and Marcia Cassab and
Edna Mendes da Silva for entree into their set. Other members of the
Brazilian community who will recognize their contribution to this work
are Wilson Loria, Flor da Silva, Vera Gonçalves, Miriam Aquino, Carlos
de Paula, Moises Apsan, Lucas Mendes, Luis Azenha, Debora Dines,
Tony Noqueira, Maria Duha, Claudio Gomes, Alda Silva, Iliana, Cleria
Marques, Vera Azenha, Dr. Jesus Cheda, Clelia Morais, Laudicea dos

Santos, Isabel Bravim, Anna Oliveira, Elena Hungria, Paula Alves, Irene Simone, Marie Gobbi, Maria Costa, Marilia Andrade, Jussara Alves, Norma Guimarães, Elzi Oliveira, Gutemberg Ribeiro, Nilo Lelis, Cid Keller, and officers and personnel of the Brazilian consulate in New York.

In Brazil a number of officers of the U.S. consulate in Rio de Janeiro were informative. I particularly thank Myca and Oswaldo Coelho for their kind hospitality in Governador Valadares. I am also indebted to Duncan Lindsey, Robert Meyers, Iris Szimintzy, Harvey Summ, James Halmo, Ray Jones, and Lambros Comitas. I thank Linda Showalter for providing me with census data, Charles Wood for his helpful bibliographic suggestions, Diana Brown for her thoughtful reading of parts of this manuscript and invaluable suggestions for improving it, Conrad P. Kottak and Roberto DaMatta for their useful critiques, and the University of Florida for my combined research leave and sabbatical. And last but certainly not least, I thank my husband, Jerry Milanich, for extra-loving care and upkeep, and my daughter, Nara Milanich, who is beginning to love Brazil as much as I do. And to all my dear Brazilian friends in New York City whom, I devoutly hope, will no longer be invisible.

LITTLE BRAZIL

CHAPTER ONE

The New Voyagers

American history prepares us for exploration, strangers, and alienation. The same is true of the British and French who became world explorers and later anthropologists in their empires' most distant territories. Nor, apparently, were the early Portuguese explorers, leaders during the age of discovery, reluctant to travel abroad. Sometime between Brazil's settlement and today, that mentality of exploration has disappeared.

—CONRAD P. KOTTAK, *Prime Time Society*

Não mude do Brasil, ajude mudar o Brasil.

Don't abandon Brazil, help Brazil change.

—*Slogan from the Brazilian government's campaign against emigration*

THESE QUOTES reflect two Brazilian realities. To people knowledgeable about Brazil, the word "migration" immediately brings to mind impoverished peasants fleeing from the country's arid northeast after one of the region's periodic droughts. Carrying their few possessions and searching for a better life, they board the crowded, open-air trucks dubbed "parrots' perches" and head to Brazil's industrial south. But today the word has taken on a new meaning. Over the last decade, as economic conditions in Brazil have deteriorated, many thousands of Brazilians have left their country and migrated abroad. This is an entirely new phenomenon and one that is out of character with Brazilian history and with the Brazilian ethos. "Emigration," as the noted historian of Brazil, Thomas Skidmore, has remarked, "is a bad sign because Brazilians are famous for their optimism about the country. Even during the military regime, people who went into exile came back as soon as they could. Optimism is in short supply in Brazil."[1]

Stories of the exodus fill the pages of Brazilian newspapers and magazines. *Folha de São Paulo* reported that in early 1989, 2,000 Japanese-Brazilians a month were leaving for Japan, including many who worked at the Japanese consulate in São Paulo. In January and February 1990, 700 Brazilians of Spanish descent sought citizenship papers at the Spanish consulate in São Paulo—up from only 90 requests for all of 1989. That city's Italian consulate was similarly besieged and was issuing an average of 550 passports a month to Brazilians whose ancestors had come from Italy. *Veja*, a Brazilian news weekly akin to *Time*, has had two cover stories about Brazilians departing for Toronto, Lisbon, Paris, London, Rome, Sydney, and a number of U.S. cities. And according to government data, between 1986 and 1990 about 1.4 million Brazilians left the country and never returned.[2]

Awareness of the flight from Brazil does not depend on the news media. In inimitable Brazilian fashion, jokes about the exodus make the rounds: "There's an easy way out of Brazil's economic and social crisis," goes one, "the airport." And many people in the large cities of southern Brazil—Belo Horizonte, Rio de Janeiro, São Paulo—personally know someone who has left. During the first two or three days I was in Rio in July 1990, I met three such people: the director of a language school, who told me about a friend's son, who is working in the United States and who just received his green card; a taxicab driver, whose daughter went to Washington, D.C., as an "adventure," worked as a live-in nursemaid, and is now married to an American; and an employee of an art gallery, who had lived and worked in New York City a year or two earlier. The other side of the coin is the growing presence of Brazilians in many U.S. cities.

When Did It All Begin?

There are no dependable data on Brazilian immigration to New York City, so I have necessarily relied on "well-informed informants," particularly longtime Brazilian residents of the city, to flesh out the historical picture. An official of the U.S. consulate in Rio de Janeiro said that Brazilian immigration to the United States began on a significant scale only during the mid-1980s. A Brazilian who has lived in New York for years essentially confirmed this, noting that the rate of immigration increased slowly but steadily through the 1970s and early 1980s and then took off in 1984 or 1985. Another longtime New Yorker dated the Brazilian "deluge" from 1987. Although they did not agree on the exact year, in dozens of conversations with knowledgeable informants, nearly all date the take-off sometime between 1984 and 1987.

To be sure, there have always been Brazilians living in New York and in other areas of the country. The 1980 U.S. census counted some 44,000 native-born Brazilians, about 60 percent of whom lived in New York,

THEY ARE EVERYWHERE

One cannot turn around in midtown Manhattan and parts of Queens without bumping into Brazilians. On a Sunday in Central Park, a Brazilian was collecting signatures for a petition urging the prosecution of the men charged with the the murder of famed environmental activist, Chico Mendes. He was amazed, he said, at the number of Brazilians who stopped to chat. At a New York summer street fair, I met a Brazilian woman selling silk-screened T-shirts and a Brazilian family hawking their native cuisine. Walking through Bloomingdale's, I heard frantic pleas for help in Portuguese; a Brazilian had just had her purse stolen.

A trendy Mexican restaurant on Manhattan's East Side swarms with Brazilians—upwards of thirty work there as busboys, waiters, bathroom attendants, and cooks. At a neigborhood Italian restaurant, the coat checker was Brazilian, as were the waiter and food handler. At a French bistro on the other side of town, the waitress turned out to be Brazilian, as were the busboy at a popular Greek restaurant in the Chelsea district and another busboy at what is widely regarded one of the city's most fashionable eateries.

The assistant handyman in my building was Brazilian; he was replaced by his cousin—also Brazilian—who is now a part-time doorman there. When I was going to the laundry room in the basement, I met a Brazilian in the elevator who works as a housekeeper in the building. The parking lot attendant at a nearby garage is yet another Brazilian.

The soft nasal lilt of Portuguese can be heard among the open-air booksellers on Fifth Avenue, the shoe shine stands in the World Trade Center and Grand Central Station, and the scattered food shops, newsstands, and beauty salons that dot Astoria, Queens.

New Jersey, Massachusetts, Florida, and California.[3] During the course of my field research, I met about three dozen Brazilians who had lived in the city for fifteen, twenty, even thirty years. One longtime Brazilian resident remembers that a fair number of his compatriots lived in Newark in the late 1960s and early 1970s, doing road construction and painting bridges. Another dated the current Brazilian shoe-shining monopoly from 1969, when her brother and other *mineiros*, natives of the Brazilian state of Minas Gerais, began shining shoes at a kiosk in Grand Central Station. Yet another Brazilian related how she and a group of friends were brought to the United States some twenty-five years ago by wealthy Brazilian and American families to work as live-in housekeepers and nannies. And one Brazilian recalled his surprise when in 1968 or 1969, he visited a Catskill resort hotel and found some of his compatriots working as busboys in the restaurant there. In addition to these immigrant pioneers, there has long been another Brazilian presence in New York City: individuals employed by Brazilian-owned or -affiliated businesses, banks, tourist agencies, and airlines, as well as UN, trade bureau, and consular officers, students, and expatriate artists, writers, and musicians.

Still, the recent flight from Brazil is of a different order of magnitude from the trickle of emigrants who left earlier. There are several related reasons for this growing exodus from a country that has no history or tradition of emigration. Brazilians in New York are primarily economic exiles, fleeing from conditions of hyperinflation that have gouged the middle class and made its standard of living harder to maintain. In 1990 Brazilian inflation reached 1,795 percent annually; by 1991, even after then-President Collor's much-heralded plan to slay inflation with a "single bullet," it was averaging 20 percent a month. Moreover, by the end of Collor's first year in office, the Brazilian economy had shrunk by 4.6 percent, the largest drop since 1947, when the measurement was first recorded, and it was not expected to begin even a minor rebound until 1993. "The group of Brazilians who are leaving the country," reported the respected daily *Folha de São Paulo*, "are tired of the sequence of economic packages that didn't turn out . . . they don't believe in the Collor Era."[4]

An inflation rate of 84 percent a month—the rate in March 1990, just prior to Collor's economic plan—means that a person with $1 worth of Brazilian currency on March 1 has only 20 cents on March 31. It is little wonder, then, that hyperinflation causes extreme economic uncertainty. A few examples of what it is like to live under these conditions are illustrative. Over an eighteen-month period beginning in 1987, the real income of the Brazilian middle class declined by 30 percent, as rents soared by 800 percent, the price of newspapers often doubled overnight, and canned goods in grocery stores were thick with price stickers, stuck one on top of the other, as store owners frantically changed prices trying to keep up with inflation. "Restaurant patrons complain that the cost of their meals goes up as they eat," noted an article on Brazil's inflation in the *New York Times*. "Shoppers complain that prices are marked up while they wait in checkout lines."[5]

That hyperinflation, and the accompanying conditions of economic uncertainty, have caused the extraordinary exodus of Brazilians, is indicated by the fact that the flood of emigration began about the time that the Cruzado plan, the Brazilian government's earlier effort to deal with rampant inflation, failed in 1986. According to the Brazilian Federal Police, 37 percent of the Brazilians who left the country that year never returned. Or, as one Brazilian emigré in New York put it, that reform plan "was our last hope for a better life."[6]

Where Are They?

Brazilians, then, have been coming to New York—and other U.S. cities— in droves. But where do they live? Is there a Brazilian residential enclave within New York, or are they scattered throughout the city? This was one of the first questions I asked when starting my research. After a year of riding the "N" and "R" subway trains to Astoria, Queens, I can answer the question definitively: Brazilians are heavily concentrated in the borough of Queens, particularly in Astoria, adjacent Long Island City, and to a lesser extent, in Jackson Heights, Sunnyside, and one or two other Queens neighborhoods. But their residential profile is more complex than that because Brazilians live in all five boroughs and in a number of cities and towns throughout the Greater New York metropolitan area.

Where Brazilians live is, in part, determined by social class and immigration status. For example, I was told by the president of the New York branch of a major Brazilian bank that Scarsdale, a lush suburb in Westchester County whose per capita income is among the top twenty-five in the nation, had become "Brazilian country." He was alluding to the fact that the chief executives and directors of the New York offices of large Brazilian companies make their homes there, as well as in other posh communities in Westchester, such as neighboring Rye, and in Greenwich and Darien in nearby Connecticut.[7]

At the other end of the social spectrum are Brazilians who live in small, crowded apartments in Newark, another Brazilian bastion. This New Jersey city is home to many working-class Brazilians employed in unskilled jobs, as construction workers, truck drivers, gas station attendants, and restaurant workers. Although I lack hard data to confirm this, it appears that Brazilians living in Newark and a few other residential pockets, such as Framingham, Mass., are from working-class backgrounds and are more homogeneous socially than their compatriots in New York City.[8]

New York City proper attracts a wide range of Brazilians, from the very wealthy to the decidedly less well off and less well educated. Then, too, New York, as an international city—some natives insist it is the center of the universe—beckons not only immigrants who come to earn money, but artists, writers, and musicians whose hopes lie in the lyrical dictum " . . . if you can make it there, you can make it anywhere." Still, the entire range of the Brazilian social spectrum is not represented in New York since very few poor Brazilians can afford to travel to New York or elsewhere in the United States.

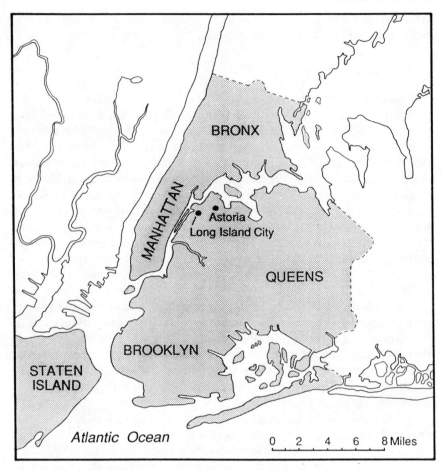

Map 1.1 New York City's Five Boroughs

Two Stops Past Bloomingdale's

"If you wanted to talk about a Brazilian ghetto, it would be Queens," I was told early on in my research, and this turned out to be true. Sixty percent of my New York sample live in Queens, and aside from a single commercial street in Manhattan, Queens is the only borough that has a cluster of Brazilian-owned and -oriented retail businesses.

Brazilians fit the general profile of new immigrants to Queens, who are mostly from urban, middle-class, relatively well-educated backgrounds in their countries of origin. Moreover, Queens is the favored borough of recent immigrants to New York City, followed by Manhattan and Brooklyn. Since the late 1960s the northwestern corridor of Queens from

1.1 Little Brazil, West 46th Street in Manhattan, is the commercial center of New York City's Brazilian community.

Flushing to the East River has become "something of a latter-day Babel." Between 1965 and 1979, over 300,000 immigrants moved to Queens, half of these to the northwestern Queens neighborhoods of Elmhurst, Woodside, Corona, and Jackson Heights, an area that has attracted the bulk of recent immigrants from South and Central America. These new-comers have turned this part of New York City into what has been called "the most diversely populated immigrant neighborhood in the world."[9]

Within Queens, Brazilians are very heavily concentrated in Astoria, the sector of the northwestern corridor that is closest to Manhattan. In my sample, 80 percent of the Queens residents live in Astoria or in the adjacent neighborhood of Long Island City, two subway stops past Bloomingdale's, New York's famed shopping emporium. Astoria is a largely working-class Greek, Italian, and Hispanic enclave, whose attractions are relatively low rents and close proximity to Manhattan, where most Brazilians work.

Astoria has a few, scattered establishments that are owned by Brazilians and serve a largely Brazilian clientele, but the only area that at all resembles a Brazilian commercial district is a street with three adjacent businesses—a grocery store, beauty salon, and car service company. Other Brazilian-owned enterprises in the neighborhood include a bar, a restaurant, a luncheonette, a store that sells Brazilian newspapers, magazines, and the latest tapes and videos from Brazil, a second beauty salon, a travel and remittance agency, and four or five more car service companies. A few of these businesses opened while I was doing my research, and if present immigration trends continue, a distinctly Brazilian commercial presence will become a more visible part of Astoria's future ethnic mix.

After Queens, Manhattan is the residential borough of choice for Brazilians; 30 percent of the Brazilians in my sample live on the "isle of joy." The largest Brazilian enclave in Manhattan is probably Spanish Harlem, where Brazilians live in densely packed, low-rise tenement buildings. In one building with thirty apartments, about 90 percent of the tenants are Brazilian, and I know of at least seven similar buildings in the same neigborhood. One local resident estimated that some 500 of his compatriots live in the area.

Another part of Manhattan with a sizable group of Brazilians is the Upper West Side, where, as in Spanish Harlem, they tend to cluster in particular buildings, often those with tiny efficiency apartments and bathrooms down the hall. Until they can find permanent quarters, some recent arrivals share cheap hotel rooms in the Times Square area, and, not surprisingly, Greenwich Village is the location of choice for Brazilian artists, writers, and musicians.

These, then, are the primary residential areas of Brazilians in New York City. There are also a smattering of Brazilians living in Brooklyn, the Bronx, and Staten Island, but they are not concentrated in any one neighborhhood. I asked perhaps 250 Brazilians where they lived in the city; less than 10 percent of them called any of these three boroughs home.

Beyond the Big Apple

This is a study of Brazilians in New York City, but they are by no means the only Brazilians in the region. A number of Brazilian nuclei dot the Greater New York metropolitan area, as well as other parts of the Northeast. Brazilians live in the towns of White Plains, New Rochelle, Mount Vernon, and Port Chester in Westchester, a suburban county just north of the city. The Brazilian enclaves there are said to be dominated by natives of southern Minas Gerais, particularly the city of Poços de Caldas, a well-known Brazilian spa and resort.

Mineola, a town in Long Island, is another suburban locale with Brazilian residents. The Brazilian population there is of sufficient size—300

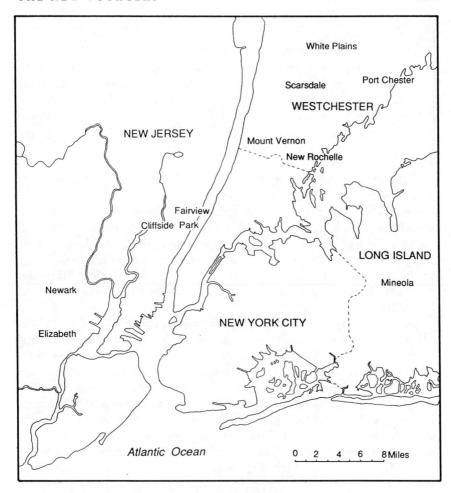

Map 1.2 The Greater New York Metropolitan Area

or so—to warrant masses in Portuguese at the local Catholic church, as
well as services in Portuguese at the Presbyterian church.

Newark is also home to a sizable Brazilian community, one large
enough to support its own weekly newspaper. Newark, which has a long-
established Portuguese population in the Ironbound District, has attracted numerous Brazilians in recent years, who find jobs in Portuguese-
owned businesses, most often construction and demolition. A significant
portion of Newark's Brazilian population comes from the city of Governador Valadares, in the state of Minas Gerais, a major exporter of Brazilians to the United States.[10]

CALLS FOR HELP

There are so many Brazilians and Portuguese in Newark, goes the joke, that when a woman was assaulted on the street there and yelled, "Help, help!" she was ignored. Why? If she had yelled, "Socorro, socorro!" instead—Portuguese for "help"—then passersby would have understood and come to her aid.

Although there are far more Brazilians in New York City than in Newark, their presence is more noticeable in Newark, not only because it is a much smaller city, but because Brazilians are more residentially concentrated there. In fact, walking down Ferry Street, the main commercial artery in the Ironbound District, one hears more Portuguese than English. But Brazilians are by no means limited to Newark; other New Jersey towns with Brazilian populations include Elizabeth, Fairview, Harrison, Kearney, Lindenhurst, North Arlington, Cliffside Park, Jersey City, and Long Branch.

Away from the New York metropolitan area, scattered pockets of Brazilians are found in a number of communities in the northeastern United States. The Catskill Mountains resort towns of Ellenville and Monticello in upstate New York are a case in point. Such well-known Jewish resort hotels as the Nevele, the Concord, Kutsher's, Fallsview, and the now-defunct Grossingers employ(ed) hundreds of Brazilians as dishwashers, busboys, waiters, and chambermaids. There are even Brazilian soccer teams from the various hotels that compete with one another. Brazilians have worked in these resorts since the late 1960s. Their major attraction is that since room and board are provided, it is easier to save money while working there.

New England also is home to several major Brazilian communities. In the state of Connecticut, Danbury, Waterbury, and Bridgeport all have their fair share of *brazucas*, as Brazilians living in the United States are called. But probably nowhere in the United States outside of New York, is there as large a concentration of Brazilians as in Boston and the surrounding communities of Cambridge, Somerville, Allston, Marlboro, Southboro, and Framingham. A weekly paper published in Boston, the *Brazilian Times*, is crammed with ads for shops featuring Brazilian food and drink, magazines, newspapers, records, tapes, and videos. There are ads for Brazilian travel and remittance agencies, beauty salons, auto mechanics, snack shops, restaurants, and nightclubs, as well as for churches of a range of denominations with religious services in Portuguese.

Brazilians also live in communities south of Boston: Rockland, Brockton, Weymouth, Hanover, Abingdon, Quincy, Whitman, and on Cape Cod, Hyannis. Take Rockland, for example, a community of 16,000, with a Brazilian population of about 2,000. This small town has two businesses that cater to Brazilians: a remittance agency and a store with Brazilian food products, newspapers, and magazines. According to an article in the *Boston Globe*, about $30,000 a month in remittance money is sent to Brazil from the Rockland area.[11]

This, then, is where Brazilians live in New York City and other parts of the Northeast. It is also worth mentioning that Brazilians are by no means limited to this region. Philadelphia, Washington, D.C., Miami, San Francisco, and Los Angeles have significant numbers of Brazilian residents, and there are also Brazilian enclaves in Roanoke, Va., and in Austin, Houston, and San Antonio in Texas.

How Many Are There?

Estimating the number of Brazilians who reside in New York City or in the New York metropolitan area is difficult at best. Equally problematic are figures on Brazilians living in other cities in the United States and the totals for the country as a whole. The problem is that official immigration data fail to capture the presence of undocumented immigrants (see Table 1.1).

Table 1.1 Brazilian Immigration to the United States, Selected Years

1965	*1980*	*1985*	*1990*	*1991*
2,869	1,570	2,272	4,191	8,133

Total Immigrants Admitted from Brazil:

1966–1979: 22,310
1980–1991: 33,475

Source: U.S. INS 1992.

The U.S. government statistics show a temporary decline and then a moderate increase in the number of Brazilians immigrating to this country between 1965 and 1991. The totals for the period are equally modest. Moreover, the official numbers—given the magnitude of immigration to the United States in those years and the size of the Brazilian population as a whole—are, quite literally, a drop in the bucket. Were one to take these figures at face value, one would have to conclude that Brazilian immigration to the United States is minuscule and that it has been fairly steady over the last twenty-five years.

The problem with these data is that they include only legal immigrants from Brazil, yet a far larger but unknown number of Brazilians living in this country are—or, until recently were—undocumented immigrants. People who are in the United States illegally, of whatever nationality, are not anxious to make their presence known nor to stand up and be counted. For example, officials of the Brazilian consular district for the northeastern United States, which is headquartered in New York City and is the busiest Brazilian consular office in the world, note that many of their compatriots living in the United States illegally are afraid to set foot inside the consulate under the mistaken belief that consular personnel will turn them over to U.S. immigration authorities. Thus, consular officials have little idea how many Brazilians live in New York City, in the greater metropolitan area, or for that matter, in the consular district as a whole.

This does not mean that no data exist on the rate of Brazilian immigration to this country. Although some of the figures that follow provide only indirect evidence and should be viewed with a critical eye, they do give some insight into the magnitude of this migrant flow.

The best source of information on the true volume of Brazilian immigration to the United States is the statistics of the U.S. Immigration and Naturalization Service (INS) on tourist visas issued to Brazilians, because it is Brazilians overstaying their tourist visas who, by virtue of that fact, become undocumented immigrants. Visa statistics, of course, do not include the Brazilians who arrived clandestinely without visas, primarily by way of the Mexican border, but my research suggests that comparatively few Brazilians come to the United States via this route.

The data on tourist visas are revealing. In 1990, 300,000 tourist visas for travel to the United States were issued to Brazilian citizens.[12] If we assume that 20 percent of those with tourist visas actually come to the United States to work—an estimate that may be conservative—this means that roughly 60,000 visas were issued to what immigration officials term "overstayers," that is, people who remain in the United States after their visas expire.[13] The 1990 tourist visa figure is also noteworthy given the anticipated decline in tourism due to the economic crisis in Brazil. One might have expected the number of Brazilian tourists to the United States to have declined after the mid-1980s because of Brazil's weak economy. But quite to the contrary, the number of tourist visas issued to Brazilians between 1984 and 1991 actually rose by more than 200 percent.

We now turn to the big picture. Approximately 1.66 million tourist visas were issued to Brazilians during the seven-year period beginning in 1984, when the Brazilian economy began a nosedive and emigration increased sharply (see Table 1.2). Once again, using the 20 percent figure, this means that perhaps 332,000 Brazilian "tourists" actually came to the United States to work. While this total does not include earlier arrivals from the 1970s and early 1980s, it does cover what I believe to be the most intense period of Brazilian immigration.

Table 1.2   U.S. Tourist Visas Issued in Brazil, 1984–1991

1984	128,000	1989	272,000
1985	148,000	1990	300,000
1986	192,000	1991	390,000
1988	233,000		

Source: U.S. INS 1986–1992.

What does this mean for the total Brazilian population in the United States? Without citing its source, a 1990 article in the respected Brazilian newspaper, *Folha de São Paulo*, estimated that there are about 600,000 Brazilians living in the United States, while *Veja*, the Brazilian news weekly, put the number at a more modest 330,000. If we add up population estimates from the regions of greatest Brazilian concentration, both in the Northeast and in the other cities cited earlier, the total may well be around 350,000 or 400,000 for the country as a whole (see Table 1.3).[14]

Table 1.3   Estimates of the Brazilian Population in the United States, Selected Northeastern Regions

Region/City	Number	Source
Northeast Consular District (New York, New Jersey, New England)	150,000–200,000	Brazilian consulate
Boston and region	25,000–35,000	Commonwealth of Massachusetts
	25,000–35,000	*Boston Globe*
	70,000	*The Brasilians*
	90,000	*Folha de São Paulo*
	150,000	*Veja*
Danbury, Waterbury, and Bridgeport, Conn.	15,000	*The Brazilian Voice*
Newark, N.J., and nearby towns	15,000	Brazilian consulate
	10,000	*Folha de São Paulo*
Westchester County, N.Y.	6,000	*Brazilian Times*
Greater New York metropolitan area	80,000–100,000	Brazilian consulate
	100,000	*The Brasilians*
	Over 100,000	U.S. census official
	7,000	1980 U.S. census
	14,403	1990 U.S. census
New York City	50,000–150,000	*Veja*

Note: The Brasilians, The Brazilian Voice, and the *Brazilian Times* are Brazilian newspapers published in New York, Newark, and Boston, respectively.

Although it is impossible to cite precise figures, there is no doubt that the number of Brazilians in the United States has risen dramatically during the 1980s. Long-term Brazilian residents of New York all agree that sometime in middecade, they became aware of increasing numbers of their compatriots on the city's streets. One Brazilian told me that when he first came to New York in 1981, he so rarely heard Portuguese spoken that when he did, he would stop the person and inquire where they were from in Brazil. Now he hears Portuguese so often that he barely notices it. Similarly, a woman who has lived in Astoria, Queens—now the major Brazilian residential enclave in the city—since 1981 told me that when she first arrived, there were hardly any Brazilians in Astoria. She dates the influx from about 1986. A Brazilian immigration attorney with offices in New York and Newark agrees that the Brazilian community has been "increasing geometrically" since the mid-1980s. Prior to that, he had a Brazilian client or two every few months; now half of his clients are Brazilian, and a day does not go by without his seeing one of his compatriots.

These, then, in very general terms, are the parameters of the Brazilian population in the United States, with some specifics on Brazilians in the Northeast and in the New York metropolitan area. The remainder of this book will focus exclusively on Brazilians in New York City.

The Secret, Silent Immigration

Over the course of a year and a half of research on the Brazilian community in New York City, a few themes kept emerging that I now believe are key to understanding both the nature of Brazilian immigration and the adjustment of Brazilians to life in New York City. Perhaps the most salient feature of Brazilians as a new ingredient in New York's cultural mix is their invisibility. Few New Yorkers seem to know that there are Brazilians in their midst, and Brazilians are never mentioned in the media or in popular or academic works dealing with the city's diverse ethnicity. Brazilians are nowhere to be found in two books on new immigrants in New York City published in the late 1980s, even though the index of one of the books, written by the city's then-director of the Office of Immigrant Affairs, actually lists twenty-eight distinct immigrant groups. Another recent book on the topic cites the large number of South Americans residing in Queens, and mentions Colombians, Peruvians, Argentinians, and Ecuadorians but never Brazilians.[15]

Brazilians are not only invisible in the academic literature on immigration, but they are an ethnic and linguistic group that has been completely overlooked by the city's social service and educational agencies. Nor is their situation likely to change soon, since the racial and ethnic categories used in the 1990 U.S. census virtually ensure their continued invisibility.

What is all the more remarkable about the obliviousness to the existence of Brazilians in New York City is that it coincides with a craze for all things Brazilian. The lambada vogue, the popularity of David Byrne's and Paul Simon's Brazilian albums, the concert tours of Brazilian pop stars, the new restaurants with Brazilian themes, and the packed bar scene at the Coffee Shop, a New York eatery that serves Brazilian food and is a trendy singles hangout, newly touched by the Warholian wand of flash-in-the-pan celebrity, have led *New York Magazine* to call Brazil "the nation *du jour* among New York style-setters."[16]

The lack of awareness of the Brazilian presence in New York, in part, stems from the sheer size of the city's Hispanic population, with whom Brazilians are continually confused. But calling Brazilians Hispanics is incorrect because the term denotes Spanish-speaking people or those of Spanish-speaking descent.[17] *Brazilians, of course, speak Portuguese.* I emphasize this because most Americans, even many well-educated ones, think that Spanish is the language of Brazil and that Portuguese is only spoken in Portugal. Most Americans simply do not know that Brazil is in any way distinct, linguistically or culturally, from the rest of Latin America.

Brazilian immigrants are also confused with Hispanics because many of them live in parts of the city where Spanish is common and they often work with Hispanics. Moreover, part of the confusion about Brazilian identity is probably due to the lack of a previously established ethnic community in New York into which new immigrants could easily blend. Unlike Chinese, Haitian, Dominican, and other recent migrants to the city, Brazilians had no previous cultural or linguistic presence there.

The irregular status of many Brazilians also contributes to what one of them called their "secret, silent immigration." Illegal aliens are not anxious to make their presence known. Virtually all Brazilian immigrants who arrived in New York City in the 1980s were undocumented for a time. But by the time this study was done in the 1990–91, the ranks of the undocumented had been reduced somewhat. While some were sponsored for green cards by their employers, most have received or are in the process of receiving legal residence through the Amnesty Program of the 1986 Immigration Reform and Control Act (IRCA). Nevertheless, most of the subjects of this study once were or still are undocumented.

Up the Down Staircase

Aside from being new to New York and largely undocumented, the majority of Brazilians know little English, at least when they arrive in this country. As a result, they generally are confined to the most menial and dead-end jobs that the city has to offer, the ones that require no papers and few language skills. Within the city, Brazilians are concentrated in the low-wage, service sector; the men wash dishes, bus tables, and shine shoes, and the women clean apartments and care for children. In the suburbs, men are most often found in unskilled construction and maintenance jobs, although there, too, most Brazilian women work as housekeepers.

Since the overwhelming majority of recent immigrants from Brazil come from middle- and lower-middle-class backgrounds, the low-level jobs that they hold in New York would be unthinkable for them at home. Middle-class Brazilian women *employ* household servants in Brazil; in New York they *are themselves* household servants. In Brazil, restaurant work, including waiting on tables, would be out of the question for anyone with more than a modicum of education, yet in New York Brazilians with university degrees are employed as busboys in some of the city's trendiest restaurants.

Brazilians use a variety of devices to cope with their downward social trajectories. Some use humor: women joke about how inept they are at housework, never having had to do it before. Others try to compartmentalize their life and work. Still others take great pains to conceal the nature of their jobs from family members in Brazil. But more than anything else, because most Brazilians come to this country, at least initially, as sojourners rather than as settlers, they are more easily reconciled to their menial jobs and the accompanying loss of status since they view both as temporary.

The Ties That Don't Bind

Before starting this research, I knew that one of its major questions would be, Does the fact that Brazilians in New York are strangers in a strange land override whatever social and economic differences exist among them? In other words, I wanted to know whether ethnicity acted as a countervailing force to the divisiveness of social class within the expatriate community.

Within a week I thought I had the answer, which was repeatedly confirmed over fourteen months of research: no, it did not. Ethnicity meant little in the face of the social and economic divisions that split the Brazilian community. For the most part, these divisions were not based on contrasts in the social and educational background of Brazilians in New York. Rather, they were related to the disparities in lifestyle and status resulting from the menial character of the jobs held by new immigrants to the city. The Brazilian community was crosscut by a pervasive differentiation into occasionally hostile—or at least, mutually indifferent—camps whose membership was based on the time and the manner of arrival in New York. In fact, I began to doubt whether a Brazilian community existed at all in the qualitative sense of the term: a group of people working together for a common end.

The fault lines among Brazilians in New York City are roughly as follows. There are the Brazilian old-timers who arrived in the city two and three decades ago. Some came from modest backgrounds but many achieved considerable financial success by starting businesses that catered to Brazilian tourists and residents. Then there is the local Brazilian elite, the well-educated and affluent executives and directors of the city's Brazilian banks and corporations. Some are in temporary posts, while others have lived in New York with their families for years. Finally, there are the new immigrants, the mostly young, mostly educated men and women from the middle sectors of Brazilian society who arrived in the city in the 1980s. By far the most numerous segment of the Brazilian community in New York, they are the principal focus of this book.

The Context: New York's Labor Market

Before I recount the arrival and settlement of Brazilian immigrants in New York City, two contextual issues, which daily shape the experiences of Brazilians and other recent immigrants to the city, must be addressed: the local job market, which brings them to New York in the first place, and recent changes in U.S. immigration policy, including the much-heralded amnesty program of the 1986 Immigration Reform and Control Act, which affects what they can do once they get there. The two issues are related because the sorts of jobs available to Brazilians new to the city are determined partly by structural changes in the New York economy and partly by the immigrants' legal status, that is, whether or not they are undocumented.

New immigrants from Brazil come to New York City for one major reason: jobs. If Brazilian immigrants did not have access to jobs at what they consider good wages, this book would never have been written because there would be few of them to write about. Of course, many Brazilians also see their sojourn in the city as an adventure, as an experience that they will recount some day to their grandchildren. But the overwhelming attraction of New York is not its spectacular skyline, its renown as a world cultural capital, or its come hither cosmopolitan flair. The drawing power of the city lies in its abundance of low-level jobs that require little English but that pay considerably more money than these new immigrants were earning in Brazil.

The city's current job market seems paradoxical at first: a time of major job losses, recession, and rising unemployment has coincided with a large influx of new immigrants seeking and finding work. But this contradiction is more apparent than real because the economic base of New York—and some other U.S. cities—is being restructured in a way that enhances the employment opportunities of certain groups. These structural changes have entailed a loss of better-paid manufacturing jobs with a concomitant increase in low-wage jobs. The proliferation of low-wage jobs is tied to two sectors of the economy: what sociologist Saskia Sassen has labeled the "downgraded manufacturing" sector and the "producer services" sector. Although very distinct from each other, both market segments have generated a wide array of largely unskilled, poorly paid, dead-end jobs, which do not require proficiency in English. It is just these jobs that offer a labor market niche to recent immigrants, and growth in this employment sector is continuing. Projections suggest that the greatest number of new jobs for the period 1980 to 1995 will have been in low-wage industries.[18]

In New York the downgraded manufacturing sector primarily consists of informal, small-scale, nonunionized companies that require few skilled or English-proficient workers. These companies produce a variety of apparel, footwear, electronics, and furniture; they are located in the sweatshops of New York's Chinatown and the city's outer boroughs as well as the living rooms of industrial homeworkers.[19]

The second growth area in the city's economy, the low-wage service sector, is tied, in part, to an increasing number of high-income, top-level managerial and professional jobs in the corporate headquarters of the city's banking, investment, trading, communications, and other producer service–related industries. The growth in producer services has created low-wage, low-skill jobs that support this sector directly and indirectly. Wage workers who provide direct support for producer services are the ubiquitous office cleaners, stock clerks, and messengers who keep the firms running. There are also the myriad jobs that underpin the high-income lifestyles of the well-paid executives employed in these companies. These include housekeepers, nannies, building attendants, drivers, restaurant workers, caterers, employees in gourmet and specialty shops, manucurists, and beauticians. Writes Sassen: "The demand for low-wage workers to service the high-income lifestyles of the rapidly expanding top-level work force is one key factor in the expansion of the informal sector in cities like New York and Los Angeles.[20]

Parenthetically, these economic trends have led to a greater polarization of New York's income and occupational structure. At a time when high-income managerial and professional jobs are expanding, there has been a contraction of middle-income blue-collar and white-collar jobs and an increase in low-wage service and manufacturing jobs. Writes Saskia Sassen: "It is in this restructuring of labor demand that we find the conditions for the absorption of the large immigrant influx."[21]

Where do Brazilians fit into all of this? Very few Brazilians are employed in the city's downgraded manufacturing sector. They are overwhelmingly found in New York's second growth area: the low-wage service sector that is part of the support system for the lifestyles of the affluent, including the much-heralded (and maligned) yuppies. Restaurant work, housecleaning, baby-sitting, call car and limousine driving, shoe shining, office cleaning, and delivery and messenger services are a few of the jobs that Brazilians hold in this segment of the labor market.

Beginning in the 1970s, then, the New York economy witnessed an expansion of just the sort of jobs most likely to employ recent immigrants. Why immigrants? The reason is that these jobs have a number of characteristics that make them undesirable to American citizens and many employers argue, with some justification, that were it not for the influx of new immigrants, they would not be filled at all. Aside from their low pay, the jobs often involve physical labor or unpleasant working conditions, or they may entail odd working hours, such as nights and weekends. They usually offer few chances for advancement, and they provide little job security. In short, they are low-status jobs that individuals who have other employment options tend to avoid.[22]

It is not just by chance that many, although by no means all, of these jobs belong to the informal sector of New York's economy. They are jobs that, while legal, are unregulated in terms of working conditions, taxes withheld, and other standards. And it is just these sorts of jobs that are the ones *least likely* to require immigrants to demonstrate their legal status. This brings us to our second major contextual issue: immigrants' status in light of U.S. immigration reform.

The Context: Immigration Reform, Jobs, and the Undocumented

There is no sympathy in the United States Congress for the middle-class illegal.

—*Former U.S. ambassador to Brazil, at a forum on immigration reform*

The Immigration Reform and Control Act of 1986, known as IRCA, has received a lot of publicity, and some of its provisions have, indeed, had a major impact on the lives of immigrants in the United States. Although I am primarily concerned with how the legislation has affected Brazilian immigrants, studies of the general impact of the law are revealing.

Just what does IRCA entail? The act had two goals: (1) to stem the tide of illegal immigrants coming to the United States through sanctions against employers who hired them; and (2) to legalize long-resident undocumented aliens through the amnesty program. While the provisions of the act are straightforward, its results have not been nearly so clear-cut. In fact, confusion and unintended consequences often have resulted from the 1986 law.[23]

Evidence suggests that IRCA cut the illegal flow of immigrants less than expected, and it may even have encouraged some unlawful new entry. For example, one study found that the rate of unlawful border crossings had been reduced less than 20 percent. Many people crossed the border for the first time carrying false documents and personal histories with them so that they could qualify for the amnesty program. One survey found that those who actually did qualify under the amnesty provisions and were no longer undocumented themselves, acted as magnets for newly arrived illegals. It seems that almost everyone but INS officials acknowledges that the law has not appreciably checked the influx of undocumented immigrants.[24]

There is also considerable question as to whether IRCA has achieved its other goal: limiting the work available to illegals through employer sanctions. While experts agree that the ban on hiring illegals has made it somewhat more difficult for them to find jobs, they do not agree on the extent to which employer sanctions have reduced the actual flow across the Mexican border. A joint study by the Rand Corporation and the Urban Institute suggests that this provision has had only a slight effect on the rate of illegal immigration. The reason for this is fairly straightforward; while it may be slightly harder to get jobs than it was before the passage of IRCA, economic conditions are such in Brazil and other sending countries that undocumented immigrants are coming anyway. Said one recent illegal from El Salvador, "Yes, it is more difficult to get here and earn money now, but people still do it."[25]

My own research indicates that the recession-induced decline in service jobs in New York City has had a greater impact on the employment of Brazilians than have IRCA-imposed employer sanctions. While a few employers demand hard evidence of legality, most only ask for a social security card as "proof" of employability, an item that is readily available to undocumented immigrants in New York and other cities for between $30 and $100. Then, too, some employers knowingly flout the law, arguing that if they cannot hire "these people" (illegals) to do menial work, such as washing dishes, they will go out of business, claiming that they cannot pay $8 an hour for such jobs and make a profit. Still, employer sanctions, having made work somewhat scarcer, may also have had the unintended effect of forcing illegals "deeper into the underground economy where few questions are asked, no records are kept and the potential for workers to be exploited is high."[26]

Amnesty: A Path to Legality?

The best-known IRCA provision is the amnesty program. The legislation allowed undocumented aliens who could prove that they were in the United States before January 1, 1982, to apply for amnesty; the application had to be made in the twelve months preceding May 1988. Those approved for amnesty were granted temporary residence, the right to work, and later, permanent resident status, along with a highly coveted green card.

How have Brazilians been affected by the amnesty program? I would hazard a guess that no more than 10 or 15 percent of undocumented Brazilians in New York City qualified for amnesty since the great migration surge from Brazil occured between 1984 and 1987, *some two to five years after the 1982 deadline* for U.S. residence.

What has this meant, then, in real terms? After all, IRCA's amnesty and employer sanctions provisions are bound by the assumption that undocumented aliens who do not qualify for amnesty will return to their own countries once they cannot find work in the United States. I have found no evidence for this among Brazilians. Quite to the contrary, like untold numbers of immigrants from other countries, thousands of Brazilians on tourist visas entered the United States with the intention of seeking jobs *after* the immigration law went into effect. While it may be somewhat more difficult for the undocumented to find work since the enactment of IRCA, jobs shining shoes, cleaning houses, and washing dishes are still widely available—with or without papers—to most who want them. Of course, since I only met and talked with Brazilians still living in New York, there may, indeed, be some Brazilians who returned home after being unable to find employment. There certainly has been return migration to Brazil, but it is impossible to say whether any of it can be linked to the inability to find jobs in the United States as a result of IRCA's employer sanctions provisions.

Brazilians are not the only recent immigrants who have taken IRCA in stride. One study found that about one in three undocumented immigrants from El Salvador and Mexico had no intention of returning to their homelands. This means that a sizable group of immigrants do not qualify for amnesty under the law's provisions—for the simple reason that they arrived in the United States after the January 1982 deadline—but who, nevertheless, intend to remain in this country indefinitely. The authors of the study conclude—and my own data on Brazilians concur—that it is very unlikely that those not qualifying for amnesty but desiring to stay will simply pack up their bags and go home. Thus, to the undoubted chagrin of the authors of the Immigration Reform Act, while many undocumented aliens would like to regularize their status, legalization per se "is not necessarily a condition for continuing to reside in the U.S." [27]

Do You Have Your "Gal Costa"?

Gal Costa is a popular contemporary singer in Brazil. When Brazilians in New York City inquire about one another's legal status in the United States, they ask: "Do you have your Gal Costa?," an oblique reference to the green card, that highly sought-after document that permits its immigrant holder to live and work legally in this country. A green card may make it easier to find work, and having one will certainly lessen an undocumented immigrant's paranoia about meeting up with an immigration agent around every corner. But more than anything else, a green card means that its holder can enter and leave the United States at will—visit friends and relatives in Brazil, and then return to the United States unimpeded.

A significant although undetermined proportion of Brazilians who were "out of status"—in the country illegally—applied for amnesty to obtain the much desired green card that comes with it. But recall that to qualify for amnesty, an individual had to have lived in this country prior to January 1, 1982. How, then, could Brazilians apply if only about 10 or 15 percent of undocumented Brazilians qualified under the terms of the law, the rest having arrived in the United States *after the 1982 cut-off*? The answer is twofold. Either they proved through various means that they were living in this country before 1982, or, even more imaginatively, they applied for amnesty through the law's special provisions for farm workers.

The peculiarly Brazilian notion of *dar um jeito* came into play here. Although difficult to translate, the term means to have a knack for getting something done, to cut red tape in order to reach a goal, or to achieve an end through minor chicanery. Brazilian anthropologist Roberto DaMatta has written that *jeitos* are part of his country's "social navigation," a way of beating the system by getting around the nation's laws and labyrinthine state bureaucracy.[28] At any rate, *jeito* was much in evidence when Brazilians were confronted with the finicky provisos of the amnesty program. Using the *jeito* of doctored rent receipts, pay vouchers, and phone bills, backdated letters, and similar items, many Brazilians "proved" that they were living in the United States prior to 1982.

A case in point: I asked Luis, an undocumented Brazilian friend, if he were going to apply for amnesty. He already had, he said, and showed me his provisional work card. This is the first step toward amnesty and allows the recipient to work legally. Luis had lived in the United States for a few months in 1977, had gone back to Brazil, and then had returned to New York in 1986, where he has been ever since. He did not qualify for amnesty because he was not in this country continuously prior to 1982, but he applied for it anyway and produced "proof" that he had been a U.S. resident since the late 1970s. Luis's friend, Ricardo, who has lived in this country since 1985, used a similar ruse. To prove his pre-1982 residence in the United States, Ricardo produced a series of love letters with 1980 postmarks sent to him in Florida by his woman friend in Brazil. In fact, he had received the letters while on a tour to Disney World that year.

Another example is José, a Brazilian who arrived in the United States well after the cutoff date for amnesty, but completed the first stage of the process and has his temporary work card. José qualified for the program by requesting a letter from a Brazilian friend, a longtime New York resident, saying that José had worked for him since 1981. José had indeed been an employee in his friend's delivery business when he first came to this country; only the date of his employment was altered for the purposes of the amnesty program.

1981: THE YEAR OF THE IMMIGRANT

Brazilians were by no means the only ones to use such methods to circumvent the terms of the amnesty program. For example, all of the Chinese immigrants interviewed for an article in the *New York Times* claimed to have come to New York in 1981, coincidentally just under the wire for participation in the amnesty program.

Source: Hays, "Immigrants Strain Chinatown's Resources."

Applying for amnesty was not cheap; informants told me that they had paid attorneys anywhere from $1,000 to $2,500 to have amnesty papers filed. But some Brazilians chose not to apply to the amnesty program because they planned to stay in the United States only for a limited time, perhaps a year or less, and were thus loath to pay the hefty legal fees that an amnesty application would entail. Then there is the case of the woman who did qualify for amnesty, having lived in New York continuously since 1980, but who decided not to apply for it because she planned to return to Brazil "momentarily" to live. That was over three years ago, and she is still living in Queens and ruing the fact that she, one of the few Brazilians to qualify for the amnesty program, did not do so.

As late as mid-1990, more than two years after the deadline for amnesty applications, a few immigrants were still trying to file for it with the help of some less than scrupulous attorneys. For a fee of about $2,500 a lawyer would file for amnesty for a client, and then not only backdate the time of the client's arrival in the United States, but also backdate the actual application form so that it fell within the filing deadline. I was not able to determine if any of these late applications were successful.

Down on the Farm

The second route to amnesty and a green card was through IRCA's provisions for farm workers. Amnesty applications under the Special Agricultural Worker (SAW) program far outnumbered those under other provisions (see Table 1.4); the program was particularly popular among some immigrants who arrived after 1982, the cutoff date for the general am-

Table 1.4 Brazilian Amnesty Applicants

Illegal entry:	620
Visa overstays:	1,141
SAW applicants:	5,998
TOTAL:	7,759 amnesty applicants

Source: U.S. INS 1991, 94–95.

Note: While the preliminary data showing that only about 8,000 Brazilians applied for amnesty seem low, they are in line with the figures for many other countries with sizable numbers of illegal aliens in the United States. Aside from Mexico, El Salvador, Guatemala and Columbia, no country accounted for as many as 20,000 amnesty applicants. See Woodrow and Passel 1990.

nesty program. Under the SAW program, undocumented individuals in the United States who had been employed as farm laborers for at least ninety days between May 1985 and May 1986 could apply for amnesty and ultimately for permanent resident status.

Brazilian *jeito* came into play here even more than it did for the general amnesty program, although, once again, I emphasize that these tactics were by no means limited to Brazilians. For a handsome fee, immigration attorneys located American farmers who were willing—also for a tidy sum—to sign an official immigration document testifying that Senhor or Senhora Fulano de Tal (Mr. or Ms. So-and-So) had worked on their farms for the requisite period of time. In fact, according to incomplete statistics from the INS, of the nearly 8,000 Brazilian applicants for amnesty, 78 percent became legalized through the farm worker provisions of the program; the remaining 22 percent were legalized under IRCA's general amnesty program. However odd these figures, they do mesh with another curious bit of INS data: the amazingly high number of applicants in the agricultural workers program—nearly 47,000—who lived in New York City.[29] Perhaps they were farming in Central Park!

Many immigrants who qualified for amnesty through the SAW program did so by claiming to have labored in the orange groves or vegetable fields of Florida. One Brazilian friend, after paying a $2,500 fee to a lawyer in New York, twice traveled to the Sunshine State to pick up documents showing he had worked on a farm there. Another paid an attorney $1,400, and then spent an additional $600 on a trip to West Palm Beach, where he visited the flower nursery where he had had a "job" to get information on his hours and dates of employment. One informant told me that he first came to the United States in April 1988, and then immediately corrected himself, claiming it had "slipped his mind" that he had lived in Florida and worked on a farm there a few years earlier. The farms around

West Palm Beach and Fort Lauderdale, in particular, seem to have employed an inordinate number of Brazilian field hands.

One of the strangest "down on the farm" stories is as follows. An immigrant applied for legalization through the farm program. Although he felt that his interview with an INS official had not gone well, he waited to hear the results for some time but returned to Brazil before he had had a response to his application. In his absence a letter arrived from "Tia Mimi"—"Aunt Mimi" is a Brazilian euphemism for the INS—denying his legalization request and stating that his application was full of inconsistencies. Inexplicably, a short while later, another letter arrived from the INS approving his amnesty application. This letter was forwarded to him in Brazil, and he used it to reenter the U.S. The day after his return to New York, he received a provisional work permit.

A similarly odd tale was told to me by a woman from Minas Gerais who is employed as a waitress in New York. She applied for farm amnesty and was interviewed by an INS official. The interviewer told her that she was "lying," that she had "never worked on a farm a day in her life," and that she could be "deported for falsifying legal documents." She said that the woman who interviewed her had "scared her to death" and that she decided not to proceed with her SAW application. She went back to Brazil; a short time later, her former roommate in New York wrote to her that she had received a letter from "Tia Mimi" notifying her that her amnesty application had been approved. She, too, returned to the United States, which, she said, she had not planned to do, and she also received a provisional work permit.

THE LAW OF THE COW

The way some immigrants used the farm amnesty program to get green cards parallels the way some Brazilians gain entrance to federal agricultural universities in Brazil. Some years ago, when it was discovered that most of the students in these schools were from urban areas and knew little or nothing about farming and rural life, a decree was passed—colloquially referred to as "the law of the cow"—setting up a two-tier admissions system: one for city residents and one for those with rural backgrounds. The quota for urbanites was quickly filled, while places remained in the rural admissions tier. Urban applicants soon learned that if they could "prove" that they were from rural areas, they would stand a better chance of being admitted. As a result, the schools were deluged with hopeful applicants from São Paulo, Rio, and other big cities whose applications were accompanied by letters testifying that they had spent their entire lives "down on the farm."

The Long Wait

Receiving amnesty takes about three years. After an application is filed and approved, the first stage of the process, work authorization, is given for one year, and applicants are not permitted to leave the United States during that time except for humanitarian reasons. The second stage, provisional residence, lasts two years; then one can leave the country for whatever reason, visit friends and relatives in Brazil, and return to the United States. In the final stage, a green card is issued, and the amnesty applicant becomes a permanent resident alien.

During the initial stage of the amnesty process, permission is granted to leave the United States and visit the home country only in cases of the death or serious illness of a family member there. At first a telegram about a sick or dying relative in Brazil was sufficient to satisfy the humanitarian proviso, but then immigration authorities began requiring a letter from a physician as well. A professional translator told me that he is asked to translate dozens of such letters from Portuguese to English intended for the INS so that first-stage amnesty applicants can get permission to travel to Brazil. Once someone showed up in his office with "this ridiculous-looking letter," supposedly from a doctor. While the translator is certain that some of these requests involve legitimate family emergencies, he wonders why it is that the relatives of Brazilian amnesty applicants get sick and die more often around Christmas and Carnival than at other times of the year.

A Question of Status

IRCA has not cut off the flow of new undocumented immigrants to the

United States.

—KAREN A. WOODROW AND JEFFREY S. PASSEL,

"Post-IRCA Undocumented Immigration to the United States"

At the start of my research, I interviewed an immigration attorney with a large Brazilian clientele. He assured me that, on the basis of his own experience, Brazilians had a far lower percentage of illegal immigrants in their midst than that of any other nationality in New York City. When Brazilians come to his office for legal advice, they are still "in status," that is, they have valid tourist visas. Brazilians like to stay within the law, he told me, so they seek his advice before they have a legal problem. In contrast, clients from other countries generally come to him after their visas have expired and they have remained in the United States illegally.

I do not doubt the veracity of this attorney, and I feel certain that the just-so-story he told me is based on his own experience. But within weeks of the interview, I knew that his information on the legal status of "most Brazilians" in the city was wrong and that a significant—but indeterminable—percentage of them were in fact undocumented. It turned out that even though some Brazilians in New York became legalized through the amnesty program, a sizable minority of recent immigrants remained undocumented. In my own sample, 16 percent were legalized through amnesty, 41 percent were undocumented at the time of the interview, and another 13 percent were employed while on unexpired tourist visas, which may be valid for up to six months (in other words, they were illegals-to-be). In all, 54 percent of the sample already were or were likely to become undocumented.[30]

Where does this figure fit in with what is generally known about illegal immigrants in the United States? First, there is simply no way to estimate their total numbers with any degree of accuracy. Estimates fluctuate, but the most widely cited figure is the 2 to 4 million from the 1980 census. Other figures for undocumented aliens in the 1980s range from a low of 1.5 million to a high of 6.25 million. Moreover, other estimates suggest that between 1980 and 1986, anywhere from 100,000 to 300,000 undocumented immigrants entered the United States each year. Thus, by 1989, well after IRCA and its amnesty provisions came into force, somewhere between 1.7 million and 2.9 million undocumented individuals were living in this country.[31]

Other figures indicate that about 10 percent of all undocumented immigrants in the United States—somewhere between 250,000 and 600,000 people—live in New York City, and that they arrive at more or less the same rate as do legal immigrants, about 75,000 a year. As is the case with Brazilians, the undocumented in New York are most likely to be visa overstayers who enter the United States on temporary visas, usually through Kennedy Airport, and remain after the visa expires. They may seek employment, which also violates the terms of their visas. But other than mode of entry, undocumented Brazilians and other illegals are similar to their legal compatriots in the types of jobs they hold and the neighborhoods in which they live.[32]

Finally, Brazilians pose one more challenge to the popular image of undocumented immigrants as young, impoverished males, largely of rural Mexican origin. In fact, Brazilians fit the description of other communities of illegal immigrants in the northeastern United States far more than they do the stereotypic Mexican. Undocumented Brazilians, like the undocumented Haitians and Dominicans in one study,[33] are largely middle and lower-middle class. Also, like many new immigrants to New York City, Brazilians are mostly of urban origin, have relatively high levels of education, and were employed before coming to the United States. A few of them are repeat migrants, and the majority have stayed in this country longer than they originally had planned. Also, like so many other recent immigrants, Brazilians arrive in New York as economic exiles trying to escape chaotic economic conditions back home. How they make it to these shores is the subject of the next chapter.

CHAPTER TWO

Bye-Bye, Brazil

Immigration regulations did not prevent entry. . . . Regulations merely caused delays in the movement of some and created stresses and strains.

—VIVIAN GARRISON AND CAROL WEISS,

"Dominican Family Networks and United States Immigration Policy"

THE LABYRINTHINE RULES and regulations of the INS are no match for the ingenuity of Brazilian immigrants desiring to come to the United States—and, with some 1.5 million to 3 million undocumented aliens in the country, presumably no match for that of other nationalities as well. The first step in coming to the United States, getting a U.S. tourist visa, is the major hurdle to entry faced by aspiring Brazilian immigrants. To get a tourist visa the would-be traveler has to demonstrate to the satisfaction of U.S. consular personnel in Brazil that he or she has adequate means to pay for the stay in the United States and has strong reasons to return to Brazil: close family ties or significant property or a good job.

In the past, before the onslaught of Brazilian immigrants entering the United States as tourists, this was a relatively simple procedure; travel agencies that booked flights to the United States secured the bulk of tourist visas for their clients. But regulations have been tightened, and getting a tourist visa these days is far more likely to mean a trip to the closest consular office for a personal interview. The current standard for a tourist visa, to paraphrase the words of an official in the U.S. consulate in Rio de Janeiro, is guilty until proven innocent—the presumption is that tourist visa applicants are going to stay in the United States and work unless they can prove otherwise.

Blame It on (the) Rio (Consulate)

The majority of Brazilian immigrants in New York City got their tourist visas from the U.S. consulate in Rio de Janeiro, since the consular district covered by the Rio office includes Minas Gerais state and the city of Rio de Janeiro, the two places where most Brazilians in New York come from.

2.1 The line for visa applicants forms early and snakes around the block at the U.S. consulate in Rio de Janeiro.

A visit to the consulate in downtown Rio is instructive. Before 8:00 A.M., when the doors open, a line of visa applicants has already formed; an hour or so later, it winds around the block. The consulate continues accepting applicants until 11:00 A.M., when everyone on line is given a number, assuring them of an interview that day. Anyone arriving after that is told to come back the next day.

The ambience of the consular offices is semicontrolled chaos. Stacks of Brazilian passports and visa applications overflow desks and tables, and down computers often delay processing. Severe understaffing has meant that only two officers are charged with interviewing applicants for tourist visas; interviews usually take only a minute or two. Still, during the busiest months, July and August—the Brazilian vacation season—up to a thousand applications a day are processed. Aside from a personal interview, all names must be computer checked to see if the individual has a police record of any kind.

Not all tourist visa applicants are interviewed, including many applying through travel agencies and *despachantes*, literally, "dispatchers," people who are hired to acquire documents or cut through red tape. Some tourist applications are rubber-stamped—those that are renewals for people who have had tourist visas before and applications from tour groups taking children to Disney World. People with multiple U.S. entry stamps in their passports also are approved quickly because they have established a record of not overstaying their visas in the past.

THE INTERVIEW

Fernando, a single man in his twenties who had taught high school in Rio, recounted the saga of his tourist visa pursuit at the U.S. consulate there. He had first tried to get a visa through a travel agency, but his request was denied, and he was told that he had to appear in person for an interview. He went to the consulate armed with all manner of documents—employment papers, a copy of his university diploma, tax receipts, and checking account stubs.

Fernando had been forewarned by a friend to try to avoid one of the interviewers at the consulate, who was infamous for denying tourist visas to one and all. Rumor had it that she regularly turned down weeping would-be travelers. While he waited for his interview, he spotted the notorious interviewer and said a silent prayer that his passport would not be among those that she periodically plucked from the large stack on the desk. He waited nervously, certain that he would be denied a visa if he were assigned to her for an interview. To his great relief, his name was called by the other consular officer.

Fernando quickly told the interviewer that he was a high school teacher, liked his job, and—of course—had no desire to stay in the United States. When the consular officer asked how much money he planned to bring with him for his trip, Fernando replied that he intended to bring $700. The official told him that INS officials like to see tourists enter the United States with at least $1,000, to make sure that they really *are* tourists and not immigrants looking for work.

Fernando is convinced that the consular officer gave him this useful bit of advice knowing that he probably planned to stay in the United States and seek a job. He believes that the interviewer was trying to be helpful because Fernando was a teacher, well educated, and well dressed and because they got along well. He is just as convinced that a selection process goes on at the consulate and that certain people are granted visas even though consular officers may suspect that they plan to stay in the United States and seek employment. I should note that Fernando has what Brazilians call *uma boa aparência*, "a nice appearance"; he is white, is good looking, and has a pleasant, outgoing personality.

To end the saga: Fernando's tourist visa was granted. I met him about a year later, while he was shining shoes in a shoe repair shop near Penn Station in midtown Manhattan.

A consular official estimated that applications for tourist visas in the Rio office in 1990 were up about 25 percent over the preceding year, but denials were also up slightly, from about 25 percent of applicants in 1989 to 29 percent in 1990.[1] The percentage of denials varies with the characteristics of the applicant although no statistics are kept on this. Since, as one consular officer told me, there is no "computer program" that indicates which applicants are likely to overstay their visas and seek employment, interviewers look for risk factors. Young, single people with no job or other source of income are the most suspect category of visa applicant, followed by those with relatives in the United States. To overcome suspicion that they will remain in the United States and look for work, applicants must, in the words of one consular employee, "show their ties to Brazil" through employment, family, income, and ownership of property. Even something as simple as paying income tax is evidence that the person earns enough to file a tax return and therefore can afford the trip. Actual payment of taxes owed "shows some respect for the law," the same consular officer told me, a hopeful sign of honesty, indicating that the applicant will not be a visa overstayer.

Two consular officers who regularly interview visa applicants are well aware of tales about their hard heartedness, and said they hoped that I would not depict them as "unfeeling ogres" in my book because they routinely deny visas and turn people away in tears. They realize that with up to a thousand visa requests a day, "mistakes are made," including denying visas to legitimate tourists. They "have sympathy" but are "just following the law." In fact, gossip about visa interviewers is rife among Brazilians in New York, much of it not very flattering.

"They're Shutting the Gates"

Whatever type of visa, we look at the applicant as a possible immigrant.

—*U.S. Embassy official, Brasília*

A New York attorney who has long worked with Brazilian clients noted that in the past Brazilians had no trouble getting tourist visas because, like the English, French, and other nationalities, they had reputations as legitimate tourists who returned home before their visas expired. But sometime during the 1980s, he began hearing stories about the problems Brazilians were having securing tourist visas, problems that have grown with every passing year. The INS, he says, will not admit that there are "suspect groups" whose tourist visa applications are scrutinized with extra care, but he has no doubt that such categories exist. Because of their growing notoriety as visa overstayers, he believes, Brazilians are now classified with other immigrant scofflaws.

Other longtime Brazilian residents of New York concurred with this attorney's assessment. "Today you have to have rich parents to get a tourist visa," I was told. You have to "prove that you are a millionaire" to consular officers before they will believe that you are not coming to the United States to work. "They're shutting the gates," a Brazilian remarked plaintively. Another informant adamantly insisted that no more than 5 percent of all Brazilian applicants actually got tourist visas.

While this figure is certainly a gross exaggeration, during the course of my research, I was continually regaled with stories of visa denials. One Brazilian friend gave me a firsthand account. While she was on line at the U.S. consulate in Rio to renew a student visa, she witnessed a consular officer deny tourist visas to three people in a row. One woman was turned down when she said that she had no family or job in Brazil, and that while it was true she was only thirty-five years old, she had already retired because of an undisclosed "illness." Two others were denied because of insufficient assets. The consular officer treated most people "boorishly," my friend said, but was courteous to her when he found out she was a Ph.D. candidate at a U.S. university.

THE LETTER NOBODY WANTS

Dear Senhor/a,

We regret to inform you that it is impossible at present to grant you a visa.

In accordance with the immigration laws of the U.S.A., it is the exclusive responsibility of applicants for temporary visas to prove that they will leave the United States before the expiration of the visa. This can be done by showing strong bonds making likely the person's return to his or her country of origin.

Although each case is given consideration, a good job and a good financial situation in Brazil are considered of extreme importance in proving that the person will return to Brazil.

This decision does not permamently deny you the right to obtain a visa. Your case can be reviewed again when circumstances indicate strong reasons for your return [to Brazil].

—*Form letter sent to temporary visa applicants in Brazil by the Consulate of the United States of America. Translated from the Portuguese.*

Tales of three, four, even five denials before a successful visa application are common. One man was approved on his third try after switching to a better job as a computer operator, and then applying at a different U.S. consulate. A Brazilian minister in New York told me about a parishioner who changed his appearance and hair style after being refused a visa four times, hoping that consular personnel would not recognize him.

When he was denied a visa for the fifth time, he gave up and came to the United States via Mexico. Another man was denied, and then approved only after paying a *despachante* $400 to file the visa application for him.

With incredulity, well-to-do Brazilians also recounted problems that their own relatives had had getting tourist visas. One woman, a well-known figure in New York's Brazilian business community, told me that her nephew was turned down on his first try even though he meant to come to the United States as a tourist. She thinks he was denied because he fit the "profile" of those who plan to stay; he is a student in his early twenties. Similarly, the daughter of a wealthy Brazilian physican at first was rejected for a tourist visa because she was unemployed at the time she applied for it. The fact that she owned two apartments in Brazil apparently made no difference to consular officials; she was approved for a visa only after her father activated his contacts at Itamaraty, Brazil's foreign office, and she returned to the U.S. consulate armed with evidence of her family's vast financial holdings.

Getting a visa at the U.S. consulate in São Paulo, the second-most-frequented consulate for Brazilians going to New York, seems to be no easier: in order to visit her son who was living in New York, one elderly woman went to the São Paulo consulate to get a tourist visa. She was turned down even though she is decidedly middle class, owns a business in São Paulo, and had no intention of staying in the United States beyond the expiration of her visa. She tried again a year later. This time she claimed that she had no children—recall that applicants with relatives in the United States are in a suspect category. She told the consular officer who interviewed her that she had been married thirty-five years and that her husband had given her the trip to the United States as an anniversary present although he, unfortunately, could not accompany her because of business. She was quickly approved for the visa, her interviewer remarking on "how few marriages lasted that long."

The Red Flag of Minas Gerais

Many tales revolve around the special problems that *mineiros*, natives of the Brazilian state of Minas Gerais, face getting visas. As visa applicants, *mineiros* are in a suspect category all their own because there are probably more undocumented immigrants in the United States from Minas Gerais than from any other state in Brazil. A case in point: a wealthy businessman, a longtime resident of Rio de Janeiro, is convinced that he was turned down for a tourist visa by the consulate there despite his financial status because of his place of birth; he is a native of Minas Gerais.[2]

One informant told me that the following sign in Portuguese was prominently displayed on a wall in the U.S. consulate in Rio de Janeiro: "Those from Governador Valadares or Poços de Caldas should not even bother to apply for a tourist visa." Both towns in Minas Gerais are well known for the number of their citizens residing in the United States. I saw no such sign when I visited the Rio consulate in July 1990, and according to consular officials, there never has been one. Still, the fact that people insist such a sign exists indicates how convinced they are that there is bias against *mineiros* in the issuance of tourist visas, particularly those from well-known sending communities. Indeed, without specifying the source of its figures, the popular Brazilian news weekly *Veja* reported that half of all undocumented Brazilians in the United States are from a handful of places in Minas Gerais, such as Governador Valadares, Poços de Caldas, and Botelhos.[3]

When I visited the town of Governador Valadares during the summer of 1990, a constant topic of conversation was the obstacles that its inhabitants face in getting tourist visas at the U.S. consulate. People liked to trade horror stories about who the latest local resident was to be denied a visa. Most of the stories centered around wealthy physicians and *fazendeiros* (cattle ranchers), people with no intention of staying and working in the United States, who were denied tourist visas, which they sought as legitimate tourists. One man and his daughter—he, a wealthy rancher who also practices law—were denied tourist visas to visit Disney World, as was another man, an engineer who had studied in the United States, and wanted to return for a three-month refresher course.

People in Governador Valadares are convinced—despite vigorous denials by officials of the U.S. consulate in Rio—that they are systematically discriminated against in the issuance of visas because of their place of origin. For example, a young woman from the town was invited to a conference of Presbyterian youth in Panama City, Fla. She and other Brazilians had been invited to the convention by an American pastor they had met at an earlier church youth conference in Brasília. She applied for a tourist visa and took time off from work to travel to the U.S. consulate in Rio for her interview. But despite vehement protestations that she was going to the United States only to attend the church conference and had no intention of seeking a job there, she was denied a visa. The other young invitees from elsewhere in Brazil had no problem getting visas to attend the same conference, and this young woman is convinced that she was denied solely because she is a *valadarense*.

The Brazilian press has carried many accounts of the problems that certain categories of aspiring travelers face in their dealings with U.S. consulates. According to an article in the *Folha de São Paulo*, about 3 percent of *paulistas*—people from São Paulo—were turned down for tourist visas, in contrast to a 30 percent refusal rate for *mineiros*. Because of the difficulties that *mineiros* have in obtaining visas, tourist agencies in Rio de Janeiro have been turning away prospective clients born in Minas Gerais even if they now live in other states. The director of a leading Rio travel agency that sells tours to Disney World thinks the actions of the U.S. consulate have some basis. "Many people first want to know if *we* get the passport [and visa] for them and *only then buy the excursion*," she is quoted as saying in an article on tourists' visa problems.[4]

One U.S. consular officer in Rio said that many *mineiros* have only themselves to blame if they are turned down since so many of their compatriots have tried to get visas through an unending variety of scams. Still, he insisted, there is no policy of discrimination against natives of Minas Gerais per se, while admitting that "it is only human nature" to deny greater numbers of those that one has strong reason to believe—based on past history—will be visa overstayers.

THE HONEYMOON TRIP

A man and a woman from Minas Gerais put an engagement announcement in their local newspaper. After it was published, they cut it out and brought it with them when they went to the U.S. consulate in Rio to apply for tourist visas. They told the consular officer who interviewed them that they were going to Miami on their honeymoon and glowingly showed him their engagement announcement. He quickly approved their application. After they arrived in New York they both got jobs, and *then* they got married.

Where There's a Will . . .

Fake visas and doctored passports are sometime tools used to slip through the United States immigration bulwark. There are, indeed, so many scams and schemes surrounding these prized items that pages could be devoted to the machinations of their acquisition and use. Brazilian *jeito*—that special knack for achieving one's goal—is much in evidence when it comes to the travel documents needed to bypass the tourist visa logjam. And the *jeitos* apparently work since many Brazilians get legitimate visas by using less than legitimate documents. Still, I cannot emphasize the point too strongly that there is nothing particularly "Brazilian" about all these scams and schemes, nothing that would-be immigrants of other nationalities do not also use.

Recall that one criterion for granting a visa is financial well-being. The solution for those on shaky financial ground? Present consular officers with letters that create highly paid, long-term employment histories. Bring in inflated bank statements and tax returns showing greater means than one actually has. Borrow large sums of money from friends and relatives and temporarily deposit it in your own bank account. Supply consular officers with newly minted business ownership papers, a surefire way of enhancing one's financial status in their eyes.

A VISA TALE

For three years, João, a *paulista*, tried to get a tourist visa to come to the United States. After he finally got one, he came to New York and found a job with a construction company, where he worked for six years. The company's owner agreed to sponsor him for a green card. While he was in the process of getting it, his mother fell seriously ill in São Paulo, and he had to go back to Brazil for a month.

When he was ready to return to the United States, the U.S. consulate refused to grant him a visa. He explained that he was in the final stages of approval for a green card, had a good job, and was a part-time college student. He had taken a leave of absence only to visit his ailing mother in Brazil. He showed consular officials his American credit cards, his U.S. income tax returns, and his New York driver's license, all to no avail. None of this convinced them to grant him a visa; he was told that he was going to have to wait it out in Brazil until his green card came through.

João became desperate to return to New York because he was worried about losing his job and missing classes, while continuing to pay rent on his apartment. Seeing no other solution, he bought another person's passport for $3,500, with a visa already stamped in it. He removed the photo, replaced it with his own, and traveled to the United States under the passport owner's name. He made sure that when he went through immigration control at Kennedy Airport, he had nothing on him—credit cards, driver's license, checks— that might give away his true identity. He got through without a hitch and today is the proud owner of a green card.

Would-be travelers to the United States from Minas Gerais sometimes buy birth certificates from non*mineiros*, believing that this will enhance their chances of being approved for a tourist visa. One of the most elaborate visa scams along these lines was pulled off by Carlinhos, a native of Governador Valadares. In 1986, after eight months of unsuccessful attempts to get a visa from the U.S. consulate in Rio, he "moved"—for the purposes of his visa application—and became a resident of Goiania, a city in central Brazil that falls within the consular district served by the U.S.

Embassy in Brasília. Fewer immigrants come from this part of Brazil, so it is said to be easier to get a tourist visa there. More important, Carlinhos no longer belonged to that infamous category: *mineiro* from Governador Valadares. He traveled to the embassy in Brasília, and in the application for his visa he used the address and phone number of a friend who lived in Goiania. He also provided the consulate with a document indicating that he was the owner of a cosmetics company there. His sister, who was living in Newark, N.J., at the time, was the one who advised him to take the "Brasília route" to a tourist visa; she had heard about it through the local Brazilian grapevine.

People who, for whatever reason, are unable to get visas in their own names, yet who desperately want to come to the United States, may use the alternative of traveling on someone else's passport, that is, a passport with a valid U.S. tourist visa already stamped in it. This practice, called "photo subbing" by immigration authorities, usually involves certain steps to ensure that the bogus passport holder will not encounter problems either when leaving Brazil or when entering the United States. When a passport is purchased, the photo of the legitimate owner is replaced by one of the individual who is going to travel on the passport. A difficulty may arise, however, because in Brazilian passports the photo has an official stamp on top of it, and there is the chance that when the traveler is leaving Brazil, the federal police officer who stamps the date of departure into the passport may notice the absence of a stamp on the photo. To avoid this, the purchasers of passports are told that when they depart from Brazil, they should go to a specific individual for their exit stamp. In other words, part of the money they pay for the passport is used to smooth their departure by finding its way into the hands of a cooperative federal employee.

> *WEEKEND PASSAGE*
> Brazilians traveling to the United States with passports belonging to someone else try to travel on Friday or Saturday. The reason is simple. When they go through immigration control the next morning, any doubts that the INS officer may have about the passport's legitimacy cannot be immediately checked out by faxing an inquiry to Brazil, because the offices of the Brazilian federal police are closed on the weekend—making it far more likely that the would-be immigrant will be waved on through.

Most prospective immigrants have neither the skills nor the contacts to pull off these document schemes by themselves. What one informant called "a visa and passport industry" has developed to serve their needs in Rio de Janeiro, Governador Valadares, Poços de Caldas, and presumably other areas of Brazil where there is a demand. It has even been suggested that clandestine immigration is partly spurred by the small businesses and travel agencies that arrange U.S. visas; indeed, some newspaper ads in Minas Gerais offer passports and guarantee entry into the United States within fifteen days.[5]

The visa side of the "industry" is charged with producing the various documents intended to show that visa applicants are people of considerable means, while con artists in the passport business also have their work cut out for them; they change photos and names, doctor places of origin, and insert pages in passports with valid tourist visas granted to other individuals. Those who work with fraudulent documents sometimes buy passports with unexpired tourist visas from Brazilians living in the United States who do not intend to return to Brazil before the visa expires. In these cases, about one month before the expiration of the visa, the passport is sent from the United States to the Brazilian purchaser. There, the passport holder's photograph is removed, and then the passport, with its valid tourist visa, is sold to a new would-be *brazuca*. Brazilians, of course, are not the only would-be migrants to the United States who engage in such practices. Similar ruses have been reported for Peruvians, Dominicans, and others.[6]

None of these schemes or their attendant documents comes cheap. One Brazilian who lived in New York and then went home to Brazil "for good," stayed only two months, and then wanted to return to the United States badly enough to pay $4,000 for the necessary documents—fake income tax returns and business ownership papers—that allowed him to get a new tourist visa. A doctored passport costs at least $1,000, and one *mineiro* told me that if he wanted to, he could sell his passport, which had a valid tourist visa in it, for $2,000. I also met immigrants who were denied visas who claimed to have paid $1,500 to $2,000 to *despachantes*—who, in turn, were said to have paid off consular personnel to get legitimate visas on their behalf. Whether this is true or not, there is no doubt that some people believe that visas are obtainable through such means.

These schemes have had mixed success. In 1989, according to the Brazilian Federal Police, at least 2,000 Brazilians traveled to the United States on false passports. Undoubtedly, many times that number entered with counterfeit tourist visas or with legitimate visas obtained through counterfeit means. On one occasion, twenty-eight Brazilians, purportedly all from Governador Valadares, arrived at Kennedy Airport and tried to pass through immigration control with doctored tourist visas. Twenty-seven were apprehended by the INS and sent back to Brazil; one somehow escaped detection.[7]

The purchase of travel documents is certainly not limited to Brazilians; a passport rental industry of sorts operates among other groups of hopeful immigrants, Dominicans, for example. For a $1,200 fee, passports with valid tourist visas stamped in them are rented from their owners and used for a single one-way trip to enter the United States. They are then returned to the owner, and subsequently rented to another traveler. Similarly, in communities in the Dominican Republic with high rates of migration to the United States, there are specialized "agent-brokers" who have complex systems for obtaining tourist visas by using forged land deeds, savings passbooks, and other documents.[8]

All of these schemes combined translate into large numbers. Perhaps 500,000 visitors annually drift from sight as their visas lapse. Estimates suggest that 40 percent of all undocumented aliens in the United States either overstayed their tourist visas or used fraudulent documents to gain entry in the first place. In fact, most undocumented Brazilians in the United States—probably well over 90 percent—fall into this category, officially termed visa abusers by the INS. Moreover, it is relatively easy to be a visa abuser or overstayer in the United States because once entrants—whether legitimate tourists or would-be immigrants—are safely beyond the swinging doors that lead out of immigration control at Kennedy Airport or any other U.S. port of entry, there is simply no system for keeping track of any of them.[9]

Arriving in the Big Apple

After landing at Kennedy Airport, Brazilian immigrants' first encounter with New York occurs in the chaotic ambience of the airport's International Arrivals Building. After a nine-hour overnight flight from Rio de Janeiro, the primary point of embarkation, they make their way off the plane weighted down with carry-on luggage and are directed to the entryway marked "Visitors." Thus begins the drawn-out passage through immigration control. Depending on the time of year, the length of the line, and the inquisitiveness of immigration officials, the wait lasts from thirty minutes to two hours.

After an overnight flight with little sleep, a delay of this length would be trying under any circumstances, but it is particularly grueling for would-be immigrants from Brazil—or anywhere else, for that matter—who do not know whether they will pass muster with immigration authorities and be allowed to enter the country. The tension on the line is palpable as passengers inch closer to their turn to be interviewed by an immigration officer, juggling their luggage to get at passports with the prized tourist visas stamped in them. In another part of the terminal, friends and relatives waiting to meet the weary travelers are just as edgy, not knowing if the new arrivals will be approved for entry and walk through the swinging doors to be greeted by hugs and kisses amidst sighs of relief or, harrowingly, if they will be detained.

The tension begins long before arrival at Kennedy Airport. To be sure, for some it is their first time on an airplane, but for most Brazilian immigrants coming to New York on tourist visas, it is not fear of flying but fear of immigration authorities that accounts for their jittery behavior. A Brazilian friend told me about a fellow passenger on her flight from Rio de Janeiro to New York. The young man who sat next to her was clearly agitated and sweated profusely throughout the trip. He apparently was fearful of his impending passage through the immigration gauntlet and, sure enough, upon arrival at Kennedy Airport, he was detained by INS officers; that was the last she saw of him.

Why all the nervousness and tension? After all, my research suggests that the great majority of prospective immigrants from Brazil arrive in New York with valid passports and legitimate tourist visas. But neither guarantees quick approval for entry to the United States by immigration authorities. Even individuals with valid documents can be detained for questioning if an immigration officer suspects that they actually plan to stay in this country and look for work. Any indication that someone is not really a "temporary visitor," in INS parlance, can be cause for further inquiry.

A few examples: If a person holding a tourist visa is asked by an immigration officer whether he or she has any close friends or relatives in this country, and the person hesitates and then responds in the negative, the officer may probe further to try to determine the truth of the matter. To immigration authorities, lying about having friends or relatives in the United States instantly sends up a red flag that the individual is a likely visa overstayer. Since many overstayers-in-the-making are aware of this, they hide the names, addresses, and phone numbers of friends or relatives living in the United States whom they plan to contact. For the same reason, savvy immigrants never tell an immigration officer that they plan to stay at a friend's or relative's apartment in New York, and they have the name and address of a local hotel with them just in case the question comes up.

Then, too, people on tourist visas are often asked by immigration officials how much money they have with them. If the amount seems too meager to cover the expenses of a vacation trip, this may signal that the person intends to stay in the United States and seek work. Once again, many travelers know this and come prepared by carrying at least $1,000 with them even if they have to borrow the money before leaving Brazil. Some take short-term loans of several thousand dollars from friends and relatives for the sole purpose of demonstrating to the INS officer upon entry that they have plenty of money and thus would not dream of staying in the United States and looking for work.

NO ENGLISH SPOKEN HERE

One Brazilian family returned to New York as "tourists" after a visit to Brazil. They had been living in the United States illegally for several years, and their young daughter attended school and spoke fluent English. They told her to be sure to speak only Portuguese when going through immigration control at Kennedy Airport in order to avoid suspicion by appearing to be an average Brazilian tourist. To their horror, as their passports were being stamped by an immigration officer, their daughter began speaking English, blurting out that she "couldn't lie" about not understanding the language. This slip led to a long and expensive legal proceeding to avoid deportation.

There is simply no way to determine how many Brazilians with valid passports and visas are deported to Brazil after judicial hearings because they initially aroused the suspicions of immigration authorities. A high-level official at the U.S. consulate in Rio de Janeiro told me that most of those picked up by U.S. immigration authorities at Kennedy Airport and sent back to Brazil have fake visas or obviously doctored passports. She insisted that those with legitimate documents are rarely deported at the port of entry. Nevertheless, her office does get INS reports of between seventy and eighty cases a month of individuals' being deported as likely visa overstayers, and she admitted that there are additional cases that the INS never reports because of understaffing.

The cases of deportation appear to be few in number in the context of the hundreds of would-be Brazilian immigrants arriving at Kennedy Airport every month. Nevertheless, nightmarish tales about entrants' being detained and deported to Brazil spread like wildfire in New York's Brazilian community. To wit: One woman's sister and niece were detained by immigration authorities at Kennedy Airport and, after a hearing, were sent back to Brazil. When the sister was interviewed by an immigration officer, she was asked if her husband was in the United States. She lied, saying that he was in Brazil. A quick computer check of his name showed that he was in fact residing in this country. On this basis, she and her young daughter were deported. The woman lost the $3,000 she had paid for airfare and other expenses for the trip. Her husband, in disgust, subsequently went back to Brazil two months after his wife and daughter were sent home.

CLOSE CALL

Jeninho had been living in New York City for more than a year when he went out to Kennedy Airport to meet his wife and young son, who were arriving from Rio to join him in the Big Apple. As they were passing through immigration control, after Jeninho's wife had told the INS agent that she had no relatives in the United States and had come to New York on vacation, Jeninho, overcome with emotion by the sight of his son, rushed forward and swept him up into his arms. The INS agent taking note of this touching family scene, immediately detained Jeninho's wife and son. They spent two days in INS custody at a motel near the airport before being released on bond. They did not appear for the court hearing and are still living in the city.

A Brazilian woman said that she was interrogated mercilessly for two hours in the "red room"—I never learned the reason for this name—by three immigration officers upon her arrival at Kennedy Airport. They took her aside and questioned her in a separate room, trying to get her to admit that she had really come to the United States to work rather than as a tourist on vacation. They questioned her in detail about her plans—what hotel she was going to stay at, what cities she was going to visit—all the while insisting that they knew that she intended to stay in the United States and find a job. She stuck to her guns, and she was eventually released because there was no proof that she planned to remain in the country illegally. She was probably detained in the first place because of her age, marital status, and origin. Being young, single, and from Governador Valadares, the Brazilian town that has gained notoriety as a major exporter of *brazucas*, was a near-lethal combination for someone trying to enter the United States as a tourist.

Another Brazilian woman was seized by INS officials at Kennedy Airport and held as a potential overstayer because she had only $500 with her. How was she going to pay for her tour of this country? she was asked over and over again. She said that at one point an officer offered to free her in exchange for sex, but that she refused and said she would rather be deported. She was held over for a hearing and the immigration judge found in her favor. That was two years ago, she told me, with a wink.

Finally, one informant said that on his second trip to the United States he had had no problem getting through immigration inspection at Kennedy Airport even though he had entered the country on someone else's passport and tourist visa, items he had purchased after having been denied a visa himself. In contrast, on his first visit, he landed at Miami Airport with his own passport and valid tourist visa. That time he was questioned closely by immigration officers about how much money he had with him, what his plans were, and so on. He noted with wry amusement that INS officials gave him a hard time when all of his papers were in order, but that when he entered the United States on another person's passport he breezed through immigration.

Perhaps the best illustration of the problems some Brazilians face when trying to pass through immigration comes from the stories recounted by Adelia, a Brazilian who worked as an official court interpreter under contract to the INS. She traveled to Kennedy Airport five days a week over a four-month period in 1987 to serve as an interpreter for Brazilians detained by immigration authorities there. Adelia estimates that while she was working for the INS, anywhere from five to fifteen people on every flight arriving from Brazil were detained for questioning; she believes that a dragnet of some sort was operating at the time.[10] People whose visas or passports seemed irregular or who were suspected for any reason of having come to the United States to stay and work were stopped and told to step aside. Those detained were put under guard and taken into a separate room for questioning. Later, they were put up for the night at an airport hotel, usually at the expense of the transporting airline whose responsibility it is to ensure that its passengers have valid travel documents. Since hearings were held only on weekdays, those unfortunate enough to be stopped on the weekend were bound over until Monday morning.

According to Adelia, this was a traumatic experience for many Brazilians. They were under guard at all times; they were accompanied to the hotel by guards, and even trips to the bathroom had to be made with a guard of the appropriate sex. Some of the guards, she was told, requested money or sexual favors from the detainees.

Adelia says she felt awkward about having to appear neutral and not being able to give any advice or comfort to her often-terrified compatriots. But she did try to help them when she could. When immigration officers found evidence in a detainee's luggage that he or she was planning on staying in the United States, Adelia would think of an alternative "cultural" explanation for the presence of the incriminating item. For example, one detainee was carrying memorabilia from a farewell party that had been thrown for her by friends and relatives before she left Brazil. When questioned about this, Adelia told INS officials that Brazilians use almost any excuse for a party and that it was common to throw "farewell parties" for people who leave on short vacation trips.

Detainees were rarely permitted phone calls and although a representative of the Brazilian consulate was present at the hearings, this seems to have been a mere formality. During the proceedings, INS attorneys strongly suggested to the detainees that they return to Brazil immediately and not challenge the legal case against them. This advice was so forcefully presented, and most of the Brazilians were so frightened, that nearly all of them—95 percent or so, Adelia estimates—went back to Brazil on the next available plane. Those that agreed to be deported had their passports confiscated, with the INS arranging substitute travel documents through the Brazilian consulate so that they could reenter Brazil. Invariably, the few who chose to stay and contest their deportation had friends or relatives in the United States, who helped them post bond.

The Disney World Connection

Only slightly apocryphal stories circulate in New York's Brazilian community of packed charter flights from Rio de Janeiro to Orlando that leave Florida for the return trip to Brazil devoid of passengers. In fact, many would-be immigrants take the Disney World route to New York via cheap charter flights that are usually part of a package tour. One Brazilian tour operator accompanies tour groups to Florida and New York five or six times a year, and is well aware that some members of the group simply vanish before the tour returns to Brazil.

Orlando is the logical entry point for immigrant families with children since immigration authorities are more apt to believe that they are legitimate tourists on a visit to Disney World. Still, over the course of my research, I met a number of single Brazilians in New York who had also entered the country via Orlando. Three young men traveled there together because they felt it would be easier to pass themselves off as tourists in Florida than in New York. Right after they arrived in Florida, they bought a used car to drive to New York because it turned out to be cheaper than paying for three plane tickets to fly there.

> ### JUST AN ORDINARY TOURIST
> One Brazilian who had trouble getting a tourist visa eventually got one after three years of trying. To avoid further suspicion that his real intention was to stay in the United States and find a job in New York, he flew from Rio to Miami with a large surfboard prominently displayed in his carry-on luggage. This was supposed to convince immigration officials that he really was a tourist.

After a trip to visit relatives in Brazil, a woman who works as a housekeeper in New York returned on a charter flight from Rio to Orlando, and then made a direct connection to New York. She told me how a large group of her fellow passengers, after passing through immigration control, went straight to the ticket counter of a U.S. airline to purchase one-way tickets to New York. She shook her head in wonder, saying she does not know how they managed since no one in the group spoke a word of English.

But a Disney World entrée to the United States is no guarantee of safe passage through the labyrinth of U.S. immigration control. I have been told stories—impossible to verify—of entire planeloads of Brazilian tourists' not being allowed to disembark in Orlando because INS officials suspected that there were many potential visa overstayers among them. An official at the U.S. consulate in Rio lent credence to this when she told me that the word is out among INS agents to carefully check documents of passengers on certain flights bound from Brazil. Then, there is the case of Eduardinho, who was picked up by the INS in Orlando after a visit to Brazil. Although he had a valid multiple-entry, four-year tourist visa, the stamps in his passport indicated that he had lived in New York for two years—a maximum stay of six months is permitted on a tourist visa. Immigration officials tried to talk him into being deported immediately, but he protested and was flown to Miami, where he was jailed for two weeks when he could not raise bond. He demanded and obtained an administrative hearing, at which the judge gave him permission to stay in the United States for sixty days because he was involved in an ongoing worker's compensation case in New York. All of this took place about two years prior to my interview with Eduardinho; he has since applied for and been granted amnesty.

The Mexican Route

If all else fails for Brazilians who desperately want to come to the United States, the Mexican route is a final option. This route is more problematic for Brazilians than for other Latin Americans, not only because of the distances involved but because as non–Spanish speakers, Brazilians run greater risks since they have more difficulty blending into the Mexican population.

Mexico also is the point of entry of last resort because of its high cost. The price is often triple what it would be for the more conventional route of flying directly from Rio de Janeiro to New York or Florida. Brazilians pay as much as $5,000 for airfare to Mexico City, transportation to the border, a *coyote* escort to cross it, travel to a U.S. border city, and a one-way plane ticket from the border city to the final destination. This was the actual cost of a trip offered by an agency in Governador Valadares to those who could not get U.S. tourist visas. In comparison, non-stop flights between Rio de Janeiro and some U.S. cities can be purchased for about $1,000 roundtrip—roundtrip tickets are required for those on tourist visas—or even less on some charter flights. The Mexican route, in contrast, never costs less than $2,000.

FIRST CROSSING

It was 1978. Tanya had lived in the United States for two years, where she had been employed as a live-in nanny and housekeeper. She missed her family terribly and returned to Brazil for three months to see them. When she applied for a tourist visa to come back to the United States, she was turned down by the U.S. consulate in Rio because she could not show sufficient income. A second application for a visa was no more successful. Desperate to return to the United States, she flew from Rio to Mexico City, thinking it was only about an hour from there to the U.S. border. After the rude geographic awakening of a thirty-hour bus ride, she got in touch with a woman who, she had been told, could help her get across the border. She paid the woman $50, and the woman arranged for a *coyote* to help her. In the middle of the night she met the *coyote* on the banks of the Rio Grande. He told her to hop on; she did so, and he swam across the freezing water—it was the middle of winter—with Tanya on his back. Tanya, today an admistrative assistant at a New York bank, has the distinction of being a Brazilian pioneer, possibly the first of her compatriots to have taken the Mexican route to this country.

Package deals to Mexico can be purchased in some cities in Brazil. A newspaper in Minas Gerais, the Brazilian state famed for its export of *brazucas*, reported that a group of sixteen Brazilians paid $3,000 apiece to a local travel agency for the flight to Mexico, a Brazilian guide to Tijuana, and a local *coyote* to assist in the border crossing. But, according to the article, the travel agency was *not* responsible for clients' being apprehended by U.S. immigration authorities and would make no refunds should that occur.[11]

Then, too, while any route can present obstacles for a would-be immigrant traveling to the U.S. on a tourist visa, the Mexican one is particularly risky. Stories abound of Brazilians being robbed and otherwise exploited at various points along the way. Bribes of $100, $200, or more to airport and border police—on both sides of the border—are commonplace; passports and luggage are stolen; and more than one Brazilian has wound up in a Mexican jail when he or she could not come up with sufficient funds to satisfy the authorities. To add insult to injury, some Brazilian clandestine border crossers, after being ordered to leave their luggage behind in Mexico in order to make the trip unencumbered, have then been told not to worry; they could buy used clothes from *coyotes* on the U.S. side of the border.[12]

Entry to the United States from Mexico also has become somewhat more difficult for Brazilians in the last few years, which may have cut down on the number arriving via this route. In contrast to past years, when Brazilians could simply buy a plane ticket to Mexico, they are now required—some say at the urging of U.S. immigration authorities—to have Mexican tourist visas. This means that when they apply for tourist visas, Brazilians must show Mexican consular officials in Brazil evidence of their financial well-being, a requirement similar to the one long necessary for a U.S. tourist visa. Nevertheless, it is still easier to get a Mexican tourist visa than to get a U.S. one.

One well-informed informant estimated that about 10 percent of Brazilian immigrants enter the U.S. "without inspection," that is, clandestinely, via Mexico. While this seems high, on the basis of my New York sample, in which only 3 percent reported using this route, other evidence suggests that the percentage does vary considerably, depending on a number of factors. For example, in a survey of Brazilians in Framingham, Mass., over 43 percent said that they had entered the United States clandestinely via Mexico, and I believe that Brazilian immigrants headed for Boston and Newark are somewhat more likely to take the Mexican route than those going to New York.[13]

DISAPPEARING ACT

A journalist for *O Globo*, a major Brazilian newspaper, interviewed thirty Brazilians from Governador Valadares who had been apprehended by the authorities in Mexico City. They were put up in a hotel there, and she interviewed them over a period of several days. Twenty-eight were headed for Boston, one was going to Newark, and one was going to California. She noticed that fewer and fewer Brazilians were around with each passing day, until only three remained at the hotel. They told her that the others had slipped away and were making their way to the U.S. border. Then they bid her *até logo*—goodbye—and also silently vanished to parts unknown.

Which route is used seems to be related to social class, education, and place of origin in Brazil. Poorer, less schooled *mineiros*—natives of Minas Gerais—are more likely to come into the United States through Mexico because they are more likely to have problems obtaining U.S. tourist visas than better-off, better-educated *cariocas* or *paulistas*—natives of Rio de Janeiro or São Paulo—who are more likely to fly directly to the United States and enter legally as tourists.

Would-be Brazilian immigrants to the United States much prefer the tourist visa path because of its relative simplicity, lower risks, and lower cost. Moreover, because the Mexican frontier route has severe drawbacks in price, time, and risk and is used only by their poorer compatriots, from the perspective of many in New York's Brazilian community, it is a stigmatized mode of entry.

The same ironic pattern—poorer immigrants' having to take the more costly and dangerous route to the United States—is noted by Eugenia Georges in her study of emigration from the Dominican Republic. In the town she studied, richer residents—those who own land or businesses—can usually get tourist visas and fly directly to the United States since, being property owners, they can convince U.S. consular officials that they will return home after their "tourist" excursions. But poorer, landless Dominicans are less likely to be approved for tourist visas; thus if they want to come to the United States badly enough, they must take the more expensive, riskier indirect route via Mexico.[14]

The following account of a harrowing entry into the United States via Mexico was told to me by Manuel three months after he arrived in New York. Manuel is a young man from a lower-middle-class family in southern Brazil whom I met when he was peddling books from a stand on Fifth Avenue.

After repeated unsuccessful attempts to obtain a tourist visa at the U.S. consulate in the Brazilian city of Porto Alegre, Manuel decided to try his luck via Mexico. This was suggested to him by a Brazilian friend living in New York. Although the friend had himself flown to New York and entered the United States legally on a tourist visa, three of his relatives had taken the Mexican route after being denied tourist visas by U.S. consular officials in Brazil.

Using false documents attesting to a well-paying job in Brazil, Manuel was able to get a thirty-day tourist visa to Mexico. He bought a round-trip ticket between São Paulo and Mexico City for $990. It was a long flight—the plane made three stops before landing in Mexico.

His friend in New York had arranged to have two people meet him at the airport in Mexico City. They were to transport him to the U.S. border, and then introduce him to a *coyote*, who would see him across. Manuel was supposed to wear a name tag to identify himself, but he said he got scared and at the last minute took the tag off. Had his escorts actually shown up, which they apparently had not, they would not have known who he was.

Not knowing what to do at this point, Manuel bought a plane ticket to Tijuana with some of the $700 or so he had with him. The flight took three hours, and by the time he reached Tijuana, it was 11:30 P.M. of the day he had arrived in Mexico.

When Manuel got to Tijuana, the Mexican immigration police threatened to send him back to Mexico City and then deport him to Brazil despite his valid passport and Mexican tourist visa. After continuing threats, he finally paid them $300, and they let him go. He now had about $300 left; he took a cab to a cheap motel, whose address he had been given in Brazil. The cabdriver tried to rob him, but he managed to hold on to his remaining dollars by convincing the driver that the 50 Brazilian cruzeiros—then about $1—that he parted with were a lot of money.

He spent one night at the motel but was unable to sleep because he was "a bundle of nerves." In the morning, he called his friend in New York, and the friend called his contact in Los Angeles, who arranged to have Manuel taken across the border to the United States. This transfer cost another $500; his friend in New York wired the money to the Los Angeles contact. Later that same day, a Mexican appeared at the motel, having been sent by the Los Angeles contact to take Manuel over the border. Manuel was jittery when the man refused to show him any identification. The man said that if Manuel wanted to be escorted across the border, he could take no luggage with him, and he was instructed to wear a black jacket to better conceal himself during the crossing. The man promised that once Manuel arrived in New York, his suitcase would be forwarded to him there. Needless to say, it never was, and all the new clothes that Manuel had bought for the trip to the United States remain somewhere in Mexico.

Manuel got into the man's car; they drove for a while, before transferring to a taxicab and eventually to a bus that took them close to the U.S. border. There, they waited about an hour for another six or seven people, all Mexicans, who were also going to enter the United States clandestinely. All wore dark clothes, as instructed, and they were told to throw themselves to the ground to avoid detection if helicopter lights appeared. Their first attempt at crossing the border was stymied when they spotted a border patrol. They turned back and spent about an hour running to another spot along the border, where, with the *coyote* in the lead and the rest of the group running behind him, they crossed over into the United States.

They spent the night in an apartment in San Isidro, California. The next morning, the group dispersed. Two Mexican women, accompanied by three children, came to the apartment to pick up Manuel and one of the Mexicans. They were told to get into the trunk of the women's car, where they were covered by a blanket with flowers arranged on top of it. They stayed in the trunk for the seemingly long ride to San Diego. Manuel said it was so hot in the trunk that he could barely breathe and he thought that he was going to die.

Once in San Diego, he was taken to the women's house, where he was picked up by a Mexican who was in the *coyote* network and driven to another house in Los Angeles, where he spent the night. The next morning, he again phoned his New York friend, who wired him additional money for a plane ticket from Los Angeles to New York. He arrived at New York's La Guardia Airport virtually penniless and with only the clothes on his back. His friend met him and took him to his apartment in Brooklyn.

The trip began on a Monday in São Paulo when he boarded the flight to Mexico and ended the following Saturday when he arrived in New York City. The trip cost close to $3,500, most of which he still owes his friend.

TRY AND TRY AGAIN

A letter to the editor of *Brazilian Times*, a weekly published for the Brazilian community in Boston, pokes fun at the obstacles that some Brazilians face when they try to enter the United States "Formerly anyone who got through immigration was a hero," the letter writer notes, and the family boasted of the feat: " 'My son,' the mother said, 'had to stay in a car trunk for fourteen hours on the Mexican border!' Not to be outdone, her friend replied: 'Well, *my son* went with a false passport, but immigration officers discovered it and he was deported. He came home last Wednesday, but we already are working on a new plan for him to try again next Wednesday. They say that this scheme is *really* good.' "

"Other Than Mexicans"

Brazilians seem to belie the popular American image of the illegal border crosser as a young Mexican male headed for work in the vineyards and vegetable fields of California. According to INS data, this image is quite an accurate one since until very recently OTMs—"Other Than Mexicans" in the lingo of the INS—made up less than 2 percent of all apprehensions in the San Diego–Tijuana area, the busiest stretch of the U.S.-Mexican border. By early 1989, however, the proportion of OTMs had increased slightly, to 5 percent of apprehended illegals. Over 58,000 non-Mexicans were detained in 1990, and it has been estimated that for every person who is caught, at least two others successfully cross the border. Moreover, apprehensions had become very cosmopolitan: "We are now picking up *coyotes* whose personal address books list names and phone numbers in Frankfurt, New Delhi, Hong Kong, Rio and Belgrade," Mexican officials are quoted as saying, and there have been reports of Mexicans sheperding Turks, Koreans, and other far flung nationals across the border into the United States.[15]

The illicit trade in undocumented border crossers, once loosely organized and local, is quickly becoming a lucrative international enterprise
run by professionals. More prominent now are multinational rings,
which front as travel agencies, use safe houses, and produce fake or illegal
documents. According to a *New York Times* report, tens of thousands of
people from East Asia, West Africa, India, and Brazil, among other countries, "are no less eager [than Mexicans] to build new lives in the U.S."[16]

North of the Border and Other Routes

Before Canada created a visa requirement for Brazilian tourists, an unknown number of them flew from Rio to Toronto, and then crossed the
border into the United States. When that was a viable means of entry, a
Brazilian *coyote* worked full-time running other Brazilians across an international bridge that spanned a river between Ontario and New York
State. In 1988, reports circulated in the Brazilian community that a group
of Brazilians were caught entering the United States illegally from Canada
by clinging to the underside of a railroad trestle that crossed a river somewhere along the U.S.-Canadian border. I met one Brazilian who flew to
western Canada, and then gradually made his way to the United States by
crossing the Canadian Rockies.

A more recent route has taken Brazilians to Puerto Rico, an entry point
of choice for many Latin Americans because, since Puerto Rico is part of
the United States, those traveling to the U.S. mainland from there do not
have to pass through immigration control. In fact, up to 30,000 Dominicans a year may enter the United States via this route.[17] In early 1991, *El
Diario/La Prensa*, a Spanish-language newspaper in New York City, reported that a boat with ninety-two Brazilians and Ecuadorians on board
was intercepted off the Puerto Rican coast by local authorities. The boat
was bound from the Dominican Republic, its load of would-be immigrants hoping to slip into the United States via Puerto Rico. The Rio de
Janeiro daily *O Globo* carried a brief news item a year earlier reporting
that sixteen Brazilians were arrested and detained in the Santo Domingo
airport for entering the Dominican Republic with improper documents.
They, too, were headed for the United States by way of Puerto Rico. According to the report, those apprehended claimed to have paid $2,000
each to the organizer of the trip, and I was told that similar packages to
Puerto Rico, including "tour guides," are sold in Governador Valadares
for $3,500.

These recent news stories suggest that more Brazilians may now be
using these alternate routes to the United States, as entry via Mexico has
become more perilous. Of course, the Puerto Rican route for undocumented entry into the United States is nothing new. For at least two de-

cades, Dominicans who have had trouble getting tourist visas have traveled to Puerto Rico on small planes or boats, spent a day or two there, and then bought airplane tickets from San Juan to New York and passed themselves off as Puerto Ricans in order to enter the United States without visas.[18]

In the last few years, the Brazilian media have been filled with reports of stowaways to the United States. In August 1988 there were horrific accounts of the experiences of forty-three Brazilian men and eight Brazilian women, all apprehended stowaways on a cargo ship. The ship left Ilheus in the state of Bahia with a cargo of cacao on an eleven-day voyage to Philadelphia. Conditions on board were grim. Each cabin housed about ten Brazilians, and they were given only one meal a day for the duration of the trip. After arriving in Philadelphia, five crew members were arrested along with the stowaways, each of whom had paid $2,500 for the "fare."

According to these same reports, INS officials suspected that the ship and its human cargo were part of a larger clandestine network smuggling Brazilians into the United States. One official is quoted as saying that the seizure looked like the "tip of an iceberg" of the operations of a criminal gang since it was the third incident that year involving vessels owned by the same shipping company.[19]

I occasionally heard similar tales during my research. For example, one man told me that his sister had paid $2,500 to a Brazilian sailor to stow away in his berth on a cargo ship bound from Vitoria, a city on Brazil's central coast, to Newark. The trip took twelve days, and three other Brazilians also were stowaways on board. The ship's captain purportedly knew nothing about them, and the man's sister disembarked in Newark, where she still lives.

AND FOR THE POOR

Poverty-stricken Brazilians are leaving the country to seek their fortunes elsewhere. It is estimated that about 15,000 Brazilians are working as miners in Venuzuela, 10,000 are in mining and construction in French Guiana, and 6,000 are miners and shopkeepers in Guyana. Thousands more work in Bolivia, Colombia, and Peru, having crossed the remote and often unmarked borders in the Amazon region between those countries and Brazil.

Source: Brooke, "Venezuela's Policy for Brazil's Gold Miners: Bullets."

There are two other modes of entry into the United States, which now seem to be used only rarely by Brazilians. At one time, I was told, Brazilians who could afford it went to Europe and applied for U.S. tourist visas at U.S. consulates there because the requirements for issuing such visas were somewhat more lax than in Brazil. This practice supposedly ended when U.S. consular regulations were tightened and made uniform. Moreover, a few Brazilians of Portuguese and Italian descent became citizens of the lands of their ancestors by taking out papers at the Portuguese and Italian consulates in Brazil. Then, since Europeans—unlike Brazilians— do not have reputations as visa overstayers and potential illegals among U.S. consular officers in Brazil, these born-again Europeans headed for the closest U.S. consulate with their brand-new passports and were granted tourist visas to come to the United States.

ANOTHER DESTINATION

The United States is not the only popular destination abroad for Brazilians. Many Brazilians of Japanese descent are going to Japan to take high-paying, manual labor jobs in Japanese industry. Between 1988 and 1991, the number of visas issued to Japanese-Brazilians by the São Paulo consulate increased nearly sevenfold; by 1992, an estimated 160,000 Japanese-Brazilians were working in Japan. Travel agencies in Brazil serve as labor recruiters, paying for the one-way fare and having it deducted from the immigrants' wages in Japan. All told, it is estimated that Japanese-Brazilians remit some $2 billion annually to Brazil.

Japanese-Brazilians take jobs that the Japanese themselves do not want because they are the "three *Ks*"—*kitanai, kiken,* and *kitsui* (dirty, dangerous, and difficult). But the attraction of these jobs is clear. Wages are ten times what they are in Brazil; by living frugally and staying in inexpensive dormitories, Japanese-Brazilians can save $1,500 to $1,700 a month. Some earn nearly $2,000 a month by working overtime.

Both working-class and middle-class Japanese-Brazilians are emigrating to Japan. About one-third of the immigrants have university degrees. But lacking fluency in Japanese, they can get only low-prestige factory jobs. Still, the Japanese-Brazilian community is awash with success stories. There is the one about the man who worked in an Osaka metal shop for two years and invested his savings in what is today a thriving luncheonette in São Paulo. Before going to Japan he had worked as a gas station attendant and street vendor.

Sources: Brooke, "A Rising Sun Beckons, to Highly Paid Drudgery"; Yoshida, "Brasileiros 'Dekassequis' Sofrem Mas Querem a Familia no Japão"; Lucena, "Aumenta Exôdo Para Japão e Estados Unidos"; *Veja*, "O Povo da Diáspora"; Kamm, "Brazil's Swelling Wave of Emigration Reflects Gloom about Nation's Future"; Kepp, "Japanese-Brazilians Find Cold Cash in Ancestral Homes"; Jones, "Latin-Japanese Workers Feel Cool Welcome"; Michaels, "*Dekasegi* Drawn by Promise of Jobs"; Brooke, "Jobs Lure Japanese-Brazilians to Old World."

Money Cares

How Brazilians live in New York, both in their first days and subsequently, depends in part on the size of the debts they left behind in Brazil to pay for their trip. At a minimum, the cost of coming to the United States is around $2,000, about equally divided between airfare and money for living expenses—recall that $1,000 is thought to be the magic number needed to get through immigration.[20] Although even this is a considerable sum by Brazilian standards, some immigrants bring even more cash with them as a financial cushion in case they are unable to get jobs right away.

About two-thirds of the Brazilians in my sample paid for the trip to the United States with money from their own savings or with help from their families; an unknown number of the sums from families were really loans from family members, not gifts, and were expected to be repaid. A few individuals sold cars, apartments, or other property to raise money for the move, and the handful who quit their jobs to come to the United States used their severance pay (*fundo de garantia*) to finance the airfare and other expenses.[21] The remaining third of the sample paid for the trip through loans, most often installment loans provided by travel agencies for plane tickets. Some individuals used multiple sources to come up with the money: their own savings, loans, and/or help from their families.

About one-third of the people in my sample, then, were in debt when they arrived in New York. These are the ones under the most pressure to find jobs immediately so that they can begin meeting their financial obligations in Brazil. Although I have no hard data on this, it appears that an indeterminate but probably significant number of Brazilians come to New York with only enough money to live on for a month or so, resolved to return to Brazil if they cannot find work within that time. If they borrowed the money for the trip, they presumably return home worse off than when they left. One well-informed informant with wide contacts in the Brazilian community estimates that about 10 percent of would-be immigrants return to Brazil within three months after arriving in the United States.

Still, some Brazilians earn money almost as soon as they get off the plane at Kennedy Airport, be it to pay off debts back home or simply for living expenses in the United States. They come to New York carrying semiprecious stones, which they then sell to help defray the cost of the trip. This is perfectly legal since up to $10,000 worth of stones can be imported duty free. One Brazilian who works in New York City's jewelry district on West 47th Street—conveniently located only a stone's throw from Little Brazil—estimates that up to 60 percent of Brazilians from Minas Gerais (or "general mines"), a state that is justly famed for its amethysts, topazes, tourmalines, and aquamarines, bring in loose stones to sell.

Another common practice also puts cash in the hands of newly arrived Brazilian immigrants: the illegal sale of their unused New York–Rio de Janeiro return tickets to other Brazilians planning to go home for good. These tickets are typically sold for between $250 and $350, a good deal less than the $600 charged by airlines.

Since this is such a common practice, the actual transaction is worth describing. The ticket sale is between two individuals, the seller and the traveler. The seller in whose name the return ticket is written accompanies the traveler to Kennedy Airport on the day of the flight. The seller goes to the airline counter with the plane ticket, shows his or her passport to the agent, checks in for the flight, and receives a boarding pass. Seller and traveler then repair to the waiting room, where the traveler is handed the plane ticket and boarding pass. The traveler gets on the flight using the seller's ticket and boarding pass and flys to Brazil. This is done all the time, and only occasionally do airline personnel, aware of this ruse, demand to see passengers' identification after they have boarded the plane.

This, then, is how Brazilian immigrants make their way to New York, how they finance the move and get the documents they need to make the trip, or barring that, how they come to the United States through a clandestine route. Their imaginative perseverance is evident in all of this, just as it is during their early days in the city.

CHAPTER THREE

First Days

The migrant travels along well developed, and smoothly functioning, ethnic
pathways to the destination location.

—DEMETRIOS PAPADEMETRIOU AND NICHOLAS DIMARZIO,
Undocumented Aliens in the New York Metropolitan Area

AFTER CLEARING immigration at Kennedy Airport or flying into New
York from Florida or a border city, the experience of newly arrived Brazilians varies somewhat, depending on whether they traveled to the
United States alone or with friends and relatives. A slight majority make
the trip by themselves—52 percent in my sample—but nearly as many
travel accompanied by others; 26 percent traveled with relatives, most
often a spouse or spouse and children, and 19 percent traveled with
friends.[1]

Brazilians' first days in New York City are colored more than anything
else by the aid and comfort—or lack of it—provided by familiar faces.
Most do get help settling into life in the Big Apple—over two-thirds of
those in my sample—either from friends (46 percent) or from relatives (23
percent), most often siblings and cousins. But some are not so fortunate.
The Brazilians who tell the most colorful, adventurous, and/or heartrend-
ing stories of their early days in New York are those—over a quarter of
my sample—who traveled to the United States by themselves and who
knew no one in the city when they arrived. These are the ones who find
themselves alone in strange hotels or, as one newcomer did, bedding down
for the night on a bench in Manhattan's Port Authority bus terminal.

Finding a place to live obviously has the highest priority for newly
arrived immigrants, and this is where having a friend or relative in the
area can really make a difference. About 60 percent of the people I interviewed had help with housing. When they first came to New York, they
lived with friends or relatives until they found jobs and moved to their
own apartments, or they stayed on and continued to share rent and other
expenses. One woman told me what a godsend it was for her and her
husband to be able to live in a friend's apartment in Queens for the first
few weeks after they arrived in New York.

More than a third of the Brazilians in my sample also had help finding jobs, help that was usually provided by the friends or relatives with whom they were staying. Most often, the host arranged a position at his or her place of work or found one through prior contacts. These networks and a little bit of luck meant that some brand-new immigrants were able to begin work right away. One Monday I met a man shining shoes at a shoe repair shop near Grand Central Station. He had arrived in New York for the first time the previous Friday; his cousin, with whom he was staying and who shined shoes in the same shop, had arranged the job for him. Another man told me with evident pride that he flew to New York on a Saturday and after a day recovering from jet lag, was working as an auto mechanic in Queens, bright and early Monday morning.

The protective cloak of friends and relatives contrasts with the first days of solo travelers who go it alone, arriving in New York with little more than the name and address of a hotel or one of the handful of rooming houses that cater to Brazilians. One man from southern Brazil knew no one in New York when he arrived and rented a room at the YMCA for a few nights. Others make their first homes in one of the cheap hotels tucked away amid the neon honky-tonks of Times Square. A few Brazilians with no contacts in New York buy a one- or two-week tour package from a travel agency in Brazil. A typical package includes round-trip airfare, airport transfers, and hotel. While this is costly by Brazilian standards, it surely makes things easier for those who speak little or no English and who would otherwise have to find lodging on their own.

The case of Ana, while melodramatic, is not atypical of lone voyagers who come to New York on tour packages. Ana, a widowed nurse born in Bahia, but long resident in Rio de Janeiro, was "fed up" living in Brazil as a single, middle-aged woman. She decided to come to New York to live although she spoke no English and knew no one—"only Jesus." She flew to the United States and went to the hotel that she had booked through a travel agent. She was terribly lonely and cried when she talked to her family in Rio by phone. She did not want them to know how miserable she was, explaining that the sniffling they heard was because of the bitterly cold weather in New York. Not knowing where to turn, Ana went to a Catholic church in midtown Manhattan and prayed for help. The next day she met a Brazilian—a fellow Bahian no less—in a luncheonette near her hotel. He took her under his wing and helped her find a job as a live-in nanny in Brooklyn. She credits Jesus with this "miracle" and has attended mass at the same church ever since.

Even some Brazilians who travel with friends or relatives or who have contacts in New York encounter unexpected difficulties. There is the case of Clarice, for example, who planned to travel to New York from her hometown in Minas Gerais with a woman friend and a male acquaintance. The man had told Clarice and her friend that they could stay with him for a while—until they were settled and found jobs—at his uncle's place in the Catskill Mountains in upstate New York.

The trio traveled together from Minas Gerais to Rio de Janeiro. After arriving at the airport, they checked their luggage and went to dinner. There the man suddenly announced that the two women could not stay with his uncle after all because he lived in a small trailer and there was not enough room for them. Clarice is certain that the promise of a place to stay was a ruse to get her and her friend to accompany the man, who was very uneasy about making the trip by himself, from their hometown in Minas Gerais to New York City.

Now the question was, Where would the two friends stay when they reached New York? Clarice had $1,000 with her, which she needed to live on until she found a job. The only place she had heard of in New York was a hotel mentioned in passing by her travel agent in Brazil: the Barbizon Plaza, across from Central Park. And so, after arriving at Kennedy Airport and going through immigration control, they hailed a taxi and told the driver to take them to the Barbizon Plaza.

When they checked in, Clarice and her friend were horrified to learn that a room cost $90 a night and did not, in her words, "even include *café de manha* (breakfast)."[2] They spent one night there; early the next morning Clarice called the number of a Brazilian woman living in New York given to her by a friend at home. The tale has a happy ending: the woman said that Clarice and her friend could stay in her apartment in Queens for a few days until they found jobs and a place of their own.

"Chicken Coops" and Rooming Houses

Crowded quarters in which Brazilians live—typically those who are newcomers to the United States—are dubbed *puleiros*, "chicken coops," in Portuguese slang. Whether in a hotel, rooming house, or apartment, *puleiros* are places that house many people to a room, rooms that typically are filled from floor to ceiling with bunk beds or wall-to-wall mattresses. More than one informant told me that some *puleiros* have fewer beds than occupants. In one *puleiro* in a Brooklyn apartment, eight Brazilians were said to share four beds by sleeping in shifts; in Queens an apartment with six beds purportedly had twelve occupants. People accommodate themselves to this arrangement, I was told, because they work in shifts—those who work nights occupy the beds during the day, and vice versa. Since I was never in a facility housing Brazilians that had fewer beds than occupants, I am not certain that such places actually exist. These stories may be only slightly apocryphal exaggerations of what really are very crowded living conditions.

There certainly are *puleiros* in New York City, albeit, I believe, on a limited scale. Moreover, *puleiros* are generally transitory residences that newly arrived Brazilians stay in only until they can find more permanent lodgings. Couples, in particular, rarely remain for long since "chicken coops" obviously afford little privacy.

For almost nine months, one Brazilian engineer paid $35 weekly to live in what he described as a *puleiro* located in an apartment in Spanish Harlem. He decried the dormitory-style living quarters with many roommates, saying how miserable he was crammed in with fellow Brazilians, who, he insisted, were "all lower class." In the same building, a Brazilian family with one child lives in a two-bedroom apartment; the family sleeps in one bedroom and rents the other one out to three Brazilian men, who sleep in bunk beds. In fact, almost the entire building, about fifteen small apartments in all, is one big Brazilian *puleiro*, with no fewer than four people per dwelling.

Despite these stark conditions, settling in New York City is probably no more difficult than what Brazilians experience in other parts of the country. One informant who lived in San Franciso for a few months when he first came to the United States described the dark basement—it was not wired for electricity—that he shared there with fifteen or twenty other Brazilians. The basement was in a hotel owned by a Brazilian, who employed the new immigrants in various jobs and charged them $45 a week per bed. Living in obscurity, the basement dwellers bought cheap meals of "bread and honey" from their employer. This man's tale and those of other Brazilians living in assorted *puleiros* are vivid illustrations of economist Michael J. Piore's remark that temporary migrants, particularly when they first arrive in the United States, put up with crowded, barebones living conditions that they would *never* stand for at home.[3]

Puleiros similar to the ones described above are found in other parts of Manhattan and in Queens. But from the very first days of my fieldwork, I began hearing about the most famous *puleiro* of them all: the Queens rooming house owned by Dona Dahlia, a Brazilian who first came to New York in the late 1970s. Her name and address circulate widely in sending communities in Brazil, particularly those in Minas Gerais. As with other *puleiros*, Brazilians who lack friends or relatives in New York stay at Dona Dahlia's for a while when they first come to the city; with a few exceptions, two months is the usual maximum time in residence and many stay only a few days or a week.

Dona Dahlia's *pensão* (rooming house), the proper term in Portuguese, has consisted of different entities over the ten years that it has been in existence. The rooming house began in an apartment, expanded to two apartments, then to two adjacent houses, and eventually to a single, three-floor semidetached house. The number of boarders also has ebbed and flowed with the tide of Brazilian immigration; anywhere from as few as ten to as many as thirty Brazilians have been in residence at any one time. Their number also varies seasonally; more usually live there in summer than in winter. The reason is simple: many Brazilians travel to New York in March or later, during the warmer months of the year. They try to avoid arriving in the dead of winter so that they can gradually get used to what is for them New York's very frosty clime. One Brazilian told me how he froze when he arrived in New York on a frigid February day, having just left Rio de Janeiro's sweltering summer heat.

Among New York's Brazilians, the crowded living quarters at Dona Dahlia's are a rich source of stories about the trials new immigrants face living in the city. Her *puleiro* is cited as an illustration of the spartan conditions that Brazilians are willing to endure in order to work in the Big Apple. An informant who had stayed at her first *pensão*, a small, one-bedroom apartment, for two weeks in 1984 told me how he had shared the floor with twelve fellow Brazilians. Later, in a slightly bigger apartment, Dona Dahlia brought in bunk beds, which slept from fifteen to eighteen people. As she herself told me, Brazilians would arrive at her rooming house and she would tell them, "Não tem vaga gente, não tem vaga"—"There's no room, folks, there's just no room"—but then she would make room for them anyway. One former resident told me how she did it; he claimed Dona Dahlia occasionally slept on the floor so that she could rent out her own bed.

The cost of a bed—or mattress—at Dona Dahlia's was $40 a week during the early days of the *pensão*, or $50 with one meal provided. For a while Dona Dahlia served meals to a few of her tenants, but then abandoned the practice. Residents now pay $50 a week without meals and cook for themselves in one of the rooming house's two kitchens, or they survive on take-out food.

While Dona Dahlia's is the best-known *pensão* in New York that caters to Brazilians, there are two or three others of more recent vintage in Queens. In fact, in March 1990, during my fieldwork, the owner of one of these rooming houses, Dona Regina, bought Dona Dahlia's famed establishment, Dona Dahlia having decided to return permanently to Brazil.

First Home: Dona Dahlia's Lodgings

Dona Dahlia's *pensão* is a three-floor, semidetached brick row house in a neat, lower-middle-class section of Queens. It is about four blocks from the area's main shopping district, an ethnic mosaic where Indian stores selling saris crowd next to Korean groceries, Arab butcher shops, Chinese restaurants, and Hispanic bodegas. There are no businesses in the neighborhood that cater exclusively to Brazilians, but O *Globo*, Brazil's most widely read newspaper, is sold at the newsstand at the entrance to the subway station, and *farinha* (manioc flour, a Brazilian staple) and *cachaça* (a fiery Brazilian drink of distilled cane alcohol) are available at local stores.

HOME AT LAST

A Brazilian friend, Nelsinho, told me the poignant tale of his arrival in New York. He flew alone from Rio into Kennedy Airport; he knew no one in New York and spoke no English. After an uneventful passage through immigration control, he got his luggage and hailed a cab to take him to Dona Dahlia's rooming house in Queens.

After driving for a while, the cab driver wrote Nelsinho a note indicating that the fare was going to be $110. Nelsinho had $1,000 with him but he knew that this was a rip off—the fare should have been no more than about $30. When Nelsinho, through gestures, let it be known that he had no intention of paying that amount, the cab driver unceremoniously dumped him and his luggage at a gas station along the Long Island Expressway.

The gas station attendant called for another cab; one of the few English words Nelsinho knew was "taxi," which is the same in Portuguese. When the attendant asked for money to pay for the phone call, Nelsinho refused because he did not know what a "quarter" was and he thought the attendant was demanding a bribe from him.

The second cab arrived and took him to the address, purportedly Dona Dahlia's rooming house, written on a piece of paper given to Nelsinho by a friend before he left Rio. No one was there and the house seemed deserted. The driver then stopped at a telephone booth and called the number written on the piece of paper. He was told that the rooming house had moved to a new location five blocks away. Luckily, Dona Dahlia had kept the same phone number. The cab driver drove to the second address, a private house. Nelsinho got out of the cab and rang the bell; a woman, Dona Dahlia, came to the front door. "Você é brasileiro? Are you Brazilian?," she inquired. Nelsinho felt his eyes sting as they filled with tears.

When I visited Dona Dahlia's in February 1990, eight men and five women—all Brazilians—were in residence. Her usual occupancy is fifteen or sixteen, in addition to two temporary spots for women who work as live-in domestic servants and do not want to stay in their employers' homes on their days off. Dona Dahlia rents futonlike beds to them for $10 a night for the two weekend nights that they typically spend at her establishment.

The rooming house is laid out to accommodate its lodgers. The living room is on the main floor. It is carpeted and furnished with two comfortable couches, a table, a color television set—Charles Bronson movies were on the whole time I was there—and little else. The only wall decoration is a wooden crucifix. Adjacent to the living room is a sitting room with additional chairs and couches and a table. During one of my visits the room was occupied by a woman manicuring the nails of another woman, while a man was ironing clothes. A continually ringing telephone was on a nearby table.

A narrow kitchen adjoins the sitting room. Since many of Dona Dahlia's lodgers cook for themselves, the kitchen cupboards and refrigerator are crammed with groceries carefully labeled with the names of individual residents. A piece of paper taped to the refrigerator lists telephone calls made to Brazil, with a checklist on which Dona Dahlia crosses off the names of those who have reimbursed her for their long-distance calls.

A door at one end of the kitchen opens on a steep flight of stairs leading down to the finished basement, where the women's quarters are located. There is a bedroom with two bunk beds that can sleep four women. The room is awash with the toilet articles, cosmetics, and other personal belongings of its boarders. The bedroom and a small bathroom with a shower are off a central area equipped with a stove and built-in storage cabinets. Two futons for weekend stays are next to these cooking facilities, as is another bed, partially hidden behind a screen, which is for a permanent boarder.

The men's quarters are on the second floor, up another flight of stairs off the living room. Two bedrooms jammed with bunk beds can house four to six men each. Small storage closets, in which individuals keep their clothes and other possessions, are next to the bunk beds. Some of the beds are made and others are unmade and piled high with laundry. A man is sound asleep in the top bunk oblivious to the noise and activity that surrounds him. The place looks exactly like a very messy college dormitory room.

A bathroom is just off the landing, as is a tiny bedroom where Dona Dahlia sleeps. She has a telephone extension in her bedroom, which is used by residents who want privacy when they call friends and relatives in Brazil. And phone calls certainly are a major diversion here; nearly everyone calls Brazil, and Dona Dahlia's phone bill is regularly $1,000, $1,200 or even $1,500 a month. As one of her former boarders put it, "The immigrants are the one's who give all their money to AT & T. If you took away the immigrants, the telephone company's business would fall off a lot."

The greater number of beds for men than for women at Dona Dahlia's roughly reflects the sex ratio of her boarders—70 percent men, 30 percent women—that she says she has had over the long term. Most of her residents are single, separated, or divorced, although I met two with spouses in Brazil and two single mothers whose children are living with relatives in Brazil. The few couples that do show up at the *pensão* are lodged sepa-

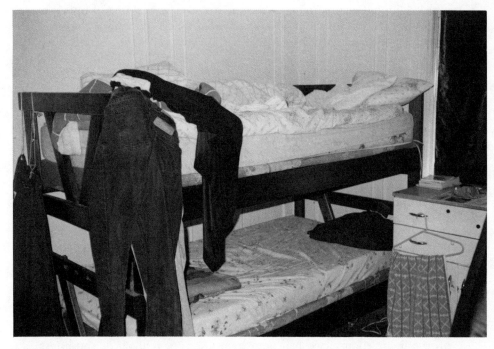

3.1 A room in the men's quarters at Dona Dahlia's pensão houses four to six men.

rately: the man goes upstairs to the men's quarters and the woman down to the basement. Dona Dahlia points out that since she has no private facilities for couples, they do not stay with her for more than a few days.

Some Brazilians wind up at Dona Dahlia's although they had no intention of staying there. They arrive in New York planning to live with friends or relatives but then find out that there is no room for them. For example, a married couple living in a small studio apartment was expected to house a cousin; very quickly, the cousin was provided with Dona Dahlia's name and address and given a gentle shove in the direction of her lodgings.

During two Sunday mornings when I visited Dona Dahlia's, residents were constantly coming and going. Some came in carrying bulging copies of the Sunday *New York Times*, while others left to take the subway to jobs in Manhattan. People who had just awakened straggled into the kitchen in their bathrobes to make coffee. One woman was boiling eggs and making rice for her lunch; others came into the kitchen to eat the prepared take-out food that has become such a ubiquitous part of the New York gastronomic scene.

THE MISTRESS OF THE HOUSE

Dona Dahlia is a very tiny woman for such an important Brazilian institution. She is about sixty years old and was born in the backlands of Ceará, an impoverished state in northeastern Brazil. She dresses very plainly and is devoid of makeup, save for long, beautifully manicured bright-red fingernails. Dona Dahlia's father owned a cattle ranch, and she describes her childhood as comfortable. She was married at the age of twelve to a man of thirty-six, whom she had met only once before the wedding; the marriage was arranged by her parents. She had her first child, a daughter, at the age of thirteen. At twenty-two, she was widowed and left with five children to raise. Dona Dahlia says she did not like being married; she has only been happy since being widowed, when, in her own words, she became *"uma mulher livre,"* an independent woman.

Dona Dahlia moved to Rio de Janeiro to find work and slowly brought the children from Ceará to live with her. Her first job in Rio was serving *cafezinho*, Brazilian espresso, at a coffee bar. Then she took a job at a jewelry factory, and eventually became factory manager. For a while, she held a second job, working a few nights a week, in addition to her regular daytime position. Later, she was hired as a nurse's aide and worked at various hospitals around Rio.

Her oldest daughter, Maria, was employed as a housekeeper with a family in Rio. The family was coming to the United States to live and wanted to take a servant with them; Maria agreed to accompany them to New York. She worked for the family and at other jobs in the city for four or five years, and then bought a Mexican restaurant in lower Manhattan. One of Dona Dahlia's sons, Luís, left Brazil and traveled to New York to help out at the restaurant. Maria, by now an American citizen, called Dona Dahlia in Rio and asked her to come to New York.

By the time Dona Dahlia was summoned to New York, she had retired as a nurse's aide, and all of her children were married. She agreed to come to the United States because she wanted to make enough money to buy "a little place for me to live," something she had never earned enough to do in Brazil. Now, after a decade running her *pensão*, she has achieved her goal. She owns an apartment in a quiet, middle-class neigborhood in Rio. In March 1990, Dona Dahlia sold her famed Queens establishment and returned to Brazil for good. She went home to help take care of two grandchildren and to "rest a little."

Immigrant Services

It was immediately apparent from talking to a number of boarders as well as to Dona Dahlia herself that her *pensão* is far more than just a place to live. It is a combination school, counseling center, employment agency, and legal aid society that provides new immigrants with most of the things they need to know and items they need to have during their early days in New York. For example, Dona Dahlia explains to new arrivals with immediate money problems how they can sell the unused portions of their plane tickets. When one lodger urgently needed cash, Dona Dahlia arranged the sale of his New York–Rio de Janeiro return ticket for $300 to a Brazilian who was about to return to Brazil for good.

Dona Dahlia has found work for lodgers through her contacts in New York's Brazilian community; she has gotten them jobs in construction and as street vendors, housekeepers, and baby-sitters. Or she counsels residents as to where they should go to look for a job on their own. She advised one woman who had worked as a hairdresser in Brazil to order business cards that advertised her services. The woman took Dona Dahlia's advice and now earns money going to people's houses to cut and style their hair.

Since it is nearly impossible to get a job without a social security card— *um social* in the parlance of New York Brazilians—Dona Dahlia can arrange this too. One resident gave her $150 and received his *social* three days later. She also sometimes lends newcomers money to buy a card on their own and is reimbursed when they find work. But, she cautions her lodgers, counterfeit social security cards should be used with care so that they will not be detected. This is why Dona Dahlia has been known to accompany new immigrants to the bank to help them open checking accounts by using her own, legitimate *social*.

Dona Dahlia has also become expert in the matter of amnesty for undocumented immigrants. Before the deadline for applications passed, she was a fount of information on how to apply for amnesty in both the regular and farm workers' programs. On more than one occasion, she signed affadavits testifying that *senhor(a) fulano-de-tal* ("Mr. or Ms. So-and-so") was a resident of her pension at some date prior to 1982, allowing him or her to qualify for amnesty. In one case she did this for a Brazilian whom she barely knew but whose brother had once stayed at her *pensão*. When the amnesty applicant finally got his green card two years later, he came back to thank Dona Dahlia for her help. She told me with evident satisfaction that her Brazilian boarders trust her advice on amnesty and that "*graças a Deus*," thank God, most succeeded in getting it.

Dona Dahlia does assorted favors for residents she likes. While they are at work, she runs errands and makes purchases for them. She even

3.2 Dona Dahlia stands in the front door of her pensão on a snowy winter day.

lent one long-term lodger $2,000 so that he could make a down payment on an apartment in São Paulo. Then, too, when she goes on one of her periodic trips to Brazil, she carries letters, money, and gifts from her boarders to their families.

Dona Dahlia collects $50 a week from each of her Brazilian lodgers, but allows a few who have just arrived in New York and are not yet employed to owe her rent until they find jobs. Most settle the debt quickly, but a few have left without paying her. The problem is far more serious when it comes to unpaid phone bills, which occasionally reach astronomical proportions. Dona Dahlia says she was badly stung twice, once for $300 and another time for $1,000, in unpaid calls to Brazil made by boarders who took off for parts unknown before the phone bill arrived.

None of this is meant to suggest that Dona Dahlia is running a charity. It is clear that she has done very well financially in her years as mistress of the *pensão*; she owns land in Brazil, an investment property, and an apartment with a telephone. Parenthetically, telephones are very expensive in Brazil, $1,000 or more, because the number of lines is limited. She has also helped set up her children in business, as well as contributing to the support of a number of grandchildren back in Brazil.

At the same time, Dona Dahlia clearly enjoys running her establishment and has made some lasting friendships among the many "guests" she has quartered. The Brazilian to whom she loaned $2,000 for his apartment refers to her as *minha mãe*, "my mother," and sat with his arm around her shoulders during part of my interview with her. One resident I met said that Dona Dahlia has "children of all ages," referring to her boarders. "She's small," the resident said, "but she has room for all of us." Dona Dahlia in turn, likes to see her "children happy." She says that when they are "without jobs or working long hours and not doing well, it gives [her] great sadness" and she "asks God to help them whether they deserve it or not because it's so hard to be in a foreign land [*terra dos outros*] without speaking the language."

At the end of our conversation, I asked Dona Dahlia to estimate how many Brazilians had stayed with her over the ten years that she had been running her rooming house. She laughed and said she had no idea. But then she told me about the one and only time she went to a Brazilian nightclub in Manhattan. As soon as she got there, people started coming over and saying "Oh, Dona Dahlia! I used to stay with you. How long has it been?" After the owner of the nightclub announced that she was in the audience, a steady stream of people came over to her table, exclaiming: "Oh Dona Dahlia what *saudades grandes*, I've missed you! How long it's been since I last saw you! Do you remember that time when you made *feijão* [black beans]? Do you remember how we used to play *buraco* [a card game]?" Dona Dahlia said that it seemed that most of the patrons there that night had lived at her *pensão* at one time or another. She did not remember many of them, especially those that had stayed with her for only a short time years ago. But they all remembered her. She compared the experience to that of a schoolteacher—a former pupil, even after many years, always remembers her third-grade teacher, but the teacher, having had so many students, is unable to remember who most of them are.

Living Arrangements

Most Brazilian immigrants in New York live with friends or relatives. Even those who know no one when they first come to the city and stay in a rooming house like Dona Dahlia's, usually move to more permanent quarters after a few weeks. These are typically shared with other Brazilians, often compatriots they met after arriving in New York. My sample was about evenly split between those who lived with relatives (35 percent) and those who lived with friends (34 percent). Another 15 percent lived with both friends *and* relatives; here, the most common arrangement was a married couple sharing expenses with one or two friends. Only about one in ten of the Brazilians in the sample lived alone, mostly older women who had been in this country for at least a decade.[4]

Living alone is not only costly in a city like New York, but its benefits—privacy and having one's "own space"—are not especially valued by Brazilians. Even if they could afford to, most Brazilians would choose not to live by themselves because of the loneliness that solitary living connotes. Americans and Brazilians have very different views of privacy; in the words of American anthropologist Conrad Kottak, "Americans need space because we remain much more private people than Brazilians." Brazilian anthropologist Roberto DaMatta cleverly encapsulates these cultural contrasts when he pairs Greta Garbo's famous plea, "I want to be alone," with its Brazilian equivalent, "Please don't leave me!"[5]

But having friends and relatives to help pay rent and utilities bills is no less important than having them for company. Since the aim of most Brazilians, at least initially, is to save money quickly and then return to Brazil, they try to keep living expenses down by sharing them. This is why married couples often take in one or two boarders and why three or four friends will rent a small apartment together and put up with the crowded living conditions that result. Although many Brazilians live in cramped quarters, the only ones in my sample who lived in a full-fledged *puleiro* environment with more than five people per dwelling were residents of

Dona Dahlia's.[6] Still, in Brazilian apartments shared by friends, one common practice is reminiscent of life at Dona Dahlia's and similar establishments. All the food in the refrigerator and kitchen cupboard is labeled with someone's name. And so you find "João's beer," "Mario's orange juice," "Claudia's milk," and "Maria's crackers."

"Garbage Decor"

Brazilian immigrants save money not only on rent but also on household furnishings. Here, too, since they view their stay in New York as temporary, they are loath to spend much fixing up their apartments. Still, certain basic items are needed and some Brazilians equip their apartments with the castoffs that Americans discard. Chairs, tables, couches, beds, various household items, and even clothes are retrieved from garbage cans and dumpsters on the streets. Brazilians refer to this as their *decoração de lixo*, their "garbage decor."

In a play written and produced in Governador Valadares about the trials and tribulations of *brazucas*, Brazilian immigrants in the United States, one very funny scene shows Brazilians scavenging through a large box marked "Garbage" in search of useful items. An old but still usable toaster is triumphantly fished out, as is an answering machine, a set of dishes, and various items of clothing. In fact, while I was in Governador Valadares, I met a woman whose brother lives in New York and, although she is decidedly upper-middle class, the outfit she was wearing—wool slacks and a sweater—had been sent to her by her brother, who had picked them out of the trash on a street in Queens.

A topic of amused conversation among Brazilians is what they managed to salvage that day from the useful items discarded by what they regard as American wastefulness. Some Brazilians have even become connoisseurs of American garbage patterns; they say that November and December are particularly good for retrieving throwaways because that is when people get rid of their old appliances, worn furniture, and still-wearable clothes in the expectation of receiving new ones for Christmas.

So many Brazilians living at Dona Dahlia's had found discarded television sets in the street that at one point there were a total of seven sets in her rooming house. Then, there was the tale about the Brazilian who was such a rapacious scavenger that he had picked up three television sets of varying sizes and arranged them, one on top of the other, pyramid-fashion, in his apartment. A newly arrived but still unemployed middle-class woman openly disdained those who picked up things from the street, but when she found a still-usable television set on the curb near her apartment, she sheepishly brought it home.

Old Clothes

Just as Brazilian immigrants try to be frugal when it comes to rent and household items in order to save most of what they earn for the return to Brazil, they are also reluctant, at least at first, to spend money on clothes. This is especially true of cold weather items, such as heavy winter coats, gloves, scarves, and hats—things that would be of little use in Brazil's tropical and semitropical climate. But winter in New York requires appropriate attire.

A church-run social service agency in Queens, combined with Brazilian ingenuity, helps resolve this particular dilemma. Among other things, the agency is a collection center for used clothing donated for the city's homeless and destitute. Vera, the woman who runs the agency, while not Brazilian herself, is fluent in Portuguese, having lived in a Portuguese-speaking country as a missionary.

Brazilian immigrants regularly appear at the agency requesting clothes, especially winter coats, wool sweaters, and the like. The agency is well known in the Greater New York metropolitan area—it is visited by Brazilians from as far away as Newark—and its address is widely circulated in *brazuca*-exporting communities in Brazil. Vera says that this service has become so popular among Brazilians that they comprise about 80 percent of those who show up requesting used clothing and that of the Brazilians who appear there, 80 to 90 percent are from Minas Gerais.

The agency keeps records on the number of people who receive clothes. During the week of my visit in early October, when the city was enjoying a brief respite of Indian summer, eleven Brazilians had appeared asking for clothes. Since Brazilians often pick up clothes for family members or friends who cannot come in themselves, Vera said that she provided these eleven Brazilians with clothes for a total of thirty-one people. This was a typical week for that time of year; many more come in during the first cold snap and throughout the winter months.

According to Vera, some Brazilian immigrants arrive in New York with few clothes, but others claim that they brought little with them because, they say, if they had taken all the clothes they would actually need, they would have been burdened with luggage and immigration officers would have suspected that they were not really tourists. Vera herself doubts this story and says it is just a way to get her to give them clothes. Some immigrants arrive at the agency claiming that their only clothes are what they are wearing. "I have just this shirt and pants," they say. "The jacket is borrowed." Vera thinks that this may well be true for the few Brazilians who come to the United States via Mexico since they are often robbed of their possessions at the border or are forced to leave their luggage behind.

Brazilians also occasionally come in asking for free food—the agency runs a major food program for the homeless—but Vera will give it only to those who are out of work, and, at least at the time I interviewed her in 1990, most of the Brazilians coming to the agency had jobs. Many who could well afford to buy food request it anyway in an effort to save money. With a wry smile, Vera adds that the other free service that the church agency offers—a stop-smoking course—has enrolled very few Brazilians.

What I have described—a sparse standard of living, crowded apartments equipped with salvaged items, and the occasional article of used clothing—accurately depicts the lifestyles of many Brazilian immigrants during their early months or even their first years in New York City. I have also tried to capture their irrepressible sense of humor about it all. But time passes and living conditions gradually improve as the return to Brazil is put off for yet another year. Some Brazilians begin to fix up their apartments, or eat out more often, or buy more expensive clothes, even though, almost to a man and woman, they *still* insist that they are planning to return home.

Economist Michael J. Piore sees this change in attitude and behavior as part of the transition from sojourner to immigrant, from temporary resident to permanent settler.[7] As their time in New York lengthens, many Brazilians become less content to live in packed quarters with few creature comforts. While even crowded, sparsely furnished apartments often sport expensive new stereo equipment, VCRs, and elaborate telephone-answering machines, it is understood that these purchases will be taken back to Brazil. But when people begin installing wall-to-wall carpeting, framing large posters to hang on their walls, buying furniture, and investing in other amenities that cannot be easily transported back home, it is apparent that they no longer see life in New York as transient.

Why Do They Do It?

We are witnesses to the invasion of young Brazilians in search of new horizons. As the years pass, we have seen it become more widespread. We have in our midst some young people who could not get an education in Brazil, others studied at government expense and then could not get jobs, and disastrously, we have a cultural elite—professionals and researchers—who, unable to find work in their fields, are giving their skills to other countries.

—Letter to Fernando Collor de Mello, President of Brazil, upon his inauguration in March 1990, from two long-term Brazilian residents of New York

Why do Brazilians, largely from middle- and lower-middle-class backgrounds, abandon the relative comfort and security of home, friends, and family to brave an uncertain new world of crowded *puleiros*, menial jobs, and alien ways, all of which must be confronted in a language in which they have little or no fluency? The answer is predominantly material. Brazilian immigrants coming to New York, and presumably those coming to other parts of the United States, are economic refugees, fleeing from conditions of hyperinflation, underemployment, low wages, a relatively high cost of living, and pervasive economic uncertainty at home. I leave it to the economists to analyze the causes of the Brazilian economic crisis. I will deal only with its consequences, its impact on the lives of Brazilians and its role as a catalyst for emigration.

Brazilians in New York City often refer to themselves as "economic immigrants," and this rubric seems appropriate; nearly two-thirds of the people in my sample cited economic/professional reasons for coming to this country. Moreover, they are very definite about what lured them here: compared to jobs in Brazil, jobs in the United States pay high enough wages to allow them to save a considerable sum of money. One can save money *and* save time. Over and over, I was told how in Brazil, after twenty years of work, owning a home was still a pipe dream for many, whereas in the United States, the wages saved from only a year's labor could mean a down payment on a house or an apartment.

This is the enticing formula in the Brazilian/American equation: the ability to earn so much more money in so much less time. A Brazilian friend said that what drew his compatriots to New York was the "economy of time." His own case is instructive. After two years of holding down two jobs in New York, he was able to help his parents finish building their house outside of Rio de Janeiro and make a substantial down payment on his own condominimum in São Paulo. He said that in those two years, he had saved what it would have taken him at least ten years to save in his former job as a high school teacher in Brazil.

Dona Dahlia is another case in point. When I visited her in Rio de Janeiro after she returned to Brazil to live, she showed me why she was so grateful for the twelve years she had spent in New York. Although from a modest background, today she owns a modern, three-bedroom apartment in a new building in a middle-class section of the city's northern zone. The apartment is fully furnished with modern appliances, including a telephone. She also owns land outside Rio and a beach house in another state, which she bought as an investment. All of this, she noted, would not have been possible had she stayed in Brazil.

Then, there is the seemingly apocryphal story of the couple who managed to save $50,000 in only two years. They took in four boarders in their apartment so that they paid no rent, and they lived very frugally, spending a minimal amount on food and nothing on entertainment. The wife worked seven days a week as a baby-sitter, while the husband held down two jobs that paid him "off the books." Today the couple are the proud owners of a house in Brazil.

"The successes of emigrants become mythologized while their misfortunes are minimized," note two researchers.[8] Back in Brazil, examples of Brazilians "making it" in the United States are pumped up, revamped, and turned into glorified portrayals of life in the United States; they filter back to Brazil by way of returned migrants. Grossly exaggerated stories of living well and saving large sums of money in little time spread rapidly because of their enormous appeal to people unable to plan their economic futures. "A car? Well you can save enough money for one in just two months!" one Brazilian was told. The American dream in the form of money grows on trees is a prominent leitmotif in these tales of good fortune.

These reports are particularly appealing given current realities in Brazil. The combination of relatively low wages, constantly changing prices due to runaway inflation, and nerve-wracking uncertainty about what tomorrow will bring have created an uncharacteristic gloom among many Brazilians about their country's economic future and their place in it. This disquieting pessimism also has spurred emigration. By the late 1980s and early 1990s, economic conditions in Brazil were being described as "the worst in this century." Things are so bad, one informant told me in March 1990, that if there were five jumbo jets a day flying from Rio de Janeiro or São Paulo to New York—and Brazilians could get tourist visas—all of the planes would be full.

Rampant inflation is one of the main culprits. Between 1980 and 1988, Brazil had an average annual inflation rate of 189 percent, and things have since gotten worse. Inflation reached 1760 percent a year in 1989; by March 1990, just prior to the imposition of President Collor's package of economic reforms, it was running at 84 percent a month. Even after the plan was in place, inflation was still galloping along at 926 percent for the twelve months ending March 1991, and by mid-1992 it was once again over 20 percent a month.[9]

"Brazil is not a serious country; if you want to earn money there, forget about it," said a Brazilian engineer living in New York City. As a result of inflation, real wages in Brazil have fallen 80 percent over the last decade. With a monthly minimum wage of only $85 (in May 1992) and a per capita income that is one-tenth that of the United States, it is easy to understand why Brazilians find U.S. wages so alluring. But it is important to emphasize that the Brazilians coming to New York *are not minimum-wage workers*. In Brazil many of the new immigrants held professional or semiprofessional positions that paid good salaries by Brazilian standards. Still, Brazilian salaries pale in comparision to what immigrants can make in the United States, even in the most menial jobs.

A few examples of what Brazilians earned before coming to New York: In São Paulo a woman with a university degree was paid $600 a month as an executive at a well-known American-owned advertising agency. A graduate in law had a position at the Bank of Brazil in Porto Alegre, a city in southern Brazil. He earned a salary of $300 a month, which he supplemented with a second job, for a total monthly income of $500. A Brazilian mechanical engineer was making $500 a month in Belo Horizonte before he quit his job to come to New York.[10] The rates of pay for skilled blue-collar labor in Brazil are also far below those of the United States. For example, the wages of a man employed as an airplane mechanic for Varig, the Brazilian national airline, came to $300 a month.

MARATHON HOPES

Wage differentials between Brazil and the United States are reflected in the amount of prize money awarded in athletic competitions in the two countries. Eliza, whom I met while she was selling books on a midtown Manhattan street, is a serious marathon runner, who came to the United States because, she said, "the Brazilian government does not support" sports or competitive events. For example, she was the second-place winner in the Rio de Janeiro Marathon and received a paltry $50 prize—the first-place prize was $100—after having trained for the event for months. She contrasts this with the huge amounts paid to the winners of the Boston and New York marathons. A physical education student in Brazil, Eliza dropped out of school to come to the United States to try to fulfill her dream of winning a major race. At the time I met her, she was in daily training for the New York Marathon.

Brazilians in New York never tire of contrasting their old and new earnings. A woman whose salary had been a paltry $200 a month as the head floor nurse in a large hospital in Belo Horizonte told me in wonder that she earned some five times more working long hours as a baby-sitter in New York City. A bartender in Queens who had studied psychology but never finished her degree noted with pride that she makes more than her sister in Brazil, who has two university degrees. A waitress in Manhattan commented that her sister, a practicing psychologist at a clinic in Rio, has a much higher-status job but a much lower income than she does. A young man, just out of high school when he left Brazil, works as a plumber's assistant in Queens for $10 an hour, or about $900 a month, compared to the $50 a month he earned as a part-time office assistant in Belo Horizonte. The ratios cited by informants were never less than four to one, that is, one month's earnings in Brazil, could be made in one week in the United States.

Of course, it will be argued, Brazil's wage structure must be seen within the context of the country's lower cost of living. But the cost of living in Brazil has been rising rapidly; by the late 1980s and early 1990s, in some large Brazilian cities, it was nearly comparable to that of major U.S. metropolitan areas. Then, with the collapse of the Collor economic plan, the return to double-digit monthly inflation, and the overvaluation of the *cruzeiro* (the Brazilian unit of currency) by up to 50 percent, the wage gap between the United States and Brazil, at least in Brazil's large cities, was no longer mitigated by a much lower cost of living.[11]

Even before the current economic crisis, certain types of consumer goods were far more expensive in Brazil than in the United States. Color television sets, VCRs, microwaves, vacuum cleaners, and washing machines cost anywhere from 50 percent to 275 percent more in Brazil than in the United States.[12] Thus, while average Brazilian wages are far lower than of those in the United States, for years the price of some consumer products has been much higher in Brazil. This does much to explain why Brazilian apartments in New York are literally crammed with VCRs, stereo systems, CD players, and elaborate telephone-answering machines.

Cheaper consumer goods aside, other aspects of the U.S. standard of living are very attractive to Brazilians, particularly those from more modest backgrounds. After they come to New York, many Brazilians begin to look at life in Brazil through an American lens, and wonder aloud how people back home make ends meet. Maria, a primary school teacher in Brazil, said that she could never have supported herself on what she earned there; she lived with her parents and only bought incidentals. In contrast, in New York, she said, "You can work as a maid and eat meat every day if you want to. In Brazil you have to be very well off to afford meat all the time." She continued the comparison: "You can even work here as a maid and pay cash for a VCR. In Brazil most people never have enough money on hand to do that. The only way to buy something that expensive is to pay for it on time."

Even Brazilians from decidedly middle-class backgrounds are intrigued by some components of the U.S. standard of living. In Brazil a residential telephone is an expensive luxury because of the limited number of phone lines, and even middle-class households may lack this ubiquitous, taken-for-granted American convenience. In contrast, within a month of arriving in the United States and with a deposit of about $100, any Brazilian with a job can easily afford a telephone. Buying power of this kind may partly compensate for the loss of occupational status that Brazilians suffer in this country.

THE PRICE OF A DRESS

"In Brazil, if you want a $50 dress, you can only buy it by paying on credit over twelve months. And by the time it's paid for, the dress is worn out. But in the United States, if you want a $50 dress, you just go out and buy it for cash. And, can you imagine, in New York, a TV costs one week's earnings? But in Brazil even a month's wages won't pay for one."

—Betty Gomes, a Brazilian who works as a housekeeper in New York City

---

And loss of occupational status is indeed acute. From the perspective of many Brazilian immigrants in New York, one of the most disturbing aspects of the current economic crisis in Brazil and the one that spurred the migration of some, is the difficulty of finding jobs in the fields in which they were trained. The educational credentials of lawyers, engineers, agronomists, psychologists, and other professionals are useless if they cannot get employment appropriate to their skills. One Brazilian immigrant who had studied law expressed frustration at the time and money spent to complete her degree and the paltry salary she earned once she got a job.

Indeed, over the last decade, this problem has become acute in Brazil, as university enrollments have skyrocketed and skilled jobs that require university training have failed to keep pace. During the 1970s, the number of university graduates grew at least five times faster than did the national labor force, but for a time, skilled white collar and professional jobs also increased dramatically (fivefold between 1950 and 1980). But with the economic difficulties the country faced in the 1980s, fewer positions requiring highly skilled personnel were created, so many university graduates had to content themselves with lower-status jobs that paid less than their training had led them to expect. This is the classic mismatch between opportunity and expectation that has long been recognized as a cause of migration. As Michael J. Piore notes in his well-regarded study of international migration, *Birds of Passage*:

> [T]he urban occupational structure of [some] developing countries is unequal to the size of the aspiring middle class . . . [even to] that group that has not only the aspirations but is also educated for and equipped to assume professional and managerial roles in the economy.[13]

The reason they left Brazil, said any number of informants with professional degrees, was their inability to get decent jobs there that used their skills. One mechanical engineer stressed that he was not the only one to migrate; many of his classmates at the University of São Paulo had gone to the United States, France, Portugal, and elsewhere because "you can't get work in Brazil." A woman with a degree in social work could find only a part-time position in her profession; she was a social worker at a hospital in Rio de Janeiro and held down a second job as a store manager. Even then, she earned so little that she continued to live at home with her parents.

A Brazilian physician, a longtime resident of New York, was very emphatic about the reason for the recent wave of Brazilian immigrants to the United States and insisted that I quote him: "THEY WANT TO WORK," he repeated over and over again, adding mournfully, "but there are no jobs for them in Brazil." The Brazilian brain drain was deplored by a number of immigrants, and one, a journalist, delivered a lengthy diatribe about unemployment among professionals in his country:

> Brazil is a rich country that has everything—but people are not valued. We need doctors but doctors are unemployed. We need teachers but they earn very little. We need engineers—there's not enough decent housing. We need journalists but . . . Doctors, for example. Brazil is a country full of sick people! We need doctors, but they earn so little. I can't understand this. It's a shame because we need all of these people. Brazil doesn't take advantage of its human capital. It's just not valued.

Runaway inflation and underemployment have led some members of the middle strata of Brazilian society to take jobs that they never would have considered before. For example, today there are said to be cabdrivers in São Paulo with university educations. While a cabdriver with a college degree would not be particularly noteworthy in the United States, in Brazil there are some jobs, such as driving a taxicab, that people with university training simply have not done in the past, even temporarily. Another example: in Rio de Janeiro middle class teenagers have begun taking temporary or part-time jobs at McDonalds and at Bob's, a sort of upscale Brazilian Dairy Queen. This would have been unheard of before the current economic crisis, when the nonmanagerial employees of such establishments were strictly working class. Finally, many married middle-class women have gotten jobs in shops and elsewhere to shore up family income. Even a few years ago, one Brazilian told me, such women "would have been ashamed to work as salesgirls."

And so economic uncertainty, long a prerogative of the Brazilian poor, has now come to the middle class with a vengeance. After years of economic optimism during which the middle strata of Brazilian society prospered, today "the middle class has been impoverished by inflation," says Brazilian economist Eliana Cardoso.[14] One long-term Brazilian resident of New York, who had not been in Brazil for eight years, went back in 1988 to visit his parents in São Paulo. He told me how struck he was by people's behavior there. They were "drinking booze like crazy," trying to blot out the high anxiety of not knowing what the next day would bring. He gave his middle-class parents as an example: "They are not out on the street begging but what they have is not worth anything anymore." His sixty-five-year-old father is still working full-time, eight hours a day, six days a week. At one time, his parents were comfortable financially, and they still own a small business and a farm. But now they are so strapped that he is thinking of trying to bring them to the United States once he gets his green card. Even his brother, a computer consultant and landowner, who is very well-off has a Plan B—emigration—should things get much worse.

Primeramão, a São Paulo weekly devoted to classified advertisements, illustrates one way people are trying to retain a middle-class income in the face of inflation and the temporary freeze on savings accounts, one part of Collor's economic package. In the month after the Collor reform plan went into effect, ads for private music and foreign language lessons increased by 30 percent, ads for the sale of jewelry and watches increased by 75 percent and ads in the barter section of the weekly quadrupled.[15]

The totality of these economic problems has led many to declare the death of the Brazilian middle class. The middle class is "suffocating," said one informant. "It doesn't exist anymore," said another. "Today in Brazil there are only the rich and the poor," averred a third. Some Brazilians in New York cited the purported disappearance of the middle class and its lifestyle as one reason why they left the country. A few specifically linked the problems of the middle class and Brazil's economic turmoil to the political realm. They talked of their bitter disappointment that after so many years of military rule, the return to civilian government did not put things right. During the dictatorship, the generals could be blamed for all of Brazil's ills, but with the return to an elected leadership, there were no convenient culprits. More than a few recent émigrés said that they had left Brazil in disgust; they were disillusioned by the ineffectual maneuvering of elected officials when confronted with the country's precarious economic situation.

The Land of Milk and Honey

Although a sizable majority of Brazilian immigrants in New York probably would classify themselves as economic refugees escaping from their country's chaotic economy, many would add that a New York sojourn also has adventurous appeal. They wanted to see for themselves what life was like in the United States or, more specifically, what life was like in "the capital of the world," as one Brazilian called New York City. After seeing the Woody Allen movie *Manhattan*, a Brazilian said that she knew that she had to come to New York, while another "dreamed" of playing volleyball in Central Park, surrounded by the city's skyscrapers. And a few told me of their own idiosyncratic reasons for coming to New York: to pursue a career as a race car driver, to become a screenwriter, even to be artificially inseminated.

A number of informants spoke of how the Brazilian media idealize the United States as a sort of promised land, "as the salvation of humankind," as a nation not riven by the stresses of social and economic haves and have-nots, as a place where "the government cares about the people" and "is not corrupt." And who can blame Brazilians for wanting to visit a country whose music pervades their airwaves, whose movies are their most popular, and whose fads and fashions are carefully emulated? "A good sign that you are in Brazil," one informant told me, "is that you see people wearing T-shirts with logos written in English." And, he pointed out, it was not due to chance but to admiration for things American that the formal name of the country was once—the United States of Brazil.

CHAPTER FOUR

Who Are They?

Their relatively more privileged incorporation into the national economy appears to have provided them with the springboard from which to launch a costly international move.

—Eugenia Georges, *The Making of a Transnational Community*

Just who are these immigrants? Are they typical of the Brazilian population as a whole in terms of their vital statistics, their class, race, religion, and education? In other words, are the Brazilians in New York a representative sample of their compatriots back home? I cannot answer this question definitively, but based on my own sample of one hundred Brazilians living in New York City, the response is mixed. In some ways Brazilians in the Big Apple do reflect the Brazilian population at large, while in others, they most decidedly do not. Today, for example, Brazilians in the city are nearly evenly divided between men and women—54 to 46 percent—although I believe that earlier in the great migration surge that began in the mid-1980s, the sex ratio was less balanced, with perhaps 70 percent men to 30 percent women. Then, too, their religious affiliation is in line with that of their fellow citizens back home; 74 percent are Catholic, 13 percent are Protestant, and 13 percent are unaffiliated or espouse other beliefs, including Spiritism.[1]

In contrast, the racial makeup of New York's Brazilians is atypical of their homeland because it is markedly skewed toward the lighter end of the color spectrum. Eighty-three percent of the Brazilians in my sample were white, 8 percent were light-skinned persons of mixed ancestry, and 8 percent were black. Thus, blacks and other "people of color," to use the Brazilian term, account for perhaps 16 percent of New York's Brazilian community, a fraction of the 45 percent reported in the 1980 census for Brazil as a whole.[2]

The Brazilian population in New York City is fairly young. Thirty-six percent of my sample were under thirty, another 43 percent were "thirty-something," 16 percent were forty to forty-nine, and only five percent were over fifty. I have no figures for younger age groups, although they are undoubtedly small; two-thirds of my sample were childless and of those that did have children, a sizable proportion of them (42 percent) had offspring living with relatives in Brazil.

Marital status changed for quite a few Brazilians after they arrived in the United States. When they first came to New York, 60 percent of the people in my sample were single, 24 percent were married, and the remainder were separated, divorced, or widowed. But by the time the subjects were interviewed after having lived in the city anywhere from a few months to a few years, the ranks of the *solteiros* and *solteiras* (single men and women) had dwindled to 43 percent, while those of the married had increased to 37 percent. But the marital status of men and women differed; while half of the women were still single, only 37 percent of the men were. Conversely, 44 percent of the men were married at the time of the interview, compared to 29 percent of the women. The figures for divorce and separation were similar for both sexes.

QUICK WORK

A Brazilian woman living in New York who was undocumented became engaged to a European man who lived in the city. He had previously applied to become a naturalized U.S. citizen. Right after he received his citizenship papers and went through the ceremony for new citizens, the couple went to City Hall and were married. From there, they made a beeline to the INS office, where she filed papers for a green card based on her brand-new marriage to a U.S. citizen.

Brazilians tend to marry other Brazilians; less than a fifth were married to Americans or people of some other nationality. Also, most of the married Brazilians in my sample (80 percent) lived with their spouses in New York. This contrasts with the pattern for some other Brazilian populations in the United States. For example, a report in the magazine *Veja* about *brazucas* in Boston describes the typical Brazilian immigrant there as a "young unmarried male," but if married, "his family nearly always stays in Brazil."[3]

These, then, are the vital statistics of my New York sample, less one relevant datum: how long they have been immigrants. Brazilian immigration to the United States on a major scale is quite a new phenomenon, one that dates only from the mid-1980s. The recency of the Brazilian influx is reflected in the histories of individual migrants. At the time I interviewed them, in 1990, over half of my informants, 56 percent to be exact, had lived in the United States for three years or less, another third had been here between four and ten years, and only 12 percent could be called "old-timers," people who had lived in the country for a decade or more.

Over three-quarters came straight to the Big Apple and stayed; only 23 percent had lived elsewhere in the United States. Of those that did, Florida and New Jersey were the most common states of residence. Finally, for 87 percent of the Brazilians in my sample, coming to the United States was their first experience living abroad.

The Case of Class

International migration requires both transportation and documentation. People have to know where to go to obtain passports and visas; they must be able to get there; they need to know how to fill out the forms that are required . . . they must be able to purchase transportation.

—MICHAEL J. PIORE, *Birds of Passage*

Brazilian immigrants in New York City do not represent the full spectrum of their nation's class structure. One very telling index of Brazilian social class—buying power—clearly illustrates this. The scale shown in Table 4.1 was developed to evaluate Brazilian purchasing power, with a particular focus on disposable income. The scale is based on the proportion and amount of household income left over after basic expenditures are met— food, utilities, telephone, school expenses, clothing, transportation, basic hygiene items, and medical care. Since the scale assumes a Brazilian middle-class standard of living, domestic help is included as a basic household expense.

Table 4.1 Purchasing Power Index by Social Class in Brazil

Index Classification	Social Class	Percentage of Population
Classes A and B1	Upper and upper-middle	6
Classes B2 and B3	Middle and lower-middle	34
Class C	Working	34
Class D	Abject poverty	26

Source: Adapted from Kottak, *Prime Time Society*, 26.

This buying power scale was developed by the Instituto Brasileiro de Opinião Pública e Estatística (IBOPE), the Brazilian Statistical Public Opinion Institute. It is useful because although data on income from wages are available, there are no good data on income from property, investments, and so on in Brazil. As a result, data on the distribution of wealth in Brazil—except in land—are difficult to come by. Even the information on wage structure is not finely tuned. For example, in 1980, the top income group earned the equivalent of at least twenty minimum wages. This income cohort included those with a wide range of incomes, from university professors to highly paid business executives.[4]

How does this picture of Brazilian class structure compare with that of New York's Brazilian immigrants? I used a number of different indices to determine my research population's class affiliations. I asked informants to what social class they thought they belonged. I also asked them if they or their parents owned significant property in Brazil—houses, apartments, cars, land. I asked about their education, their work histories in Brazil, and the occupations of their parents. Finally, I recorded my own impressions of their social class based on all the information that they had provided. The line between middle- and lower-middle-class affiliation was based on property ownership and occupational and educational data on my informants and their parents. For example, if an informant or his or her parent had a professional degree and/or owned significant property, I classified that informant as middle class; if the parent or informant owned a small business or if the informant had been a nurse or schoolteacher in Brazil, I classified the informant as lower middle class. Tables 4.2 through 4.5 show the results of these inquiries.

Table 4.2   Social Class of Informants

Social Class	Self-Identified	Interviewer-Judged
Upper-middle class	11 percent	11 percent
Middle class	47	30
Lower-middle class	31	50
Lower class	11	9

The most salient statistic is the marked contrast between the national class distribution of Brazil (see Table 4.1) and that of my Brazilian informants in New York City (see Table 4.2). Whereas Brazil's upper, upper-middle, middle, and lower-middle classes comprise 40 percent of the country's population, a far larger proportion—about 90 percent—of my New York sample falls into these categories. In contrast, the two lowest classes account for 60 percent of the Brazilian population as a whole, while only about 10 percent of my New York informants are so classified. To sum up, a far higher percentage of Brazilian immigrants in the New York sample are upper-middle, middle, or lower-middle class and a far

Table 4.3 Property Ownership in Brazil

Respondent owns significant property	
Yes	62 percent
No	38
Respondent's parents own significant property	
Yes	84 percent
No	14

lower percentage of them are working or lower class than is true for Brazilians in their native land.

The patterns of major property ownership among New York's Brazilians and their parents also suggest roots in the middle strata (see Table 4.3). In Brazil, car ownership, in particular, is limited to the middle and upper classes; thus, we can use the data on social class in Brazil in Table 4.1 as a surrogate for data on property ownership in Brazil.[5] If, indeed, only Classes A and B are so endowed in Brazil, then about 40 percent of the Brazilian population own major property. This contrasts with a figure of 62 percent among my New York informants and a figure of 84 percent for their parents. However, some of the major property owned by immigrants themselves in Brazil—although not that owned by their parents—was bought with hard-earned dollars from their jobs in New York.

Table 4.4 Occupation in Brazil

Occupation	Respondents	Respondents' Fathers[a]	Respondents' Mothers[b]
Salaried employee	44 percent	26 percent	7 percent
Professional	22	6	2
Teacher	9	0	7
Business owner	7	22	5
Self-employed	5	14	4
Skilled worker	4	13	1
Unskilled worker	6	6	2
Manager	2	5	0
Housewife	1	0	68

[a] Eight percent deceased or unknown.
[b] Four percent deceased or unknown.

Two items stand out in the data on occupation (see Table 4.4). One is the high rate (22 percent) of business ownership for the parental generation, a good indicator of membership in the Brazilian middle and lower-middle classes. The other is the large proportion of professionals (also 22 percent) in my New York sample. Brazilian professionals included people with law and journalism degrees, engineers, an agronomist, a social worker, a psychologist, and a veterinarian.

More noteworthy still is the remarkably high educational level of the New York–based Brazilians: 46 percent have attended university, and of these, 31 percent are university graduates (see Table 4.5). By way of comparison, only 24 percent of Americans have college degrees. And the figures for Brazilian women in New York are even more striking; nearly 60 percent have some higher education (see Table 4.6). In contrast, in 1990 in Brazil, only 28 percent of the population had completed secondary school, and only 12 percent had gone on to higher education.[6] These New York immigrants, then, are singularly well educated when compared with their compatriots back home.

Table 4.5   Education of Informants

Primary school	8 percent
Junior high	9
Some high school	7
High school graduate	30
Some university	15
University graduate	31

Table 4.6   Education of Informants by Sex

	Males	Females
Primary school	4 percent	13 percent
Junior high	15	4
High school	48	25
Some university	9	22
University graduate	25	37

How They See Themselves

Migrants to the U.S. . . . were characterized by preferential access to material resources, human capital and social connections not equally distributed among the population.

—EUGENIA GEORGES, *The Making of a Transnational Community*

The figures on the social and educational attributes of Brazilians in New York City were confirmed by innumerable conversations I had with a large number of Brazilians who live there. Informants generally agreed that the middle sectors of Brazilian society account for most of the migrants to the Big Apple; neither the bottom nor the top rung of the social ladder is represented in significant numbers. To be sure, many people told me that there are wealthy Brazilians in New York, but that "they don't emigrate. They come as tourists."

A few long-term New York residents, however, contended that as the Brazilian economy plummeted in the late 1980s, the social class of emigrants began to rise. A Brazilian physician who has lived in the city for years was quite insistent that "upper-class college graduates," as he called them, have started showing up as immigrants in New York. He cited medical colleagues and other people with considerable capital to invest.[7] The owner of a large remittance agency believes that a "better quality immigrant" has been coming recently; he put lawyers, doctors, and engineers in that category. "Sure, there have always been some professionals," he said, "but now the numbers are way up because they can't get jobs in Brazil." The owner of a midtown boutique that caters to Brazilian tourists agreed and went on to describe the newcomers:

I know a number of upper-middle-class business and professional people arriving in the United States who want to invest in businesses here or practice their professions. They don't plan to remain illegals and they certainly did not come here to take menial employment. These are not the very rich, but they do live well in Brazil. They've only been coming to New York since last year [1988], as economic conditions at home deteriorated. This is the class of people who had their suitcases packed and were ready to leave Brazil if Lula [the socialist candidate for president of Brazil] had been elected.

This upward social shift was also alluded to in a different context. A Brazilian in the New York music world remarked on how the city has long attracted young musicians from his country. They come to the city to explore career opportunities, he said, and work at whatever jobs they can find to support themselves. But with the continued decline of Brazil's economy, well-known, established musicians are now heading for New York and looking for work in their profession.

There is another side to the question of the social class of recent arrivals. A handful of informants averred that of late, less rather than more affluent immigrants from Brazil had been arriving in the city. For example, a professional interpreter told me that the social class of Brazilians coming to the United States "used to be better." "Even if they didn't have that much formal education, they had better manners," he remarked. However, I found absolutely no evidence for a recent wave of immigrants from the lower stratum of Brazilian society.

While in very recent years, there may have been a slight broadening at the top and at the bottom of New York's Brazilian immigrant social hierarchy, those of middle- and lower-middle-class origin clearly predominate. One Brazilian resident who owns a radio call car company in Queens said that of the thousand or so job applications she received from Brazilians over a two-year period, not one came from someone who would be considered poor by Brazilian standards. Most of the applicants own their own homes in Brazil, she said. Thus, "they may be poor here [in New York] but not there."

A woman who heads a social service agency in Queens that has a large Brazilian clientele describes her clients as "mostly middle class." The majority occupied white-collar positions in Brazil, with a sprinkling of professionals. Some clients show her snapshots of the homes they left behind, and she tells them that she "can't believe that people who own such things aren't satisfied living in Brazil." But the answer is always the same: they came to the United States to earn *verdinhas* ("little green things," Portuguese slang for dollars).

Lower-middle-class Brazilians also constitute a major presence in New York, informants acknowledged. Many émigrés were nurses and primary school teachers in Brazil—notoriously underpaid professions there—who came to the United States "just to see the possibilities." Others owned small businesses—auto repair shops, restaurants, pharmacies—that were badly hit by the souring economy back home. But most Brazilians with whom I spoke took care to distinguish such petit bourgeoisie from the impoverished of their land. And they were unanimous in pointing out the improbability of poor Brazilians' making the trip to the United States.

A Cut Above

Our subjects appear to be almost an elite.

—Demetrios G. Papademetriou and Nicholas DiMarzio,

Undocumented Aliens in the New York Metropolitan Area

The data on Brazilians in New York City clearly show that contrary to conventional wisdom, it is not necessarily the poorest of the poor who migrate internationally or who turn into illegal immigrants when they arrive at their destinations abroad. This finding is in line with other recent research. Over the last few years, such countries as the Dominican Republic and Peru also have become exporters of middle-class migrants to the United States. In her study of Dominican migration, Eugenia Georges found that urban business owners and other people in the middle stratum of society had initiated migration to this country. When faced with the loss of economic opportunities at home—not unemployment—the lure of higher wages in New York beckoned. The migrants, Georges notes, "came from the more privileged segments of the population." Similarly, in a study of another Dominican community, Patricia Pessar found that most migrants to the United States were from the ranks of landowners with substantial holdings, specifically those who raised cattle and grew cash crops.[8]

The high educational levels of many groups of recent immigrants to the United States also belies conventional wisdom. A research project on undocumented individuals in the New York area found that over one-third of the study population of Haitians and Colombians had some university education. As it turns out, the educational credentials of new immigrants are similar to those of Americans as a whole.[9]

What are we to make of these findings about Brazilians, Dominicans, and others that challenge the stereotypes of uneducated, economically desperate migrants, people who are willing to do almost anything to leave the poverty of their homelands and live illegally in the United States?[10] As economic conditions deteriorate at home, why is it the relatively comfortable middle and lower-middle classes, rather than the traditional "wretched refuse" who are now coming to our "teeming shores"? The answer can be summed up in two words: resources and information. When discouraged by the lack of good jobs or economic opportunities at home, it is members of the middle sectors who have the discretionary income to pay for the high costs of migrating internationally, as well as the social contacts to know how to do so.

Indeed, the actual cost and process of migration is often affected by social class. For Brazilians and Dominicans, and undoubtedly for others as well, the difficulty of entering the United States is related to one's social class and financial resources back home. Paradoxically, poorer people often have to spend more money to come to the United States than do wealthier ones. U.S. consular officials demand that people applying for tourist visas demonstrate that they do not intend to stay in this country and work. Potential tourists must show home ownership or other property, good jobs, savings accounts, and so on. Since poorer people are far less likely to have these things, they have to pay for fake documents to "prove" their economic well-being, thus adding anywhere from $1,000 to $3,000 to the cost of migrating. Members of the middle class, on the other hand, who are more apt to own their own homes or to have savings, do not have to rely on falsified documents to secure tourist visas, thus avoiding this additional expense.

In Brazil, in fact, the current difficulty in acquiring a U.S. tourist visa may make the Brazilian immigrant flow *more* middle class than would be the case were there no strict requirements to demonstrate financial soundness. In other words, a presumably unintended consequence of these requirements may be to select for more middle-class overstays. The alternative for the less well-off is either not to come at all, or to increase the expense and risk of migrating by buying false documents or coming to the United States via Mexico.

The middle class, however, paves the migration path for the less well-off. In fact, there appears to be a sequencing of migration based on social class. In his study of international migration, *Birds of Passage*, Michael J. Piore points out that the middle class usually migrates abroad first. It is members of the middle class, especially the urban middle class, who have the education and the resources to find out about obtaining passports and visas, about airplane fares and other transportation costs, and about the general ins and outs of moving to a new country. Only after informational networks that facilitate international migration are established— travel agencies, visa brokers, and the like—are people from lower social strata able to follow the migratory path abroad.

This observation may shed light on the spatial and class distribution of Brazilian immigrants in the northeastern United States. While migrants to New York City are mostly middle and lower-middle class, there are pockets of poorer, working-class Brazilians in Framingham, Mass., and in other enclaves in the Boston area, as well as in Danbury, Conn., and Newark, N.J.[11] Moreover, coincidence alone cannot explain the disproportionate share of Boston-, Danbury-, and Newark-based Brazilians who hail from Governador Valadares and other towns in the Rio Doce Valley of Minas Gerais state. For example, 87 percent of the Brazilians in Framingham studied by Bicalho were from the state of Minas Gerais (three-quarters of them from the Rio Doce Valley region), and one Brazilian informant, a long-term resident of Newark, estimates that well over half of his compatriots there and in neighboring Elizabeth are *valadarenses*, that is, from Governador Valadares.[12] In contrast, the origins of the Brazilians in my New York sample were more varied; 41 percent were from Minas Gerais, 38 percent were from Rio de Janeiro, 9 percent were from São Paulo, and the remaining 12 percent were from other states in Brazil, primarily Espirito Santo and Paraná.

The specific links between social class, place of origin in Brazil, and city of residence in the northeastern United States are complex. In attempting

4.1 Apartment construction in Governador Valadares in Minas Gerais is tangible evidence of the impact of immigrants' remittance money.

to understand them, we must digress and use the town of Governador Valadares, the famed exporter of *brazucas*, as a case study.

"The Last One to Leave, Turn Out the Light"

The idea of migrating to work in the United States is not something that just

happens. It is socially and culturally constructed.

—Leo Chavez, *Shadowed Lives*

Because of its citizens' lengthy history of migration to the United States—which dates back to the mid- or late 1960s—Governador Valadares, in the state of Minas Gerais, is a community saturated with information about traveling to the United States, about what it is like to live there, and about what opportunities exist for immigrants there. The town itself is awash with travel agencies—some thirty-five or forty serve a population of about 210,000. Most families in town have at least one relative in the United States and although no one knows the actual figures, it has been estimated that there may be 30,000 to 35,000 *valadarenses* living in the United States, about 15 percent of the entire population of Governador Valadares. One prominent sign of the wealth that dollars have brought is the town's Mercedes-Benz dealership.

VALADARES JOKES

There are now so many Brazilians from Governador Valadares in the United States that there are jokes about it. The town, jokingly renamed Governador Vala*dolares*, is said to be a *fantasma*, an apparition that does not really exist, because nearly everyone has left for the United States. It is also said that for the few people who remain, "mass is celebrated in English."

When I was visiting the largest Brazilian-owned remittance agency in Manhattan, I struck up a conversation with a woman who was from Governador Valadares. She told me that it is not true that everyone has left Valadares for the United States. "I know there are at least two people still there— my mother and my sister."

A "culture of out-migration" exists in Governador Valadares and the towns of the Rio Doce Valley. The term, coined by political scientist Wayne Cornelius, is applied to communities that have extensive, long-established patterns of international migration; many children in them grow up expecting to migrate as part of their life experience. Moreover, long-term migration patterns lead to strong ties between sending communities and the destination(s) abroad, in this case, ties between Governador Valadares and several U.S. cities. According to sociologist Alejandro Portes, "[P]eople emigrate to where they find connections and a measure of familiarity."[13] Economic factors are important but *information* about economic opportunities is equally crucial in the decision to migrate, information that is more likely to be available to individuals who already have friends and relatives living in the United States.

The culture of out-migration in Governador Valadares is evident even to the casual visitor. Emigration and related subjects—the latest exchange rate for dollars or the cost of a charter flight to Orlando—are constant topics of conversation. The local newspaper, *Diário do Rio Doce*, features a regular Sunday column by a lawyer who gives advice on U.S. immigration laws and how to "get legal" in the United States. Newspaper accounts of the successes of earlier migrants from the town fuel emigration fever. Typical was an interview with a wealthy entrepreneur, the owner of a large local concern, who got his start with the money he saved during the five years he worked in a restaurant in Boston. Some local talent even wrote and produced a slick musical comedy about migrating to the United States, an instant hit that was sold out for its nine-day run.

The musical *O Último a Sair Apaga a Luz* (The Last One to Leave, Turn Out the Light) featured songs with lyrics about the ups and downs of emigration set to such tunes as "New York, New York," "California Dreaming," and "Monday, Monday"—the last retitled, "Money, Money."[14]

WHERE THE DOLLAR IS KING

In Governador Valadares, the talk is of dollars: How much is the dollar today? Where can I get the best rate of exchange? When I was there, the newspaper and television news were full of reports about two local men who had been arrested as counterfeiters. They did not bother with Brazilian cruzeiros; they were printing U.S. currency.

Major purchases—houses, apartments, cars—are paid for in dollars. In the town's newspaper, about half of the real estate prices are quoted in dollars. At some bars, you can pay your tab in dollars, and cabdrivers will accept them for fare. And the salesclerk at the local Benetton outlet was more than happy to accept dollars for a purchase made there.

Although there are no specific studies of immigrants from Governador Valadares in the United States, there is enough information from various sources to suggest who they might be. As the town's secretary of tourism told me, "All classes of *valadarenses* are going to the United States, from the rich to the poor; even the children of *fazendeiros* [ranchers] are going there." Indeed, it appears that a wide range of people from Valadares are emigrating to the United States. For example, cooks and orderlies from one of the local hospitals have gone to the United States, as has an orthopedic surgeon, who went with his family. Parenthetically, he kept his clinic in town and plans to save money from his American earnings to buy a cattle ranch when he returns home.

Three *valadarenses*, long-term residents of New York, told me that the majority of their fellow townspeople now in the United States are lower-middle-class "economic immigrants," defined as "people who don't own their own homes." The single most important reason that *valadarenses* go to the United States, it was explained repeatedly, is to save money to buy an apartment or a house in their hometown. A common pattern is for an émigré to buy two dwellings, one for his or her personal use and one to rent out as a source of extra income.

These same informants went on to suggest that perhaps 20 percent of *valadarenses* in the United States are of working-class origin, people who were able to come to the United States *only* because of the money sent by relatives who already had jobs there. Although I am unable to say under what circumstances Brazilians from Governador Valadares's lower stratum first came the United States, the following statement is more than just

a bit of class snobbery. According to a decidedly upper-middle-class resident of the town:

> Emigrants used to be more middle class but since 1986 or so, their level
> has declined. Now when you go to the local branch of the Bank of
> Brazil—can you imagine—there are women in rubber thong sandels
> buying dollars! These people ruined it for the middle class because now
> no one from Valadares can get a tourist visa.

Thus, it appears that a range of social classes are represented among
valadarenses in the United States. But what does social class have to do
with place of origin in Brazil and place of residence in the United States?
The presence of a pervasive culture of out-migration in a particular town
or region makes for emigrants from diverse economic and educational
backgrounds. Not only are a wide range of citizens exposed to information about emigration, but remittances sent back from relatives who already have made the move abroad enable still others to follow suit. In
other words, a culture of out-migration provides both the ideology and
the material base—in the form of remittances from relatives abroad—that
enhance the possibility of emigration for people from a wide range of
backgrounds.

In Governador Valadares and in the nearby towns of the Rio Doce
Valley, then, people who ordinarily could not dream of financing such a
trip themselves become emigrants through the good graces, in the form of
either gifts or loans, of family members who migrated earlier. Simply put,
a culture of out-migration amplifies the emigration prospects of poorer,
less educated people. This explains the anomalous presence of working-
class immigrants from Governador Valadares in the United States—
anomalous because given the current realities of the Brazilian economy
with its rock-bottom wages and runaway inflation, it is a struggle for such
people just to support themselves and their families, let alone to think
about emigrating to a foreign land.

As a result of these processes, *valadarenses* in the United States seem to
come from a broader range of social milieus, including the working class,
than do emigrants from any other part of Brazil. This also contextualizes
the comparatively modest educational levels of Brazilian immigrants in
Framingham, three quarters of whom come from the Governador Valadares–Rio Doce Valley area. Thirty-seven percent of the Brazilian residents in that Massachusetts town had only a primary school education,
53 percent went to secondary school, and 6.2 percent had university degrees. These figures mesh to some extent with a report in *Veja* that "the
level of instruction" of Brazilians in Boston is "rarely above the basic
level."[15] By way of contrast, recall my New York sample: only 8 percent
of the Brazilians in it did not go beyond primary school, but 31 percent
had completed university.

To make the final link in the chain, all of this suggests that there is a larger working-class component in the Brazilian immigrant population of those U.S. cities where *valadarenses* congregate—Boston, Newark, Danbury—than in others, such as New York, that also attract Brazilian immigrants. In fact, in New York, immigrants from large Brazilian cities—Belo Horizonte, Rio de Janeiro, and São Paulo—seem to predominate, and they are largely middle and lower-middle class.

This is a plausible interpretation of the distribution of Brazilian social classes in the northeastern United States. If the majority of immigrants from Governador Valadares and the surrounding region go to the Boston area, to Danbury, and to Newark,[16]—presumably because they already have friends and relatives there who can help them find jobs and housing—then we would expect these cities to have heavier concentrations of less well-off, less well-educated Brazilian immigrants, in comparison to those in New York. This explanation makes sense and avoids invoking the chauvinistic argument that a native New Yorker would likely make: "*But, of course*, immigrants from large cosmopolitan cities such as Rio and São Paulo would head for the Big Apple! *Where else would they go?*"

Hometowns

At Sigo You Receive Payments in DOLLARS in 24 Hours in the Following Cities: Rio de Janeiro, São Paulo, Belo Horizonte, Governador Valadares, Ipatinga, Poços de Caldas, Vitoria, Brasília, Curitiba, Ponta Grossa, Florianopolis, and Camboriu.

—*Advertisement*

Brazil is a vast country about the size of the United States excluding Alaska. It is a country of stark contrasts in wealth and human well-being. Parts of the northeastern region of the country are among the most desperately poor in the world, with abysmal infant mortality and literacy rates, malnutrition, and rampant poverty. In bold contrast to this privation is the southern third of the nation. Brazilians often say that if the industrialized south, with its world-class metropolitan centers, its humming factories, and its relatively advanced infrastructure were severed from the rest of Brazil, the region would be classified as an industrialized country.

Brazilian immigrants in New York City hail largely from southern and south-central Brazil, the relatively prosperous part of the nation (see map 4.1). They primarily come from Minas Gerais and Rio de Janeiro—79 percent of my sample come from these two states—and to a lesser extent from São Paulo, Paraná, Espirito Santo, and a smattering of others.

Moreover, they are overwhelmingly urban; 88 percent were city dwellers immediately prior to emigration.[17]

HOMETOWN POLITICS
A Message for Mineiros in the U.S.A.
Mineiros, encourage members of your family living back home in Minas Gerais to vote for Luis Santos for state governor. Here's what he will do for you and your family: He pledges to come to the immediate rescue of the dignity of the *mineiro* who has been harmed by discrimination on the part of [U.S.] consular authorities in Brazil.

—Ad appearing in *The Brasilians*, a newspaper published in New York City.

Natives of the state of Minas Gerais, *mineiros*, seem to have a dominant presence among Brazilian populations in the northeastern United States. In the town of Framingham, near Boston, 87 percent of the Brazilians hail from Minas Gerais, and in Newark, the figure probably is well over half.[18] While *mineiros* were not as prevalent in my New York sample—41 percent lived in the state before leaving Brazil, and 44 percent were born there—their celebrity far outweighs their numbers. Brazilians view *mineiros* as quintessential emigrants and, in New York at least, often overestimate their presence in the expatriate community. For example, I was told early on that at least 60 percent of the Brazilian immigrants in New York City were from Minas Gerais and that *cariocas*, natives of Rio de Janeiro, almost never come to the United States because "they can't bear to leave the beach." It turned out that this was not true; in fact, on the basis of my sample and conversations with perhaps 250 Brazilians living in New York, many of them from Rio; *cariocas* appear to be the second-largest group in the city's Brazilian population, not far behind *mineiros* in numbers.

IT'S A SMALL WORLD
My husband and I went to a Brazilian-owned remittance agency in midtown Manhattan to wire flowers to Brazil. This was to thank a family in Governador Valadares for their hospitality during our stay there. After we gave the woman who waited on us the name and address of where the flowers were to be sent, she excitedly blurted out, "Why Dona Maira was my English teacher in Valadares!"

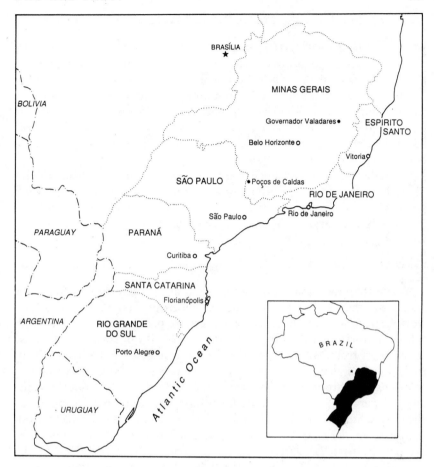

Map 4.1 Southern and South-Central Brazil

At the start of the great emigration surge to New York in the mid-1980s, however, people from Minas Gerais were probably more preponderant than they are today. Dona Dahlia told me that when she first opened her rooming house most of her boarders were *mineiros*, but that the numbers of *cariocas* and *paulistas* (natives of São Paulo) had increased with each passing year. But *mineiros* are still a major presence in the city and undoubtedly the foremost remitters of money to Brazil. At a large, Brazilian-owned remittance company in New York City with branches throughout the Northeast, about 50 percent of all remittances to Brazil are sent to Minas Gerais, and of these, about 70 percent go to Governador Valadares and neighboring towns. The size and impact of these remittances on the receiving communities can well be imagined.[19]

IS ANYBODY (STILL) HOME?

The small town of Resplendor in Minas Gerais is located some 650 kilometers northeast of Belo Horizonte, the state capital. Nearly 18 percent of the town's citizens, some 3,000 people, have left to seek their fortune in the United States. Because of the exodus, Resplendor's population went from 19,500 in 1980 to just under 17,000 by 1989. The flight began in the mid-1980s, according to the town's mayor, who attributes it to the influence of nearby Governador Valadares.

Although the economy of Resplendor is based on cattle ranching and agriculture, the most active economic sector today is civil construction, which has increased nearly 70 percent as a result of the remittances sent back home by sons and daughters living in the United States.

Source: *Folha de São Paulo*, July 23, 1989

While the most famous *mineiros* of all are people from Governador Valadares, they are not the most numerous group from that state in New York City; in my sample, there were far more people from the state capital, Belo Horizonte, than from Valadares. This is not surprising because immigrants from Minas Gerais, like those from other states, overwhelmingly lived in major cities prior to leaving Brazil. Of the native-born *mineiros*, most resided in the state capital (63 percent) or another major city (21 percent), such as Rio de Janeiro or São Paulo, before coming to the United States; only 16 percent came to the United States directly from towns or smaller cities, such as Governador Valadares. Thus, while there are people from Valadares and nearby towns in New York City, unlike their counterparts in Boston, Newark, and Danbury, they do not constitute a majority of Brazilian immigrants.

One informant suggested that some natives of Governador Valadares conceal their origin and claim to be from Belo Horizonte or elsewhere in Brazil. Why would they do that, I asked? "Well, there are certain negative images surrounding the town," he said. "It has a reputation for violence." *Valadarenses*, he told me, are stereotyped by other Brazilians in New York as grasping, untrustworthy, and provincial. I soon realized that this man's comment was too circumspect; these stereotypes were usually applied not just to *valadarenses*, but to *all mineiros*, although at times, people from that town were singled out for special denigration. Put bluntly, I found widespread anti*mineiro* sentiment in New York's Brazilian community, as witness the following comments: "I don't want to seem prejudiced or anything, but *mineiros* are extremely nationalistic," said one *paulista*. "They have a tough time adjusting to the mainstream. They're not as cosmopolitan as *paulistas* and *cariocas*, or even *bahianos* [natives of Bahia] and *gauchos* [natives of Rio Grande do Sul]. *Mineiros* are basically mercenary—people who come here, work two or three years, and then go back." "Lots of immigrants are from Minas Gerais," a native of Rio said, "but all they talk about is Brazil. They don't want to learn English; they don't want to adjust. All they say is "Brazil this and Brazil that." It's irritating sometimes. You say, God damn it, go back to Brazil! What are you doing here? . . . They are also like that in Brazil. Even when they go to other parts the country, they never leave home. They are always talking about Minas."

But *mineiros* also have their defenders, and not just other *mineiros*. They have reputations as hard workers, who often hold down two jobs and work nights and weekends. A man from São Paulo was particularly laudatory: "The U.S. Immigration Service should throw open the doors to *mineiros* because they're so dedicated; they don't even miss work when they're sick." Unlike some Brazilians, he noted pointedly, "people from Minas Gerais are not spoiled by the beach!" This was a thinly veiled reference to the other side of the stereotype coin. Rio de Janeiro, hometown of the "Girl from Ipanema," is famed for its beaches, and these, in turn, are used to typecast the city's residents. For example, a man from Belo Horizonte assured me that "*cariocas* don't work." Said another from São Paulo, "Because of the Rio lifestyle, *cariocas* don't last long in New York. They're beachcombers. They don't adjust to New York because they're not used to working, they're used to the good life. New York is not for them."

TOWN TO TOWN

Residents of Governador Valadares mainly migrate to Boston, Newark, N.J., and Danbury, Conn. Brazilians from other towns or states also tend to settle in particular places in the United States. People from the states of Goias and Bahia go to San Francisco; there is also an enclave of people from Goias living in Austin, Texas. Natives of the city of Belem, at the mouth of the Amazon River, head for Miami. Citizens of Lajes, in the state of Santa Catarina, are found in Concord and Franconia, N.H. *Mineiros* from Poços de Caldas make their way to White Plains and Mount Vernon in Westchester County, N.Y. Residents of the tiny town of Tiros, in central Minas Gerais, live in Long Branch, N.J.

All of this sounds familiar to anyone who has spent time in Brazil, where *cariocas* are caricatured as bronzed, scantily clad, beachgoing, samba-dancing hedonists who would rather play than work. But, then, regional stereotypes are rife in that country, the land of "conservative, family-oriented" *mineiros*, *paulistas* who are "good at business but not at having a good time," and so on. These are traditional Brazilian stereo-types that are peculiarly alive and well in their transplanted New York setting.

Family Ties

Networks developed by the movement of people back and forth in space are

at the core of the microstructures that sustain migration over time.

—ALEJANDRO PORTES AND RUBÉN RUMBAUT, *Immigrant America*

International migrants go to familiar territory when possible, and nothing makes a place more familiar than having family there. The benefits bestowed by a network of kin in a city such as New York are manifest. Relatives can lower the cost of the first days or weeks in New York because they offer the immigrant a place to stay. They may help the newcomer find employment either through personal contacts or through knowledge of the job market. Relatives can be founts of advice on city living and they may provide a warm shoulder to cry on when the recent arrival is overcome with *saudades* (longing, homesickness, "the memories which touch a soul") for family and friends back in Brazil. There is no question, then, that the presence of kin networks reduces the cost—both material and psychological—of migration.[20]

Just how many Brazilian immigrants had the security blanket of relatives already living in the Big Apple when they first arrived there? In my own sample, only 30 percent were so blessed; another 10 percent had relatives living elsewhere in the United States. Nevertheless, it is the 70 percent who had no kin living in New York at the time they arrived that is significant and reflects the recency of Brazilian immigration. Contrast that figure with a study of undocumented immigrants from the Caribbean in the New York metropolitan area, two-thirds of whom had relatives already living in the United States.[21]

However, this does not mean that only 30 percent of my informants had kin in New York. In fact, if we include spouses and children as well as other relatives who came to New York *after* the interviewee, then a far greater number—just over 60 percent—had relatives living in New York by the time this study was done. Also recall that a fair number of Brazilians married after they arrived in the city, and a few had children born there.

Still, by far the major cause for the increased number of immigrants with kin in New York is what sociologists call "chain migration"—a pattern in which "new migrants are successively brought to the city on the initiative of kin who are already there."[22] One migrant is followed by others; chain reactions pull still more migrants along via family networks.

Each migrant brings a new set of ties to people in the home community, and people at home, in turn, have more ties to those in the destination locale. A self-perpetuating migrant stream begins to flow as migration becomes easier. In the words of anthropologist Douglas Massey, "[E]very new migrant reduces the cost of subsequent migration for a set of friends and relatives, and with the lowered costs some of these people are induced to migrate which further expands the set of people with ties abroad. . . ."[23]

The Tree of Migration

The best way to breathe life into the links of the migratory chain is through real people. Claudio, a professional soccer player in Rio de Janeiro before coming to New York, is a champion of the technique. Since arriving in the Big Apple more than five years ago he has helped twelve relatives and friends follow in his footsteps. With his earnings as a street vendor and, later, as a shoe shiner at a busy kiosk near Grand Central Station, he helped pay their airfare—repaid once they got jobs in New York—and he let them bed down in his apartment—rent free—until they found permanent places of their own. During his first six months in the United States, he helped four cousins come to this country. During the next six months, he assisted his youngest brother, followed by a friend, and then the friend's cousin, and so it went.

Claudio estimates that every year, on average, each Brazilian immigrant helps two more Brazilians come to the United States. He likens the whole process to the branching of a tree. One Brazilian helps two or three others, and they, in turn, help two or three more. While his calculation of Brazilian largess seems quite high, there is no doubt that a significant number of Brazilian immigrants in New York traveled to the city through the good financial and emotional graces of Brazilian friends and relatives already living there.

The practice is so common, and the various combinations of relatives and friends brought over so diverse, that there is no distinct pattern, except that siblings are usually involved in the process. A few cases will illustrate the point. A *paulista* came to New York six years ago. He then helped bring over his sister, her husband, and a nephew. Then his mother arrived, but she went back to Brazil after two years. She now plans to come to New York once again, this time accompanied by a divorced daughter. Another example is a man from the northeastern state of Ceará who has lived in New York for four years. With his help, his brother and sister joined him, and he put them up in his apartment in Queens. His local kin group expanded as a sister-in-law, a niece, and a cousin arrived, along with his mother, who visits periodically. Today he has six relatives in New York and is hoping to bring yet another sister, who envisions a career as a singer on Broadway. A different variation on the theme is a woman from Rio, who came to New York with her husband. She then sent for her sister, her brother-in-law, and their infant son. They, in turn, helped pay the airfare of a brother, his wife, and a niece. An unmarried sister with a small child has also arrived, along with her mother in tow to baby-sit for her growing brood of New York–based grandchildren.

The general rule seems to be that the longer the immigrant has been in New York, the more relatives she or he has managed to bring over. The owner of a limousine service who has lived in the city for more than a decade has sponsored so many relatives—"dozens and dozens," he said— that he could not name them all. Another case in point is an old-time migrant, a resident of the city for fourteen years. Now a successful administrative assistant at a bank in New York, her four sisters, four brothers-in-law, and numerous nieces and nephews are all the indirect beneficiaries of her initial largess. Not only did she help find jobs for these myriad kin, but at one point she had eight of them living with her in her small studio apartment in Queens.

One sometime arrangement in the migratory sequence is that of the married man who arrives alone in New York, finds a place to live, works a few months or perhaps a year, and then sends for his wife—and children, if any—from Brazil. For example, a man who had been an accountant in Rio came to New York and got a job as a waiter. His wife, a psychologist, and two children stayed behind in Brazil. After his employer agreed to sponsor him for a green card, his family came to New York, and today his wife is working as a caterer out of their Queens apartment. But this migratory pattern seems not all that common among Brazilians in New York. In my sample, three-quarters of the immigrants were unmarried at the time they arrived in the city, and of those that were married, about half had traveled to the city accompanied by their spouses. In a few cases, however, men who were single when they first came to the United States went back to Brazil, married, and then returned to the United States with their new wives.

Still, the arrangement whereby immigrant men travel alone to the Big Apple while their families stay behind in Brazil may be more common among certain groups of Brazilians in New York. This may also be the case for the female side of the equation—single or divorced women who come to New York and leave their children in the care of relatives back home. As one single woman, who had just arrived in New York, leaving her two children in Brazil, told me, "I like it here but a piece of me is in Brazil." Once again, the town of Governador Valadares provides the standard. Three native sons who live in New York estimated that about a third of the fifty or so *valadarenses* whom they know in the city are either single or divorced women or married men who send remittances to their spouses and/or children in Brazil. The sister of one of my *valadarense* informants regularly sends $150 to $200 a month to support her child there.

Most of the immigrant women in my sample were single and those who were married lived with their husbands in New York. In other words, I have encountered no instances of married women's immigrating to the United States without their husbands. Women who do come alone are unmarried, divorced, or widowed. Many of these women are also involved in the chain migration process; they help bring their sisters, brothers, cousins, and, occasionally, mothers to the United States.

The category of unmarried women also includes single or divorced mothers with children being cared for by relatives in Brazil. They and their male counterparts—married men with families back in Brazil—were described to me in similar terms, as "money machines," the "bankers" of their families, who "save every penny" they earn to send to Brazil and spend little on themselves. In some cases, their families come to depend on the remittances they send and they become stuck in New York; without the money they send, their families cannot meet expenses.

One incipient kinship arrangement found among New York's Brazilians deserves mention because, while not yet common, it seems likely to become more prevalent as the Brazilian migration stream ages and as more immigrants have children. Only about a third of Brazilian immigrants in New York are parents, and of those, perhaps 60 percent have their children living with them in the city. Despite these relatively small numbers, however, the custom of the Brazilian grandmother–child minder is emerging. Brazilian immigrants with children, particularly young children, often underwrite the cost of a grandmother's trip to New York. She comes to live with the family and takes care of her grandchildren while their parents work. This "sending for grandmother" pattern is certainly not unique to Brazilians; it has also been reported for other immigrant communities in New York, such as the Dominican one.[24]

A Special Kind of Marriage

In this discussion of family ties, marital status, parenthood, and migration patterns, one arrangement, although it serves legal, rather than familial or emotional, ends should nevertheless be mentioned. This is the "green card marriage," in which a foreigner marries a U.S. citizen or permanent resident alien in order to obtain a green card, that much-coveted document that permits its holder to live and work legally in the United States. The most common pattern is for a Brazilian man or woman— I could detect no gender differences in the frequency of green card marriages—to marry a U.S. citizen of Hispanic origin, most commonly a Puerto Rican.

A GREEN CARD MARRIAGE WITH A TWIST

One gay Brazilian who is an undocumented immigrant moved into an apartment with his American lover. They were planning to go through a "marriage" ceremony in Philadelphia and were then going to try to get the Brazilian a green card by presenting themselves to the INS as a married couple.

Green card marriages usually do not come cheap. The going rate in 1990 was $4,000 to $5,000 paid to the would-be American spouse. The price had recently gone up from about $2,500 because changes in the law had complicated and lengthened the process. Now the INS demands proof that the newlyweds filed a joint tax return for the first two years of their marriage. The couple, then, must stay in touch with each other during that period. They are also required to be present for a final joint interview with an immigration officer before the green card is approved for the alien spouse. Finally, once the green card is in hand, there is the expense of the divorce, which, depending on the circumstances, can cost as much as $2,500. In all, a green card marriage and divorce package costs between $6,000 and $7,000.

There are all sorts of variations on the green card marriage theme, and the mishaps involved are sometimes sources of hilarity. One Brazilian woman related how she borrowed a bridal gown and her new husband rented a tuxedo before they took "wedding" pictures to show to the immigration agent—just in case. I was also told about one green card couple who had never lived together—one was in New York and the other in Virginia—who spent hours rehearsing for their final interview with an immigration agent, memorizing the names of each other's relatives, their personal habits, and so on. Then, there was the woman in Newark who is said to have legalized four or five husbands of various nationalities, who are now scattered around the northeastern United States. Finally, I was told that for a hefty fee, some gay American males agree to take foreign women as brides.

Green card marriages, of course, are not limited to Brazilians. Among Hispanics in New York City they are referred to as marriages *por negócio*, "business marriages," and in the late 1970s, the going rate was around $1,000 for such nuptial arrangements. Green card marriages with friends who are U.S. citizens or resident aliens, in which no money changes hands, are called *casamientos de favor*, in Spanish, "do a favor marriages." They also exist among Brazilians, although they are less common than "business marriages," probably because Brazilian immigration is still quite recent. Since few Brazilians have become naturalized U.S.

citizens, the pool of Brazilians eligible to serve as green card spouses is quite small, and Brazilians still have little close contact with native-born Americans who might agree to "do a favor" unions.[25]

TRIALS OF A GREEN CARD INTERVIEW

Green card marriages have become well known in the United States, thanks to such movies as *Green Card*. One green card marriage that I was told about nearly went awry during its final stages when the couple was interviewed by an INS agent.

The husband, an American citizen, was unemployed and had arranged for a friend to pose as his boss in case an immigration official called to check on his employment record. During the interview, the agent questioned him about how long he had held his current job. After he responded, the agent dialed his friend's number to see if the story checked out. The "boss," of course, having no idea what the correct response was, put the agent on hold, saying that he had to "check his records."

Five minutes passed, during which the Brazilian wife—who was to be the recipient of the green card—became increasingly anxious. As the minutes ticked by and the agent became ever more impatient, he knocked over the glass of milk he had been drinking, soaking himself and all the documents on his desk including the woman's Brazilian passport. He jumped up, slammed down the phone, dabbed his pants with a handkerchief, and tried to sop up the mess on his desk. At that point, he grabbed the soggy passport, stamped it with the requisite stamp approving the woman's green card, and, much to their relief, summarily dismissed the couple.

Who Lives with Whom?

At different stages of migration and settlement different types of living

arrangments may be necessary or desirable.

—LEO CHAVEZ, "Households, Migration and Settlement"

Brazilian immigrants in New York City live in households composed of varying combinations of relatives and friends. Anthropologist Leo Chavez has distinguished four household types found among immigrant groups relatively new to the United States.[26] What he calls "no-family households," made up of single people sharing an apartment or domestic servants who live in the homes of their employers, are typical of the early stages of a migration stream. Typically, people who reside in such households are single migrants who intend to get a job, make money, and then return home. In his study of Mexicans and Central Americans, Chavez found that almost half of the undocumented migrants who had been in the United States less than two years lived in this type of household. But, he adds, "no-family households" become less common as migrants turn into settlers. Here, too, given that most Brazilian immigrants are new to this country and that most view themselves as temporary sojourners, it is little wonder that nearly 40 percent of my New York sample lived in households of this type.

There is also the "solitary," or one-person, household, a relative rarity among new immigrants to this country. As we have seen, for both economic and cultural reasons, this is the least common living arrangement among Brazilians in New York City; only about 10 percent of the people in my sample lived alone.

Chavez goes on to identify two kinds of kin-based households. The first is the simple family household, consisting of a married couple with or without children or a single-parent family; in either case, the household includes only one family unit. Then, there are complex family households, made up of varying combinations of kin. Among my Brazilian sample, 24 percent lived in simple family households, and the same percentage lived with a variety of relatives. The importance of multiple family incomes can be gauged from the fact that three-quarters of these households had two or more family wage earners. Then, too, 15 percent also had nonkin in residence, that is, one or more friends who shared expenses.

Chavez sees an evolution of immigrant household types. No-family households are very important in the early stage of migration, when single migrants predominate, and become less important the longer migrants are in the United States. The extended-family household is also more often found among recent migrants, while simple family households grow in importance as the stay in this country lengthens.

Brazilians conform to this scenario to some extent, although the simple family household of husband and wife seems to be more common than might be expected for such a new immigrant group. This is undoubtedly related to the class origins of so many of New York's Brazilian immigrants. People from the middle strata of society, if married, are more likely to migrate as a family unit because they have the financial resources to do so.

But, as we will see in the next chapter, despite their deep middle- and lower-middle-class roots, their comparatively high level of education, and the touch of worldliness that comes from living in major urban centers, when they arrive in New York City, Brazilian immigrants join the mass of other hopeful newcomers from all over the globe and resignedly take some of the most menial jobs that the city has to offer.

CHAPTER FIVE

Making a Living

The [U.S.] government could easily find these people, but the economy of the
country needs this illegal labor power to work.

—*Brazilian immigrant in Boston, quoted in* Veja *magazine*

AT THE CORE of the Brazilian immigrant experience in New York City
are jobs. Most Brazilian immigrants come to the Big Apple, at least initially, for one reason and one reason only: to earn money, to save money,
to send money home to Brazil. And to make money, they take whatever
jobs are available—busing tables, shining shoes, cleaning houses, driving
a call cab, dancing in a go-go bar, pouring cement, or selling books on the
street. Brazilians do whatever kind of work they can get that does not
require documents or much command of English. For Brazilian immigrants, legal status and language are the twin crucibles of the New York
labor market.

Jobs are indeed the focus of immigrant life, and when seeking work,
Brazilians confront New York's complex labor market. Where do they fit
into it? The employment data on Brazilians and other immigrants new to
the United States are best explained by what economists call the segmented model of the labor market. In a segmented market, not everyone
competes for all jobs, and the demand for immigrant labor is found in a
particular segment of the market, specifically, in its so-called secondary
sector. In the simplest terms, the secondary sector consists of low-paid,
low-status, unskilled jobs that Americans try to avoid. Moreover, this
sector is labor intensive, but in contrast to other labor-intensive segments
of industrialized economies, many jobs here cannot be exported to countries with large pools of cheap labor. But these are generalities that do not
explain the peculiar fit among the immigrant labor force, the specific features of the secondary sector, and the actual jobs in it.

What, then, are the characteristics of the secondary sector? Employers
in this sector of the job market have no incentive to stabilize their labor
force because workers are easily replaced. Thus jobs are usually unstable
and short term, and even seniority is no guarantee of higher pay or job

security. Moreover, since this sector of the job market expands and contracts more than others, employers value flexibility in the size of their work force and in the conditions of its employment. Thus this sector of the market is characterized by high labor turnover.[1]

Restaurant work is an apt illustration. Most restaurants are open long hours and require two shifts of workers. Business not only varies by time of day, but may wax and wane seasonally. Restaurant owners try to adjust their labor force accordingly, for example, by hiring more dishwashers and busboys during busy midwinter lunch shifts and laying them off during the dog days of August. Or, to use an obvious but pertinent example. All of the better restaurants in New York City have coat checkers, women—they invariably are women—who check customers' coats at the door. The seasonal nature of this job is evident: it evaporates in the city's sultry summer heat.

Moreover, since jobs in the secondary sector are nonunionized, employers can enforce work discipline in direct and sometimes capricious ways. In contrast, labor-management relations in the primary sector of the job market are generally more formal and regulated. But in the secondary sector, workers can be dismissed from their jobs with little cause and no notice, or they can be arbitrarily assigned to new work shifts. And people who want to keep their jobs go along with such decisions without protest. Clearly, then, the sine qua non of such a system is a large, docile work force, one that has no alternative source of employment. In the absence of such a work force, labor costs would be higher, and many marginally profitable enterprises in the secondary sector would go out of business.

Secondary sector jobs, then, have little to recommend them. They are poorly paid, have few, if any, fringe benefits, lack security, may require night or weekend work, and afford little or no opportunity for advancement. Who would want them? Certainly not Americans, including those from native disadvantaged groups, argue some economists.[2] But so close is the fit between recent immigrants—especially undocumented ones— and the labor requirements of this sector, that employers would have had to invent them if they did not already exist. This is why supporters of an open door immigration policy have called immigrants "virtually an unmixed blessing" for the U.S. economy.[3]

But what is it about immigrants that makes them tailor-made for these jobs? For one thing, they are less likely than native workers to contest dismissals or substandard working conditions. They are less apt to complain about long hours, subminimum wages, or other violations of the U.S. Labor Code. In a word, immigrants, particularly those without papers, are easier to exploit than the American-born. But does the presence of cheap, docile immigrant labor adversely effect native workers, as is commonly thought? Although the evidence is mixed, more than one study suggests that recent immigrants to the United States, whether legal or undocumented, have had almost no effect on the earnings or employment rate of U.S. citizens. Some experts have concluded that "immigrants . . . are either doing jobs that the American-born do not want, or they are filling slots in the economy with a nearly insatiable hunger for willing workers."[4]

While immigrants' impact on native workers is still subject to debate, everyone agrees that the former dominate certain niches in the U.S. economy, particularly in cities with large immigrant populations, such as New York. The strong association between some types of businesses and particular ethnic groups is common knowledge—for example, the old Chinese laundry and Greek coffee shop and the new Korean greengrocer and Indian newsstand. What is perhaps less well known is the degree to which new immigrants as wage workers dominate other, secondary sectors of the labor market: restaurant and hotel work, office and home cleaning, home child care, delivery and messenger services, unskilled construction jobs, and certain kinds of factory work. In sum, immigrants dominate the most labor-intensive segments of the secondary sector.

This is where Brazilians come into the picture. As one Brazilian friend told me, "The Brazilian community is mostly one of employees, not employers." There are no Brazilian-owned businesses, comparable to Korean groceries or Indian newsstands, that cater to a non-Brazilian clientele. In other words, Brazilians lack what sociologists call an ethnic enclave, a concentration of immigrant businesses that serve the ethnic market as well as the population at large.[5] To be sure, there are a handful of Brazilian-owned enterprises that meet the needs of the community itself, but very few Brazilians in New York City have started small businesses of their own; it is true that Brazilians are employees, not employers.

Just What Do They Do?

Positions at the bottom of the hierarchy . . . create a fundamental dilemma because . . . the bottom of the hierarchy can never be eliminated. If the bottom jobs were somehow cut off, the jobs directly above them would be at the bottom. The locus of the problem would be changed, but the problem itself would remain. Migrants provide a solution . . . essentially because they come from outside and remain apart from the social structure in which the jobs are located.

—MICHAEL J. PIORE, *Birds of Passage*

What is the particular niche that Brazilians occupy in New York's multi-faceted secondary labor sector? The most concise answer is found in the long-term job histories of the one hundred individuals in my New York sample. This broad, longitudinal job history approach is useful because it shows not only Brazilian immigrants' most common jobs, but also their range and, where applicable, their progression up the employment ladder. Also, recall that one characteristic of the secondary sector of the labor market is frequent job turnover, and many of my informants had switched jobs just before or right after they were interviewed. Thus a work history approach that includes all jobs an individual has had catches the range and rhythm of immigrant employment far better than a snapshot description that is limited to current jobs.

Table 5.1 Jobs Held by Brazilians since Their Arrival in New York City

Women (150 Jobs)	N	%	Men (175 Jobs)	N	%
Domestic service	84	56	Dishwasher/busboy	36	21
Salaried white-collar	14	9	Other restaurant work	16	9
Restaurant work	10	7	Driver	16	9
Street vendor	8	5	Construction	16	9
Beautician/manicurist	6	4	Street vendor	11	6
Seamstress/designer	6	4	Shoe shiner	10	5.5
Teacher	4	3	Houseman/cleaner	10	5.5
Go-go dancer	4	3	Messenger/delivery	8	4.5
Home care attendant	3	2	Hairdresser/barber	8	4.5
Miscellaneous	11	7	Garage attendant	6	3.5
			Mover	6	3.5
			Doorman/handyman	5	3
			Salaried white-collar	3	2
			Factory worker	3	2
			Musician	3	2
			Miscellaneous	21	12

Notes: No single job or job category included in "miscellaneous" came to more than 1 percent of the total jobs held. Four women and three men were unemployed at the time of the interview.

The one hundred Brazilians in my sample held a total of 325 jobs, ranging from a one-month stint as a street vendor for a woman who had just arrived in the city to the countless jobs held by another woman who had lived in New York for fifteen years. Table 5.1 groups the myriad jobs into the following categories so that general employment patterns emerge: domestic service includes housecleaning, cooking, and child care; street vendors include book and food sellers; drivers include call car, taxi, and limousine drivers; construction includes home renovation, demolition, and house painting; for women, restaurant work includes the jobs of waitress, cashier, barmaid, bathroom attendant, and coatcheck attendant, and for men, restaurant work includes the jobs of waiter, chef, chef's assistant, food buyer, and assistant manager.

A few observations are in order about the data on my Brazilian sample's employment in New York City. Women have held a narrower range of jobs than have men. By far the most important source of employment for women was domestic service, a category that encompasses live-in housekeepers, day maids, nannies and baby-sitters. In fact, over 80 percent of the women in my sample had been domestic servants at some point in their immigrant careers. No single occupational category employed anywhere near as high a percentage of men. But both sexes have held an unexpectedly wide range of jobs, some of which are not usually associated with immigrants.[6] This reflects the fact that 12 percent of the Brazilians in my sample were "old-timers," people who have lived in New York a decade or more. Some of these long-term city residents have moved up the occupational ladder and no longer have jobs typical of new immigrants. This explains the fairly high percentage of women in salaried white-collar positions. One example of this employment progression is Mariana, who has been in the United States for fourteen years. During her first years, she worked as a live-in nanny and later as a housekeeper for various families. After receiving her green card and perfecting her English, she found a secretarial job. Today, she is an administrative assistant at the New York branch of a major Brazilian bank.

How do Brazilians, untutored in the city and its ways and usually with little command of English, find jobs? They are much like other new immigrants in New York in this regard; they find them through friends and relatives. In some ethnic job enclaves, word-of-mouth labor recruitment is extremely important not only to workers themselves, but to their employers. Employers, especially in low-wage businesses, come to rely on immigrant hiring networks because they can supply a stable pool of inexpensive labor. This is yet another benefit reaped from hiring immigrants; not only can employers pay them lower wages than those of native-born Americans, but the recruitment and training of these workers is turned over to their compatriots.[7]

Shoe shining is a case in point. In New York, Brazilians have a near-monopoly on jobs in this employment domain, and all of the Brazilian shoe shiners I talked with had found their positions through word of mouth in the Brazilian community. Moreover, while shining shoes hardly requires much training, shoe shiners must be familiar with the techniques and products of the trade, something they learn from their compatriots the first day on the job.

GHOULISH WORK

In Governador Valadares until recently, rumor had it that the three most common jobs that Brazilians held in the United States were shining shoes, working in restaurants, and washing and dressing corpses in funeral homes. While the first two are, indeed, important sources of employment for Brazilians, there is no evidence that Brazilians ever worked in mortuaries. This was simply one of the local myths that circulated about life in the United States.

From Nine to Five—or Six or Seven or Eight

. . . if we only consider wages, immigrants are not always much cheaper than

low-wage national workers; it is also their powerlessness which makes them

profitable.

—SASKIA SASSEN, *The Mobility of Labor and Capital*

Low wages are a hallmark of immigrant labor in the secondary sector of the city's economy. Salary data suggest that most newly arrived Brazilian immigrants make somewhat above the minimum hourly wage, and those employed in construction can earn $10 to $12 an hour, still far less than unionized workers earn for similar jobs. Then, too, overtime pay and other benefits are generally nonexistent. For example, a Brazilian friend who worked as a plumber's assistant earned $7 an hour, but on some days he was required to work additional hours at no extra pay. Moreover, in the recession-ridden economy of the early 1990s, there was stiff competition for the few jobs available to new immigrants—those in construction, for example—that paid considerably above minimum wage.

But what about the penchant of some employers for exploiting new immigrants, especially those without papers? In fact, research suggests that outside of agriculture and the apparel industry—neither of which employs Brazilians—relatively few undocumented immigrants earn less than the minimum wage. Still, employers' real savings may come from the "off the books" nature of many of these jobs rather than from the payment of subminimum wages per se. In other words, employers' major cost-cutting measures are skirting contributions to social security, unemployment compensation, and other workers' benefits.

This is not to imply that some employers do not also cut costs by paying their workers less than the minimum wage. One study of undocumented workers in the New York area found that about 16 percent were earning less than the legal minimum, and another study of undocumented Mexicans, many of whom work in Korean grocery stores and other ethnic enclaves, notes that they are often paid as little as $180 for a seventy-hour work week.[8] However, in my own research, I rarely encountered cases of similar wage exploitation, although a few did exist. One Brazilian woman who was employed as a cashier in a Manhattan delicatessen, for example, worked six days a week, eight hours a day, and earned the princely sum of $158, a week, or about $3.30 an hour, far less than the minimum wage. In another case, an employer who renovated houses offered to sponsor a Brazilian immigrant—a highly skilled cabinetmaker—for a green card if the latter would work for him for a mere $200 a week. The offer was politely declined.

Still, by working many hours, often at night or on weekends, some Brazilians manage to earn what they consider good incomes. Driving a call car is a job whose earnings expand for those willing to put in long, grueling hours. Drivers who work twelve-hour shifts, six days a week, generally net between $400 and $500. One driver told me of his exhaustingly long hours, for which he earned a take-home pay of $50 to $60 a day in fares and tips.

Other Brazilians compensate for their low wages by having more than one job. Twenty-two percent of those in my sample held two jobs at the time they were interviewed; restaurant work was the most common second job. Many labored incredibly long hours, with little time to do anything but work, eat, and sleep.[9] One such worker was Fernando, who was employed in two full-time jobs. His schedule was frantic. He arose at 6:30 A.M. and took the subway to midtown Manhattan to begin work at 7:15 A.M. shining shoes at a shoe repair shop near Penn Station. He worked there until 6:00 P.M., and then caught the subway to a Japanese restaurant in Greenwich Village, where his evening shift as a dishwasher began at 6:30 P.M. He worked in the restaurant's kitchen until 11:00 P.M., grabbing a bite to eat between chores, and then took the train back to Queens. He was so tired, he says, that he often fell asleep on the train and missed his stop. And he kept up this pace six days a week. One American woman told me in amazement that a Brazilian who works at a restaurant with her five nights a week, asked her if she knew of a second job that he could get because, he said, he "just sits around all day."

Working long hours is certainly no guarantee of job security. Take the case of Fernando, the hard-working shoe shiner–dishwasher. He and a Brazilian friend were employed at a shoe repair shop for fifteen months, working ten to eleven hours a day for $15 plus tips. Fernando was a model employee, and the shop's owner entrusted him with depositing the cash receipts at the bank. Much to Fernando's chagrin, when business picked up slightly, a third Brazilian was hired to shine shoes. Fernando complained to his boss that the additional shoe shiner sharply cut into his own and his friend's earnings because each now had fewer customers and their tips had fallen off by a third. The owner replied that he, the owner, was in charge of the shop and that if Fernando did not like the new arrangement, he would do well to leave.

Aside from low pay and little job security, most jobs held by immigrants new to the city lack fringe benefits of any kind. One Brazilian with wide contacts in the immigrant community told me that he knew of only one of his compatriots who received benefits—sick leave, paid vacation, and health insurance. In fact, when I questioned informants about this aspect of their jobs, many laughed and replied, "Benefits? What are those?" But some Brazilians who had nonunion construction jobs were well aware of the contrast between their working conditions and those of unionized workers doing similar jobs. The lack of overtime pay for weekend work was a bitter pill, as was the absence of workers' compensation for one Brazilian who had been seriously injured on the job.

> ### LOOKING FOR WORK
> The economic downturn in New York has affected Brazilian immigrants. One informant says that Brazilians looking for work learn one English word right away. The word? "Slow," as in "Business is slow."

A typical response to all this might be, Well, yes, it is true that immigrants are paid little and have no job benefits, but they "get a free ride" because they do not have social security and income taxes withheld from their meager earnings. This is not necessarily the case. One study of undocumented Mexican women found that, contrary to conventional wisdom, the great majority—about 72 percent—worked "on the books" and paid social security and income taxes. Most of those who were paid in cash were employed as household servants. Similarly, a study of undocumented immigrants in the New York metropolitan area found that nearly all had social security taxes withheld from their paychecks and that about 70 percent also paid state and federal taxes.[10]

Although I have no hard data, it appears that the rate of working off the books for Brazilians is somewhat higher for women than for men because so many women are domestic servants. In terms of men's jobs, shoe shiners almost always work off the books but restaurant employees are less likely to do so. It is the nature of the job more than the legal status of the worker that determines who is paid off the books, although undocumented immigrants are more likely than those with green cards to work in informal, off-the-books jobs, such as domestic service and shoe shining. But the really interesting question here that is never asked is, How many immigrants regularly pay into the social security fund but never receive a cent in benefits because they leave the United States before retirement?

Given the alienating ambience in which Brazilian immigrants work, it is not surprising that they are little tied to their jobs and change them frequently. This became apparent on many occasions during my research. I often returned to a shoe repair shop or a street corner or a restaurant to visit Brazilians I had previously interviewed only to find other Brazilians working in their places. One bookseller who vanished from her usual spot on Fifth Avenue was replaced by another Brazilian woman, who had no idea where the first one had gone. Of the ten Brazilian shoe shiners employed in July 1988 at a shoe shine stand near Grand Central Station, only two were still working there some eighteen months later. Over the eight months that I tracked the career path of one Brazilian man, he worked as a part-time handyman in a Manhattan apartment building, as a street vendor selling books in midtown, as a home care attendant for an elderly man in Staten Island, as a bakery shop clerk on the Upper East Side, and as a call car driver in Queens. One well-informed informant said that if after one year, I tried to locate all the Brazilian immigrants whom I had previously interviewed, 95 percent of them would be in new jobs.

Paperwork

Brazilian immigrants in New York City change jobs easily because work is quite widely available. But how could this be if many of them are undocumented? Recall that a primary goal of IRCA was to reduce the flow of undocumented aliens into the United States by making it unlawful for employers to hire them. Under IRCA, employers would be subject to fines for hiring people without proper documents so that jobs would dry up and illegal aliens would pack up their bags and go home. But, as noted in an earlier chapter, that is not how it turned out.

According to published reports on other immigrant groups—which are consistent with my own findings—work documents are cheap and easy to come by in cities with large undocumented immigrant populations, such as Los Angeles and New York. And, says an INS spokesperson, "The message has clearly gone back to people who desire to work in the United States that all you need is a driver's license and a fraudulent Social Security card to meet the burden of proof for employers."[11] Fake social security cards can be purchased on the street for as little as $20. One survey of 900 undocumented immigrants arrested at their places of work found that over 40 percent of them were carrying counterfeit social security and/or green cards. IRCA has even led to the fabrication of new documents, which are meant to satisfy the legislation's own requirements; for example, an identification card that costs $500 and that states that its holder has completed the first step toward legalization under IRCA's amnesty program.[12]

False documents are seen as a major obstacle to the full implementation of IRCA, and an INS official has called them "the premier fraud problem facing the immigration service."[13] But, the problem is an inevitable outgrowth of the legislation itself. As long as some sort of legal-looking document is proffered, many employers will hire a person without checking further; the law does not require them to authenticate any one of the seventeen documents that the new hire may show to "prove" work eligibility.[14] Some employers are so anxious for workers, documented or otherwise, that they tell immigrants where false documents can be obtained so that they can hire them. This is particularly true in locales and in industries that have long relied on cheap, illegal immigrant labor. If low labor costs are paramount, then complying with the law is easy: a document, any document, will do.

HANDY READING

An immigrant who earns his living by purveying fake documents—social security cards, drivers' licenses, green cards—was carrying a paperback book in his coat pocket entitled *Prenuptial Agreements*.

Because their labor is in demand, undocumented Brazilians and other immigrants without work papers buy and use tailor-made green cards, social security cards, and other needed identification forms with impunity. But these usually do not come cheap. A professionally produced green card can cost $600 to $1,000, although as one purveyor of false documents told me, it is quite easy to pass off fake green cards since most Americans have no idea what a legitimate green card looks like. Moreover, one does not usually have to have a green card in hand, counterfeit or otherwise, to get a job. The promise of a future one can be sufficient. For example, Ricardo was hired as a part-time security guard in an office building after showing the managing agent a photocopy of a letter that the INS had sent to his friend indicating that the friend's application for a green card was being processed. In the letter, the friend's name had been whited out and Ricardo's name written in its place.

The only item that many employers require of a potential worker is a social security card. Since it is ubiquitous and purportedly easy to counterfeit, a social security card—a *social*, in the idiom of New York's Brazilians—costs a lot less than a green card. Still, the price of a *social* varies considerably and if one is needed on short notice, it is more expensive. But social security cards are not necessarily counterfeit; real cards belonging to someone else are also sold. In other words, genuine cards that have

AN UNSOCIABLE SYSTEM TO SECURE A SOCIAL SECURITY CARD

Dealing with immigration authorities in New York City can be daunting. I accompanied a Brazilian friend to the INS office in lower Manhattan so that she could get the papers necessary for a social security card. She had already been granted a nonimmigrant visa that allowed her to work for a U.S. firm for a specified period of time. She had spent three months and $1,000 in legal fees to secure this visa. Thus, she was legally entitled to be employed.

After we arrived at INS headquarters, we waited for about half an hour on a long, snaking line in a crowded room without a breath of air on a hot, muggy day in early September. When my friend's turn came, she showed her papers to the INS clerk, who gave her a white slip and told her to go upstairs to Room 301.

She was helped right away in Room 301, but the INS official there seemed unsure what to do with her case. At first he said she already had permission to work and needed no other document. When she insisted that the social security office had told her that she had to get a work permit from INS before it would give her a social security card, he conferred with another clerk, and then agreed that she needed an additional document.

The INS clerk then told my friend to go to yet another room to get a photocopy of her entry permit. This she did, but when she returned to the same clerk, he told her that she also had to have a photocopy of the letter granting her a temporary work visa and a receipt for a $35 processing fee. She went back to the room with the photocopying machine, and then waited on line for another fifteen minutes or so to pay the fee. She then returned to the clerk in Room 301, who took her papers and, without comment, thrust a slip of paper at her indicating that she had to return for an 11:30 A.M. appointment at INS headquarters in mid-October, *six weeks later*. Thus, she had to wait another six weeks to get the document necessary for a social security card—after she had been legally granted the right to work. When she returned to the INS office in October for her appointment, she waited in line for three hours before she finally was given an employment authorization card.

Parenthetically, my friend is a graduate of a U.S. college and speaks fluent English. Since very few of the INS clerks spoke anything but English—although most of the clients in the INS office appeared to be Spanish-speakers—the difficulty that many, if not most, immigrants have can well be imagined.

been lost or stolen or that belonged to someone now deceased are bought by new immigrants in need of work papers. One immigrant I met had worked in restaurants and as a porter for over four years, all the while paying into a social security account in someone else's name. He rued the fact that when he finally was legalized through the amnesty program and received his own legitimate social security card, his prior contributions came to naught. Still, undocumented immigrants avoid getting a genuine social security card in their own names, erroneously believing that doing so will put the INS hot on their trail.

A driver's license is another document much sought by Brazilians and other new immigrants. Not only is it essential for call car and limousine drivers—both common jobs for Brazilian men—but in the United States, a driver's license is an all-purpose identification card, and some employers will accept it as proof of an immigrant's work eligibility. Drivers' licenses are usually the real thing, that is, they are not often counterfeited. Since states have different requirements for a driver's license, one document seller makes the trip for his clients, taking their papers to Florida, for example, to apply for a license since it is easier to get one there than in New York. Some time ago, before the draft was ended, one Brazilian resident of New York City used a friend's New Jersey address and paid $75 to an auto school in Newark to arrange a New Jersey driver's license for him—with the unintended consequence that after getting the license, he received a letter from the Selective Service telling him that he had to register for the draft!

The INS, of course, is not unaware of these ploys by Brazilians and others. Immigration officials have requested that the Brazilian consulate not do official translations of Brazilian drivers' licenses since they can be used by an undocumented national to get a New York State driver's license. The consulate has complied with the request, and will translate Brazilian licenses only for Brazilians who have green cards or are in the United States in some official capacity. The response? One enterprising Brazilian has had consular stationary printed up so that, for a price, "official translations" of Brazilian drivers' licenses continue to be available to one and all.

With or without documentation, Brazilians get jobs. While they must have a driver's license to operate a call car, they can clean houses, shine shoes, and wash dishes with nothing more than an informal reference from a friend or relative and a willingness to work. But what are these jobs like? What does it mean for a woman from the middle strata of Brazilian society to work as a maid in the Big Apple? And what is it like for a Brazilian man to bus tables in one of New York's chic eating establishments or sell books on a freezing city sidewalk? What do Brazilian immigrants earn in these jobs, and what is the price they pay for doing them? It is to these topics, I now turn.

CHAPTER SIX

From Mistress to Servant

In the United States, inequalities of class, race, ethnicity, gender

and migration status are central to the asymmetrical relations of

housework.

—SHELLEE COLEN, "Housekeeping for the Green Card"

IN NUMBERS ALONE, domestic service is the most important job category for Brazilian immigrants in New York City, and, with some notable exceptions, it is nearly an all-female one. My own data indicate that upwards of 80 percent of Brazilian women who came to the city as immigrants have worked at some point as day maids, live-in housekeepers, full-time nannies, or part-time baby-sitters in the homes of affluent and not-so-affluent New Yorkers. But because of the nature of the work, the attitudes towards domestic servants in Brazil, and the structured inequality implicit in the mistress/master and servant relationship, no job category is more problematic for Brazilians themselves.

The job market for household workers in the New York area has boomed in recent years. The increased demand for domestic servants over the last two decades in New York City and elsewhere in the country is linked to the slow demise of the full-time housewife-mother. Her disappearance, in turn, is set against a backdrop of inflation, the decline in average male wages, and the increasing need for two family incomes to maintain a middle-class standard of living. And as more and more women have taken jobs, especially married middle-class women and women with young children, the cleaning, cooking, and child care that was their traditional lot has fallen, in part, to hired servants.[1]

Into the breach has come the new immigrant. Although New York is not yet like San Diego and some other cities where, in the words of one report, "domestic work has become institutionalized as an occupation performed almost exclusively by female illegal aliens," housecleaning and child care are far and away the most important sources of employment for undocumented Brazilian women.[2] One of my Brazilian informants commented on this in no uncertain terms: "If it weren't for us who would clean the houses and take care of the children?" she asked. "Who would clean New York's dirt? Americans don't want these jobs. The Immigration Service makes it hard for immigrants, but the U.S. economy really needs us."

TWO-WAY COMMUNICATION

A Brazilian woman works as a part-time housekeeper and baby sitter for a group of nine professional families in New York City, all of whom are friends. Each family bought a Portuguese-English dictionary to ease communication problems. Some of her employers told the woman how delighted they were that she was teaching their young children Portuguese, and one said how pleased she had been to be able to say a few words in Portuguese to a Brazilian whom she met at a dinner party.

When Your Home Is Not Your Own

Domestic servants are often "live-ins," that is, they live in the apartment or house of the family that employs them. In Portuguese this work is called *morar dentro*, "to live in," or *trabalhar dentro*, "to work in," or simply, *dentro*, "in" or "inside." Living-in has major benefits but also hidden costs. The obvious benefit is that room and board are free, so the immigrant avoids spending her hard-earned dollars on food and rent and can save money much more quickly.

Living-in is especially suited to immigrants brand-new to the city. As live-ins, they do not have to find a place to stay or arrange for utilities or learn how to use public transportation to reach their place of work. Hence live-in housekeeping is very often a woman's first job when she comes to this country. Fully half of the women in my sample had worked as live-ins, and for all but two, it was the first job they held in the United States. It is also much sought-after work. One woman, who had been in New York for three months and was living at Dona Dahlia's rooming house when I met her, asked me if I knew of any live-in positions; she said that that was the job she wanted so that she could have a room of her own—however simple—and save on rent.

In the late 1980s in Manhattan, the going rate for a live-in housekeeper was $250 to $350 a week plus room and board, although I met one Brazilian nanny who lived with a married couple and earned $500 a week caring for their two small children. The rate in the outer boroughs and in New Jersey was generally lower, about $200 a week. But even at the lower end of the pay scale, a frugal live-in could net $800 to $1,000 a month with no living expenses—a lot of money, indeed, by Brazilian standards.

NANNYGATE

President Bill Clinton's nomination of Zoë Baird for Attorney General became a cause célèbre when it was revealed that she and her husband had employed an undocumented alien to care for their young son. Her nomination was quickly withdrawn. The next day, two Republican gubernatorial candidates in New Jersey sheepishly admitted that they, too, had once employed illegal aliens as domestic help.

Suddenly the topic of "illegal aliens" was on everyone's lips and on the front page of the *New York Times*. Only rarely does an American-born worker seek a nanny job, according to an immigrant nanny quoted in the *Times*, because "these days, most Americans see it as some kind of slavery." "Illegal baby sitters" were said to be the new yuppie "sin." But despite the controversy, some quoted in the article were reluctant to give up this relatively inexpensive source of household help, and one mother of newborn triplets said she would seek a brand-new illegal immigrant. "I want someone who cannot leave the country, who doesn't know anyone in New York, who basically does not have a life," she is quoted as saying. "I want someone who is completely dependent on me and is loyal to my family.

Source: *New York Times*, January 24, 1993, A1.

The downside of this type of domestic service is its inherent potential for exploitation. Living-in is never just a nine-to-five job; many live-ins are on call at all times except their days off. One Brazilian *babá* (nanny) told me how she cooked, cleaned, and cared for a three-year-old six and sometimes seven days a week. The live-in's job is never done because, like the housewife's, her home and place of work are one.[3]

In a study of West Indian live-ins in New York City, Shellee Colen suggests that the potential for exploitation is reduced when a servant does not live with her employer's family seven days a week and can "distance herself from the social relations on the job." She found that those immigrants who could get away from their work and regularly see friends or relatives were more content with their jobs than those who remained apart from the immigrant community and lived an isolated existence in their employers' homes. Anthropologist Nancy Foner came to the same conclusion in her study of Jamaican live-ins; they felt very isolated, having had little contact with their compatriots during the work week.[4]

This is why Brazilian live-in housekeepers and nannies prefer to stay in rented rooms in boarding houses or in the apartments of Brazilian friends on their days off. Dona Dahlia's establishment has three or four futonlike beds set aside for off-duty servants. They cost $10 a night, and live-ins usually rent them for one or two nights every weekend. One live-in house-keeper paid $100 a month to store most of her clothes and other belong-ings at Dona Dahlia's, where she spends her days off. Live-in servants explain their willingness to pay for these accommodations by saying it distances them from their work, something they simply cannot do in the homes of their employers.

Along for the Ride

One group of Brazilian live-ins in New York City is socially distinct from the middle- and lower-middle-class Brazilian women who generally hold these positions. It comprises women brought to New York by their Bra-zilian employers, usually the families of diplomats or highly paid business executives. A few of the women came with American families living in Brazil, who asked their housekeepers or nannies to accompany them when they returned to the United States. In either case, the employers pay the airfare and arrange for the documents required to bring their domes-tic servants with them to this country.

But here, too, there can be serious costs. Some of the women involved in these arrangements described their lives with their employers' families as something akin to slavery. A few told me that they worked a seven-day week for room and board and nominal pay. I was regaled with stories of Brazilian women "escaping" from their employers, fleeing in the middle of the night in winter with little more than the clothes on their backs, and disappearing into the swirling maelstrom of the city. The women who left the families that brought them to this country continued working as do-mestic servants, sometimes as live-ins for American families, but most eventually got their own apartments.

Of note here is that the few Brazilian women from very poor families whom I met in New York came to the United States via this route, that is, at the behest and expense of their employers. Moreover, these women were among the only Brazilians who experienced genuine upward mobil-ity after coming to this country. Their standard of living improved dra-matically; their earnings in New York allowed them to live in a manner unimaginable for people of their social class in Brazil.[5]

Petula's case is illustrative. A black woman of seventy, she came to New York in 1968 with the American family who employed her in Rio de Janeiro. She told me that she "was born and raised in misery" in Bahia, in northeastern Brazil, and that as a child from an impoverished family, there were days when she went hungry. Before coming to the United States she worked as a maid for various families in Rio.

Petula has been working in New York as a *babá* and housekeeper for twenty-two years; today she lives by herself in a sunny, well-furnished apartment in a low-income housing project on Manhattan's West Side. The tables in her living room are covered with richly framed photos of the families she has worked for in New York, including the family that originally brought her to the United States. Petula is now semiretired, works three days a week cleaning apartments, and receives social security benefits. While she said that her income never reached $1,000 a month when she was employed full-time, she lives at a level of material comfort that is incomparably superior to what she would have had if she had stayed in Brazil. When asked if she would come to the United States again if given the opportunity, she replied that she has never regreted coming to this country, although she "suffered a lot at first." She said the United States is like "a great big Santa Casa de Misericordia," a charitable enterprise.

An Interethnic Twist

Quite by chance during the course of my research I came upon a totally unexpected ethnic link, which I came to call the Hasidic-Brazilian connection." By this I mean the fifteen or twenty ultraorthodox Jewish families in the Boro Park section of Brooklyn that employ Brazilian women as live-in housekeepers and nannies for their large broods of children. How did this come about? How did these Jewish families, whose entire lives center around their religion, come to employ Brazilian immigrant women, most of whom are Catholic?

It turned out that most, if not all, of the Hasidic families in question have some connection with Brazil. Either the husband or wife was born in Brazil or lived in Brazil for a time and speaks some Portuguese; others had businesses in Brazil.[6] In one case, an American Hasidic family that lived in São Paulo brought a Brazilian with them to work as a live-in maid when they returned to the United States.

Adina, a Brazilian woman who worked for a Hasidic family for five years—four years as a live-in and one as a commuter—found the job when she answered a newspaper ad for a housekeeper. Much to her astonishment, her new employer turned out to be a Brazilian from São Paulo who was married to an American Hasidic man. Adina says she learned very little English while she worked for this family since she spoke Portuguese to her employer as well as to the couple's children. In fact, language is a volatile issue among the Brazilian women who work for Portuguese-speaking Hasidim. They claim that their employers take advantage of them, paying them less because they do not have to know English to work in these households. One woman explained that this was why she earned only $250 for a six-day work week, cooking and cleaning for a family with eleven children!

Adina, who was a social worker in Brazil before emigrating to the United States, told me how quickly she learned all the rules of maintaining a kosher home and how she was complimented on her ritual adeptness by the mistress of the house. Still, culture clashes sometimes sparked the relations between Hasidim and their Brazilian domestic servants. One Brazilian found fault with her basement accommodations, but most complaints centered around food, one woman saying she could "never get used to the heavy Jewish cooking." Then, too, a few of the Hasidic families expected their servants to live as they do, which meant that television was banned from the home.

Working as a live-in domestic in New York City, whether for orthodox Jews, wealthy Brazilians, or secular Americans, is almost always a temporary phase in the migration cycle of Brazilian women. Usually within a year or two, they find apartments to share with other Brazilians and continue to work as maids and housekeepers, albeit on a "live-out" basis. This pattern holds for other ethnic groups as well. Nancy Foner found that Jamaican women in New York City were likely to work as live-in servants only until they received their green cards; most of those who continued to work as housekeepers or nannies after receiving the card moved to their own apartments.[7]

Day Work

Cleaning the homes of New Yorkers is the single most common job held by Brazilian immigrant women in New York City. Typically, the women live in Queens and take the subway five or six days a week to their jobs in Manhattan. The ideal is to be employed by a few individuals or families, cleaning their apartments once or twice a week on a regular basis; some will not accept jobs that are less frequent because the income is too erratic. A Brazilian woman who has been a housekeeper since she first arrived in New York in the early 1980s says that she much prefers to work for one family on a full-time basis, rather than cleaning the apartments of several people once or twice a week. She explained that it is far easier to clean a single apartment, even a large one, because "you have things under control and once the apartment is in good shape, you just do upkeep rather than a lot of heavy-duty cleaning."

Like much of the work immigrants do, cleaning peoples' homes offers little job security. In this context, a major complaint is that when New Yorkers escape the city's summer heat, their housekeepers are left in the lurch. Some women said that their work and income fall off dramatically in the summer months, when people go on vacation, lock up their apartments, and let the dust pile up in their absence. But this is the price of being confined to the informal economy because, aside from shining shoes and street vending, cleaning apartments is the only job employing many Brazilians that almost never requires a green card.[8] References and a little English are needed, but people looking for someone to clean their apartments hardly ever ask to see a green card. As one employer said to me, "Finding a maid in New York City is hard enough without getting into the legal details." And references present no problem either. Jobs are passed along between friends and relatives in the Brazilian community, and either one can easily supply a reference.

The average earnings of household servants vary, depending upon how many hours a day and how many days a week they work; they can be paid hourly, daily, weekly, or by the job. In 1989-1990 the going rate for apartment cleaning in Manhattan was $10 an hour, with flat rates ranging from $30 or $40 for a studio to $50 or $60 for larger apartments. By working very long hours and cleaning two apartments a day it is possible, although uncommon, to earn $500 a week. Most of the Brazilian women in my sample who work full-time five or six days a week earn somewhere between $250 and $400, and part-timers clear about $150.

In addition to housework, some of these women also care for children. One told me how she worked an exhausting ninety-hour week for $480, minding her two young charges while cleaning the house, washing and ironing clothes, and preparing dinner. Many affluent dual-career couples in Manhattan employ Brazilian women who do not live with the family but commute on a daily basis from their homes. One woman worked for such a family at a starting salary of $300 a week, which had reached $475 a week by the time she left three years later. Women who have no housekeeping chores but care for children on a full-time basis are paid from $150 to $300 a week.

The wages for nearly all these jobs are paid off the books, with neither social security nor state or federal income taxes deducted from them. And when Brazilians switch to jobs that have taxes withheld, they are vociferous about their dislike of the impact this has on their earnings. Clarice, a Brazilian woman who has a green card and a good command of English, explained that this is why she chooses to continue to work as a domestic servant: "Just compare what I earn as a housekeeper working off the books," she said, "with what I would make 'on the books' in a beginning position in a bank or an office."

Clarice then calculated the figures for me. She is employed by a family three full days and two afternoons a week for $300, with no taxes taken out of her wages. On the other two mornings, she does the laundry and ironing for a second family and is paid $12 an hour, or just under $100 a week, also off the books. Thus, she nets around $400 a week, and that, she notes, is far more than she would earn at an entry-level job in a bank or a business, to say nothing of the social security, federal, state and city taxes that would be withheld from her paycheck. She also points out that her expenses are lower when she works as a domestic; she eats lunch at her employer's and can wear whatever she wants to work. Clarice cited her friend's experience to confirm her figures. Her friend had worked as a housekeeper but then found a job at a bank. She did not stay long, however. Quickly concluding that a white-collar could not buy food or pay rent, she went back to her more humble, but better-paying job cleaning peoples' apartments.

Putting on the Ritz

Among Brazilian immigrants, domestic service, although clearly dominated by women, is not limited to them. I met a few Brazilian men with jobs cleaning homes or working as housemen, butlers, or private chauffeurs. In all, 13 percent of the men in my sample had worked in domestic service at some point since arriving in this country.[9] I also encountered married couples with joint positions as live-in servants. The division of labor in these jobs is along traditional lines; the woman cleans, does the laundry, and cooks or cares for children, and the man is a valet-gardener-butler and/or chauffeur. For example, for five months in the mid-1980s, João and Maria Carvalho worked as a maid-gardener-chauffeur combination for a family with six children, who lived on an estate in a lush New York suburb. Room and board were provided, in addition to a combined salary of $400 a week.

Probably the most common domestic position for Brazilian men is as a private chauffeur, driving limousines for wealthy individuals or families. For $550 a week, Alberto chauffeured a family around the city and to their country estate every weekend and tended to their stretch limousine. This salary is on the high side, with the usual range from $350 to $400 a week for a full-time chauffeur.

Brazilian immigrants of both sexes are employed as household servants in the homes of some very wealthy and well-known New Yorkers. One Brazilian woman is one of a squadron of servants who work in a family's twenty-two-room apartment on Fifth Avenue, while a Brazilian man is the cook and chauffeur for a philanthropist who owns an art-filled penthouse in one of the city's most luxurious hotels. Yet another Brazilian woman cleans the New York pied-à-terre of a Los Angeles–based film star. Then there is the Brazilian man who attends to the apartment and studio of an international fashion photographer and the one who is the chauffeur of a famous clothes designer. A Brazilian couple are caretakers at the country estate of one of the nation's best known families, and a

Brazilian woman has served as live-in companion for one of America's wealthiest heiresses, crisscrossing the country with her and alighting at one of her many homes. In certain rarified circles it appears to be chic to have a Brazilian servant.

The Price They Pay

Whether in the homes of the truly affluent or in those of the less well-to-do, domestic service is problematic for Brazilian immigrants in New York City. Their class backgrounds and the low status and regard for household workers in their own country, make these jobs, more than any others, antithetical to their own lives and personal experiences in Brazil. Newly arrived Brazilian immigrants enter the U.S. labor market and are quickly shorn of their former status. This disjunction between social roots and current employment provides a crash course in downward mobility. Nowhere is this truer than in domestic service.

Many examples bear this out. Again and again during the course of my research, I met well-educated women working as household servants: social workers, lawyers, and engineers employed as live-in housekeepers and day maids; teachers and registered nurses—one the former head floor nurse at a large hospital in Belo Horizonte—holding down jobs as *babás* and baby-sitters. As one Brazilian employed as a maid explained to me, it is not just that the Brazilian immigrants she knows would never work in Brazil in the kind of jobs they have in New York, but back home, *they would not even know anyone who held these kinds of jobs.*

THE MAID'S SERVANT

A majority of middle-class Brazilian women who work as domestic servants in New York are accustomed to employing maids in their homes in Brazil. Some of these women draw the line at doing their own housework in New York; they hire other Brazilian women to do it for them.

The discontinuity between Brazilians' jobs as domestics in New York and their social origins back home can fuel a gnawing resentment. For example, Elena was infuriated that the woman who employed her as a housekeeper in her Manhattan apartment assumed that she had also been a maid in Brazil. When Elena indignantly told her employer that, in fact, she had been a law student in Rio while working as a part-time paralegal, her employer seemed not to believe her and told Elena that she was "just lucky to be here earning so much money." Rosalinda, from an upper-middle-class family in Rio, worked as a live-in housekeeper for three different families during her first year in the United States. She complained bitterly about two of the families, saying that they treated her like a "maid." She was hired as a *babá* in her last live-in position, and when her employer told her to wash the floor, Rosalinda angrily shot back that she "did not do that kind of work" and that at home in Rio, "her mother had three maids, one who did nothing but floors and windows."

Some Brazilian immigrants deal with the loss of status by putting themselves in a sort of disassociative state while on the job. Susana, a university graduate in geography from a lower-middle-class family in Campinas, in the state of São Paulo, cleans house for several families in New York City. She says that at first it was very hard to work as a maid because in Brazil maids are *uma classe muita baixa* (very low class) and she felt "inferior" doing this kind of work. But since putting herself on automatic pilot, she feels better about her work; zombielike, she cleans, is paid, and leaves.

Brazilian women also use humor to deal with their plummeting employment status. Lisa, having grown up in a home with two servants, was at first horrified at the thought of doing housework for someone else. She was a student and then a housewife in São Paulo before her husband, a bank manager, lost his job. Then they emigrated to the United States. Lisa joked about her downward slide, regaling me with stories about her life as a maid in New York City. One story was about a fussy employer who "didn't believe in mops," insisting that she get down on her hands and knees to wash the floor. Another concerned an employer who suggested they sit on the bed together to discuss Lisa's chores, and then instructed her—rather oddly, she thought—to be sure to clean the bathroom last. After the other rooms were done, Lisa went into the bathroom only to find that the walls were covered with nude photographs of her employer in various poses holding a large dildo. She fled the apartment without being paid.

Ineptitude is also a source of humor. One Brazilian woman worked as a domestic servant for a wealthy French family soon after she arrived in New York. In her first days on the job, she slipped and hit her head while cleaning the family's large sunken bathtub. This was to be expected, she noted wryly, because *she* had never done housework before; her family in Brazil had always *employed* maids. And ineptitude can even be a source of pride. One Brazilian housekeeper noted with a certain glee that she had "simply ruined her boss's gym clothes" since she had "so little experience doing the laundry."

To be sure, Brazilians are not the only new immigrants who have to come to terms with lowered stations in life. Nancy Foner describes how Jamaican women working as household servants in New York City dealt with their decline in occupational status. Most of her study group had held white-collar jobs—as secretaries, teachers, stenographers—in Jamaica before migrating to New York. They were comforted by the fact that their social status in New York's Jamaican community was based on the more prestigious jobs they had held at home rather than on the ones they held as immigrants. For example, a woman was thought of as a teacher among her compatriots, not as a domestic servant. But in the final analysis the benefits of higher earnings simply outweighed the costs of lower prestige. The women saw their present jobs solely as means to an end—a higher standard of living or a brighter future for their children.[10]

Similarly, for a handful of Brazilian women the time spent in domestic service is worth it because of the bright green card at the end of the long dark employment tunnel. In her study of "housekeeping for the green card," anthropologist Shellee Colen notes that because of the provisions of U.S. immigration law, housework and child care are among the only jobs available to immigrant women that permit employers to sponsor them for a green card. For women who lack kin in the United States, domestic service is usually the one feasible route to legality. Immigration legislation, in effect, helps alleviate a shortage of domestic labor and quiets demands for federal support of child care by ensuring a large pool of relatively cheap and vulnerable workers.[11]

And child care is, indeed, the bait that hooks families, often dual-career ones, into green card sponsorship. Most women on the domestic path to a green card take care of children, usually on a live-in basis. To qualify for a green card through this provision of the law, immigrant women are expected to have had at least one year of prior experience in child care—a requirement easily satisfied with a bogus letter from a "former employer." The sponsoring family, in turn, must demonstrate a certain income level. Once the papers are filed it usually takes two to three years and $1,000 to $3,000 in legal fees before a green card is issued.

This is a system ripe for exploitation because the women in question, being in a sort of legal limbo, have few other job options. Moreover, they have a powerful incentive to stay with the sponsoring family, no matter what the conditions of employment. The system works, as Colen has so aptly put it, as if "the promise of a green card should be enough compensation" for low wages and heavy work loads.[12]

Dining Out

What domestic service is to women, restaurant work is to men. Nearly half of the Brazilian men in my sample had worked in restaurants at some point since coming to New York, making this category the single largest source of employment for men. Moreover, Brazilians, like most recent immigrants, predominate in unskilled and semiskilled positions in the full-service—as opposed to the fast food—sector of the restaurant industry. Then, too, just as live-in housekeeping is common among Brazilian women new to the city, dishwashing and busing tables are the most frequent first jobs among Brazilian men; one-third of the men in my sample listed "busboy" or "dishwasher" as their initial position.

Although dishwashing and busing tables are the most typical restaurant jobs held by Brazilian immigrants, they are by no means the only ones. In higher-priced restaurants, such as those that abound in Manhattan, the work of preparing and serving food is labor intensive and is divided up into many individual tasks. Aside from the cooks and their assistants, there are salad makers, who do nothing but wash and prepare greens. Then, there are "food handlers," people who go from table to table grinding pepper and sprinkling grated cheese onto customers' plates. Beyond waiters and busboys, there are food assemblers, whose sole task is to take completed orders from the kitchen and put them on trays for pickup by waiters. There are also kitchen cleaners, food buyers, food haulers, assistant managers, maitre d's, bartenders, reservationists, coat checkers, and restroom attendants. Brazilians are found in all of these jobs in Big Apple restaurants.

There is a gender hierarchy in New York restaurants based on wages and working conditions. Restaurant work is overwhelmingly male, and the few Brazilian women in it are mostly confined to the seasonal or relatively low-paid positions of coat checker and restroom attendant. In all my months of research, I met only a handful of Brazilian women working in more remunerative restaurant jobs, such as waiting tables and tending bar.

Restaurant work is also organized into a well-defined occupational hierarchy. Cleaning and sweeping the kitchen at night after the restaurant closes—usually a minimum-wage job—is the lowest rung on the ladder. Washing dishes is next, an undesirable position because of its low pay and steamy working conditions. Busing tables pays somewhat more because busboys receive a share of the waiter's gratuities and the job demands at least a modicum of English. Being a waiter is the top-of-the-line job for most Brazilians employed in restaurants, although a few have become chefs, food buyers, managers, and maitre d's.

It is possible to climb the occupational ladder in restaurant work, one of the few fields employing Brazilian immigrants in New York in which real job mobility exists.[13] Roberto provides a case in point. Six years ago he began work in a trendy Tex-Mex restaurant in Manhattan's Murray Hill neighborhood. He knew little English and was hired to do odd jobs: sweeping, unloading food shipments, and so on. Roberto moved up through the ranks in the restaurant, working as a dishwasher, cook's helper, and salad maker; today he is one of the establishment's principal chefs. Although he had no prior cooking experience, he learned to make the restaurant's Tex-Mex specialties while he was employed there. Another path of restaurant mobility is Sergio's. He has been working at one of New York's chicest Italian bistros for nearly three years. He began as a dishwasher earning $250 a week, was promoted to busboy at $500 a week, and now has a weekly income of $750 from the wages and tips he makes as a waiter. Still, despite what can be excellent pay in New York, in Brazil jobs waiting tables are low-wage and low-status ones, and Brazilians often view them in the same light in New York.

Restaurants are the quintessential establishments staffed through the immigrant grapevine. As soon as a vacancy occurs, word spreads rapidly among the restaurant's immigrant employees, and a friend or relative of one of them is quickly summoned to fill the job. Moreover, once a particular ethnic group comes to dominate a specific niche in the labor market, continued reliance on network hiring may hinder the entrance of other groups.[14]

A good example of ethnic apprenticeship writ large is the yuppie Tex-Mex restaurant mentioned earlier. Today, there are about thirty Brazilians working there in three shifts as dishwashers, busboys, waiters, bartenders, cooks, hostesses, restroom attendants, food buyers, and so on. The first Brazilian was hired around 1985; through word-of-mouth recruitment, upwards of 200 Brazilians found jobs there over the next six years. The original owner of the restaurant was apparently pleased with this ethnic contingent because when she sold the restaurant and bought another establishment, she took a group of Brazilian employees along with her. Today, with an ongoing immigrant network, her new restaurant also has a large number of Brazilians among its workers.

While restaurant work remains the single most important source of employment for Brazilian men in New York City, there are ominous signs in the industry. According to a report in the *New York Times*, as a result of the recession, the number of restaurant jobs fell from 135,600 in 1988 to 128,000 in 1991.[15] While this is a drop of less than 6 percent, it is already being felt by immigrant workers; some Brazilians told me that they were having a harder time finding restaurant jobs.

Tooling Around Town

As anyone who has ever hailed a cab in New York City knows, taxi driving is a job with "high immigrant penetration," to use the sociological jargon.[16] In fact, few Brazilians drive yellow cabs in Manhattan, the taxis that cruise the city's streets picking up passengers along the way. But many Brazilian men do drive radio service cars; for the men in my sample, it is the second most common form of employment after restaurant work.

And, like restaurant work, it is also a largely male occupation; one call car company has two Brazilian women among its sixty-five drivers, a typical ratio.

APRIL FOOL

On April 1, 1990, a rumor began circulating in New York's Brazilian community that the newly inaugurated president of Brazil, Fernando Collor de Melo, had been shot by an assassin. The rumor was first broadcast on Brazilian call car radios, and the story spread like wildfire. Many Brazilians called home to check out the rumor. One driver phoned his brother in Rio; when his brother said he didn't know what he was talking about, the caller sheepishly admitted that he had completely forgotten that it was April Fool's Day.

In the car service branch of the business, requests for customer pickups are made through a company switchboard and relayed by dispatchers to drivers who have radios in their cars. More than half of the Brazilian drivers own their cars and pay a weekly fee to receive calls through the companies' dispatchers, while the remainder lease company-owned cars at a daily or weekly rate. Fees and arrangements vary by company. One company, which owns twelve cars, rents them to drivers for $250 a week, which includes use of the company's dispatchers; the company also covers car insurance. Drivers with their own cars pay $50 a week for access to the car service switchboard. Drivers at another company pay $42 for a twenty-four-hour rental of one of the company-owned cars. In still another arrangement, owner-drivers pay $30 a week plus 25 percent of the fare to receive calls through the company's dispatchers.

The majority of Brazilian drivers are affiliated with one of the five or six Brazilian-owned car service companies in Queens. Others drive radio call cars for non-Brazilian companies, many owned by Israelis. Seventy to 80 percent of the drivers at the Brazilian-owned companies are Brazilian, and the smaller firms employ only their own compatriots. The companies owned by Brazilians vary in size, with anywhere from ten to eighty drivers, although the number of affiliate drivers fluctuates widely, as drivers leave one call car company for another and as business varies seasonally. A driver at one of the larger car service companies has been with the firm for one year, and he is considered a seasoned employee.

Starting a car service company is one of the few entrepreneurial endeavors undertaken by Brazilian immigrants in New York City. The companies were founded by immigrants who drove their own cars and then set up a dispatcher service for other drivers. The initial investment was relatively modest if no additional cars were bought. The largest Brazilian company, which has had up to eighty drivers and seven dispatchers, began as a two-person operation in 1986. To be sure, there are other Brazilian entrepreneurs among new immigrants in New York, but they are in diverse businesses, and their success is usually based on individual creative talent. Unlike the Brazilian owners of car service companies, they are not examples of an ethnic aggregation in a particular commercial niche.

Like so many other jobs Brazilian immigrants hold, the income from driving a call car varies, depending upon the number of days a week and the number of a hours a day a driver puts in. Most drivers net at least $300 or $350 a week. Earnings of $400 to $500 a week are not unusual, but they mean driving long hours, six or even seven days a week. Many drivers regularly put in twelve-hour days and I was told, perhaps apocryphally, of workaholics who were sometimes on the road for eighteen hours at a stretch. One driver, a native of Rio de Janeiro, picked me up in a blinding snowstorm in Astoria, Queens, at 7:30 P.M. on an icy January evening; he said that he had been driving since 5:00 A.M. that morning. As we inched across the Queensborough Bridge to Manhattan, he did not exactly inspire confidence when he told me how excited he was because he had never seen snow before, not to mention ever having driven in it.

Aside from the long hours, driving a cab in New York City is not an easy job. One Brazilian driver said that it was "the worst job" he had had because of the ever-present danger. The New York tabloids are full of stories of car service drivers' being mugged or even murdered. Then, there are the expenses for gas, a chauffeur's license, repairs, and insurance for owner-operated cars, to say nothing of the cost of parking tickets. Still, many Brazilians prefer driving call cars to the other jobs they can get. After all, they say, you can make your own hours and be your own boss. And, while driving a cab is not something an educated person in Brazil would do, unlike domestic service and restaurant work, it does not carry the stigma of manual labor.[17]

Aside from call car service drivers, an unknown number of Brazilians drive yellow cabs, the only ones that can legally pick up passengers on the streets of Manhattan. I know of two or three Brazilians who own the very costly taxi medallions required to operate a yellow cab in New York City, but most of their compatriots drive cabs that they rent for a daily or weekly fee. Still, there are very few Brazilian yellow cab drivers compared to the ubiquitous Indians, Haitians, Russians, Dominicans, Egyptians, and others who cruise the city's streets. One savvy informant suggested the reason why. To drive a yellow cab in Manhattan, a special hack license is required. And to get a hack license the would-be cabbie must show a green card—an item that many Brazilians notably lack. But to work for a car service company, only a driver's license is needed, and a license is quite easy to obtain no matter what one's legal status.

Then, there are the Brazilians who drive the massive stretch limousines that became such a cumbersome presence on the streets of Manhattan during the Reagan-Bush era. These Brazilians work for the growing number of limousine rental companies in the city, at least two of which are owned by fellow Brazilians. Like their counterparts who drive more modest conveyences, the earnings of Brazilian limousine drivers vary with the days and hours they work. But here the decision about how much time to put in is not the driver's; it depends on the limousine company's need for the driver's services, which in turn depends on the volume of clients on any given day. And it will come as no surprise that limousine rental is a recession-sensitive industry. Thus, while the pay for driving a limousine is good—$9 an hour plus what are often generous tips—work is very irregular. One limousine driver told me that he works anywhere from three to seven days a week, which translates into wild swings in pay from lows of $250 or $300 to as much as to $700 for a particularly hectic week.

Here, too, there is a tale of Brazilian entrepreneurship. The owner of one of these limousine rental companies, a man of modest background from Minas Gerais, came to New York two decades ago and worked as a dishwasher, shoe shiner, and doorman. He bought his first limousine in 1974; today he owns ten limousines and employs seven drivers, all Brazilian. Most of his clients are the Brazilian bankers, business executives, and diplomats who come and go with such alacrity from the city.

"Sweet Pushcarts Gently Gliding By"

Far removed from the rarefied quiet of clients in sleek chauffeured limousines, crowds swarm amidst the cacophony of horns and wailing sirens in another business setting: that of New York's street vendors and their customers. Over the last decade or so—much to the chagrin of shop owners and police—the city's sidewalks have been turned into a great street bazaar, where vendors sell books, maps, calendars, watches, jewelry, T-shirts, hats, ties, scarves, and gloves, as well as all manner of food and drink, from traditional American hot dogs, Cokes, pretzels, and ice cream to such decidedly ethnic fare as falafel, cappuccino, shish kabob, and gyros.

Amid this miscellany of food and wares are the immigrants—Brazilians among them—who account for most of the sidewalk sales force. Street vending, in fact, is not only very common among Brazilian newcomers to the city, it is the only job that employs roughly equal numbers of women and men. And, like live-in housekeeping and dishwashing, it is a quintessential first job. The call for English is minimal—little more than

a knowledge of numbers to quote prices—and no papers, not even a social security card, are needed. But, with some exceptions, most notably
the city's Greek community, street vending is generally not a job to which
people make a long-term commitment. One Brazilian who works in the
trade suggested that upwards of 90 percent of Brazilian street vendors
had been in New York less than six months and that, on average, they
stayed on the job only four or five months before moving on to other
work.

Just what do Brazilians sell on the city's sidewalks? Mostly books and
food. Book sales are the only form of street vending in the city that can be
carried on legally without a license; the courts have ruled that requiring
a license to sell printed matter would abridge First Amendment rights.
Still, during the course of my research, the city began requiring book
distributors to have a license to load and unload their wares from parked
vans. I was told that many vendors went out of business rather than pay
the steep $1,000 fee for the license, and for a while at least, there were
noticably fewer booksellers on city streets.

There is no way of knowing the size of the Brazilian sidewalk sales
force, although one wholesaler estimated that on any given day, 200 to
300 Brazilians sell books on Manhattan streets. Still, he noted, the numbers change constantly, as vendors come and go. They vanish from the
streets in heavy rain or snow and on bitterly cold winter days, but they are
out in force in almost any weather in November and December, when
sales are at an annual peak and putting in a seven-day work week can
mean $400 or $500, cash in hand.

Book distributors pay their sidewalk sellers a flat daily rate and a small
commission on any sales over a specified amount. Or there may be no
commission and a daily rate that fluctuates with the value of the books
sold. In either case, the vendor's earnings usually range from $30 to $50
a day, although they can reach $70 in the frenzied pre-Christmas shop-
ping season.[18] Still, it is difficult to generalize about average weekly income because it is—quite literally—as changeable as the weather. In a
week of six sunny days, for example, one vendor earned $300, but the
following week, it rained for three days, and her income plummeted to
$150. Sellers receive no pay when they cannot work because of inclement
weather. Moreover, book vendors put in very long hours for their uncertain earnings; ten hours a day is typical. They begin at 8:00 or 9:00 A.M.
and work until 6:00 or 7:00 P.M., with only one brief break, when the
distributors for whom they work—many of them also Brazilian—show
up to mind their wares.

The distributor's job is an integral part of street vending. Every morning distributors deliver books to their sidewalk sales force. At midday
they visit all their vendors to relieve them for a fifteen- or twenty-minute
lunch and bathroom break. Then, in the evening, distributors make their

rounds once again, retrieving the unsold books and settling their accounts in cash with the men and women who sell their wares.

The number of Brazilian book distributors in the city is also unknown, but here, too, figures vary as people go in and out of business. I was told that at one time a Brazilian distributor had nearly a hundred book vendors working for him, most of them compatriots. But because it requires some initial capital, this is not an enterprise for new immigrants. Money is required to buy books in bulk from a wholesaler, and a van is necessary to pick up the books and deliver them daily to the street vendors at their various stations around Manhattan. One Brazilian distributor estimated that about $5,000 is needed to cover the start-up costs of buying a used van and supplying books to four or five vendors. He gets his books—2,000 to 5,000 volumes at a time—from an American wholesaler and pays 10 to 30 cents apiece for most books (more for the large, illustrated "coffee table" variety). After expenses for wages, gas, car insurance, and parking tickets—a regular part of doing business—he nets about $500 a week.

Brazilians do not sell only books. Many of them also sell food from the colorful umbrella pushcarts that are such a ubiquitous part of the Manhattan street scene. Brazilians hawk hot dogs, shish kabob, soft pretzels, and cold drinks at busy intersections near some of the city's most famous landmarks: Rockefeller Center, Times Square, and Macy's—"the largest department store in the world." But the real Brazilian food specialty is peanuts cooked in a sweet syrup right on the cart. Brazilians sell more of this street fare—said to have been concocted by Argentines, who own many of the carts that sell it—than any other item.

Once again, numbers are illusive because of high job turnover, but I was told that somewhere between fifty and seventy-five Brazilians sell street food on any given day, although collectively the numbers are far higher since many Brazilians have had this job at some point in their immigrant careers. Unlike booksellers, vendors selling food must be licensed by the city. There are also questions of territory, which occasionally lead to disputes between pushcart owners, but generally those selling the same food try to space themselves far enough apart so that they do not directly compete with one another.[19]

Hours depend on the fare sold. Before 10:00 A.M. at one of the garages that store pushcarts near Times Square, Brazilians can be seen washing down their carts before taking them out for the day. "The public does not buy peanuts before 11:30 in the morning," I was told, so pushcarts that sell them do not appear on the street until midday. Most food vendors remain on the job until 6:00 or 6:30 in the evening, when the last stragglers at work descend from the city's office towers and make their way home.

Like other street sales, income from food vending varies by weather and location. Most vendors will sell their fare when it is raining, but in heavy downpours, they either do not take their carts out at all or go home early. Then, too, many will not work on bitter cold days when temperatures fall well below freezing. Vendors say that when it is icy out, pedestrians rush by, not stopping for peanuts or other street fare, and that business is best on balmy days in spring and summer. While most vendors try to be on the city's streets six days a week, they actually average somewhat less than this as a result of days lost because of inclement weather.

What do Brazilians earn from their days spent selling street fare? A Brazilian who hawks sugared peanuts near Macy's is paid a commission of 30 percent of her sales. On a slow day she earns as little as $30—working from 11 A.M. to 7 P.M.—but overall she averages $40 to $45 a day. When I met her she was taking home between $250 and $300 for a seven-day week. Most food vendors work on a commission rather than for a fixed salary, but on very slow days, some cart owners will pay their vendors a minimum of $35 or $40 even if their commissions do not amount to that much.

Although Greeks own a majority of the food carts on city streets, a few Brazilians own pushcarts and are vendors themselves or employ others, usually fellow Brazilians, to sell for them. As with all job data concerning Brazilians, one can only make an educated guess at the numbers involved; perhaps twenty Brazilians own pushcarts, ranging from one to twenty carts apiece. A Brazilian and his Argentine partner operate twenty carts that sell peanuts; they employ both Brazilian and Argentine vendors. Or street vending can be a family affair. A native of Minas Gerais who bought three carts mans one himself; his brother sells from another; and his father, who has since returned to Brazil, once operated the third cart. Two Brazilian brothers jointly own eight carts that specialize in shish kabob. They no longer work on the street themselves; they manage the business while eight Brazilian employees handle the carts. These cases illustrate occupational mobility in the street-vending business. The path proceeds from cart employee to single-cart owner and, for the successful few, to multicart owner/manager who hires others to do the actual street selling.

Pushcart entrepreneurs are generally not immigrants right off the plane because the initial investment is considerable. A small hot dog cart costs about $2,500, and a large one can be as much as $6,000. A peanut-making cart runs to about $3,500 because of the heating element needed to cook the syrupy peanuts on the street.

Is cart ownership profitable enough to justify these rather high start-up costs? The answer depends on when and with whom this question is raised. Some cart owners complain that business has fallen off sharply with the recession. A three-cart owner who sells only peanuts said that his profits were down by about 50 percent from the previous year or two because of increased costs and fewer sales—people were more reluctant to shell out a dollar for a small bag of peanuts. Even in a prime midtown location with high pedestrian traffic, he said, business was off; a year earlier one of his carts had average sales of $250 to $270 a day, which had since fallen to the $150–170 range. But large, well-located carts selling shish kabob and other substanial fare can still be very profitable, with net proceeds of up to $400 on very busy days. I was told about one native of Governador Valadares who sold shish kabob from his own stand and managed to save $20,000 in just two years.

Of course, very few Brazilians make this kind of money, and most express mixed feelings about street vending. One vendor told me that he much prefers this job to busing tables—no one tells him what to do and it is interesting work because he "gets to talk to all kinds of people on the street"—but most Brazilians abandon their fresh air work at the first opportunity. They leave, they say, because they hate being out in all kinds of weather and they are not compensated for their trials because the pay is so irregular.[20]

Building the Big Apple

Brazilians work in New York's construction industry, particularly in unskilled jobs in home and office renovation and painting. Construction, in fact, is tied with call car driving as the second most common line of work for Brazilian men in the city proper, and it is probably the single most important source of male employment for immigrants who live in the suburbs. Brazilians do all kinds of heavy, unskilled labor—demolition, paving, cement mixing, brick making, and hauling building materials. They do not work in the building trades as masons, electricians, carpenters, and so on, in part, because they are not trained in them. Recall that most Brazilian immigrants had white-collar jobs at home and that in the Brazilian ethos, manual labor, even skilled manual labor, carries a certain stigma.

Brazilians are but one of many groups of newcomers to New York who work in construction; there is, in fact, a strong immigrant presence in those parts of the building industry that are neither licensed nor unionized.[21] Moreover, Brazilians are likely to work for other immigrants, albeit immigrants who have been in the United States for quite some time. In Queens and on Long Island, Brazilians work for Greeks in house and apartment renovation and painting, and they work for Portuguese-owned renovation and demolition companies in Queens and New Jersey.

Construction is the only line of employment that Brazilians hold that consistently pays well above the minimum wage. On the high side of the pay scale, I met one Brazilian who works for a paving company and earns $15 an hour. More typical is this man's brother, who is paid $10 an hour for helping to repair water mains. Yet another Brazilian has worked for an apartment renovation and painting company for six years; he started at $250 a week and was earning $400 a week by the time I met him.

While these wages are comparatively high, the downside of construction is the seasonality of many jobs in the industry. During the winter, construction jobs involving outside work generally come to a halt from December 15 to March 15. Brazilians scramble to find other temporary jobs or, like one Brazilian blessed with a new green card via the amnesty program, spend the winter break visiting family and friends in sunny Brazil. Most of the construction jobs available to those without papers are short term, and layoffs and job changes are frequent. But some actually see this as an advantage. As one informant explained, construction jobs are sought after not only because of their comparatively high wages but because they are considered fairly safe vis-à-vis the INS. Construction workers change job sites often, in the belief that this will make it harder for immigration inspectors to find them. Whether this is true or not is difficult to say, but some Brazilians certainly believe it to be the case.

A CAPITALIST LAGNIAPPE

One Brazilian who works as a part-time doorman in an apartment building in Manhattan keeps up to date on the U.S. economy by regularly reading *Forbes* magazine, which he salvages from the building's recycled garbage before it is hauled away.

The Entrepreneurial Spirit

There are no Brazilian equivalents of Korean grocery stores or Indian newsstands. One reason that so few Brazilian immigrants own businesses is that most see themselves as sojourners, rather than as settlers; thus they are reluctant to make the long-term commitment that starting a business often entails. After all, if they are only going to be in the United States for a limited time, why should they invest their hard-earned dollars in this country? Better to save up one's money and start a business in Brazil.[22]

Longtime Brazilian residents of New York often comment about how few Brazilian-owned businesses there are in the city and recount the same handful of immigrant success stories. Most will mention Carlinho, the owner of a limousine service, who started from scratch, or one of the Brazilian-owned car service companies in Queens. Or they will point to the Brazilian immigrant who became a successful clothes designer after coming to New York, or the man from Belo Horizonte who owns a Park Avenue antique shop and does floral arrangements for society weddings and parties. Or they might cite the handbag manufacturer whose wares have been featured in American fashion magazines. And this is where the list will end.

However, most Brazilians in New York City, whether long-term residents or recent arrivals, are unaware of the small-scale entrepreneurial activities of some of their compatriots. There is, for example, the family from São Paulo that sells Brazilian food, beer, and soft drinks at the city's street fairs. Then, there are the dozen or so Brazilian women in Queens who do catering from their homes. They cook readymade meals, which they sell to other Brazilians, or they cater parties. These and other unglamorous Brazilian enterprises—an auto body shop, an electronics repair shop, a delivery service, a paving company, a towing firm, a painting company—are usually overlooked when Brazilians rue their compatriots' lack of business acumen.

BRAZILIAN STREET FARE

With a map of Brazil, Brazilian flags, and a mini-lesson about the country—language, population, religion—prominently displayed on a board in front of their food stand, a Brazilian family cooks and serves *pasteis*, savoury meat, shrimp, or olive-filled pastries, and Brazilian desserts and beverages at one of the myriad street fairs held in Manhattan on warm spring and summer days.

Their fare has been well received by New Yorkers, they note with pride, and they can net $1,500 to $2,000 on a busy two-day weekend. Still, selling street food is a risky business; if it rains they can lose all of the food they have prepared since they have no means of storing it.

The business is run on a part-time basis by a brother, a sister, her husband, their son, and a family friend. Because of the popularity of their food at street fairs, they may open a *pastelaria*, a Brazilian-style fast food restaurant that specializes in *pasteis*.

Far better known are the Brazilian entrepreneurs in New York with businesses directed at the Brazilian community in the city, tourists and immigrants alike. These are the owners of restaurants, travel and remittance agencies, the monthly Brazilian newspaper, and the electronics stores catering to tourists that dot Little Brazil, West 46th Street in Manhattan. Then, there are the Brazilian-owned newsstands, grocery stores, bars, luncheonettes, and beauty salons in Astoria, the city's main Brazilian residential neighborhood.

One immigrant success story involving marketing to fellow Brazilians is that of Marta, a woman from Minas Gerais who opened a small store in 1981 on West 46th Street. She sold Brazilian newspapers, magazines, records, tapes, and a few food items. As New York's resident Brazilian community grew, Marta moved to larger quarters across the street. She added a coffee bar and remittance service, began importing a limited line of Brazilian products, and opened an adjacent beauty salon. By starting branch stores in Newark and Astoria, Marta pursued the burgeoning Brazilian population's buying power out of Manhattan into the Greater New York area.

In fact, the closest thing to a hotbed of entrepreneurial activity targeted at the Brazilian community is found in Astoria. One *mineiro* owns a combination grocery store-newsstand, in addition to a travel agency. Two Brazilian siblings run a unisex hair salon, whose clientele is about 70 percent Brazilian. There is also a bar and a couple of luncheonettes owned by Brazilians in the vicinity, as well as the aforementioned car service companies.

Other Brazilians have steered clear of pedestrian enterprises geared to their compatriots, preferring instead to hitch their entrepreneurial stars to the recent trendiness of their homeland and its music. And trendy it is. At a late-night performance, the urbane cabaret singer Bobby Short called out to his audience in his sophisticated drawl: "*Uma vez mais. Uma vez mais.* Do you know what that means? It means "one more time" in Portuguese. Now, isn't *that* chic?" This is right in line with the 1990 issue of *New York Magazine*, which labeled Brazil "the country du jour among the city's stylesetters." At least ten restaurants and nightclubs in Manhattan have responded to the modishness of things Brazilian by specializing in that nation's food and/or music. In fact, if one had the time, the money, and the inclination it would be possible to go to nightclubs that feature Brazilian music or shows on a regular basis at least six nights a week in New York. Then, there is the fashionable new singles bar on the city's waterfront—incongruously called Amazon Beach—that has nothing whatever to do with Brazil other than its name, the tropical drinks that are served, and the fact that it was the site of the "Don't Bungle the Jungle" charity party for rain forest preservation. At least three expatriate bands ply the New York nightclub circuit with a Brazilian beat, and two or three companies of Brazilian singers, dancers, and musicians have been formed to capitalize on the Brazilian entertainment craze. One group, Carioca Nights, has twenty-five dancers and musicians; all but two are Brazilian. They perform at private parties, bar mitzvahs, nightclubs, and carnival balls, on Circle Line cruises around Manhattan Island, at Trump Castle in Atlantic City, and in television specials. The company was founded by Elena, a *mineira*, and does four or five shows a month. She

6.1 Stores selling small electronics line West 46th Street, Manhattan's Little Brazil. They cater primarily to Brazilian tourists.

6.2 Newspapers from about a dozen Brazilian cities are available on West 46th Street.

charges $2,500 per show and pays the performers $90 each for shows in New York and $125 if they have to travel well beyond the city. Elena supplies the costumes and elaborate feathered headdresses, which she keeps carefully stored in her Queens apartment. A few members of the troupe work full-time as dancers or musicians, while most hold the more pedestrian jobs usually associated with new immigrants.

A similar company, Brazil Alive!, was started by Ronaldo in 1984. Today he employs twenty Brazilians, although in the first years he also hired American performers because "at that time there were not enough Brazilian dancers and musicians in the city." The group is much in demand, says Ronaldo, because of the popularity of the lambada, a Brazilian dance that first became the vogue in France before making a well-publicized debut in the United States. Parenthetically, the lambada had become such a craze in New York by the late 1980s, that "lambada outfits" for women—low-cut halter tops and very short, flouncy skirts—were being sold in the city's department stores and adorned the windows of Macy's.

None of Ronaldo's employees support themselves from the shows alone; they are also baby-sitters, cabdrivers, maids, and students. Aloisio is typical. He is an accomplished lambada dancer and does at least one show a week—often two or three—but still paints houses when he is not performing. He earns $70 or more for a show in the city and up to $150 if travel is required. In Brazil, where he was employed as a computer programmer, he only danced "for fun." When I met him, Aloisio had been in the United States for just a few months but he had already traveled to a number of cities with the troupe, including Philadelphia and Miami, to do shows in nightclubs and at private parties.

But, Aloisio insists, many Brazilian performers are not as fortunate as he. He cites the case of Music Brasil, a band of Brazilian musicians that plays throughout the New York metropolitan area. A few years ago when they first started playing regularly at a nightspot in New Jersey, nearly every band member was undocumented. They became, in Aloisio's words, "night slaves," who were paid next to nothing for playing into the wee hours of the morning. But they were reluctant to quit because the club's owner had promised to sponsor band members for green cards.

Odd Jobs

The vast majority of Brazilian immigrants in New York City work at one or another of the jobs already discussed, but their employment niche is more varied than this. Brazilians work, albeit in relatively small numbers, in at least another dozen job categories. Some are obvious. Retail establishments employ Brazilian immigrants who have been in the United States for some time and have both a good command of English and a green card. Delicatessens, bakeries, gift stores, gourmet shops, fish markets, and shoe and clothing stores are among the retail outlets where Brazilians work.

> ### REALLY ODD JOBS
> One Brazilian, who had spent a year making bagels in Brooklyn and boasted to me of how many varieties he knew how to make, left that job to become a dog obedience trainer in Manhattan. I met Brazilians who worked as flower arrangers and bouncers, as locksmiths and dog walkers—and one who did nothing but dismantle used cars.

A number of Brazilians are hairdressers in Manhattan and Queens, including a dozen or so employed in the two beauty shops in the city owned by Brazilians. One beautician, who has his own hair salon in Curitiba, a city in southern Brazil, periodically returns to New York to ply his trade when he needs additional money to invest in his business back home. And a handful of Brazilian women in New York work as manicurists, either in salons or as independents performing their services in customers' homes.

Brazilians also are employed as parking lot attendants in Manhattan, positions that are more often associated with Hispanic immigrants, especially Colombians. But in two large companies in the city, which are said to own upwards of 150 parking garages, anywhere between 10 and 50 percent of the attendants in each garage are Brazilian. Wages run around $6 an hour plus occasional tips, but parking attendants almost never receive fringe benefits. Still, some manage to make a decent living by working extremely long hours; one attendant I met regularly put in an eighty-hour week. This work attracts undocumented immigrants since most employers only ask for a social security card and a driver's license. But the downside of this, as with so many jobs that employ newcomers to this country, is the potential for exploitation. I was told that the managers of parking garages "prefer to employ illegal aliens" because they know that if they complain about wages or hours they can be easily dismissed.[23]

FAR FROM THE MADDING CROWD

Some Brazilian immigrants who live in New York City leave temporarily to take jobs as lumberjacks in Maine, Colorado, and other states. A labor contractor hires men to perform the work, most often planting pines. The men are paid by the number of seedlings planted or trees cut. They are supervised by foremen, who make sure the seedlings are properly spaced.

Lumberjacks can earn good money, but the work is hard and jobs are seasonal. Living conditions are usually spartan, with five or six men housed together in a van or a trailer. Some men complain that there is no place to eat or bathe. Because of this, one Brazilian told me how he went to Maine to work as a lumberjack, lasted one day on the job, and then hopped a bus back to New York City, where he resumed his job shining shoes.

Then, there are the Brazilian men employed as delivery "boys" for take-out restaurants and their compatriots who work as couriers weaving through Manhattan traffic on bicycles to deliver business letters, documents, and small packages. Although earnings have declined since the stock market crash of 1987, during the height of the go-go era on Wall Street, when no expense was spared, couriers who worked long hours could earn as much as $400 a week through hourly wages and generous tips.

Another job held by a handful of Brazilians will be familiar to anyone who in recent years has had even a glancing acquaintance with midtown

Manhattan. Distributors of fliers advertising all manner of businesses and services crowd the city's sidewalks; standing at busy intersections, they shove the fliers at passing pedestrians. This is a perfect first job for brand-new immigrants; neither a word of English nor papers of any sort are necessary, and the distributor is paid in cash at the end of the day. Although weather can be a problem, "flier people," as they are called, earn about $4.25 an hour, with no benefits, and can net $40 for a ten- or twelve-hour day.[24]

One job category notably absent from this entire discussion is factory employment. With a single exception, in many months of research I neither met nor heard of any Brazilians with factory jobs. The lone exception is a small Greek-owned furniture factory in Queens that now employs about eight Brazilians and that used to employ perhaps twice that many. The absence of Brazilians from factory work is noteworthy because certain kinds of factory jobs employ significant numbers of new, undocumented immigrants. The notorious sweatshops in Chinatown are but one example. Immigrant job networks are crucial in securing factory employment, but for some unknown reason, Brazilians have never become involved in factory work. But, as we will see in the chapter to follow, Brazilian immigrant networks are flourishing indeed in two odd jobs, shoe shining and go-go dancing.

CHAPTER SEVEN

Shoe Shine "Boys" and Go-Go "Girls"

IN THE LAST CHAPTER, we looked at the jobs held by most Brazilian immigrants after they arrive in New York City: domestic service, cabdriving, street vending, restaurant work, and construction work, as well as assorted odd jobs. But if one were to walk down a street in Rio de Janeiro, Belo Horizonte, or São Paulo and randomly ask some passersby what kind of work their compatriots do in New York, the chances are the most common reply would be, "Well, there's shining shoes and then there's go-go dancing and . . ." In other words, shoe shining and go-go dancing are stereotyped as the jobs that "most Brazilians" have in the city—as the ones that Brazilians are associated with. One reason for this fixation is the media attention given to these jobs. Articles on *brazucas* in Brazilian newspapers and magazines usually mention *ingraxates* (shoe shiners) and invariably include prurient references to and eye-catching pictures of *dançarinas* (go-go dancers).[1]

While Brazilian immigrants do, indeed, shine shoes and dance in bars in New York City, it is not the numbers involved that have made these job niches such well-known Brazilian specialties. Take shining shoes, for example. Although no one knows exactly how many shoe shiners ply their trade in New York, their numbers are surely miniscule compared to the multitude of busboys and dishwashers in the city's restaurants: while many Brazilian men work as shoe shiners, many more wash dishes and bus tables. And simple common sense tells us that far fewer Brazilian women in New York City work as go-go dancers than as domestic servants. It is not their numbers, then, that have brought renown to Brazilian shoe shine "boys" and go-go "girls" rather, their fame rests on the near-monopoly that Brazilians have in these jobs. Brazilian men dominate shoe shining in Manhattan; Brazilian women prevail as go-go dancers in the city and, indeed, in bars throughout the Greater New York metropolitan area.

"Put a Shine on Your Shoes"

It is the networks [immigrants] establish for access, and the informal training
that takes place in these enterprises, that make it possible for them to maintain their foothold in the city's economy.

—MARCIA FREEDMAN, "The Labor Market for Immigrants in New York
City"

The shoe-shining "industry" in New York is a quintessential example of
an immigrant employment network in action. I have met Brazilians who
within forty-eight hours of arriving in New York, were hard at work
shining shoes at one of the bustling shoe shine stands that dot the canyons
of Gotham. Midtown and lower Manhattan are abuzz with the soft, nasal
lilt of Portuguese. You can hear it spoken at New York landmarks—
Rockefeller Center, Times Square, the World Trade Center, the Empire
State Building—at the city's transportation hubs—Grand Central and
Penn stations, and in the small shoe repair shops scattered along such
well-known thoroughfares as Broadway, Wall Street, and Madison Avenue.

But as with all work done by Brazilian immigrants, numbers are illusive here. One Baptist minister from Brazil who heads a congregation in
Queens said that he had been told that 8,000 of his compatriots shined
shoes in the city. When I replied that this figure seemed very high and that
it was doubtful that there were that many shoe shiners in New York,
Brazilian or otherwise, he told me about the day that he ventured into
Manhattan by subway from Queens to look for potential congregants.
Over the course of two hours he visited fifteen shoe repair/shoe shine
shops in the financial district around Wall Street. Each shop had at least
two Brazilian employees, and most had more than five. He emphasized
that this was just the tip of the shoe-shining iceberg, since there were
many more such shops in this part of Manhattan, which he had not had
time to visit, not to mention those in midtown. One Brazilian entrepreneur, a longtime resident of the city, insisted that around 500 of his
compatriots were working as shoe shiners in the Wall Street area alone.
Yet another Brazilian, himself a shoe shiner with wide contacts in the
Brazilian community, provided what I believe is a more realistic figure; he
estimated that there are between 300 and 400 Brazilian *ingraxates* working at any one time in the shoe shine shops in Manhattan.

While their numbers may be subject to debate, no one disputes the
ethnicity of most New York shoe shiners. All agree that 90 to 95 percent

7.1 Shoe shining employs many Brazilian men at shoe repair shops and kiosks in midtown Manhattan.

of shoe-shining jobs in the city are held by Brazilians and that this ethnic homogeneity is remarkably consistent.[2] In most shops, all the shoe shiners are Brazilian, although in some an occasional Hispanic—usually a Colombian or an Ecuadorian—is found in their midst. And in a few instances the managers are also Brazilian.

Just how did Brazilians come to dominate this small sector of the city's variegated job market? Their first inroads into shoe shining can be traced back to the mid-1960s. Mario, then a young man from Minas Gerais and now retired in Brazil, was probably the first of his compatriots to shine shoes in the Big Apple. His brother followed him into the trade, and by 1969, a small contingent of Brazilians was shining shoes in the vicinity of Grand Central Station, a group that included some immigrant pioneers from Governador Valadares. Their numbers gradually increased as networks of friends and relatives found shoe shine jobs for newcomers to the city, and by the early 1980s, this job sector—once the bailiwick of African Americans—was dominated by Brazilians.

Today, many Brazilians work for a Manhattan chain of shoe shine shops owned by a Romanian émigré. At one time, there were close to sixty shops in the chain, but some closed, and now there are about half that number. Hispanic and Greek store managers hired by this company told me that they had had to learn some Portuguese to be able to communicate with their Brazilian employees. One Greek immigrant, who has managed a shoe repair shop for more than a decade, estimated that he had worked with upwards of 200 Brazilian shoe shiners over the years.

Brazilians often say that the reason that they got into this line of work is that Americans simply will not do it even though the pay is fairly good. "Americans would rather work in a bank and earn $150 a week than shine shoes," they told me. Although the range of pay is quite wide, shoe shining can seem like very remunerative work from the perspective of people accustomed to Brazilian white-collar wages.

Shoe repair shops and shoe shine stands either pay no wages at all or they pay a token $10 or $15 a day. Earnings, therefore, depend entirely or largely on tips, and tips vary with the season, the weather, the time of day, and how many regular customers a man has.[3] Mornings are busier than afternoons, and some men will leave at midday in order to avoid competing with one another for too few clients. On rainy days, customers nearly vanish; business also tends to slack off in the summer, when more people wear sneakers and sandals. Business picks up in colder weather, and tips are more generous in the weeks before Christmas. Of course, this variability in income and the inability to control its fluctuation is a salient feature not only of shining shoes, but of many jobs held by Brazilian immigrants.

Earnings from shining shoes average about $40 a day in summer and $50 or $60 a day in winter. Still, on a busy day, a man with many steady customers working at a shop in a good location can pick up $70, $80, or occasionally $100 in wages and tips. In the winter, one shoe shiner with many regular customers averaged $400 a week, while in the summer his income slipped to $250 or $300. But another shoe shiner with few steady clients earned considerably less; over eighteen months his earnings ranged from a low of $120 to a high of $300 a week, still very good pay by Brazilian standards.

As these cases illustrate, income from shining shoes varies widely because so much of it depends on the number and generosity of a man's regular clients. Some "regulars" will tip $5 or even $10 per shine, while one man who works in a shoe shine shop adjacent to Grand Central Station is paid up to $60 a week by a Japanese customer who leaves his shoes to be polished. The goal, then, is to have a stable of steady customers who are generous tippers.

What about the businesses that do not pay their shoe shiners any wages at all? How do they attract workers? In these stores—they are usually in areas of heavy pedestrian traffic, with a steady stream of customers—the men work only for tips, and they have to buy their own supplies: shoe polish, brushes, rags, and so on. In effect, they provide free labor and supply work materials at no cost to the owner of the establishment. In return, they are given the right to collect tips.[4] No money is withheld for social security or income taxes since no wages are paid. But even in those shops that pay a daily rate, wages are almost always paid in cash and are rarely subject to withholding.

Brazilian shoe shiners have devised various strategies to maximize their clientele, tips, and earnings. When most of those employed at the same shop are friends and/or relatives, the men try to divide customers evenly among themselves. They rotate customers on a regular basis as they enter the shop, not deviating from the sequence unless a client requests a specific shoe shiner. In that case the shoe shiner will attend to the customer even if it is not his turn. After working at a shop for a while, the shoe shiners get to know most of the regular clients and, more to the point, how much they tip. Tips range from nothing at all to a paltry 50 cents to a princely $10. With the rotation system, each man has about the same number of clients, and the shoe shiners share high- and low-tipping customers. While it is the luck of the draw which man gets which, this strategy makes it less likely that one man will get all the generous tippers and another will be stuck with nothing but cheapskates.

Shoe shiners who try to beat the system are not looked on kindly by their coworkers. When a customer of miserly repute appears at a shoe repair shop near Penn Station, one shoe shiner regularly says to his colleagues, "You take him. I'm tired." Or if a low tipper shows up, followed by a high tipper, and it is this man's turn to get the next customer, he will slow down his pace so that one of the other shoe shiners will get stuck with the low tipper and he will wind up with the one who tips well. While his fellow workers deeply resent this man's behavior, they can do nothing about it since the man, a Colombian, is a good friend of the shop owner, also Colombian. "This doesn't happen when all the *ingraxates* are Brazilian," one informant told me with disgust, "because when a position opens up we only recommend friends for it that we can trust."

In line with the importance of tipping, shoe shiners immediately size up new clients as they come through the door. A well-dressed, no-nonsense businessman with a copy of the *Wall Street Journal* under his arm is judged a likely good tipper, whereas camera-toting tourists, particularly foreign tourists, are not. If a customer shows up who is a known or suspected frugal tipper he will get a "one, two, three" shine, also known as a *fumaça*, a "smoke," that is, a perfunctory job.

A "ONE, TWO, THREE" JOB

A Brazilian friend who works as an *ingraxate* (shoe shiner) accompanied me to a bustling shoe shine shop on Lexington Avenue, in midtown Manhattan, so that I could see the system he had described in action. We pretended not to speak Portuguese—we wanted the shoe shiners to treat us like ordinary customers. "They think we're tourists," my friend whispered to me—in other words, poor tippers. And it was true that no one seemed overly anxious to shine his shoes or my boots. We overheard one shoe shiner say to another that he would give us an *um, dois, tres*—a "one, two, three."

Much to their surprise, we both tipped generously and my Brazilian friend noted that if we were to return to the same shop the following week, they would remember us and would be more than happy to have us as customers.

Brazilian shoe shiners put in long hours usually from 7:00 or 7:30 A.M. until 5:30 or 6:00 P.M. Most work five days a week, but the few who work at shoe shine stands that are open on Saturday may decide to pick up an extra day's pay. Some shop owners exploit Brazilian shoe shiners by insisting that they work grueling hours for tips alone. I met a man who worked in one such enterprise for six months; he had to arrive by 6:00 A.M. and stay until 6:00 P.M. even if there were no customers. These were the rules, he was told, if he wanted to retain the "right" to earn tips in this well-located shop. Another *ingraxate*, who had worked at the same store for more than two years, was summarily dismissed for some minor infraction. Since the majority of Brazilian shoe shiners are undocumented immigrants, they have no recourse but to accept such treatment or to leave and find other work.

Shining on High

In addition to the Brazilian *ingraxates* who work at New York's myriad shoe repair shops and shoe shine stands, Brazilians also work as independent shoe shiners, plying their trade in the city's office towers. Talking to the men who have these jobs evoked vivid images of hundreds of Brazilians shining shoes high up in the glittering skyscrapers of Manhattan. Some consider this work more desirable than shoe shining in shops or at stands because the independent earns not only tips but the money that customers pay for the shoe shine as well. Then, too, working hours can be shorter, or at least more flexible, than those in a shop. Independents also glory in the fact that they are their own bosses and can work the days and hours that they prefer.

The income of independent shoe shiners depends on the size and location of the office buildings in which they work and the length of time they have been there, both of which add up to the same bottom line: the number and generosity of customers. Although I was told that income can be doubled by working in an office building, most of the independents I met earned only somewhat more than those working in stores and at shoe shine stands. On the high end, one independent averaged $50 to $60 a day in summer and $100 to $120 a day in winter. But another *ingraxate*, who plys his trade in two different buildings, nets only about $250 a week after he pays $40 to the Brazilian from whom he "inherited" the job.

DASHED HOPES

Nilo was working as a shoe shiner in a shop near Penn Station when he was offered a job as an independent in a small office building in midtown. He saw this as a golden opportunity to earn more money, since business had fallen off sharply in the shop where he worked and he was only making about $40 for an eleven-hour day.

Nilo's hopes were dashed by the second day in his new job. After investing $150 in a shoe shine box and materials, he made only $16 the first day and $13 the next day working as an independent. One problem was that a lot of women were employed in the building, and women almost never get their shoes shined at work. Then, too, an entire floor was occupied by a jewelry concern, which let no one into its offices for security reasons. A general reluctance to allow an unknown shoe shiner onto the premises also contributed to Nilo's problems. Only one floor in the entire building turned out to be lucrative—he earned $12 from a single office on it. He would have stayed, he said, if the whole building was like that. Instead, he quit and went back to his old job.

Such "inheritance" fees can be a major expense for Brazilians who work as independents. In a few cases Brazilians pay management for the right to work in a specific building. More commonly, they pay a weekly fee or a flat sum of money to the individual who held the job before them; this is nearly always another Brazilian who is changing jobs or returning to Brazil. The price depends on how much money can be made from shining shoes in a particular location. For example, a shoe shining position in a bustling office tower in which an independent can earn $120 a day might sell for $1,000 or even $1,500, while a job in a smaller, less well-situated building might be had for $600.

Fifty-story skyscrapers typically have four or five *ingraxates* working in them and buildings in the financial district in lower Manhattan are full of independents because they are considered particularly desirable. One Brazilian who works as an independent got an excellent deal when he paid another Brazilian who was about to leave the country only $600 for two positions in the World Trade Center complex; he has since bought a third position there. He works alone and averages about $450, a week, charging $2 a shine and making most of his money in tips.

The business of shoe shining in office buildings has attracted Brazilian entrepreneurs. Two men from Minas Gerais bought positions in one lofty skyscraper and proceeded to employ three other Brazilians to shine shoes for them. They carry beepers and send the men to the offices that request their services. Another Brazilian makes the rounds of office buildings, asking the building managers if shoe shiners are permitted on the premises. If a manager says yes, he then goes to shoe shine stands and shoe repair shops where Brazilians work and asks if anyone wants to "buy" a position in a building as an independent.

Some *ingraxates* who work in these shops complain that their *own* business is off because there are now so many Brazilian independents working in office buildings. This is because businessmen who have their shoes shined in their offices seldom patronize street-level shoe shine stands and shoe repair shops.

The Hidden Profession

Go-go dancing is to women what shoe shining is to men. Go-go dancing, like shoe shining, is seen as a quintessentially Brazilian job, as one the Brazilian community in New York and their compatriots back home associate with Brazilian immigrant women.[5] But that is where the similarity between the two jobs ends. While Brazilian men were no more self-conscious talking about shining shoes than about busing tables or doing other menial jobs, Brazilian women who were go-go dancers were very reluctant to discuss their work. In fact, it was much easier to find out about the various less than licit ploys involving the acquisition and use of tourist visas and green cards than to learn the most basic facts about go-go dancers and go-go dancing as a profession.

The difficulty that I had interviewing these women is strong evidence that most of them do not think of go-go dancing as "just another job." Again and again during my research, I met Brazilians who said they had friends who were go-go dancers who would be "delighted" to talk to me about their work and who would be "more than happy" to recount their experiences in it. But when it came time to set up an interview or do a questionaire, their go-go–dancing friends flatly refused to cooperate. One man, for example, told me that his Brazilian roommate worked as a go-go dancer and that he was sure that she would tell me about her job. But when I called him a few days later, he sheepishly admitted that his roommate had told him in no uncertain terms that she had no intention of being interviewed about go-go dancing by me or anyone else.

On one occasion, after refusing to discuss her job in person, a Brazilian go-go dancer reluctantly agreed to a phone interview with my Brazilian research assistant. But even over the phone, she was less than forthcoming; she would not say which bars she worked at or even how long she had been a dancer. Another interviewee was even more prickly. In conversation she let it drop that she was once a *dançarina*—Portuguese for go-go dancer—and then she caught herself and denied she ever said she had such a job. She claimed that she had been "misunderstood" and that she actually had worked as a barmaid. But she agreed to talk about go-go dancing as long as the questions were posed in the third person: How much did her friends earn as go-go dancers? What were their working hours? How did they feel about their jobs? At times she became rattled and said "I" instead of "they" when replying, but quickly recovered and went back to the pretense that go-go dancing was something only *other* women did.

> ### BATTLE DRESS OF A GO-GO
> A Brazilian described go-go dancers as having "string bikinis full of dollar bills." Some go-gos use stage names when they dance in order to maintain their anonymity. One told me these sobriquets are their "noms de guerre."

If Brazilian go-go dancers are reticent about their work with an inquisitive anthropologist, they are even more secretive about it with their families in Brazil. They tell their friends and relatives back home that they are employed as baby-sitters, as housekeepers, or as waitresses. One woman from an upper-middle-class family in northeastern Brazil told her parents that her considerable income came from working long hours at two jobs: as a bartender and as a baby-sitter. Informants said that since many go-go dancers are from Minas Gerais—a state former Vice President Dan Quayle would appreciate, one famed for its "traditional, conservative family values"—it was especially incumbent on them to lie to their families about the kind of work they do in New York.

Some women who work as go-gos even hide that fact from their Brazilian friends in the city. One woman told me about a friend of hers who purportedly worked as a baby-sitter. The friend lived very well indeed, buying expensive clothes and furniture. This woman became convinced that her friend had another source of income since she could not possibly earn enough money as a baby-sitter to support her opulent tastes. When the two became roommates, the woman had further proof of what she had long suspected. Her friend, it turned out, went out most nights, only to return in the wee hours of the morning; she refused to say where she had been, saying only that she "liked to get out of the house and get some fresh air."

To be sure, not all Brazilian go-go dancers are ashamed to talk about what they do, and some insist that they see it as "just a job." One go-go had no apologies for her work. "I dance," she said with a defiant air. "I don't like cleaning people's houses, and I have no intention of quitting because I can make the best money dancing." Another explained that when she dances, she tries to distance herself from what she is doing: "You get there, do your work, earn your money and leave. I don't become involved psychologically." But one former go-go conceded that despite the excellent pay, working as a go-go "is just not worth it."

There is no way of knowing how many Brazilian women are employed as go-go dancers in bars and nightclubs in New York. One Brazilian who was a pioneer go-go dancer herself in the mid-1970s, estimated that there are now between 2,000 and 3,000 go-go dancers throughout the Greater New York metropolitan area—including Long Island, Westchester County, and New Jersey—and that about 80 percent of them are Brazilian.[6] Some bars, she noted, even advertise that they feature "all Brazilian girls in our samba show." In fact, the 80 percent figure was cited over and over again by Brazilians with some knowledge of the profession.

Three or four talent agencies book go-go dancers for bars and night-clubs in the metropolitan area. One lists some 200 Brazilians among its stable of dancers, and another, whose manager was born in Rio de Janeiro, lists 300 dancers, most of them Brazilians. Many other dancers operate independently and contract with bars on their own. One go-go dancer who lives in Queens said that she personally knows at least forty Brazilian women in the profession in New York, and that there are even more in Newark, Elizabeth, and other towns in New Jersey because of the many go-go bars in that area. A news article about Brazilian immigrants in Newark even suggests that the only jobs available to Brazilian women there are as domestic servants, go-go dancers, and barmaids.[7]

How did Brazilian women come to corner the market on go-go dancing in the New York area? Just as with shoe shining, there seems to have been an early connection to the town of Governador Valadares. One *valadarense*, a longtime New York resident, said that the first women to emigrate from Valadares in the late 1960s and early 1970s worked as domestic servants in New York. In those days, maids were paid $70 or $75 a week for very long hours. At some point, one or more of these women discovered that they could work as go-go dancers and make $45

or $50 a night in wages and tips. Word of these earnings presumably
filtered back to Brazil, and others followed. The Metropole, a go-go bar
near Times Square, is said to have employed many of these pioneer dancers, a fact confirmed by a women from Minas Gerais who, along with her
sister, began dancing there in 1976.

The flow of immigrant go-gos continued through the mid-1970s—one
informant emphasized how easy it was for Brazilians to get tourist visas
in those days—as the lure of earning $400 or even $500 a week proved
irresistible. Some dancers fanned out of the city, finding work at bars in
and around Newark, in Westchester, and on Long Island. A Brazilian
journalist has reported in a story on go-go dancers that the Valadares
connection is still alive and well in Newark; that Governador Valadares
is the hometown of many go-go dancers in that city.[8] Parenthetically, the
association between Valadares and go-go dancing has spawned a new
business there: the export of Brazilian-made string bikinis (*tangas*) to Brazilian dancers in New York, New Jersey, Connecticut, and Massachusetts. Periodically, entrepreneurs from Governador Valadares fill their
suitcases with these tiny bits of cloth (with good reason, string bikinis are
also called *fio dental*, "dental floss") and travel to the United States to sell
their wares to their go-go–dancing compatriots.

Just who are these "go-go girls," as they are usually called? This was
as difficult to determine as it was to interview them, but what little data
I have suggest that they come from a range of backgrounds in Brazil.
Nevertheless, most dancers hail from Minas Gerais and Rio de Janeiro, a
reflection of the geographic origin of the majority of Brazilian immigrants
in New York City, and most are young—in their twenties and early thir-
ties—although I was told that some Brazilian go-go dancers are over forty.

Brazilian go-go dancers range from women from what Brazilians call
"good families" in Rio, who have two or three years of university education and become go-go dancers "to try their luck in the United States," to
single mothers from Governador Valadares, whose children in Brazil depend on their remittances for support. One divorced mother of two came
to New York to earn money and left her children with relatives in Brazil.
She could not get work in the city and was about to return to Brazil
discouraged and in debt when she found a job as a go-go dancer. Since
then her finances have improved immeasurably, and she regularly sends
money to her family back home. Then, there is the accountant from
Governador Valadares. Back home she worked long hours in her profession and complained that by the end of the month she never had any
money left. But, she noted with amazement, after only three months of
working as a go-go dancer in New Jersey, her closets were filled with new
clothes. Finally, there is the young woman from Minas Gerais who has
been dancing in bars in Queens for nine months. She has one goal in
mind, now nearly realized—saving enough money to make a down pay-

ment on a house for her mother in Belo Horizonte. Informants say that while most women who work as go-go dancers send at least some money to their families in Brazil, the bulk of their earnings are set aside for their own future use. This usually means buying an apartment or other property in Brazil or starting a business there. But these brief snapshots only hint at the strong monetary lure of the profession.

The Wearing of the Green

Some Brazilian women who become go-go dancers in New York arrive in this country with no more thought of doing such work than of becoming Miss America. Intent on making money, they get jobs as booksellers, housekeepers, or baby-sitters. They earn the minimum wage or a bit more, but before long they begin to hear from friends about the money to be made in go-go dancing. It is enticing. Some women then go to one of the city's booking agencies to see if they can break into this remunerative profession.

THE MAKING OF A GO-GO

This account was provided by Clarisa, a young woman from Brasília, who worked as a go-go dancer for nearly two years in Queens, Manhattan, Westchester, and New Jersey. At the time of the interview, she had just quit dancing and had taken a job in a shop selling Brazilian products.

When she first came to this country, Clarisa found work as a go-go dancer through a booking agency in Times Square. She bought a counterfeit social security card and told the agency that the papers for her green card were being "processed by her lawyer in Florida." This sufficed, and she was directed to proceed to the "interview."

When potential go-go dancers first go to an agency, they are told to strip down to their panties so that the booking agent can see if their bodies are "good enough" for go-go dancing. Most women are accepted, Clarisa says, since some bars, particularly those with a Hispanic clientele, will hire plump women.

Clarisa went to the agency once a week to get her bookings. She danced in a different bar every night, going from Queens to New Jersey and back again. Some bars are "classier" than others in terms of atmosphere, clientele, type of show, and size of tips. And the better the bar, the "fussier" it is about the dancers' appearance.

Clarisa says she is happy that she stopped dancing—"people look at you differently when you dance"—even though at her current job she makes far less money and works longer hours. But, she avers, she will not go back to dancing unless she becomes "desperate for money."

The earnings of go-go dancers vary with the bar, its location, and its clientele; income is from both wages and tips. In New York City, in addition to tips, bars pay their dancers a flat rate of from $50 to $120 a night, or a minimum of $10 an hour. Bars in New Jersey pay $13 to $20 an hour, but the tips are quite a bit less than in New York. Dancers agreed that it is better to work in bars that pay less but where the tips are generous—individual tips generally range from $1 to $20—than in bars that pay more but have a miserly clientele. But there are other considerations as well. One dancer who lives in Queens told me that she prefers to dance in local bars because when she works in New Jersey her expenses are so much higher; she gets off work in the wee hours of the morning and has to spend $30 for a cab back home to Queens.

Earnings also depend on the number of days and hours a woman works. Go-go dancers work five, six, or occasionally, seven days a week. They might arrive at work at 8:00 or 9:00 P.M. and stay until 3:00 or 4:00 A.M. To be sure, the women are not dancing all this time. A dancer will do a set of twenty or thirty minutes, usually with one or two other dancers. Then she will change clothes, and sit at the bar with patrons for about a half-hour while other dancers do the the next set. She then changes back into her costume and dances again. These shifts of dancing and sitting with patrons last anywhere from five to eight hours. Then, too, go-go dancers can find work at almost any hour of the day or night, or they can work double shifts since some bars open around noon and have continuous performances until closing time.

> **THE DANCING DENTIST**
>
> Marisa and her husband, both dentists, arrived in New York with the goal of saving enough money to pay off a $30,000 debt for the purchase of dental equipment for their practice in Brazil. She held low-wage jobs as a domestic servant until a friend told her about the money she could earn as a go-go dancer. Somewhat reluctantly, Marisa and her husband decided she should give it a try. After about eighteen months working as a go-go dancer at bars and nightclubs in Queens, Marisa had reached her goal; with $30,000 in hand, she and her husband returned to Brazil. But, she said with a wink, before leaving New York, the money she had earned as a go-go was awfully good and she hoped her former employers would keep a place open for her "just in case."

A go-go dancer's nightly earnings can range from $100 to $300, depending on the location of the bar and the number and generosity of its patrons, although most dancers average $150 to $200 a night.[9] For example, Nicola's, a go-go bar in Queens pays Gloria a set rate of $52 for an eight-hour shift, and various other bars in the area pay her between $50 and $70 for a night's work. She has earned up to $1,000 a week from wages and tips, but this meant dancing seven nights before particularly free-handed audiences. At the time of the interview, Gloria complained that she was averaging only $700 a week, explaining that customers were tipping less because of the weak economy. Still, Gloria noted with pride, she had earned $23,000 over the nine months she had been working as a go-go dancer, more than double what she had made during her entire first year in New York, when she was employed as a manicurist, book vendor, and maid.

One go-go dancer, Clarisa, used to work in bars all over the New York metropolitan area and made as much as $1,500 during an especially lucrative seven-day week or as little as $500 over a particularly quiet five-night stretch. In one bar in Westchester County, she is paid $115 by the house, for a grueling double shift lasting from noon to 2:00 A.M., and with tips her earnings can come to as much as $700. Clarisa also lamented the decline in tips, which she blamed on the recession, but was quick to point out that go-go dancing still pays far more than any other job available to Brazilian immigrant women.[10]

While most or all of what go-go dancers earn is not taxed, net income still depends on whether or not they pay a booking agent to locate jobs for them. Dancers who use agents pay a commission of 8 to 10 percent on the nightly wage that they receive from the bar but not on their tips, which, they assured me, is where the real money is. Some dancers prefer to pay agents rather than freelance because with an agent, they do not have to make the rounds of bars themselves and they have a wider range of establishments from which to choose. Still, if a particular bar and a particular dancer are compatible, the dancer may avoid an agent's fee by booking her performances directly with the bar manager.

One Brazilian couple who own a booking agency in New Jersey are famed in go-go–dancing circles. Former dancers themselves, they earn a 10 percent commission on all the jobs they book for their bevy of Brazilian clients. For an additional $25 they will also chauffeur a dancer to and from the bar, an attractive proposition to women who get off work in the middle of the night and have to hail cabs in what may be unsavory neighborhoods. Even some dancers who own cars prefer to use the agency's escort service in order to avoid unwanted attentions from customers after the show. The Brazilian booking agents are doing very well financially; they own three cars, an apartment, and a suite of offices. They can hardly handle all the business, they say, because "the appetite for Brazilian go-gos is insatiable."[11]

Look But Don't Touch

Go-go dancers work in a nearly all-male environment. The only women in the bars that feature go-go dancing are usually the dancers themselves and a barmaid or two; with few exceptions, all of the bar patrons are men. But aside from the constancy of their audience, the dancers' working conditions vary, depending on the jurisdiction and the neighborhood in which the bar is located. The state of New Jersey has more stringent laws regulating go-go dancing than does the state of New York. Striptease, for example, is legal in New York but not in New Jersey. In New Jersey, women may not dance topless—the women wear tiny string bikini bras instead—and clients may neither touch the dancers nor stuff tips into their skimpy outfits. Moreover, bar owners in that state cannot oblige dancers to sit with customers and push drinks after the show. The women tend to see these regulations as protective rather than restrictive, and some say this is why they prefer to work in bars in Newark or neighboring towns rather than in New York. Also since some go-gos speak little English, they opt to work in Newark, where they are more likely to have Portuguese-speaking customers because of the presence of a large Portuguese community in that city. But the downside is that tips are usually lower in bars outside New York City.

Since New York has fewer legal restrictions, bars have more latitude in the type of show that they may present, and topless dancing is standard. Guidelines vary; some bars will not permit dancers to touch their breasts or to "flash" or do "floor shows" in which they briefly expose their genitals. But, as one go-go put it, "the sleazier bars let the girls do whatever they want." And the dancers decide for themselves what they are willing to do. One told me that she would never do a "floor show," touch herself, or let customers touch her. Dancers also differ as to whether or not they are willing to sit with clients and coax them to order drinks; some bars require it, while others do not. A dancer usually earns more if she mingles with customers—the goal is to get a tip from everyone who has watched the show—and bar managers favor dancers who sell a lot of drinks. Dancers who work in go-go bars in Manhattan are generally expected to encourage patrons to buy drinks, and in some establishments they get a percentage of the price of each drink sold.[12]

The Show Must Go On

Nicola's, a go-go bar in Queens, is of average size and its layout resembles those of other go-go bars I visited. A large, circular bar in the center of the establishment is surrounded by bar stools. This is the only seating avail-

7.2 Go-go dancing is a lucrative occupation for some Brazilian women.

able; there are no separate tables or chairs where patrons may sit. The go-gos perform on a raised dance floor in the center of the bar area, while barmaids make their way around the base of the platform, taking orders and serving drinks to the largely male clientele. The room is in semidarkness, with colored spotlights fixed on the dancers.

I arrived at Nicola's at 9:30 one evening accompanied by two Brazilian friends. When I got there, only one woman was among the twenty or so patrons seated around the bar; most of the customers appeared to be Hispanic and South Asian. Nicola's employs five or six go-go dancers on any given night—typical go-go bars have as many as six or as few as two dancers—and the women, who usually dance in pairs, take turns performing. That night, there was a Brazilian go-go dancer, a Colombian dancer, and three American dancers.

At Nicola's, the dancers come on stage wearing a variety of skimpy costumes—a ruffled, low-cut, midriff-baring top and tight, spandex miniskirt, for example, or a scanty, sequined "cowgirl" outfit. Over the course of the performance, with soft rock music playing in the background, a dancer will do a slow striptease until she has taken off all of her clothes except a string bikini bottom and high stiletto heels. Much of the "dancing" consists of a variety of sensual movements in which the go-gos touch their breasts, bend over to the floor to expose their buttocks, and writhe and gyrate in explicit sexual pantomimes. Nicola's is said to prohibit "floor shows." After the performance, which lasts about twenty minutes, the dancers kneel down before each man at the bar and solicit money. That night, all of the customers appeared to give each dancer a dollar or more in tips, some laughing drunkenly while stuffing the bills into the go-gos' tiny bikini bottoms.

After the set is over, the go-gos go backstage and change into the skimpy outfits they were wearing before the performance. As per the bar's requirements, the dancers then reappear and sit next to customers, talking and encouraging them to buy drinks. After her set, Gloria, a Brazilian dancer, sat at the bar with us and ordered a Coke. She did this, she said, only because "the manager would object" if he saw her "talking to customers without ordering a drink." She did not mind, she said, because between wages and tips, she expected to earn about $150 that night.

But for many Brazilian go-go dancers, their well-paying jobs come at a serious cost. Most complain of being subject to a never-ending barrage of sexual advances. They must constantly fend off unwanted proposals from customers, who lie in wait for them outside the bars when they get off work. Patrons and male bar employees hound them for dates; a few even propose marriage. One Brazilian woman, a former go-go dancer, said of the job, "It was dirty work and there were lots of problems. The customers not only try to grab us and make dates, but the men who work at the go-go bars"—bartenders, bouncers and managers—"also see the dancers as fair game." She herself lost a job at a bar when she refused to go out with the manager and his friends.

Still, she estimated, perhaps 70 percent of the dancers she knows date customers, at least on an occasional basis. A few acquire "sugar daddies" who support them so that they work less and dance only two or three nights a week. While some bars officially prohibit "fraternizing" between dancers and customers, such "rules" are rarely enforced; other bars adopt a laissez-faire stance on the matter or even encourage the dancers to make dates with regular patrons.

The red flag issues of prostitution and drugs often come up in conversations with Brazilians about go-go dancing. Some informants insisted vehemently that go-go dancing has nothing whatever to do with prostitution and that few or no Brazilian dancers take money for sex. But others were just as insistent that many Brazilian go-gos become prostitutes, particularly those that get involved with drugs. A real "yes, they do"—"no, they don't" tug of war goes on between defenders and critics of go-go dancing as a legitimate profession. One former go-go alleged that half of the dancers she knows use cocaine. Then, there was the story—repeated several times—about the "gorgeous Brazilian go-go 'girl'" who had "never touched drugs in her life" until she got involved with cocaine through an unsavory boyfriend; she spent all her money on drugs and "lost her looks." But a woman who has befriended many Brazilian go-gos insisted equally emphatically that while prostitution and drug use occasionally occur among go-gos, both are rare. The truth probably lies somewhere between the two claims. As a former dancer put it in describing her own career, "When I was a go-go it wasn't difficult to steer clear of prostitution and drugs, although the bars do lend themselves to these activities. Sure, I might recommend this job to someone because of the money but I would certainly counsel her about its dangers."

And so, while the numbers of Brazilians involved are relatively small, shoe shining and go-go dancing are seen as quintessential Brazilian ethnic enclaves. But what is the best way to summarize the economic niche of most Brazilian immigrants in New York City? As we have seen, more Brazilian men and women have jobs in the city's two largest immigrant employment sectors—restaurant work and domestic work, respectively—than in any others.[13] Street vending and cab driving are other prototypical immigrant occupations employing many Brazilians. However, with the exception of shoe shining and go-go dancing, Brazilians are not identified with any specific ethnic employment enclave or ethnic specialization. There is no Brazilian equivalent of the Korean grocery, Indian newsstand, or Greek coffee shop.[14]

While work is the raison d'être for Brazilian immigrants to the city, it is not all there is to life there. New York is, after all, one of the world's greatest and most difficult metropolises in which to live. How Brazilian immigrants see life in the city, and what they do there when they are not working are the subjects of the next chapter.

CHAPTER EIGHT

Life and Leisure in
the Big Apple

Brazil is beaches and beautiful people; the United States is making money.

—*Brazilian immigrant in New York City*

Hᴏᴡ ᴅᴏ Bʀᴀᴢɪʟɪᴀɴ immigrants see life in the United States? What do they make of New York, with its myriad wonders and inordinate problems? Their views are decidedly mixed. One Brazilian passionately proclaimed that she "loves America," calling it "the great mother of all people" (*a grande mãe de todos*). While life can, indeed, be hard in the United States, she said, her compatriots' complaints about this country irritate her and she has to stifle the urge to tell them: "So why don't you just go back to Brazil then?" Another immigrant admitted that although she had "suffered a lot here," the United States was still "the best school in the world." A compatriot agreed, proclaiming that her six years in New York had taught her more than had twenty years in Brazil. When she went home for a visit, her parents remarked on how different she was, how much more mature. "I was a girl when I left and a woman when I returned," she said with a proud shake of her head. Still others spoke of "greater opportunities" in the United States than in Brazil or of the supposedly "greater respect" that people show to one another in the United States or simply of "the adventure of living in a first world nation."

But these upbeat views of life in "the great mother of them all" are only one facet of the picture. Some immigrants cast their experiences in starkly negative terms. One spoke in disgust about the "fantasies" many Brazilians have when they leave for the United States. They arrive and "are deceived by the type of life they lead here." Many do not want their families to know how unhappy they are and how poorly they have fared and stay on because they are "ashamed" to return home so soon. A woman from Rio de Janeiro was vehement about the "deception" of Brazilian immigrants, conditioned as they are by the U.S. media to think of the United States as "a beautiful place." Returning migrants contribute to this delusion. They go back to Brazil and say, "The United States? Why, it's the most wonderful place! You can be rich in two weeks." But the reality is far different, she noted bitterly: "Someone should tell them what really happens here—the price you have to pay. I want to tell them, Hello people, wake up. It's not the paradise that people imagine. This is *not* the golden dream."

The Good, the Bad, and the Ugly

One Brazilian immigrant told me, "New York has everything, the good, the bad, and the ugly." He might have been speaking for most of his compatriots when describing life in the Big Apple as a decidedly mixed blessing. But just what is it that Brazilians like and dislike about their newly adopted land? The chance to make money and other economic benefits are the most frequently cited pluses. "I'd rather be poor in the United States than a millionaire in Brazil," said the Brazilian owner of an auto body shop in Queens, "because you live better poor here than rich there." He explained that in New York he can work for a week and earn enough money to eat for a month, something he could never do in Brazil. Others mentioned the relatively stable U.S. economy, which allows them to plan and save. Brazil has had high inflation for so long—even before the current era of hyperinflation—that people find it difficult or impossible to make future plans. As one Brazilian pointed out, in contrast to his homeland, "Here, you know that next month the money you save is going to be worth approximately the same as it is today."

Some Brazilians are favorably impressed by seemingly minor differences between the two countries. A number cited the fact that in the United States people generally receive their wages every week or two, while in Brazil salaries are typically paid only once a month; with an inflation rate that can hover around 20 percent a month, this means a significant loss in earnings. Then, too, more than one immigrant noted approvingly that most Americans can simply go out and buy something they want—compact disc players, stereos, television sets, and VCRs, were the items most often cited—while in Brazil you have to think long and hard before making such purchases and even then buy them on time or not at all.

Certain polarities in Brazilian and American culture also appeal to immigrants. A successful Brazilian entrepreneur finds life more formal and "patterned" in this country than in his own; this is a plus for him because it leads to "greater productivity." Still, he joked about how Americans try to cram themselves into a common mold, citing his own experience interviewing Americans for jobs in the New York office of the Brazilian construction company he directs: "Americans must all take the same course called 'how to find a job' because they all say that they enjoy playing tennis. I guess the instructor tells them that tennis is an appropriate sport to mention in an interview." Then, there is the Brazilian who places a high premium on the American sense of privacy, a value that he finds notably lacking among his compatriots. "Why Brazilians just show up at my apartment uninvited," he remarked with chagrin—something his American friends would never do, he said.

Other immigrants are attracted by the things that make New York City famous—the glittering lights, the soaring skyscrapers, the electric street life, the multitude of cultural events. One immigrant decribed her sheer delight at visiting the Empire State Building and the Statue of Liberty for the first time. But because of the single-mindedness with which they save money, most immigrants do not take advantage of New York's entertainment and cultural fare, although a few do. One woman from Minas Gerais told me how she had been "swimming in a cultural bath" since coming to New York, spending her hard-earned wages on theater, opera, and ballet tickets. Another called the city a "cultural paradise" because of its museums but admitted that most Brazilian immigrants spend so many hours working that they have little time left to take advantage of New York's attractions.

Then, there are the appealing intangibles of city life. In a conversation about New York, one Brazilian woman recounted how enchanted she was by her first snowfall and how she is still dazzled by the skyline at night. Her friend countered that *her* favorite part of city life is autumn in Central Park. She showed me the brightly colored leaves she had pressed between the pages of a book, saying that on her next trip to Brazil she was going to take them to her relatives there. Living in a tropical climate, they had never experienced the change of seasons.

Sometimes a simple act of kindness casts a positive light on life in the city. One Brazilian related how, lost in the city's labyrinthine subway system, he asked a woman for directions. The woman gave them to him and then got on the train that had just pulled into the station. Suddenly realizing that what she had told him was wrong, the woman hopped off the train just before the doors slammed shut and headed his way to give him the correct information. The helpfulness that she displayed was an example of "American generosity," one of the reasons he "loves New York."

A rather odd reason for looking favorably on life in New York comes from a Brazilian who reads the *New York Times* every day. He is well aware of the city's critical social and economic plight, but, he says, he sees it as an "outsider," as someone uninvolved in what is happening around him. After work he goes home, reads, listens to music, talks to his wife, and feels entirely removed from New York's problems. And he likes it that way. In contrast, in Rio de Janeiro, his hometown, he is haunted by the specters of crime and poverty; there, he is a part of society, not just an observer of it.

Then there are the Brazilians who are so taken with the Big Apple that they sound like inveterate New Yorkers; they become as chauvinistic about the city as any native. One Brazilian immigrant who has achieved considerable success in his adopted city cheerfully agreed with the song lyric, "If you can make it here, you can make it anywhere." Another immigrant, a widow from Rio de Janeiro, declared that she had "returned to life in New York." Although she sometimes misses Brazil, "once you've lived here you can't live anywhere else." Yet another woman, a long-term U.S. resident, remarked that while it is true that many of her compatriots go back to Brazil, some turn right around and come back to the city because "New York is like a vice—people get addicted; they just keep coming back for more."

The Illusion of the "Little Green Things"

Brazilians' single most common complaint about life in New York City is how they were deluded in their belief in the "little green things" (*verdinhas*), Portuguese slang for "dollars." They blame themselves and other Brazilians for their misconceptions about what a dollar will buy and what it takes to earn. A man who travels back and forth to Brazil buying and selling semiprecious stones compared Brazilians who come to New York to people who leave Brazil's poverty-stricken northeast and travel to São Paulo in search of jobs. Both migrant streams involve "the same deceptive dream of riches."

Such terms as "delusion," "illusion," and "deception" were a leitmotif in conversations with Brazilians about life in the United States. One engineer from Minas Gerais told me how the "illusion of the little green things" had fooled him into believing that in a few short years he was going to be able to save $50,000 for his return to Brazil. There is also the "illusion" of the U.S. minimum wage. "Sure, $4 an hour is a lot in Brazil, but here it's nothing," said the same engineer. "On earnings of $900 a month in New York, I live no better than if I were making $50 a month [the Brazilian minimum wage] at home." Then, there is the woman who pays $750 a month rent for a house in Queens that, she says, "isn't fit for her maid to live in" and the limousine driver who found that the reality of life in New York is not what he thought it would be: "You can actually go hungry here if you don't work really hard," he said increduously. This is why one Brazilian, a seasoned New York resident, tells her friends to come to the city "only for adventure, not to earn money." Contrary to

Brazilians' "sweet illusion of life in the Big Apple," she said, "money is *not* growing on the trees in Central Park."

But, in reality, there is probably less illusion about life in the United States than the rhetoric of some Brazilians would suggest; most such statements seem to be exaggerations of true expectations. I met almost no Brazilians who actually thought they would strike it rich in New York and return to Brazil with a small fortune. Informants always referred to unspecified "other people" who were so deluded; it was always "someone else" who fancied that after two years in the United States, he or she would return to Brazil with $50,000 or $70,000 in hand. While it is true that when they first arrived, many Brazilians were shocked by the high cost of living in New York City, almost all came with relatively modest notions about the amount of money they could hope to save; $10,000 or $20,000 over two to four years were the most common figures cited. The goal for most was to buy, or at least make a down payment on, a piece of property in Brazil—an apartment, a house, a small business. For a few, it was to send remittances to their families back home. Recall that the appeal of jobs in New York, despite the city's high cost of living, is what one Brazilian called "the economy of time"—an immigrant's ability to save a given sum of money in so much less time than it would take to save a similar amount in Brazil.

This brings us to Brazilians' second major complaint about life in New York: how hard they have to work. Given the relatively low wages that immigrants earn, the expense of living in a city such as New York, and the common goal of saving money for the return home, Brazilians necessarily labor very long hours, often at two jobs. Here, too, the vocabulary of "delusion" is often heard, and returning migrants are blamed for their compatriots' fantasies. Brazilians have "no real understanding of what it is like to work in the United States," I was told, because migrants who have gone back to Brazil "brag about how easy it is to earn lots of money in a short time." Then, when Brazilian immigrants in New York face the reality of twelve- or thirteen-hour days, sometimes under arduous conditions, they are disillusioned indeed. And, as one put it, contrasting these conditions with the eight-hour days they typically put in at their jobs in Brazil, "Of course, they suffer."

Culture Shocks

Aside from what they endure at work, Brazilian immigrants, like all immigrants, are subject to a daily barrage of culture shocks, both great and small. A Brazilian Baptist minister suggests that some Brazilians suffer from "cultural, linguistic, and culinary shock" after they arrive in New York. Moreover, he claims that a large part of his job involves counseling

Brazilians beset by the strains of life in New York. One Brazilian who has lived in the United States since the mid-1970s tries to prepare her Brazilian friends and relatives for life in the Big Apple. Soon after they arrive she gives them a mini-lesson in American culture, emphasizing how it contrasts with the Brazilian way of doing things. The first lesson is about the sense of privacy in the United States. She tells Brazilians, "The doors of people's houses are not open like they are in Brazil. Americans value their privacy, and you should never just show up at an American's home without arranging a date first."

CULTURAL CONTRASTS

"In the TV news in Brazil . . . issues of reproductive technology, such as test tube babies and surrogate motherhood, proved popular. Brazilians found such stories particularly interesting because they confirmed the stereotype of American society as developed but flawed. The United States may be technologically innovative, but it is an Anglo-Saxon nation that lacks a Latin soul. Because of this, American culture sometimes carried its know-how and inventiveness to inhumane extremes. Such stories appeal to Brazilians because they suggest that power, influence and technology are insufficient to warrant full international respect. In contrast, they suggest that Brazil, despite its troubled economy and polity, has something enduring and valuable that many other nations lack: warmth and humanity."

Source: Kottak, *Prime Time Society*, 93.

Brazilian immigrants face other problems in New York. Foremost among them is language. Over and over, I was told that "people who don't speak English suffer a lot in New York," or that "to come here without English is suicide." Some blamed the solitude that many Brazilians feel on their lack of fluency in English; without it, they cannot fully participate in the life around them. Indeed, loneliness particularly plagues Brazilians without family members in the city. To live isolated from kin is always viewed as a hardship by Brazilians irregardless of other circumstances. In this respect the contrast between life in Brazil and life in the United States is especially striking. In Brazil, said one immigrant, "a family sits down and has dinner together. Here, families don't eat together. They have a hamburger and fries from Burger King and then they go to sleep." In Brazil, relatives—grandparents, cousins, married siblings—typically see one another on a regular, even daily basis. Kin tend to live near one another, often residing in apartments in the same building in large cities, and a great deal of Brazilian social life revolves around the ex-

tended family.[1] "Solitude" or the "solitary life" are terms Brazilians use
to express the linguistic and social isolation of being far from friends and
relatives. Some claim that this isolation changes their fellow Brazilians.
They become "more distrustful, more tense." Then, too, many live with
the fear of crime, especially those whose jobs require them to travel on the
subways late at night or who live in high-crime neighborhoods.

NEW YORK BARRICADES

Paulo has four locks on the door of his apartment, a fifth-floor walk-
up in a tenement building in East Harlem. He has taken many home videos
in the apartment and sent them to friends and relatives in Brazil; they invariably inquire about the large number of locks on the door.

The same kind of criticisms that Americans voice about life in New
York are echoed by Brazilian immigrants. Aside from the city's high
crime rate and homelessness, they deplore the mounds of garbage decay-
ing on the streets, the frenetic pace, the coldness of pedestrians rushing
by, the curtness of salespeople. You "live like a machine in New York;
there is a specified hour for everything—work, sleep, play," one Brazilian
lamented. Then, there are the general complaints about life in the United
States. The "American personality" is often deemed "colder," or at least
"more restrained," than the Brazilian one. A woman from Rio de Janeiro
told me how disgusted she was by the government in her own country,
only to find when she came to the United States, "child abuse, old people
abandoned in nursing homes, working parents neglecting their children."
Another *carioca*, a successful executive with a long distance moving firm
in New York, related how, as a woman and a foreigner, she had had to
fight hard to gain respect in business. And a man from Minas Gerais
deplored the racial discrimination in this country, comparing it unfavorably to Brazil, which he labeled a "racial paradise."

A number of Brazilians spoke wistfully of longing to combine features
of Brazilian and American life and culture. They lauded Brazilian warmth
and sociability, while admiring the American work ethic. Undiluted Brazilian qualities, particularly those of the "100 percent *carioca*," a carica-
ture of the carefree native of Rio, were seen as too much of a good thing.
One woman from that city told me that by living in New York, she had
come to embody the best of both worlds. She is, she said with obvious
pride, "the fruit of two cultures," a hardworking, successful businesswoman who has also kept her warmth and sensitivity and her decided
knack for having a good time.

> *BASIC VOCABULARY*
> One Brazilian told me how he had become adept at reading the New York tabloids once he learned their most common words: "murder," "arson," "mutilation," "mugging," "rape," and so on. He has a harder time reading the *New York Times*, he says.

Given these varying opinions about life in the United States, what do Brazilian immigrants tell their friends and relatives back in Brazil when the latter ask whether they, too, should try their luck in the Big Apple? Many immigrants say that while they do not regret their own decision to come to New York, they would not advise most of their compatriots to make a simlar move. A psychologist from Rio de Janeiro thinks that migration for economic reasons alone is just not worth it and cites the trials and tribulations of a Brazilian acquaintance. The Brazilian, a young man in his early twenties, comes from a small town in Minas Gerais and works as a parking lot attendant in Manhattan. Prior to coming to New York, he had never been in a big city before, and he became lonely and despondent after his arrival; now he is beset with severe emotional problems. "His suffering is just not worth the money he is making here," opined my informant. Another Brazilian agrees that it makes no sense for most of her compatriots to migrate to New York. While the city does offer job opportunities and even some chance for advancement, the problem, as she sees it, is that many Brazilian immigrants are just too single-minded in pursuing their goal of saving money, for the return home. To do so, they live a meager existence in New York; they share crowded apartments to cut down on expenses, live only with other Brazilians, and never learn much English. Her conclusion? "To save money in New York you have to sacrifice your life." Yet another Brazilian, a long-term resident of the city, said that my question about advice to prospective migrants was a "tricky one." For some people, the difficulties of life in New York, particularly when they first arrive, far outweigh any benefits. "It's a big fight," she said, and she would make sure her friends back home knew this before they headed for the United States.

Other Brazilians are more upbeat about their compatriots' ability to adapt to life in New York. A woman from São Paulo believes that it is relatively easy for urbanites from southern Brazil, particularly those from large cities, such as Rio and São Paulo, to cope with life in New York; in contrast, Brazilians from small towns or from the less cosmopolitan parts of the country have a much more difficult time. But one long-term New

York resident expressed faith in the adaptability of all emigrating Brazilians. Recall, she said, that Brazil, like the United States, is a multicultural nation; "it too is a land full of immigrants."

The Fearsome Aunt

When you are an illegal you learn the underside of life.

—*Undocumented Brazilian in New York City*

The specter of Tia Mimi—Aunt Mimi, Portuguese slang for the U.S. immigration authorities—is a worrisome presence in the lives of undocumented Brazilians. The fear of being caught by immigration officials haunts the lives of undocumented Brazilians and colors the quality of their experience in New York. While much of the fear is groundless, tales spread like wildfire about the few Brazilians who are seized by immigration authorities. In early 1990, for example, a story about Tia Mimi's purported apprehension of thirty undocumented Brazilians on a chicken farm in New Jersey was recounted time and again by members of New York's Brazilian community. Perhaps one reason that Brazilians without papers are so anxious about being picked up by INS agents is that in Brazil everyone carries a national identity card, which must be presented to the authorities upon request. Many Brazilians may not realize that there is no equivalent document in the United States and that New York police will not arbitrarily stop them on the street and ask for their papers.

Fear of detention and deportation takes hold almost from the moment that would-be immigrants step off the plane at Kennedy Airport, and for some undocumented Brazilians, much of their subsequent behavior is shaped by it. For example, the owner of a large remittance agency told me that many Brazilians give false New York addresses when filling out forms to send money to Brazil under the mistaken belief that to do otherwise puts them at risk of being apprehended as illegals. Then, too, some Brazilians will not open a bank account; they would have to give their address and are afraid that the bank would put Tia Mimi on their trail. The same fear shades their dealings with the Brazilian consulate in New York City. Some immigrants avoid going to the consulate for any reason because they think that consular officers will report them to U.S. immigration authorities. Brazilians employed by the consulate confirm these anxieties; one woman who works there told me that many of her compatriots are "scared to death" to set foot in the consulate.

TIA MIMI

A Song by Lucinho

Look out for Aunt Mimi,
Look out for Aunt Mimi,
Don't go out or she'll get you.

I am going to act like a polar bear
and hibernate with five liters of rum;
I'm not going to go out in this mess.
I'm far from home
and always hiding from immigration.
Just like me, there are thousands
who want to escape this situation.

Look out for Aunt Mimi,
Look out for Aunt Mimi,
Don't go out or she'll get you

I have no money in my pocket,
and here I'm known as an "illegal."
These people are after me
and things aren't going well
If they get me I'll lose my job
and they're going to have to house and feed me.
Then things will be better
and I won't ever go back.

Look out for Aunt Mimi,
Look out for Aunt Mimi,
Don't go out or she'll get you

Translated from the Portuguese and reprinted with permission courtesy of Lucinho
Bizidão.

Undocumented Brazilians tend to avoid contact not only with their own consulate, but with authorities of any kind—Brazilian or American—fearing that any communication will end in their apprehension and deportation. Moreover, their illegal status and the fear that it generates leads a few to take jobs that pay subminimum wages, while making them loath to complain if employers do not pay them for their work. For the same reason, some are reluctant to report crimes committed against them to the police. One Brazilian told me that even living arrangements are colored by fear; his compatriots reside together under crowded conditions not only to save money but for security; they feel there is safety in numbers.

Brazilians, of course, are not unique in these anxieties. Immigrant rights groups report that a common misconception among illegal aliens of whatever nationality is that if they were to go to the authorities for any reason at all, they would be turned over to the INS. They believe this, even though since the mid-1980s, an executive order has prohibited city agencies from turning undocumented immigrants over to federal authorities unless there is reason to believe that they have committed a crime. "Part of the problem with the undocumented is that they don't know what rights they have," the director of an immigrant rights group told the *New York Times*.[2]

FEAR AND LOATHING IN QUEENS

I personally witnessed the near-paranoid fear of Tia Mimi that haunts many Brazilians. On a cold Sunday morning in February, my husband and I, accompanied by a Brazilian friend, visited Dona Dahlia's rooming house in Queens.

My Brazilian friend had lived at Dona Dahlia's and still had many friends there; I had visited her house before and interviewed some of her boarders. Still, when our little entourage arrived, except for Dona Dahlia, none of the Brazilian residents would have anything to do with us. One by one, they began vanishing from sight.

What was the explanation for this peculiar behavior? The problem was that my husband had a camera and, at my request and with Dona Dahlia's permission, he was taking pictures of her rooming house for this book. Later I learned that her Brazilian boarders were so afraid that we were part of an INS plot to catch and deport them that after we left, some of them took their money and other valuables to friends' houses for safekeeping in case Dona Dahlia's was raided by INS agents.

The fear of deportation among Brazilians and other undocumented immigrants, said a Brazilian consular official, is exaggerated because most of the illegals who are picked up and deported meet this fate when they first arrive in the United States, having failed to pass muster with immigration officials upon entry at Kennedy Airport. In fact, relatively few undocumented aliens are picked up in the "interior"—away from the border or port of entry—either at their workplaces or in their neighborhoods. The fears of most undocumented Brazilians are due to what the consular official called "a lack of information"; the actual risk of being caught simply does not warrant their level of anxiety. In his three years at the consulate, the official had heard of only one undocumented Brazilian who was arrested by U.S. immigration authorities and subsequently deported. The reality is that the INS does not have sufficient personnel to actively pursue illegal aliens, Brazilian or otherwise.

None of this is meant to imply that undocumented Brazilians run no risk of being caught by U.S. immigration authorities. The INS does make occasional raids, usually when agents are tipped off that a large number of undocumented immigrants are working in a particular location. Indeed, there were at least two raids against undocumented Brazilians in New York City while I was doing my research there. In February 1991, the INS raided a shoe shine shop in midtown Manhattan; I was told that most of the Brazilians who worked there were able to flee out the back door without being apprehended. At about the same time, there were a series of raids on go-go bars in New York and also on the homes of some of the dancers. For about three months following the crackdown, dancers without green cards could not get work in the city. Many took jobs in go-go bars in New Jersey, which had not been subject to INS raids.

Then, too, over the course of my research I was regaled with stories of Brazilians informing on one another to the immigration authorities and was told that the "Don't do that to me or I'll call Tia Mimi" threat was a common one among members of the Brazilian community. It was said, for example, that the raids on New York go-go bars had been instigated by a Brazilian dancer who denounced her compatriots to the INS. And when an undocumented Brazilian living quietly with his family in a small town in Connecticut was suddenly picked up and deported by the INS, this too was said to be the work of an informer. Revenge and greed were held responsible for these betrayals of compatriots. I was told that the INS paid informers $500 for tips on the whereabouts of undocumented aliens and that some immigrants simply could not resist the lure of easy money. Nevertheless—and I want to emphasize this—I was not able to document a single case of such a denunciation, and I remain skeptical that they actually occur with any frequency.

But life in the Big Apple is not all work and steering clear of Tia Mimi. After living in New York for a year or two, Brazilian immigrants become more relaxed about their undocumented status, and some even begin to enjoy themselves. As the months go by, many are no longer content to go from home to work and back home again. They begin spending some of their hard-earned dollars on an occasional night out at a restaurant or a nightclub, they get together for a party at a friend's house, or they start playing on one of the ubiquitous soccer teams that crosscut New York's myriad ethnic communities. It is to these leisure activities that we now turn.

Having Fun

How do Brazilian immigrants in New York City spend their time during the few hours a week when they are not working? What do they do for entertainment? The paucity of leisure in New York is unlike what most were accustomed to in Brazil. Because of the long hours at work and the persistent desire to save money, the social life of Brazilian immigrants in New York City is a truncated version of what it was back home. This is why in this regard virtually every Brazilian I talked to compared the United States unfavorably with Brazil. "Leisure is very costly here," they said, meaning two things: Leisure is expensive because it takes time away from work, resulting in the unhappy equation: the more leisure, the less money earned. Moreover, leisure activities—going to the movies, to plays, to bars and restaurants—cost a lot in a city like New York.

Some Brazilians, especially those from Rio de Janeiro, fondly reminisced about the spontaneity of social life in Brazil. They spoke glowingly of young people's going to the beach and to bars and restaurants with groups of friends. A *carioca* painted an idyllic word picture of handsome men and women with lean bronzed bodies sipping *caipirinhas*—a potent mix of Brazilian cane alcohol, limes, and sugar—at an outdoor cafe in Ipanema. A *mineiro* with glistening eyes recalled picnics with friends at a waterfall near his hometown. Another Brazilian basked in the recollection of the monthly parties she used to throw, and yet another described the *saudades* (homesickness, longing) she feels when she thinks about weekends back home, "the days of sociability," as she called them, when family and friends came together for a leisurely lunch or cookout.

Brazilians contrast their attenuated social life in New York with these blissful portraits of their idle hours back home. "In New York when I'm not working," said one woman, "I stay home with my husband, watch TV, and maybe have a glass of wine." On weekends in New York, noted another, "people go shopping instead of getting together with family and friends. All the stores are open and the health clubs are full." Some Brazilian immigrants even denied that their compatriots in New York enjoy any leisure at all. One young woman told me how struck she was by the "materialism" of the Brazilians she met in the city, by how differently they acted in the United States than in Brazil. For immigrants, she said, "money is in first, second, and third place; all they do is work. They don't go to the movies or the theater or read books. They have no social life at all."

Although I personally met only one Brazilian immigrant who claimed to do absolutely nothing but work, eat, and sleep, I did hear many tales about such single-minded money-makers. There was the one, for example, about the five or six young men, all employed as dishwashers, who shared a small tenement apartment in Spanish Harlem. It was said that they only went home to sleep since they ate most of their meals on the job. Aside from paying for rent and transportation, they saved every penny they earn. "They are not here to live, only to make money," a Brazilian who resides in the same building remarked with some distaste. While this case may be apocryphal, I was often told how reluctant Brazilian immigrants are, particularly when they first come to New York, to spend money on restaurants, nightclubs, or concerts. This is partially borne out by my own data on one hundred immigrants in the city. Half said that they ate at restaurants, at least occasionally, but only one-third had ever attended a concert featuring Brazilian music, and a mere 20 percent went out to nightclubs.

A NIGHT ON THE TOWN

Xadrez, a popular Brazilian night spot, is on the second floor above a Spanish restaurant on a busy, ethnically diverse thoroughfare in Queens. A flight of stairs leads up to a pleasant, whitewashed dining room with large color photos of scenic sights in Minas Gerais—the home of the restaurant's owner. An open barbecue takes up one corner of the room. The restaurant specializes in *churrasco á rodizio*, a sort of round robin barbecue in which waiters pass from table to table with large skewers of grilled meats, forking pieces of beef, pork, and chicken onto customers' plates. Heaping platters of rice, black beans, french fries, and potato salad accompany the meal.

When we arrived at 10:30 on a Saturday night, the place was half-full. Customers were eating dinner, and tapes of Brazilian music played in the background. As the evening progressed, more and more people arrived; by midnight, there was not a seat to be had. About seventy or eighty patrons were there that night, and I am quite certain that I was the only non-Brazilian among them.

Earlier in the evening, two musicians had begun playing a variety of popular Brazilian music, including carnival songs and such golden oldies as the classic samba "Brazil." The small dance floor was packed, and two couples—professional dancers—put on a very slick performance of lambada dancing. The place rocked with the strains of bossa nova, lambada, samba, and afoxe. People sitting at tables jumped to their feet and began dancing in place when a favorite carnival song was played. When we left at 2:30 A.M. the place was still packed and the music and dancing still going strong.

When they do go out, Brazilians tend to congregate in restaurants and nightclubs that feature Brazilian food and/or music. A popular eatery in Manhattan is a Portuguese-owned restaurant that features an "all you can eat" lunch buffet for $4.95. The place is usually packed, especially on weekdays, when Brazilians and Americans line up to take advantage of the bargain prices. This is the one Brazilian restaurant in Manhattan that has a steady immigrant clientele. Immigrants patronize the other Brazilian dining establishments far less because they are deemed "too expensive"; these restaurants cater instead to Brazilian tourists, the resident Brazilian elite, and Americans looking for a new and different ethnic fare.

When I began my research in 1988, there was one Brazilian-owned bar and cafe in Astoria, the largest Brazilian residential neighborhood in the city, but by 1991, at least two more had opened in response to the continuing migration from Brazil. Entering the Last Chance Café, the original Brazilian hangout, one could well have been in Brazil. The atmosphere of the cafe, established in late 1984 by a woman from Minas Gerais, is working-class Brazilian—spare, with simple formica tables and chairs, no tablecloths, and a handwritten menu with the specials of the day tacked on the wall. A jukebox and two video arcade games are off to the side. The Last Chance Café has a primarily Brazilian clientele, although a few Hispanics and an occasional American are brought there by Brazilian friends. A limited menu features such Brazilian fare as black beans and rice, *frango à passarinho*, literally, "chicken in the style of a little bird," small pieces of chicken fried in garlic, and Brahma, a Brazilian beer.

Brazilian immigrants do not limit themselves to Brazilian-owned establishments. For example, one popular nightspot in Astoria is Opal Nera, a dark, smoky Italian bar and restaurant that has live dance music on weekends. An ethnically mixed crowd stands three or four deep at the bar or is seated at snug booths and cocktail tables. There are Greeks, Italians, Americans, Puerto Ricans, Dominicans, Bolivians, and the night I was there, ten or fifteen Brazilians. The music is a combination of 1950s polkas and rock and roll hits, with merengues, cha-chas, and an occasional lambada thrown in. The old standard, "Brazil," and a well-known carnival song are played in obvious deference to the establishment's Brazilian patrons.

With the growth of the Brazilian population in parts of the city such as Queens, a few Hispanic nightclubs have begun to feature "authentic Brazilian nights," with lambada music and "beautiful bikini girls." Still, it is hard to tell if these shows are meant to attract a local Brazilian clientele or if they are just capitalizing on the general popularity of things Brazilian. The latter is certainly the case in the Manhattan nightclub that has a "Lambada Night" on Saturdays. Although produced by a long-term Brazilian resident of the city, the show is not geared to the Brazilian community in New York, or at least does not get its patronage. In fact, on the night I was there, the only Brazilians present were the producer, his wife, four or five assistants, the lead singer, and a few musicians; there seemed to be no Brazilians at all in the audience. With or without Brazilians, this production managed to combine the worst features of the New York "club scene" with American caricatures of Brazil. A long line of people were kept waiting on the sidewalk in the cold as a singularly rude door-man decided whom he deemed important enough (or attractive enough) to allow in early. Once inside, the clubgoer was treated to archetypical Carmen Miranda decor, with fake palm trees and a scantily clad singer in a tall headdress with fruit dangling from it.

At another club in Manhattan, however, this same impresario produces a Brazilian show with live music on Sunday nights that does attract a large Brazilian clientele. Starting at 10:00 P.M. and lasting until the wee hours of the morning, Brazilians from all over the Greater New York metropolitan area come to drink, dance, and meet friends. Among the 300 or so Brazilians in attendance, I met immigrants who work as maids, dishwashers, drivers, street vendors, and musicians. Once the music starts—the Brazilian band plays everything from sambas, lambadas, and forrós to contemporary Brazilian rock—the place has the ambience of a club in Rio de Janeiro. The steamy dance floor is packed with gyrating figures, some of them dressed in the flashy, revealing outfits typical of Brazilian *boîtes* (nightclubs).

These Sunday night gatherings are a meeting place. People know one another and come over to greet friends with warm Brazilian-style *abraços* (hugs) and kisses on both cheeks. But most immigrants do not come here very often. The expense and the Sunday night time slot make partying until all hours difficult for those who have to go to work early Monday morning. Three Brazilian women who work as domestics laughed when I asked if they go there every Sunday. "Of course not," they cried—this was a rare night out; they treat themselves to this club only about once every three months.

CONCERT GOING, BRAZILIAN-STYLE

It is easy to spot Brazilians at a concert because they are the ones who get up from their seats and dance to the music. That is what happened at the Oludum concert in New York. The Olodum band, from the Brazilian state of Bahia, gained fame in the United States after they made a recording, *Rhythm of the Saints*, with Paul Simon. Their premiere U.S. appearance was sold out.

During the concert, some people kept leaving their seats and heading toward the back of the theater. The Americans in the audience became disconcerted. After all, it is rude to leave a performance in the middle of a set. As it happens, the members of the audience who were getting up from their seats and appeared to be leaving were actually going to the back of the theater, where there was more room to dance. I have no doubt that all of them were Brazilian.

I thank Professor Michael Turner of Hunter College—CUNY for this anecdote.

Besides restaurants and nightclubs, some immigrants attend the increasingly frequent concerts of such Brazilian superstars as Milton Nascimento, Caetano Veloso, Gilberto Gil, Maria Bethania, and João Gilberto, all of whom played the Big Apple during the course of my research. While one informant said that only the Brazilian elite can afford the tickets to these events, in fact, people from varying strata in New York's Brazilian community attend them at least occasionally. For example, at Milton Nascimento's sold-out performance at Radio City Music Hall, about 50 or 60 percent of the audience of over 2,000 were Brazilians, and there are simply not that many elite Brazilians in the city.

The Sport of Choice

Another popular diversion among members of New York's Brazilian community is that quintessential Brazilian sport, *futebol*, or soccer. There are a number of soccer teams in the city on which Brazilian men play. Some teams have regular games, say, every Tuesday and Thursday evening at a sports complex in Manhattan, or on Saturday afternoons at a city high school, or, weather permitting, on Sundays in Central Park and Flushing Meadow Park in Queens; other teams play more sporadically. Some are composed exclusively of Brazilians—the Athletic Club of Minas, for example—while others are of mixed ethnicity.

Nearly a quarter of the Brazilian men in my sample play *futebol* on a regular or occasional basis, although only 11 percent are members of organized teams. But these rather modest figures belie the importance of soccer as a spectator sport for Brazilian immigrants in New York City because many men, women, and children attend games played by their compatriots. For example, on Memorial Day and Labor Day weekends, at least 300 Brazilians cheered from the sidelines as Brazilian soccer teams competed at an outdoor playing field in Manhattan. These sporting events, sponsored by the largest Brazilian-owned remittance agency in the city, had a decidedly Brazilian touch. Many spectators wore green and gold clothing—the Brazilian national colors. Brazilian flags fluttered overhead, and vendors sold *guaraná* and *salgadinhos*, Brazilian soft drinks and savory snacks.

Brazilian immigrants in New York also got together to watch Brazil play in the 1990 World Cup on television. The two gatherings I attended were in the front yard of a private house in Queens. A large color television set was set up on the window ledge, Brazilian flags flew, and bedsheets strung along the fence afforded some privacy from the rather perplexed neighbors. Between thirty and fifty Brazilians, about two-thirds of them men, were at each gathering—the second game was better attended because it was the quarter-finals and was on a Sunday. With the exception of myself and a Hispanic male, all those present were Brazilian. Nearly everyone was dressed in green and gold, with T-shirts proclaiming "I love Brazil" and "I love Rio" much in evidence.

Beer could be purchased for a dollar a can from the Brazilian host and a large platter of *kibe*, a fried Brazilian snack of Lebanese origin, was passed around. When Brazil scored the lone goal of the first game, the crowd went wild. People started jumping up and down and hugging and kissing one another; they threw their arms in the air and danced the samba to imaginary music. A woman shaking a pair of tambourines and a man pounding a large drum added to the general din. In stark contrast, the second game turned into a glum affair when Argentina—Brazil's arch-rival—scored and Brazil was eliminated from the World Cup. One woman choked back tears, while a man moaned despairingly: "Now we're not going to have Carnival," meaning a big victory celebration. But one optimist in the group pointed out that the next World Cup was only four years away and that all those present might see the games in person. After all, he noted, they were scheduled to be played in the United States.

TELEVISION ABROAD

Every three or four weeks, a Brazilian who has just arrived in New York brings videocassette recordings of Brazil's enormously popular evening soap opera, "Pantanal," a melodrama set in the wild interior of southern Mato Grosso state. The six- or seven-hour tapes, about a week's worth of the program, are dutifully passed from friend to friend so that they will not miss Brazilian television's hit of the season even though they are living in the Big Apple.

Among Friends

One Brazilian said that in his own country people entertain at home more than they do after they immigrate to the United States and have to spend long hours at work. But the other side of the leisure coin is the time and expense of going out for a "night on the town" in the Big Apple compared to an evening spent at home with friends. After all, said one Brazilian, it not only costs money to go to a restaurant or a nightclub, but it also may mean a trek into Manhattan by subway or out to Newark by car.[3]

Informal get-togethers and parties with friends are important social activities among many Brazilians in the immigrant community. Carlos, a Brazilian cabdriver, told me that his entire social life revolves around gatherings held nearly every weekend with the same group of ten or twelve Brazilian friends at one of their homes. When members of the core group invite their own friends along, as many as thirty people may show up. Whatever their numbers, they eat, drink whisky, and listen to tapes of Brazilian music. The food is potluck. Clarisa, a member of the group, cooked a large *bacalhau* (codfish) casserole and told a few close friends to come over for dinner, but to her amused chagrin, there was barely enough to go around, when nineteen Brazilians appeared on her doorstep that evening.

Then, there are the (slightly) more formal parties, usually thrown to celebrate a specific event—a marriage, a birth, or a farewell bash for an immigrant returning to Brazil. One I attended celebrated the marriage of a Brazilian man from Minas Gerais to a Brooklyn-born woman. About three-quarters of the guests were Brazilian, including a number of fellow *mineiros* who worked at the restaurant where the groom was employed; the rest were American. The two nationalities did not mix. The Brazilians crowded into the kitchen to drink beer and eat the platters of food that included black beans and *farofa*, toasted manioc flour. As the evening wore on, a few Brazilian couples began dancing the lambada in the living room, while most of the Americans moved to the bedroom to watch MTV, drink Coke, and eat Doritoes.

For many Brazilian immigrants, summertime in New York means beaches and barbecues. Picnics in Central Park and outdoor cookouts are favored warm-weather activities. On summer weekends, knots of Brazilians cluster around a trio of their compatriots playing *batucada*, rhythmic African-Brazilian music, in Central Park. Trips to the shore are especially popular among *cariocas* homesick for the famed beaches of their city by the sea. Clarisa, her boyfriend, and four or five other couples go to Far Rockaway Beach or Jones Beach on Long Island nearly every sunny summer weekend. Brazilians say they can always spot their compatriots at the beach because Brazilian women are the only women who wear *tangas*, tiny string bikinis.

ASTORIA BEACH

One *carioca* (native of Rio de Janeiro) told of her attempt to get a suntan by simulating the condition of a beach in Rio. On the first warm and sunny day in late spring, she donned her string bikini, filled a bucket with salt water, and gingerly made her way to the roof of her low-rise apartment building in Queens. Once she had lain down and doused herself with salt water to ensure a quick tan, a cloud drifted over the sun and a chilly wind began blowing. Thus ended her afternoon "at the beach."

8.1, 8.2 Brazilian street parades and carnivals feature colorful costumes and lively music. This one wound through the streets of Manhattan's East Village.

Things Brazilian

Parades, street fairs, and Carnival parties targeted at New York's Brazilian community comprise another category of entertainment.[4] Over the
course of my field research, parades with Brazilian themes were organized, street fairs celebrating Brazilian Independence Day were held, and
myriad Carnival parties and galas were scheduled each Lenten season.
The street parades, with anywhere from fifty to two hundred participants,
wound their way through Manhattan's Lower East Side, blocking traffic
and drawing curious stares from drivers, pedestrians, and the homeless
living in Tompkins Square Park. The parades featured a Brazilian-American percussion group, floats with Brazilian themes, and elaborately costumed dancers.[5] Some of the women wore the voluminous white skirts,
colorful ropes of beads, and white turbans traditional to the Brazilian
state of Bahia; other women were in bikinis and Carmen Miranda-like
headdresses, and male costumes ranged from sequined suits to tiger
outfits.

The parades were sparsely attended compared to the major event in the
Brazilian calendar, the annual Brazilian Independence Day celebration
and street fair in New York City, which draws thousands of Brazilians
from as far away as Boston.[6] The festival, held on "Brazil Street" (West
46th Street) on a Sunday in early September, was started in 1985 by Jota
Alves, the founder of *The Brasilians*, a monthly newspaper published in
New York. He says he decided to put on the event only after the Brazilian
government was returned to civilian control. There was nothing to celebrate while the military was in power.

From its inception, the fair grew as word of it spread and the city's
Brazilian community burgeoned. Today, for many Brazilians, it is *the*
ethnic event of the year, the one that gives their community visibility. A
large green and gold banner proclaiming Brazil's Independence Day is
strung across West 46th Street. Crowds of people—many also dressed in
green and gold—press against the dozens of booths selling Brazilian food
and drink, posters, handicrafts, tapes, T-shirts, banners, and all manner
of items with Brazilian logos. These booths, set up by entrepreneurs-for-
the-day, compete for attention with Brazilian-owned businesses advertising their wares and adherents of one religious denomination or another
passing out fliers with information about their services. Brazilian music
blares from loudspeakers, and the festival invariably ends with hundreds
of merrymakers dancing the samba in the street amidst mounds of beer
cans, paper plates, and other festival-related trash.

While the Independence Day festival draws the largest crowds, Carnival is the most quintessentially Brazilian event celebrated by the immigrant community in New York.[7] During the 1990 Carnival season, nine

8.3 The Brazilian Independence Day street fair provides an opportunity for entrepreneurs to sell their wares.

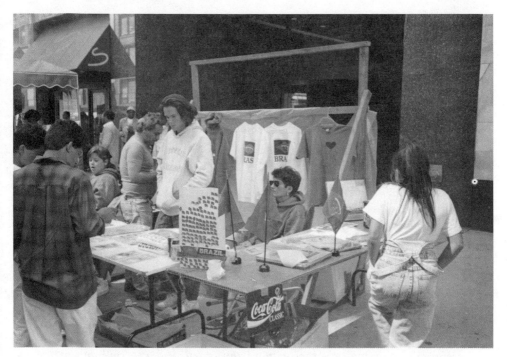

8.4. At the street fair, merchandise with Brazilian logos is a common sight.

separate Carnival galas, parties, and concerts were organized in the city, in addition to those held in Newark and other communities where Brazilians live. In New York City, the celebrations ranged from costly costume balls at such well-known hotels as the Waldorf-Astoria and the Roosevelt and such chic discos as Regine's to parties at a number of nightclubs and a "Carnival in the Rain Forest" concert at the Cathedral of St. John the Divine sponsored by "environmentally conscious businesses" —Ben and Jerry's Ice Cream and The Body Shop among them. I attended what was likely the least expensive—and least chic—Carnival party held in New York that year. For a $15 admission fee, people gathered in a dark, crowded club on Manhattan's Lower East Side to listen to a Brazilian band, dance, and drink beer, wine, and *guaraná*, a Brazilian soft drink. In contrast to most Carnival events, very few people were in costume, and of the 500 or so in attendance, not more than half were Brazilians; Americans and Hispanics also were much in evidence. This suggests that the many Carnival-related activities in New York are not just the result of the increasing presence of Brazilians in the city; they also reflect the burgeoning popularity of things Brazilian.

BRAZILIAN NEWS

In 1991 two enterprises were started to meet the growing demand for Brazilian news and entertainment. One company, Brazil Up-Date, began offering subscribers a weekly four-hour videotape for $13.95 plus postage. The tape included a selection of news, sports, music, and variety shows recorded direct from Brazilian television, "using the latest equipment and edited without commercials."

The other company provided a 900 telephone number to call "from anywhere in the U.S.A." for the latest quotes on the exchange rate for the Brazilian *cruzeiro*, sports scores, and news at a cost of $1.49 a minute. One recorded tape had information on car prices in Brazil and recent figures on the number of AIDS cases in that country.

Aside from parades, street fairs, and Carnival parties, there is also an expanding media market aimed at the Brazilian segment of the Big Apple's ethnic mélange. A weekly radio program that features Brazilian music, with a Portuguese-speaking disc jockey, has been on the air for quite some time. More recently, a Spanish-language radio station began rebroadcasting major soccer games from Brazil, and a second music and news program in Portuguese went on the air. In the fall of 1991, a regularly scheduled Brazilian television program appeared for the first time on New York's Spanish-language channel. The two-hour weekly program consists of Brazilian television shows, including a popular situation comedy, sports highlights, and news.[8]

The Story of a Street

Just how did Manhattan's West 46th Street come to be known as Little Brazil? The story begins in the late 1950s, when two hotels near West 46th Street became the favored accomodations of Brazilian tourists and Brazilian airline personnel. To cater to them, the hotels started offering excursions especially for Brazilian visitors to the city. Soon stores selling small electronics sought by Brazilians began appearing on the street. Blenders, toasters, television sets, and other electrical appliances were sold for a fraction of what they then cost in Brazil.

In the early 1960s, first one and then a second Brazilian restaurant opened its doors; by the mid-1960s, West 46th Street was coming to be known as *a rua brasileira*, "Brazil Street." Varig, the Brazilian national airline, the Bank of Brazil, and the Brazilian consulate were all conveniently within a four-block radius.

It also may be no coincidence that West 46th Street is just one block from West 47th Street, New York's "Jewelry Row." Ever since the 1960s, some Brazilians coming to the city have brought semiprecious stones with them to sell. Although most denied that there was any link between this practice and the location of Little Brazil, one Brazilian remembers an uncle's regularly going to West 47th Street to sell the amethysts and aquamarines he had carried with him from Minas Gerais. Whatever the case may be, today a number of Brazilians involved in the jewelry trade are just a stone's throw from Brazil Street.

By all accounts, Little Brazil boomed during the 1970s; at one time it was dotted with perhaps twenty or twenty-five Brazilian-owned businesses. Travel agencies, restaurants, and above all, small boutiques catering to Brazilian tourists lined the street. They sold all manner of goods favored by Brazilian visitors: small electronics, sweatshirts, cosmetics, film, and cameras. Because of relatively low prices (and the fact that the merchants hardly ever collected the sales tax), some tourists bought in quantity and then resold the goods at a profit in Brazil.

Most West 46th Street merchants agree that business peaked in the late 1970s and early 1980s and, with some exceptions, has been in gradual decline ever since. A government-imposed exit tax on Brazilian tourists, restrictions on foreign imports, the fact that many electronic items once bought in New York are now manufactured cheaply in Brazil, and most important, the general weakening of the Brazilian economy, which has meant a decrease in tourism, are all blamed for the loss of business in Little Brazil. As one shop owner put it, "We are in crisis since Brazil is in crisis because we make our living from Brazilians. When Brazil has a recession, we have a recession."

During the 1980s, many of the West 46th Street boutiques that catered to Brazilian tourists closed. Since they did not cater to New York's resident Brazilian community, they were not helped by the flow of Brazilian immigrants to the city. Then, too, some boutique owners moved to Miami to open stores to take advantage of burgeoning Brazilian tourism in Florida, much of it spurred by Disney World.

Today few stores on Brazil Street can survive on Brazilian tourists alone—rents are high and there are simply not enough tourists to support them. Because of this, perhaps three-quarters of the shops that were strictly tourist oriented have gone out of business. But others have made it through changing times. The two Brazilian restaurants, for example, whose clientele was once about 70 percent Brazilian and 30 percent American, now have this ratio reversed. Fortunately for them, New York is a city full of restaurant-goers anxious to try out new and "exotic" cuisines.

The influx of Brazilian immigrants in the late 1980s and early 1990s did breathe new life into Little Brazil as a meeting place and as a small corner of Brazilian life in the swirling metropolis. Brazilian tourists still congregate there, and although West 46th Street is not a regular shopping area for Brazilian residents in the sense that Chinatown is for local Chinese-Americans, Brazilians who live in the city visit the street at least occasionally. They go to buy one of the newspapers that arrive daily from some ten cities around Brazil or a copy of *Veja*, the Brazilian news weekly, or a package of *farinha* (manioc flour), or a just-released tape by a Brazilian singer. Some immigrants regularly go to the street to wire money home at the city's largest Brazilian-owned remittance agency or to buy plane tickets at one of the travel agencies that cater to Brazilians. And there is another sign of the new immigrant times: most Brazilian-owned businesses on Brazil Street report a steady stream of Brazilian drop-ins inquiring about jobs.

Despite this activity, in some ways Little Brazil is less Brazilian than it was in the past. The construction of large office buildings on the street and the influx of other ethnic groups have diluted its distinctive Brazilian character. Korean, Chinese, Japanese, Italian, and Argentine eateries dot the block, along with luncheonettes and take-outs of no known nationality. Moreover, some of the businesses on West 46th Street that cater to Brazilians—shops with such names as Rio Electronics or Hello, Brazil— are actually owned by Americans, Koreans, Japanese, and Argentines who speak no Portuguese and have never set foot in Brazil. Maybe this is a true sign of success; the street has became so famous as a magnet for Brazilians that non-Brazilian entrepreneurs have tried to cash in on it by passing themselves off as compatriots.

Between Two Worlds

The songs of birds are prettier in Brazil.

—*Brazilian immigrant in New York City*

Brazilian immigrants in New York City are people between two worlds. As they themselves often say, "We are here, but our heads [or hearts] are in Brazil." Many are in New York, but are not of it. This is evident in a number of ways. While nearly every immigrant has at least some contact with non-Brazilians at work, more than half of those in my sample say that all of their friends in New York are Brazilian; another 30 percent have a few American or Hispanic friends as well.[9] As one informant told me, most Brazilians do not have American friends and are not invited to American homes because "people in New York don't have much interest in foreigners except to hire them to work as baby-sitters or maids." Moreover, almost two-thirds keep up-to-date about happenings in Brazil by regularly reading Brazilian newspapers or magazines, and some 60 percent keep in touch with their ethnicity by frequenting businesses in Little Brazil, buying Brazilian records, tapes, videos, or food products, and/or going to Brazilian restaurants.

Lack of proficiency in English contributes to feelings of isolation and otherness. Sixty percent of the Brazilians in my sample said that their English was fair to poor, while only 13 percent said that it was excellent or fluent. Although many had taken classes in English at one time or another in Brazil or in the United States, only one-quarter of the Brazilians I interviewed were currently studying English. These findings mesh with Luis Guerra's study of English-language acquisition and acculturation among Brazilian immigrants in New York City. He found that both men and women function only at the "novice-plus" level of English proficiency. Moreover, he suggests that language facility and acculturation to "American ways"—which tend to go hand in hand—are more a function of job type than of length of time in the country. Car service drivers and busboys are uniformly less acculturated than housekeepers, baby-sitters, and construction workers, who in turn are less attuned to American culture than waiters.[10]

Finally, because of their frequent contact with friends and relatives in Brazil, many Brazilian immigrants in New York say their "heads are in two places." Whether or not they travel to Brazil themselves depends on how long they have been in the United States and, more important, on their legal status. With a green card, which confers resident alien status, one can enter and leave the United States at will as long as the stay abroad does not exceed one year. Consequently, the general rule is that the longer immigrants have lived in the United States, the greater the likelihood that they have green cards and thus the more probable that they have been back to Brazil for a visit. Nevertheless, despite the recency of the Brazilian migration stream and its high percentage of undocumented aliens, a surprising 57 percent of my sample had visited Brazil at least once since arriving in the United States. Slightly fewer (54 percent) have had friends or relatives from Brazil visit them. But the most constant means of contact with the homeland is via telephone; 95 percent of the immigrants in my sample call Brazil on a regular basis. In fact, they spend sizable sums on long distance calls; most spend between $85 to $150 a month, while quite a few (sheepishly) admit that their bills regularly come to $200 a month or more. Brazilians certainly take AT&T's advertising campaign "phone home" to heart!

The ties that bind immigrants to friends and relatives in Brazil are perhaps best illustrated by the number of immigrants who send remittances there since some studies suggest that regular, frequent, and high rates of remitting money indicate a close association and identification with the home community as well as a higher probability of return.[11] Just over half of the Brazilians in my New York sample send money home on a regular or an occasional basis. Sixty percent send money to their parents, some 20 percent send money to their spouses and/or children, and the rest send money to other relatives, usually siblings. Still, my data suggest that a substantial number of those sending remittances to their parents are actually saving money for their own return to Brazil—to buy an apartment, start a business, or make a major purchase or investment of some sort.

The "head in two world" syndrome—residence in New York combined with regular contact with Brazil and the determination of most Brazilian immigrants to return home within a few years—shapes their sense of community in New York. After all, most would argue, if we are in this city only temporarily, if we are just working and saving for the day we go back to Brazil, why should we care about building a life in New York? Why should we spend our limited time on anything but making money? This lack of community building has resulted in a paucity of Brazilian institutions in New York, a topic to which we now turn.

CHAPTER NINE

Little Brazil: Is It a Community?

The predominance of kinship in ordering social life explains the relative absence in Brazil of such voluntary associations as parent-teacher groups, garden clubs, and the like. People give greater value to kinship relations than to relations based on common interest or even occupation.

—CHARLES WAGLEY, *The Latin American Tradition*

[Immigrants] simply do not see themselves as being around long enough to make most issues of community development and structure relevant.

—MICHAEL J. PIORE, *Birds of Passage*

DURING THE FIRST WEEK of my research in New York City, I went to a Brazilian street parade. I sensed a strong feeling of Brazilian ethnicity and community there, and I wrote in my field notes: "A parade like this could not take place in a dispersed community with no sense of its own distinctiveness. Brazilianness is alive and well in New York City." At the time I assumed that all the participants in the parade were Brazilian; in fact, at most, 20 percent of the dancers and musicians were Brazilian. Nor did I know that this was a surface event that only gave the appearance of community—a Potemkin village with precious few underpinnings.

As it turned out, the lack of community ethos and community associations was one of the most striking and, for a time, most puzzling features of the Brazilian immigrant scene. But several factors help explain the paucity of social cohesion and ethnic structures among Brazilian immigrants in New York City. For one thing, Brazil lacks the tradition of clubs and mutual interest associations that exists in the United States. As anthropologist Conrad P. Kottak notes, "[T]he typical American belongs to dozens of non–kin based groups. These include churches, political parties, clubs, teams, occupational groups, organizations, associations and committees. In Brazil, where home and extended family hold their own so vigorously against the external world, non-kin associations are fewer."[1] Brazilians are far more likely than Americans to live close to family members and to spend much of their leisure time with them. Getting together with relative strangers to discuss gardening or stamp collecting or to plan a cake sale strikes Brazilians as rather odd.

For Brazilian immigrants in New York City, the absence of a cultural tradition of club formation coalesces with their near-universal intention of returning to Brazil. Most immigrants do not envision being in the United States long enough to justify putting their scant time and energy into local associations of any kind. From their perspective they are actually sojourners, not settlers; they are here today, but in all probability will be gone tomorrow. Moreover, to join a club or an organization might be a sign of permanence, an indication that they were really planning to stay in the United States, a suggestion that most Brazilians vehemently deny. Finally, the absence of community cohesion may simply reflect the recency of this migration stream. The lack of community organization among Brazilian immigrants, then, must be understood in structural and temporal rather than in personalistic terms—the ones most often cited by Brazilians themselves. Brazilians lack common interest groups and associations because of economic, social, and cultural factors, not because of the failure of strong community-oriented leaders to emerge or because of the grandiose schemes, self-serving projects, or other shortcomings of those that have come forth.[2]

The Ideology of Disunity

Brazilians often talk about the absence of an esprit de corps in their community and compare themselves unfavorably in this regard to New York's other new immigrant groups. All the Brazilians present at a gathering in Queens insisted that they alone among ethnic groups in the city lack a sense of community. Lamented one, "We have no club, no school, no union, no support from other Brazilians." "Everyone in New York has a community association except us," said another. Over and over, I was told that there are no Brazilian ethnic, social, or professional groups, no Brazilian occupational specialties akin to those of Korean greengrocers and Indian newsstand dealers—only commercial enterprises, such as those on West 46th Street. "We are 80,000 strong," complained my research assistant, a Brazilian with a degree in anthropology, "and we don't have a single social club, not even one."

One Brazilian old-timer in New York told me of his unsuccessful attempt to get support from a Brazilian business association to start a club for Brazilian immigrants in the city. This group, comprising long-resident entrepreneurs, many with businesses on West 46th Street, directs its charitable efforts exclusively to the needy in Brazil. Thus, on another occasion, despite pleas for help to this group on behalf of a Brazilian immigrant who needed $1,000 to bury her husband, who had died suddenly of a heart attack, none was forthcoming; the money was eventually raised by members of the Brazilian Catholic congregation in Manhattan.

Brazilians in New York also lack a physical community, a distinctly Brazilian neighborhood or shopping district with which they can identify. Even the single block of Little Brazil in Manhattan is not entirely their own—there are Japanese, Argentine, Korean, and Italian restaurants along it, as well as businesses of no distinct nationality. And in Astoria, Queens, the primary Brazilian residential area in the city, almost no outward signs of Brazilians' presence exist. A few scattered stores selling Brazilian products, a bar, and a handful of other Brazilian-owned businesses are overwhelmed by the strong Greek flavor of the neighborhood.

Moreover, because the Brazilian business sector is so circumscribed, newly arrived immigrants from Brazil, in contrast to their Chinese, Indian, Pakistani, Korean, and Greek counterparts, have no ready source of jobs within their own community. They have no economic basis of ethnic solidarity.[3] Quite the contrary, said one informant, the few Brazilians who do own businesses "not only don't help new immigrants, they exploit them by paying them less and working them longer hours." Nor do established Brazilian enterprises, such as the New York branches of major Brazilian banks, airlines, and other companies do very much to support the handful of community-based groups that do exist in the city. After a year of vigorous fund-raising, the founder of a small Brazilian cultural center on Manhattan's Lower East Side managed to come up with only $2,000 to help fund the center's activities.

Yet another example of the absence of community involvement is the lack of support for this cultural center's classes in such traditional Brazilian specialties as *capoeira*, the martial arts dance, and *batucada*, Brazilian percussion music. These classes, and similar ones that are given privately, have attracted only a handful of the thousands of Brazilians residing in New York City. For example, of the dozens of students in the *capoeira* classes that have been taught in New York since the mid-1970s, only about five of those now enrolled are Brazilian. Ninety percent of those who signed up for a samba school are not Brazilian, and Brazilians accounted for only 10 percent of the *batucada* players who participated in the Carnival street parade. These groups, it would seem, primarily serve American aficionados of Brazilian music and culture, rather than Brazilians involved in their own heritage.

The story is similar for "TV Brasil," a weekly half-hour program of Brazilian news, sports, and music. Started in 1988, the program was aimed at New York's Brazilian community. At first, interest in the show was quite high, and Brazilian businesses advertised on it. But, said the program's producer, since most Brazilians are in New York only to save money for the return to Brazil, advertisers began to feel that their ads were not attracting new customers; after a few months, they stopped buying airtime. Also, unlike the Hispanic market, the Brazilian market is not large enough to interest national advertisers. "TV Brasil" 's producer tried to get Coors Beer to buy ads on the program by exaggerating the size of the Brazilian market in New York; she claimed it was 200,000. Even then, Coors turned her down, saying that the market was too small.

After about two years "TV Brasil" 's producer despaired of ever getting sufficent support from the Brazilian community. Consequently, she eliminated its Brazilian news and sports components and changed the format to an all–music and video program called "Sounds Brazilian." Now, when she gets calls from Brazilians complaining that they miss the news about Brazil, she tells them testily, "The show's not for you anymore because when it was, you didn't support it." Indeed, the audience for the new show is largely people who like Brazilian music, rather than Brazilians themselves. Today, its main advertiser is a Rio de Janeiro–based company that runs tours to Brazil for Americans.

All this is in marked contrast to the myriad community associations and media outlets found among many other recent immigrants to the city. As just one example, there are forty-six Korean churches in New York City alone, most of which have their own church-based clubs and activities, in addition to the Korean community's innumerable professional, recreational, political, social, and civic clubs and organizations. Even the tiny Yemeni community has clubs that cater to its needs.[4] But Brazilians are not the only new immigrants in New York who lack community organizations; in this respect, Israelis and Brazilians have a lot in common. Moshe Shokeid, an anthropologist who published an ethnography on Israelis in the city, found that "Israeli immigrants in New York . . . have not initiated even one viable institution of their own . . . not even one active voluntary association. . . ." Shokeid also noted that although Israelis, like Brazilians, "often express a need for ethnic gatherings and corporate action . . . they appear completely incompetent in this sphere. . . ."[5] Not coincidentally, most Israelis, like most Brazilians, vehemently deny their immigrant status; they say they are mere sojourners in New York, counting the days until the return home.

Brazilians themselves offer various explanations for their lack of community spirit and organization. One woman who has lived in New York since the mid-1970s blamed it on the growing size of the Brazilian population in the city; when she first arrived, few Brazilians were living in New York, and everyone knew everyone else. "We had more of a sense of community then," she said with nostalgia. Another Brazilian cited the feelings of distrust that permeate a community with so many undocumented immigrants. Because of fear of informers, he said, people are uneasy about getting together in clubs or elsewhere with compatriots they do not know very well. A Brazilian journalist, a longtime resident of the city, agreed, saying that the lack of community was due to Brazilian "paranoia" about the INS. Although denunciations to the authorities are probably rare, when they do occur, people become "paranoid that whenever they have a disagreement with another Brazilian they will be reported to Tia Mimi." Others decried the lack of spirited, unselfish leaders who might have taken a hand in community building. A Brazilian pastor noted the dearth of Brazilian professionals who might assume leadership roles: "Why there are only eight or ten Brazilian doctors, lawyers, and dentists in all of New York City." But the wryest explanation was offered by a man from Minas Gerais, who pointed out that until very recently, Brazilians simply had had no experience as immigrants: "They have not been immigrants since the Portuguese discovered Brazil in 1500. They discovered it and then they just sat there."

Still, a majority of Brazilians were realists about the lack of community spirit. They said that they and most other Brazilians were in New York for one reason only: to make as much money as quickly as possible for the return to Brazil. They do not get involved in clubs or other activities because that would take time away from this one overriding goal. Or as one Brazilian emphatically put it, "We don't have an immigrant spirit because *we are not immigrants.*"

The Litany of Complaints

Brazilians in New York give you nothing but headaches.

—*Brazilian immigrant*

Economist Michael J. Piore graphically describes the material motives that fuel the lives of new immigrants. They are, he says, "people divorced from a social setting, operating outside the constraints and inhibitions that it imposes, working totally and exclusively for money."[6] His analysis cogently explains why Brazilians complain that their compatriots in New York behave very badly toward one another. The litany of complaints about such behavior was so endless and so redundant that it was the rare informant indeed who did not tell me that Brazilians "step on each other," "don't help each other out," "don't want other Brazilians to get ahead," "cheat on each other," "steal from each other," "only think of themselves," or some other variant of this baldly derogatory theme. Over and over, immigrants repeated that they had few or no Brazilian friends, or that when they heard people speaking Portuguese on the street or in the subway or in a store, they steered clear of them because they did not want to "get involved with other Brazilians." As one immigrant put it, "Brazilians run from each other."

Some said that even before they left Brazil, they were advised by return migrants to stay away from Brazilians in New York, or that shortly after they arrived in the city, friends and relatives warned them not to have anything to do with other Brazilians there. At first, many were perplexed by this advice because, as one told me, "normally when you travel outside of Brazil you enjoy meeting other Brazilians—you can speak Portuguese and you identify with them." But, she added, Brazilians quickly learn this is not the case in New York.[7]

FROM THE SUBLIME TO THE RIDICULOUS

A few Brazilians are so down on their compatriots that blame reaches farfetched proportions. One Brazilian immigrant in New York says that he never eats in Brazilian restaurants in the city because they are too expensive: "I can eat the same rice and beans in an Hispanic restaurant and they charge a lot less." He also complained about how much it cost to send money to Brazil after a Brazilian remittance agency raised its rates: "Brazilians create inflation wherever they go," the man said in exasperation.

The tirade was never ending. Brazilians, said at least a dozen different informants, are "the most disunited ethnic group in the city" (*a raça mas desunida na cidade*). This is why, they said, it is so difficult to get Brazilians to act in their own collective interest. Old-timers do not help newcomers with advice about jobs and housing; "they just pass on the suffering." Why? I asked. "Because the only reason Brazilians come here is to make money. Nothing else matters, including personal relationships." A woman from Rio illustrated what she meant: A Brazilian whom she considered a friend charged a weeks's wages for finding her a job as a live-in housekeeper. Even though she hated the job and left after a very short time, her "friend" refused to return the finder's fee. Another informant provided a comparable example: a man from Governador Valadares asked another *valadarense* who was returning home to carry some cash to his family there. The traveler agreed to deliver the money only after being paid for the "favor." Experiences like these, informants say, account for their lack of Brazilian friends. "I know a hundred Brazilians in New York City, but only four [or eight, or ten] of them are my friends, the rest are worthless," was a habitual remark, along with, "I can count the number of my Brazilian friends on the fingers of one hand."

Another leitmotif of these conversations was that Brazilians undergo an extreme Dr. Jekyll and Mr. Hyde metamorphosis in New York, where they are transformed into selfish, self-centered individuals. "It's unfortunate that people become so cold and egotistical here because it creates ill will among us," one immigrant opined. Said a woman from São Paulo who works as a domestic servant in New York, "I am ashamed of my race here. Brazilians change when they come here, and they begin to think only about money." A journalist from the same city agreed, arguing that because of their single-minded pursuit of money, his compatriots live by a different ethic in the United States than in Brazil. Immigrants, he said, "don't let anything get in the way of their greed; they step on each other; there are more disagreements here, and relationships suffer." And one Brazilian counterposed the ambience of New York, where "nobody cares about anybody and everyone's alone," against a syrupy characterization of camaraderie in Brazil, where "everyone's like a dear brother."

The attitude of "looking out for number one" was often linked to jealousy and competitiveness, said to be twin scourges in the immigrant community. I was told that the first question Brazilians ask each other when they meet is, "Do you have a green card?" And the second question is, "How much does your job pay?"[8] One immigrant said that when Brazilians see their compatriots arriving in New York, their first thought is, Have they come to grab my job? Some Brazilians are, indeed, fearful of losing their jobs to other Brazilians, particularly if the job pays relatively well. And this perceived competition for jobs, along with widespread fear of Tia Mimi, can be a lethal combination. Suspicion and distrust is heightened every time a tale circulates of one immigrant's denouncing another to the INS. In recounting the story of how her son was denounced to immigration authorities by a fellow Brazilian who was after his job, a woman said the ambience was akin to that of a "combat zone."

Immigrants from Minas Gerais were often singled out for special condemnation in these diatribes against Brazilian rapaciousness. While "all Brazilians exploit each other," I was told, "*mineiros* are the worst of the lot." Unlike the more worldly *paulistas* and *cariocas*, people from Minas Gerais, it was said, had little experience with big city life, were "square," and were "generally ignorant." *Mineiros*, a man from Rio averred, "have bad intentions" and are the source of many problems in the immigrant community because there are so many of them.

What is most intriguing about the endless stream of complaints by Brazilians about their compatriots is that without one another they could not survive in New York. Nearly every Brazilian immigrant I met in the city got his or her start there with the aid of Brazilian friends or relatives. Two-thirds of the Brazilians in my sample received help from other Brazilians in finding a place to live, and over one-third had help in locating a job. Even long after arrival, the informal immigrant employment network continues to operate; it helps Brazilians who have lost their jobs find others, or it helps them locate positions with better wages or hours.

Then, too, what little leisure time Brazilian immigrants have is spent with their compatriots. Informal gatherings, parties, nights out at a restaurant or club, and sports events are usually all-Brazilian affairs. Moreover, Brazilians regularly do favors for one another. When an immigrant who had gone back to Brazil was discontented there and wrote to his former roommate in New York that he regretted having left the United States, she offered to send him a plane ticket, assuring him that he could repay her once he returned to the city and found a job. This and dozens of similar examples of mutual aid certainly belie the stereotype of the grasping, self-centered Brazilian.

And it is also true that amidst the litany of complaints, some immigrants acknowledge the help they receive from their compatriots and suggest that the rhetoric about the community's pulling apart at the seams is exaggerated. "It's more talk than practice," said a journalist, who pointed to the wide network of Brazilian friends that most immigrants have. "Just read their address books. They're filled with Brazilian names." "Sure, they bad-mouth each other," another immigrant said of his fellow Brazilians, "but look at who helps them, look at who all their friends are." As further evidence of at least occasional community spirit, some immigrants noted the thousands of Brazilians from all over the northeastern United States who attend the Brazilian Independence Day street fair in Manhattan. Similarly, whenever a Brazilian singer or musician plays in a New York club or gives a concert, there is always a sizable contingent of Brazilians in the audience, noisily affirming their ethnicity.

The Image of Limited Good

Amidst the barrage of complaints about fellow immigrants, one group was singled out for special vilification: Brazilian businessowners in New York City. Although relatively few Brazilians are employed by fellow Brazilians, this did not stop any of my Brazilian informants from offering vitriolic secondhand accounts of what it is like to work for one of their compatriots. Instead of helping their fellow Brazilians, I was told repeatedly, Brazilian employers "exploit" them. The owner of one thriving business in Brazilian products was said to pay her employees $300 for twelve-hour-day, seven-day weeks, ignoring complaints about working conditions because she was well aware that the employees lacked green cards and were unlikely to go to the authorities.[9] And Brazilians who worked for well-to-do Brazilian families as live-in servants told tales of "slave" conditions wrought by "employers from hell" who had them work day and night for subminimum wages.[10]

Some immigrants' complaints about Brazilian business owners were specifically directed at old-timers in the community, people who have lived in New York for fifteen, twenty, and even thirty years. These Brazilians—generally from fairly modest backgrounds themselves—have had varying degrees of success as entrepreneurs in the city, and many own businesses on West 46th Street. Having lived in the city for years, they have carved out business niches for themselves; they own travel and remittance agencies, restaurants that feature Brazilian food, stores that sell small electronics and other goods aimed at the Brazilian tourist trade, and shops that stock Brazilian newspapers, magazines, tapes, and other items sought by resident Brazilians. These established entrepreneurs appear to be doing quite well, and and I was told that they aim to keep it that way. Old-timers are loath to help their more recently arrived compatriots, averred many new immigrants, because they are seen as a potential source of future competition.

In this respect, the behavior of some old-timers reflects the mind-set that anthropologists call "the image of limited good," the idea that all desirable things in the world—money, power, prestige, health, and various material goods—are finite so that every time someone gets more of these "good" things, someone else necessarily gets less.[11] Not only does this mind-set result in a less than open arms welcome to new immigrants, it also makes for less than cordial relations among the Little Brazil merchants themselves. As one of them told me, "If someone opens a shop, he looks at me as an enemy, not as a friend." Moreover, he insisted, this is not just a healthy spirit of competition: "Many businesses compete with each other but they still have their clubs and associations that work for the common good. But not my countrymen on 46th Street." Another Brazilian said that his compatriots were "monopolistic," and that to them, "competition means killing the other guy." What has this meant for the community? I asked. "Well," he replied in a tone of disgust, "it means that you can only have one newspaper, one travel agency, one remittance agency, or one of anything. Otherwise war breaks out. Brazilians just don't see competition as healthy."

The image of limited good has led to some sharp cleavages among the merchants of Little Brazil, who operate on its assumption that "more for someone else inevitably means less for me." There are, for example, the three Brazilian merchants whose enmity toward one another is legendary. The problem? They own similar enterprises. I encountered this mind-set in João, a Brazilian who works in Little Brazil. We became friendly, and somewhat later, I befriended João's former employer, also Brazilian, with whom he had had a falling-out. João told a mutual acquaintance that his former employer had "stolen" my friendship—a limited good from his point of view—as if I could not be friendly with more than one person at a time.

9.1 Vendors at the street fair sell a variety of Brazilian food, including churrasco, Brazilian barbecue, and guaraná, a Brazilian soft drink.

9.2 In 1989, the Brazilian Independence Day street fair was held despite a steady downpour.

THE BRAZILIAN STREET FAIR: A CASE STUDY IN DISUNITY

The fifth annual street fair celebrating September 7, Brazil's Independence Day, was to take place on West 46th Street in early fall of 1990. The street fair had grown vastly since its modest inception in 1985, attracting Brazilians from as far away as Boston. Estimates of the crowd ranged up to 150,000, and the fair gave the Brazilian community a modicum of visibility. In fact, the year before, New York mayor Ed Koch had attended the fair and proclaimed it "Brazil Day" in the city.

But the 1990 fair was canceled three weeks before it was to take place. The announcement was made in New York's Brazilian newspaper, which reported that there had been problems getting a permit from the city. Rumors flew in the Brazilian community. Some said a fair permit was not issued because the man who had taken it out the previous year had returned to Brazil and no one else had applied for a new permit in time. Others said that this man wanted to "sell his rights" to hold the fair and that no one was interested in "buying" them. Still others claimed the city had denied the permit because of a street fight involving broken bottles during the fair the year before; three or four people were said to have been seriously injured. No, said others, the real reason the city would not allow Brazilians to hold a fair was the mounds of garbage left on the streets after their previous fairs.

The original organizers of the fair seemed unconcerned about this turn of events and the widespread disappointment in the Brazilian community caused by the fair's cancellation. For the following year, one organizer told me, instead of a street fair, he might sponsor a commercial fair at a large convention center that would feature Brazilian products. He said that this would provide "a better Brazilian image than selling hot dogs on the street."

In 1991 another group of Brazilian businesspeople wrested control of the fair from the original organizers, who, it was said, were planning to sue for infringement of their copyright. A smaller street fair did take place that year, but its relatively poor attendance was likely due to the lack of publicity; the event was not mentioned in the local Brazilian newspaper since the paper's owner was no longer running the show. And the tug of war continues. In 1992, the street fair was back in the hands of the original organizers—and received a lot of publicity in New York's Brazilian newspaper.

A House Divided

The tension between old-timers and more recent immigrants is not the only fault line in the Brazilian community. A schism also exists between the merchants of Little Brazil and the Brazilian establishment. One informant distinguished what he called the "retail" segment of the community, the businesses on West 46th Street, from the "wholesale" segment—the "people who have the real power," the executives at the New York branches of Brazilian banks, airlines, and major companies, or in other words, the Brazilian establishment. The two factions are separated more by background—differences in education and social class in Brazil—than by current economic well-being. In the words of this same informant:

> To begin with, the 46th Street merchants are not very well educated. Their background is hard work, and they made good. These people have been here a long time, and they got an early edge in those markets—travel agencies, stores, restaurants. But regardless of the money that they have and the power that they seem to have, the Little Brazil crowd can't manage to get the name that they want because they are shunned by the other establishment, the one that really has the money and the power. So the 46th Street merchants feel out of place because of their background, and the two groups just don't mix.

This analysis was confirmed by a number of Brazilians familiar with both segments of the Brazilian community, including one high-ranking consular official. Executives of Brazilian banks and business enterprises, he said, are "prejudiced against the 46th Street merchants." The business elite, he went on, "will not accept them because of their lower-middle-class origins even if they have done very well financially." This resident diplomat claimed that he had attempted to bridge the chasm between the two community factions. He tried—unsuccessfully—to have the West 46th Street merchants included in a business organization dominated by the Brazilian elite. The Brazilian consulate sponsored a mass at St. Patrick's Cathedral to commemorate Brazilian Independence Day. The mass was "meant to reach out to the Brazilian community," said the diplomat, and he sent personal invitations to members of the elite as well as to many merchants in Little Brazil asking them to attend. (Parenthetically, the mass replaced the old practice of celebrating the day with a cocktail party at the consulate, an event, the diplomat implied, that had been limited to the Brazilian establishment). But all his efforts were in vain; the Brazilian elite continued to treat the merchants of Little Brazil and other Brazilian residents of the Big Apple as "second-class citizens."[12]

Political orientation and politics are also fault lines for some members of New York's Brazilian community, albeit far less critical ones than social origin and time of arrival in the city. Political divisions became apparent during the 1989 presidential election in Brazil, the first direct election of a Brazilian president since the military coup of 1964. Two political groups were organized among Brazilians in New York, one in support of Fernando Collor de Melo (who won the election, but was later impeached) and the other favoring the Labor party candidate, Luis Inacio da

Silva, known far and wide as Lula. The Pro-Collor Committee was started by a Brazilian businessman long resident in the United States, and he appeared to be its main active member, although a few other long-term residents lent their names to the organization. The other political group, the Labor Party (Partido Trabalhista, or PT), which supported Lula, was larger and better organized. Anywhere from fifteen to thirty people attended the PT's biweekly meetings; about half were Brazilian students studying in New York, and the rest were recent immigrants. At these gatherings, political and economic developments in Brazil were discussed; a drive to collect signatures for a petition supporting the prosecution of the murderers of Chico Mendes, the noted Brazilian environmentalist, was organized; and Amazon Week events at New York University were planned. The group also put out a newsletter.

Still, despite what appeared to be widespread interest in the results of the presidential election, relatively few Brazilians registered to vote at the consulate. A number cited the early closing date for registration—June, for the November election—and complained that the consulate had done little to publicize the need to register months in advance. In fact, the consulate did put a voter registration notice in the *New York Times*, but few Brazilians immigrants read that paper. Consular personnel, in turn, blamed the poor electoral turnout on immigrants' irrational fear of U.S. immigration authorities, and it is true that, some undocumented Brazilians are afraid that contact with the consulate puts them at risk of being apprehended by Tia Mimi. But whatever the reason, of the many thousands of Brazilian citizens who live within the purview of the New York consulate, only about 800 voted in the election, and only about 600 voted in the runoff. Of note, however, and in contrast to election results in Brazil, Lula won a sizable majority of the votes cast by Brazilians in the Big Apple.

Home Away From Home

Relations between the staff of the Brazilian consulate in New York and the Brazilian immigrants living in New York mirror the tensions within the community as a whole. The celebratory mass mentioned earlier is illustrative. The mass was sponsored by the consulate, and the diplomat who organized the event said that he viewed it as an attempt to "reach out to the community." But most of the 200 or so people who came to the late afternoon mass were either connected to the consulate or belonged to the Brazilian elite; a sprinkling of merchants from Little Brazil also attended. Not more than 10 percent of those in attendance came from the ranks of new immigrants, who are by far the largest segment of the local Brazilian community. In fact, the very well-dressed crowd standing on the sidewalk in front of Saint Patrick's Cathedral after the mass and exchanging pecks on the cheek included more Brazilian men in business suits than I had seen gathered in one place before.

Why so few immigrants? First, the scheduling of the mass on a weekday afternoon precluded many Brazilians with jobs from attending. Moreover, there were no public notices about the mass, at least not in places where immigrants would be likely to see them. No posters were put up or fliers distributed in Little Brazil, although it is only four blocks from the consulate and is a common site for publicizing Brazilian concerts, soccer matches, and other events of interest to the community. Neither was the mass announced in the local Brazilian newspaper. Notification was limited to Brazilians on the consulate's mailing list. The salient point is that consular officials had no notion of how to reach beyond the elite and the merchants of Little Brazil to extend invitations to the Brazilian community at large.

Then, too, relations between Brazilian immigrants and Brazilian consular employees are often strained; members of the immigrant community frequently complain about their treatment by the consular staff. "The consulate does nothing to help people," said one immigrant. "All it does is renew passports and register births. Consular employees get housing subsidies and good salaries for doing nothing." Another immigrant, who had been employed by a large Brazilian company in Iraq for five years, contrasted her positive experiences at the Brazilian consulate in Baghdad with her experiences at the New York consulate, where, she said, "the service is just awful." Yet another Brazilian spoke bitterly about his one visit to the consulate, saying he never intends to set foot in it again. "They treat us like aliens," he said. "When you go there they assume you are an illegal until you prove otherwise."[13]

A high-ranking consular officer acknowledged these complaints and admitted that many employees simply assume that most Brazilians who show up at the consulate are illegal and treat them accordingly. But, he said, he has repeatedly told consular personnel that undocumented Brazilians "are illegal only in the eyes of the U.S. government, not in the eyes of Brazil" and that they are to be "treated like Brazilian citizens." A junior officer told me that these admonitions had worked to some extent and that the consulate had become "less isolated" from the Brazilian community. Still, I found consular staff and officers quite uninformed about the immigrant community. Their primary concern was that immigrants be generally "well behaved," not be involved in drugs or other criminal activities, and most important, "cause little trouble" for consular personnel.

The antagonism between consular employees and immigrants also arises from traditional Brazilian expectations about proper social behavior. Brazilian anthropologist Roberto DaMatta suggests that Brazilians intensely dislike being at the mercy of impersonal bureaucratic rules and that if they have problems with such rules, they count on getting help from the authorities as well as from relatives and friends. In his words, "In Brazil, to be 'human' means to pay attention to the singularities of each case and to be sympathetic with that case." To be treated otherwise "means to be regarded as an impersonal being, to whom one simply and automatically applies the cold and impersonal letter of the law."[14] These cultural understandings lie at the core of the problematic relationship between consular personnel and ordinary Brazilian immigrants. The former are described as "cold," "unhelpful," and "formal." They are unwilling to engage in the classic *jeitinho brasileiro*—the Brazilian mode of cutting a little red tape or bending the rules slightly to solve a problem. This is especially irksome to immigrants since they and the consular employees alike, are, after all, strangers in a strange land. It infuriates Brazilians when they are treated in an impersonal, off-putting manner by fellow Brazilians who have adopted the American stance of "We don't bend the rules for anyone."

Brazilian Institutions in the Big Apple, Elite and Otherwise

The consulate is the only Brazilian institution in New York with which nearly everyone in the Brazilian community—old-timer and new immigrant, business executive and shoe shiner—has contact. The handful of other Brazilian organizations in the city either are directed by and intended for the elite, are dominated by the merchants of Little Brazil, or are aimed mainly at the immigrant segment of the community. Here, too, social background, time and conditions of arrival in the United States, and current occupation segregate Brazilians from one another.

There is the Brazilian Cultural Foundation, for example, an elite organization that sponsored a major 1990 exhibit, "Portugal-Brazil: The Age of Atlantic Discoveries," at the New York Public Library. Two and a half million dollars were raised from Brazilian, Portuguese, and U.S. companies and foundations to fund the project. The foundation, with offices on Park Avenue, was started in 1977 by Brazilian and American business executives interested in promulgating Brazilian culture in the United States. The organization has sponsored concerts by visiting Brazilian singers, musicians, and dance companies and has put on exhibits by visiting artists. It does not, however, fund musical or artistic events by local Brazilian talent. One of the foundation's current projects supports Portuguese classes for American students at two public high schools in the city. But here, too, the goal is disseminating Brazilian culture to non-Brazilians, rather than serving the resident Brazilian population. Portuguese-language instruction for the children of Brazilian immigrants, for example, is not on the foundation's roster of projects; such classes are not feasible, I was told, because the children go to schools in different parts of the city. But the foundation's future plans do include a Casa do Brasil (Brazil House), a combination conference center, library, and gallery that will showcase Brazilian art and culture.

With a business rather than a cultural focus, the Brazilian-American Chamber of Commerce is another institution that is run by and serves the elite. Members of this group include the leading lights of the Brazilian-American business community: the heads of large Brazilian enterprises with offices in New York, the local directors of Brazilian banks and airlines, and executives of U.S. companies that do business in Brazil. Its nonelite counterpart is the Brazilian Lions Club, whose membership comprises mostly Little Brazil merchants and other long-time Brazilian residents with small businesses in the city. This club's charitable activities— collecting used clothes, for example—are limited to projects that help the needy in Brazil; its charity work does not extend to immigrant compatriots in New York.[15]

Even New York's monthly Brazilian newspaper is not meant for the local immigrant community. Unlike Brazilian newspapers in Boston and Newark—both geared to Brazilian immigrants living in those cities—the paper in New York predates by more than a decade large-scale Brazilian immigration to the Big Apple. As a result, it has always been aimed at Americans interested in Brazil and long-term Brazilian residents of the United States. Today the paper's only feature specifically aimed at new immigrants—the largest sector of the Brazilian community in New York—is a question and answer column by an immigration attorney.[16]

The Empire Loisada Samba School—"Empire" for New York, the Empire State, and "Loisada" for the Lower East Side, its location—is probably the only secular Brazilian organization in the city with immigrant participation; it could be considered the plebian equivalent of the Brazilian Cultural Foundation. The group organizes an annual parade featuring elaborately costumed samba dancers and floats with Brazilian themes and offers classes in *capoeira*, the Brazilian martial art, and *batucada*, African-Brazilian percussion.[17] In a real sense, though, Empire Loisada is not of New York's Brazilian community, immigrant or otherwise, but about the popularity of things Brazilian; the majority of participants in the parades and classes are not Brazilians at all, but aficionados of Brazilian culture. At any rate, the last I heard of the group was that, having lost its office space in a city-owned building, it was nearly defunct.

Two other organizations primarily aimed at the immigrant segment of the Brazilian community never really got off the ground because both involved grandiose schemes with little financial underpinning. The Bra-

zilian Community Improvement Center, started by two longtime Brazilian residents of Astoria, was incorporated in 1987 as a nonprofit enterprise by the state of New York. While the founders' intentions may have
been genuine, the plans for the center were wildly out of proportion to its
likely ability to finance them. A community center, to be run by a full-time
coordinator and housed in a local public school, was to have a day care
center, a medical clinic, a hotline for Brazilians, English classes for new
immigrants, instruction in Portuguese for Brazilian children, music, judo
and *capoeira* classes, a program for teenagers, a monthly dance for
adults, and a program to combat alcholism. In short, this was to be an
all-purpose community center for Brazilian immigrants. A petition drive
was organized to convince city authorities of the community's interest in
such a center, but, lamented one of the center's organizers, because Brazilians "are a minority within a minority," being neither Hispanic nor Portuguese, the funds were not forthcoming from the city, and the entire
project fizzled.

Club Brasil was a similarly high-sounding enterprise meant to serve the
Brazilian community, including the immigrant sector, and it, too, was
dreamed up by a long-term Brazilian resident of the city. For an annual
membership fee of about $80, the club, which was to be based in Manhat-
tan, would provide a variety of services to Brazilians: a subscription to a
Brazilian magazine, discounts on airline tickets, and admission to nightclubs that feature Brazilian shows. Members would have access to a list
of Brazilian service providers—doctors, lawyers, translators, mechanics,
and so on—and could get free legal and employment advice in addition to
low-cost medical insurance. This organization was to serve the entire Brazilian community in New York, residents and tourists alike, as well as
Americans with an interest in Brazil. One of its goals was to promote
tourism to Brazil, an aim not unrelated to the business of Club Brasil's
organizer: he owns a travel agency. This scheme also seems to have foun-
dered, from lack of trust, lack of interest, or, most likely, both.

Elementary Forms of the Religious Life

Religious life is the only aspect of New York's Brazilian immigrant community with a considerable degree of institutional development. Just over
half (55 percent) of the Brazilians in my sample went to religious services
with some regularity. The pattern of doctrinal allegiance was similar to
that in Brazil: 75 percent attended a Catholic church, 11 percent were
Baptists, slightly over 6 percent were Seventh-Day Adventists, another 6
percent went to Pentecostal services, and the remainder belonged to a
variety of creeds including Spiritism. Moreover, New York City has a
number of churches with Brazilian clerics and Portuguese-language serv-

ices. Catholic masses are said in Portuguese in Manhattan. There are Baptist services for Brazilians at two churches in Queens and at one in Manhattan, Seventh-Day Adventist services in Queens and in Manhattan (in addition to a social service agency run by that denomination in Queens), Pentecostal churches with services in Portuguese in Brooklyn and Queens, Spiritist centers in Queens and Manhattan, and local branches of such distinctly Brazilian religious groups as the Igreja Universal, a denomination founded in Brazil in the 1970s, Candomblé, an African-Brazilian religion, and Seicho-No-Ie, a religion imported to Brazil from Japan.

The principal Catholic church serving the Brazilian community in the city is Our Lady of Perpetual Help (Nossa Senhora do Perpetuo Socorro) on Manhattan's East Side. In May 1990 an invitation was issued by the Archdiocese of New York asking the "Brazilian Catholic community" to attend the church's inaugural mass. A flier in Portuguese was distributed, which read:

UNION = POWER
A United Community is More Powerful!
Brazilians, Your Presence is Necessary.

The history of a Portuguese-language mass for Brazilians in New York highlights the city's changing ethnic composition. For three or four generations, Our Lady of Perpetual Help had been a Czechoslovakian national parish. But as the descendants of the original Czech congregants moved to the suburbs, attendance at mass fell precipitously, and the main sanctuary of the church was closed as an economy move. At one point, the Archdiocese of New York had considered shutting the church entirely. Enter the Brazilians. In 1989, a successful Brazilian businesswoman began lobbying Catholic authorities in New York for a mass in Portuguese for her compatriots. She located the Church of Our Lady of Perpetual Help, with its dwindling congregation, and got in touch with Father Franklin, a Portuguese-speaking American priest who had lived in Brazil for many years. The businesswoman, Father Franklin, and a representative of the archdiocese went to the Brazilian consulate to inquire about the number of Brazilians in the New York area. "About 60,000," they were told. Persuaded by this figure, the archdiocese agreed to sponsor a mass in Portuguese.

The businesswoman purchased a statue of Nossa Senhora Aparecida, a Brazilian saint, and arranged to have it shipped free of charge from Rio to New York on the national Brazilian airline. The statue was installed in its new home at an inaugural mass on May 13, 1990, the anniversary of the date that an apparition of the saint first appeared in Brazil. The standing-room-only crowd included representatives from the Archdiocese of

New York, officials of the Brazilian consulate, and members of the Brazilian community. The proceedings were filmed by a Brazilian television network and broadcast on the nightly news in Brazil.

Every Sunday afternoon, the Portuguese-language mass at Our Lady of Perpetual Help begins, says Father Franklin, with a twinkle in his eye, at "Brazilian time," 4:10 or 4:15 P.M., not "American time," 4:00 P.M. sharp. On a typical Sunday, most of the hundred seats are filled; attendance ranges from 70 to 120 congregants (the higher number for baptisms and around Christmastime). A core group of some sixty Brazilians goes to mass regularly; it includes the businesswoman who was the catalyst in instituting the mass and a Brazilian physician, the only long-term Brazilian residents of the city who are regular participants in the service. The rest of the congregants, whom Father Franklin describes as "simple lower-middle-class people," are newer immigrants. About equal numbers of men and women attend mass, in contrast to Brazil, where churchgoing is a decidedly female activity. Most are young and single; relatively few married couples attend, and even fewer children—only a half-dozen on a typical Sunday. Father Franklin performed only ten baptisms over the eight-month period following the inaugural mass, but expects the number to increase. Although most congregants say that they are in the United States only temporarily, he believes that as more marry and have children, more of the Brazilian sojourners will become permanent residents, as did the Portuguese settlers of his former parish in Philadelphia.

His Brazilian congregants, says Father Franklin, are "grateful" to have mass celebrated in Portuguese, but they lack a place for other social activities. Hence they gather after mass to chat, and when Father Franklin finally locks the church for the evening, the conversations continue on the sidewalk outside. He is hopeful that "as word spreads," the mass for Brazilians "will grow into something" and the church will become a center for the community.

BRAZILIAN RHYTHM

Three elderly American women regularly attend the Brazilian mass celebrated in Portuguese at the Church of Our Lady of Perpetual Help in Manhattan. Although they do not understand a word of the language, they told the parish priest that they attend the mass anyway because they "love the music and the hand clapping."

The Pentecostal church in Brooklyn already plays a central role in the lives of a small segment of New York's Brazilian community. Although nearly all of this church's members live in Queens, they make the long

trek to Brooklyn at least once a week to attend one of the four weekly
services in Portuguese at a Hispanic Pentecostal Church there. The 120 to
150 members of the congregation—the numbers vary as some people
leave for Brazil and others join—are urged to follow a circumspect lifestyle; alchohol and smoking are strictly prohibited, as is general carousing (*fazendo uma farra*). Members are encouraged to socialize with one
another within a religious ambience, at services held in church and in
private homes, at bible classes for children and adults, and at youth group
gatherings. Even secular events are set in a religious context. A communal
birthday party is held at the church on the first day of each month for
congregants who had birthdays during the preceding month. Group out-
ings to the beach in summer help church members "steer clear of other
Brazilians"—meaning Brazilians who do not adhere to the church's pre-
cepts on smoking and drinking. In fact, the entire social life of some adherents centers around the church. Martinho, for example, who shines
shoes in Manhattan and whose family is back in Brazil, does little else but
work long hours and travel three or four times a week from his home in
Queens to church services in Brooklyn.

Religious devotions for Brazilian Pentecostalists begin with a small
church choir singing rousing hymns in Portuguese, accompanied by the
pastor on the piano. A lively give-and-take between pastor and congregation follows. Asks the pastor, "Why are things in life so hard? You, José,
read this passage from the Bible and tell me what it says about this."
Everyone reads the same passage aloud. He questions his flock about its
meaning, and people call out their responses. Then it is time for the sermon. That Sunday evening, the subject is prostitution, which, avers the
pastor, "includes all sex outside marriage." He talks about failed marriages, citing cases from Brazil: "Often the problem is that the man drinks
and he's not a *crente* [a believer, that is, a Protestant]." He rhapsodizes
about "the pureness of the body of a *crente*" and rails against drugs,
adultery, and general debauchery as defilers of bodily virtue. The sermon
and the repartee with the congregation are lively and upbeat. The pastor,
who is a a superb performer with a masterful command of phrasing and
timing, ends the sermon on a light note: "Just remember, first matrimony,
then bed. *Make sure it's not the other way around.*"

A half-hour of spirited singing and handclapping accompanied by
piano, guitars, and drums follows. The service ends emotionally; with
eyes closed, arms raised, and some faces streaming with tears, people pray
aloud. Newcomers are introduced and asked to give their names, tell
where they come from in Brazil, and tell how long they have been in New
York. A collection plate is passed, a final prayer is said, and the service is
over; it has lasted two and a quarter hours. Then churchgoers begin the
long trip back home to Queens by car or subway.

BORN AGAIN

The pastor of the Pentecostal church in Brooklyn talked of the church's ability to transform people's lives. He cited the case of one Brazilian, an illegal immigrant, who worked as a maid in New York. She had saved $3,000 and used it to buy a counterfeit green card. Then she joined the church and felt guilty about having bought a falsified document. She returned the green card to the man who had sold it to her, whereupon, "because of God's work," she said, the man returned her $3,000. Later, she told the pastor, "God willing, I'm going to get a real green card."

Members of the Pentecostal congregation are proud of their ethic of mutual assistance. They help one another find jobs and provide food and other aid in times of need. Indeed, immigrant employment networks are in full swing here; six congregants, for example, work as busboys at the same Tex-Mex restaurant in Manhattan. One recent convert cited a specific instance of the kind of help members of the church offer. He drives a radio call cab in Queens; when he had trouble starting the car early one morning, he called a mechanic, a fellow congregant, who "dropped everything and immediately came over" to help him out. As I was leaving the church service, one member said to me, "And they say we Brazilians are not united, that we don't help each other. You can see for yourself that's not true here."

The profile of Pentecostal parishioners is similar to that of the rest of New York's Brazilian immigrant community in my sample. Congregants are divided about evenly by gender; they are young, mostly in their twenties; and the majority are single—only about ten married couples, belong, and fewer still have children. Then, too, on the evening I attended services, the congregation of sixty or so was overwhelmingly white, well dressed, and middle and lower-middle class; church members include a lawyer, a doctor, an English teacher, and an engineer. But, while representative of the Brazilian immigrant community in New York, the congregation seemed more prosperous and of a higher social class than is typical of adherents of Pentecostalism in the United States.[18] Still, in religious affiliation they differ markedly from both their compatriots in New York and those back home in Brazil. The church's pastor estimated that 70 percent of his parishioners were *crentes*, that is, Protestants, before coming to the United States.

Congregants of the Baptist Church of the Portuguese Language in Queens form another active Brazilian spiritual conclave. The church has about 200 adult parishioners, virtually all of them Brazilians, and holds services twice weekly. The church is growing rapidly, says its pastor, who has baptized about sixty congregants since his arrival from Brazil in 1986. And here, too, the majority—about two-thirds—were already *crentes*, in this case, Baptists, before coming to New York.

Between ninety and one hundred people were present at the Sunday morning service I attended during the Christmas season. Perhaps fifteen children were scattered among the audience of young adults, about equally divided between men and women—more of them married than single, according to the pastor. The church was decked with poinsettas, and Christmas lights and flags from various nations, including Brazil, hung from the rafters. Accompanied by an organist, a choir of twenty-five sang hymns and North American Christmas carols with lyrics in Portuguese. The sermon, also in Portuguese, was about the importance of Jesus Christ in the celebration of the season, the minister saying that he would like to see the name of Jesus instead of the word "Christmas" written on calendars around the world. Then he gave his own version of the Santa Claus tale: "On Christmas Eve, Santa arrives on horseback to bring presents to good little boys and girls," perhaps because reindeers are rather obscure animals to Brazilians. Following the sermon—which contained none of the fire-and-brimstone allusions to licentiousness of the Pentecostal service—some parishioners asked the pastor to say a blessing for their parents or other relatives back home in Brazil. After the service, most of the congregation adjourned to the church basement for a Brazilian lunch of beef, rice, and black beans.

One denomination of Brazilian origin, the Universal Church (Igreja Universal), has U.S. outposts in Manhattan, the Bronx, Brooklyn, and Newark. Although its branches in the metropolitan area opened between 1986 and 1992, a time when Brazilians were flocking to the city in record numbers, the Universal Church is not aimed at serving the local Brazilian community, and its services are in English, not Portuguese. Indeed, Brazilians account for only about 20 percent of the congregants—a total of some fifty people—in the four New York area churches.

Branches of the church were established in New York for quite a different reason. "Since the city is a crossroads drawing people from all over the world," the church's local pastor explains, "we hope that the church's converts in New York will start new congregations when they go back to their own countries." And, he noted with pride, although "in New York progress is slow," one local parishioner, an Argentine, had already returned home and started a branch of the church in Buenos Aires. Clearly, the church's intention is to try to replicate the success it has had in its homeland; today the Universal Church has some 800 branches in Brazil, all established since 1977.

The Universal Church's theology is reminiscent of some North American ministeries in its stress on success, particularly financial success, here on earth.[19] It is a "living faith that really changes people," said the New York pastor, "not like a Catholic mass which people just sit through and leave." Nor is the Universal Church akin to evangelical churches that "promise salvation only after death and that do not believe God helps converts in this life. We have many testimonies of people who have prospered and whose prayers have been answered after joining the church." For example, he said, after one morning service, a member gave all the money she had with her to the church. The very next day she was rewarded when her tenant, who was always in arrears and sent the rent check late, suddenly paid up in full.

The Manhattan branch of the Universal Church is located in a small building on the Lower East Side, which it shares with an Hispanic Pentecostal congregation. Sunday services are held in an unadorned room with folding chairs; the only decoration is a crimson velvet curtain with a sign in large gold lettering, "Jesus Christ is Lord," that serves as a backdrop for the Brazilian pastor. The congregation of perhaps twenty-five appears to be working class and is of mixed origin; present are Americans, Hondurans, Panamanians, people from the English-speaking Caribbean and India, a Russian, and four Brazilian women with five children.[20] About one-third of the congregants are black.

The focal point of the service, which is in English except for a few asides in Portuguese directed at the Brazilian parishioners, is prayers for better jobs and improved financial opportunities. Much of the sermon is a plea to help raise $23,000 for additional construction on the Brooklyn branch of the church. The pastor requests that envelopes he had given out the previous week be returned. After a few parishoners hand them in, he distributes more envelopes and urges his flock to donate as much as possible because "you will truly benefit from your generosity." He ends the sermon with the tale of an elderly member of the congregation who gave her rent money to the church and shortly thereafter reaped a financial windfall.

Far removed from the Universal Church with its emphasis on worldly success are the local followers of Spiritism, another sectarian movement with roots in Brazil. Brazilian Spiritists, or Kardecists, as they are sometimes called, adherents of the teachings of Allan Kardec, a nineteenth-century French philosopher, meet in Queens and in Manhattan. The Queens group, which usually has twenty or twenty-five participants, gathers on Monday evenings in an Hispanic Spiritist center, while a core group of ten Spiritists also meets on Thursdays; this meeting is closed to outsiders.

On the frigid winter evening I visited a Spiritist session, only eight people attended, six men and two women, including Nara, the organizer of
the group, a practitioner of Spiritism even before she left Brazil more than
a decade ago. Seven of the participants were Brazilian, and one was a
Colombian, whom, the others joked, had learned Portuguese by attending the sessions; all were white.[21] The room in which the session was held
was adorned with primitive paintings of Jesus and an elaborate table covered with offerings, candles, a menorah, and paper flowers. A Christmas
tree and Christmas lights were still up even though it was well past the
holiday season. The Brazilian Spiritists assured me that none of the decor
had anything to do with their group; it all belonged to their Hispanic
counterparts, with whom they shared the premises.

At their sessions in Brazil, Spiritists discuss the works of Kardec and
other spiritists; they meditate, pray, and use relaxation techniques.[22] The
session in Queens was similar. The small group sat in a circle on folding
chairs. The session began with a woman reading a poem by Castro Alves,
a famous nineteenth-century Brazilian poet who championed abolition.
Then she read some text by Chico Xavier, a well-known Brazilian Spiritist, and concluded with an articulate commentary on both pieces. A man
offered a lengthy monologue about the nature of Spiritism and mediums,
and the value of "spiritual evolution." These commentaries, lasting about
three-quarters of an hour, were followed by relaxation exercises. The
lights were dimmed, and one of the men, in a low, soothing voice, told
everyone to close their eyes, to relax, to let the tension out, to feel "the
cells reviving in their bodies," to feel themselves being "rejuvenated."
Next was the laying on of hands—what Brazilian Spiritists call *passes*. To
achieve spiritual cleansing, members took turns placing their hands above
one another's heads to draw out tense, impure emanations. This took
place in complete silence. The lights were finally turned up to mark the
end of the session; members of the group briefly talked among themselves, and then headed for the subway to their respective homes in other
parts of Queens and in Manhattan.

This is a sampling of religious observance among members of New
York's Brazilian immigrant community. There are other denominations
as well. Queens has a sizable Seventh-Day Adventist congregation, whose
members attend Saturday services and often live with one another because, they say, this makes it easier to maintain their strict dietary rules
against drinking coffee and alcohol and eating pork. There are also purported to be small spiritual conclaves in private homes. It is said, for
example, that ten or twelve *umbandistas*, practitioners of Brazilian Umbanda, a religion that blends Spiritism, folk Catholicism, and African-
Brazilian beliefs and rituals, hold sessions in a member's apartment in
Queens.[23] I was also told of another group that meets privately in

Queens, followers of Candomblé, an African-Brazilian religion practiced primarily in the state of Bahia. I mention these gatherings in tentative language since I was unable to confirm their existence.

As we have seen, the communion and amiability that suffuses at least some of these Brazilian religious gatherings are in stark contrast to the disunity that pervades the community as a whole—a disunity bound up with a crosscutting set of social and economic distinctions that separate Brazilians into sporadically contentious and at best, mutually indifferent factions. These divisions are the subject of the chapter to follow.

CHAPTER TEN

Class Pictures

WHEN I BEGAN this research project, I knew that one set of focal questions would be about social class. Is it a decisive category among Brazilian immigrants in New York City? Is social class as all-encompassing and as life defining among Brazilians in the United States as it is in Brazil? Or, given their common status as strangers in an unfamiliar land, as aliens in the maelstrom of an unknown city, would traditional social distinctions fade in the comforting haven of a common language and a common origin?

I found the answers almost immediately. One of the most striking features of New York's Brazilian community is the degree to which differences in social standing overwhelm shared national and linguistic identities. But the divisions I am calling "social class" are not based so much on the traditional criteria of social class—economic, educational, and family background—because most of New York's Brazilian immigrants come from their nation's relatively privileged middle and lower-middle strata. Rather, class distinctions in New York's Brazilian community are largely grounded in the disparities in lifestyle and position resulting from the menial character of the jobs held by nearly all new immigrants and by the undocumented status of many of them.

The social structure of New York's Brazilian community is an atrophied version of Brazil's in that it lacks the homeland's largest and poorest segment. In Brazil the working class and the abject poor comprise 60 percent of the population.[1] But probably no more than 10 percent of New York's Brazilian population are from these bottom strata; most Brazilians in the city, whether new immigrants or longtime residents, come from the lower middle class or above. The Brazilian social pyramid in New York, then, does not have the broad, lower-class base that characterizes Brazilian society as a whole.

The Case of the Phantom Lower Class

Despite the near-absence of the bottom segment of the Brazilian class hierarchy in its New York incarnation, many elite and middle-class émigrés deny that this is so. I was repeatedly told about the many Brazilians in the Big Apple who are "from a low social level," are "uneducated," "lack manners," or "are poor representatives of Brazilian soci-ety." In one of the first interviews I had, I was informed that "lower-class Brazilians" dominate the shoe shine trade.

These observations are not just the snobbish musings of members of New York's small Brazilian elite, who could be expected to consider the rest of the expatriate community to be their social inferiors. Many mid-dle- and lower-middle-class Brazilians in New York also insist that there are large numbers of Brazilians living in the city who are variously de-scribed as semiliterate, less cultured, poorer, or from a lower social level of Brazilian society than they themselves. But, when asked for specifics— Who are these people? Where do they live?—informants were always vague. "Well, I don't know any of them *personally*," was a typical re-sponse. "I only know they exist because I hear them speaking bad Portu-guese on the street."

Clarice, a woman from a lower-middle-class family in Minas Gerais who has lived in New York since 1981, contended that after the mid-1980s, the general educational level of Brazilians arriving in the city had declined. More recent immigrants "lack a certain culture," she said. "They come only to make money, not to see the world and they don't take advantage of the city. Why just the other day I heard a group of Brazilians talking on the subway and I could tell from their Portuguese that they were not very well educated." When I asked Clarice if she could give me the names of any people who fit this description, she said she could not. Another example is Elena, a retired nurse from Rio de Janeiro; Elena was hopeful that as economic conditions worsened in Brazil, her social life in New York would improve because "more middle-class peo-ple would be coming to the United States." "Now," she explained, "I have no friends, only acquaintances since I have nothing in common with the Brazilians whom I know here." Marta, a woman with wide contacts in the Brazilian community, estimated that half of all Brazilians in the city are *pobres* (poor people). She described this group of fellow Brazilians in some detail:

> They work very hard—after all, that's the only reason they're here. They live under primitive conditions, with lots of people sharing an apartment, and they don't eat well because they're saving all their money to return to Brazil. Basically, they're poorly educated *mineiros*—at most, they have high school. They come from the lower class (*classe baixa*) and are only a little better off than *favelados* (shan-tytown residents). And do they suffer! They hardly speak English be-cause they live with other Brazilians, and all they do is complain about life in the United States. They hate New York, but they really don't know much about the city. They're just not integrated into society here, and to make matters even worse, they live in fear because they're illegal.

I asked for names and addresses, please! But the story was always the same: informants could not provide me with these details because, they said, they did not personally know any Brazilians in New York from such modest backgrounds.

HIGHER EDUCATION

The cultural grid that distinguishes "us" from "them" explains why some Brazilians make a point of differentiating the quality of the universities in Brazil that their compatriots in New York had attended. One member of the resident elite, for example, said that many immigrants who are university graduates nevertheless have poor educations because they went to "inferior" institutions, while another questioned the credentials of new immigrants who hold degrees in law, psychology, agronomy, and other fields. "But what *kind* of schools did they attend?" she demanded to know. And two university-educated immigrants explained that because of the explosion in university attendance in Brazil, simply having gone to university was no longer "a sign of elite status."

It is true that the last two decades have seen huge growth in private institutions of higher learning in Brazil. Since about 1970, the university system has expanded tenfold to accommodate middle-class pressure for university slots. Not surprisingly, many new institutions in the private sector are said to have inferior standards. Nevertheless, what is telling about these remarks about the "quality" of Brazilian universities is simply the fact that they occur. Keep in mind that even today Brazil is a country in which only a small percentage of the population goes to *any* university at all.

Source: *Academe*, "From Political to Economic Siege in Brazil."

I mentioned this elusive segment of the local Brazilian population in a conversation with three university-educated immigrants. "It's true," they all chimed in. "Many of our compatriots in New York are poorly educated and never went beyond junior high school."[2] When I told them that I had met relatively few immigrants with so little schooling, they claimed that this was because educated Brazilians were reluctant to introduce me to their unlettered compatriots; they were "ashamed" of them. Another immigrant offered a more convincing solution to the puzzle of the phantom lower class: it comes from the propensity of Brazilians to point to unspecified "other people" as being poorer, more corrupt, less well educated, or in some other way inferior to themselves and to their social group. Such established cultural discourse must be especially comforting to middle- and lower-middle-class Brazilians in New York City, whose own social standing is made problematic by their low status jobs as immigrants. We may be badly off now, they seem to be saying, but at least *we* come from good families and are well educated—*unlike those other Brazilians.*

My data on remittances to Brazil provide some insight into the purported presence of a large Brazilian lower class in New York. One can assume that immigrants whose families in Brazil regularly receive and rely on remittances to meet ordinary living expenses are less well off financially and more likely to be lower class than those whose families do not, making this variable a reasonably good indicator of class standing. What are the figures, then? A little over half of the Brazilians in my sample send money home on a regular or an occasional basis. Forty-five percent of those that remit money to Brazil send it at least once a month; the rest send money less often, and many of these only send it on special occasions. But a substantial number of those sending regular remittances to their parents in Brazil are not sending money for family support. They are saving money for their own return home; they are making down payments on an apartment or saving to start a business or make an investment. Still others are sending money to Brazil on a regular basis to pay off the debts they incurred by traveling to New York.[3]

The *type* of remittance that immigrants send home, then, is a good indicator of social class. An occasional monetary gift to a relative for a birthday or for Christmas is very different from a frequent infusion of cash to sustain family members back home. And both types of remittances should be distinguished from a regular transfer of funds to pay for the immigrant's personal property, investment, or debt. While approximately one-quarter of the Brazilians in my sample remit money to their families in Brazil on a regular basis (at least once a month) many of them are sending it for their own future use or to pay off personal debts. In other words, regular remittances for family maintenance are fairly rare among the Brazilians in my sample and are largely limited to those single or divorced men and women who left children in the care of relatives in Brazil. In short, the data on remittances provide no more indication of a sizeable Brazilian lower class in New York City than do any of the other economic and educational data I collected or my personal experience over some twenty months of field research.

Social Segments

What I have dubbed "the phantom lower class" is not entirely the figment of my informants' imaginations. As previously noted, roughly 10 percent of the Brazilians in my New York sample are from very modest backgrounds in Brazil. Many of the immigrants in this category came to New York many years ago as domestic servants with Brazilian or American families and ultimately achieved a standard of living that would be the envy of people of their social class in Brazil. Women seem to outnumber men in this small slice of the local Brazilian universe since it appears that only women are brought to this country as servants. But, gender aside, in some ways the small resident lower class and the far larger, newer immigrant population are comparable. Take employment, for example. I have met women of vastly different social and educational backgrounds with very similar jobs in New York City. A case in point is: Clarina, who worked as a live-in nursemaid (*babá*) in Rio de Janeiro before coming to New York with the family of a Brazilian diplomat in the late 1970s. Although literate, she did not go much beyond elementary school. Today, she lives in her own apartment in the Bronx with her husband and small son; she works as a part-time housekeeper for three families in Manhattan. Rebecca, in contrast, is from a solidly middle-class family in Minas Gerais. She completed three years of university and has been employed as a live-in *babá* in New York for two years. Clarina, then, is doing the same work she likely would have done had she stayed in Brazil, albeit for much higher wages, while Rebecca, whose family in Brazil employs servants, is herself working as a servant because she earns more as a domestic in New York than she ever could at her chosen career—teaching school—in Brazil.

Aside from these immigrant segments of whatever social stripe, New York also has a small long-resident Brazilian community. But here, too, fault lines exist among its three primary elements: salaried employees, the Brazilian elite, and the merchants of Little Brazil.[4] Salaried Brazilian employees of the New York branches of Brazilian banks, airlines, media outlets, and other Brazilian-owned companies and employees of Brazilian governmental agencies—the consulate, the UN legation, and the Trade Bureau—are in the United States legally; they include secretaries, bank tellers, administrative assistants, translators, middle-level managers, journalists, and media specialists. They tend not to socialize with either recent immigrants, the West 46th Street business owners, or the resident elite; most have American and Brazilian friends working in similar occupations.

The last ingredient in this social stew is the resident Brazilian elite, who live in upscale Manhattan neighborhoods or in the affluent suburbs of the greater metropolitan area—Bronxville, Scarsdale, and Rye, in New York's Westchester County, and Darien, New Canaan, and Greenwich, in Connecticut. The elite counts among its members the heads of the New York offices of Brazilian banks and large Brazilian companies as well as high-level Brazilian employees in American firms. A majority are on temporary assignment to New York, but a sizable minority are permanent residents. Most are married, and many have children; they range in age from young, recently married couples to people in their sixties. Members of the elite have little to do with the rest of the Brazilian community in New York, preferring to socialize among themselves and with other *gente fina* (upscale people), be they Americans or foreigners living in that most cosmopolitan of cities.

LADIES WHO LUNCH

A large number of elite Brazilian women—sometimes as many as sixty or seventy—meet once a month at a luncheon. This informal group, which now has some eighty members, was started in about 1982 by a Brazilian woman living in Westchester. The luncheons are held at one of the women's homes, in the suburbs or, less often, in a Manhattan apartment. The women come from all over the metropolitan area to attend—New York City, Long Island, New Jersey, and Connecticut.

I went to one such luncheon at a lavishly decorated penthouse apartment on Manhattan's East Side. About forty women were at the gathering, held on a weekday afternoon. The lunch was of the pot luck variety, with everyone— or probably more accurately, everyone's cook—contributing. Most of the dishes were Brazilian specialties; beer and soft drinks were also served.

The women at the luncheon were expensively dressed—one was clothed from head to toe in creations by Chanel. With three or four exceptions, all the women were Brazilian; the rest were married to Brazilian men. Most were from São Paulo or Rio de Janeiro, with a scattering from other parts of Brazil. They ranged in age from their mid-twenties to their sixties and had lived in the United States anywhere from six months to more than thirty years.

A majority of the women's husbands were executives with Brazilian banks or large Brazilian or multinational corporations. About six of the women were single or divorced. The wife of a high-level Brazilian diplomat also attended. Perhaps in deference to her, a recording of the Brazilian national anthem was played. Everyone rose, and watery eyes were much in evidence.

A handful of the women were themselves employed. One was an economic consultant; another, an investment advisor; and a third worked for a social service agency. Because of their immigration status, many of these women could not legally hold jobs. Many others, however, had resided in the United States for years and had green cards making them eligible for employment. Nonetheless, only about a half-dozen of the forty or so women present held jobs outside the home. Societal contrasts were striking here. After all, how many American women today could attend a leisurely lunch requiring them to be away from their jobs until 3:00 P.M.?

While the New York lifestyles of the Brazilian elite and their newly arrived immigrant compatriots are very different, the two groups do have one thing in common. Just as recent immigrants talk about a social segment of Brazilians inferior to themselves, members of the Brazilian elite underrate the educational level and social background of fresh arrivals from their homeland. Members of the resident Brazilian community in New York, elite and salaried employees alike, see the Brazilian immigrant population as the local analogue of the sprawling lower classes in Brazil because, in effect, immigrants occupy an equivalent niche within the context of New York's Brazilian community. This positioning makes sense given the near-absence of true representatives of the Brazilian lower class in the city, along with the fact that middle- and lower-middle-class immigrants in New York work as maids, dishwashers, and the like—jobs that are held *only* by those on the bottom rungs of Brazilian society.

Cognitive dissonance—the sense of unease arising from mismatched perceptions—is surely at work here. After all, writes anthropologist Roberto DaMatta, Brazil is a society "intensely preoccupied with authority, hierarchy, and . . . a place for everything, and everything in its proper place."[5] How, then, could educated Brazilians be employed in such servile positions? But by insisting that recent arrivals from Brazil are "ill bred, low-class people" (*gente baixa e mal educada*), members of New York's resident Brazilian community can classify them in a familiar, reassuring, and intelligible category. Moreover, by dismissing new immigrants as lower class—and thus, "lucky" even to be in New York—these more privileged members of the community distance themselves from the plight of their less fortunate comrades, who are doing the sort of dirty, disagreeable work that higher-status Brazilians have always shunned.[6] Finally, the elite may be particularly well served by obfuscating the class backgrounds of recent émigrés from their homeland. To recognize them for what they really are would be to own up to the harsh reality that because of the dire state of the Brazilian economy, "middle-class" and "Brazilian" are increasingly becoming a contradiction in terms.

Lest the reader doubt the strength of these feelings about social class, the reactions of some Brazilians in New York to my data on the class origins and current occupations of Brazilian immigrants is telling. The reactions—which took me by surprise—reveal both the tensions among the various segments of the Brazilian population in New York and the desire of many long-term residents to present a sanitized version of their community to the American public at large. Simply put, some Brazilians do not want it widely known that many of their compatriots work in menial jobs. As one said, "They don't want their dirty linen washed in public."

During my research I published a brief portrait of the new immigrants I was studying in a local Brazilian newspaper. One Brazilian, a small business owner and long-term resident of the area, was furious that I reported that educated, middle-class Brazilians were working as servants, busboys, and shoe shiners in New York. My article, he claimed, dealt with only one segment of the community, and it gave Americans a "poor image of his countrymen." A community represented by "go-go girls, shoe shine boys, and maids" would be "looked down on" and would be "confused with Hispanics." Another old-timer in New York faulted me for not writing about Brazilians who occupy higher-status positions in the city—artists, business owners, and "Brazilians who are well situated on Wall Street."[7] Yet another implored me to "please, please write about the success stories."

Class Acts

Brazilians are far more preoccupied with class distinctions than Americans. In Brazil, moreover, class differences are often starkly apparent in behavior. I encountered a vivid example of this in New York when I interviewed Clarina, the woman from a poor Rio family who some years ago was brought to the city as a live-in servant by the family of a Brazilian diplomat. Clarina exhibited the same patterns of deferential behavior toward someone of "higher" status that I had seen so often in Brazil.[8] She greeted me at the door of her employer's apartment with a limp handshake, keeping her head slightly bowed and her eyes lowered. She addressed me using the respectful, formal term for "you" (*a senhora*) and refused to sit next to me on the upholstered furniture. "A maid has her place," she said, and she would be "ashamed" to sit on the couch. Instead, she pulled over a straightbacked dining room chair to sit on during the interview. She told me that even though "things are different in New York," she had been "raised to know her place" while growing up and working for families in Rio. Clarina, in other words, behaved exactly as a household servant is expected to act in Brazil. While she explains this by citing her upbringing, it is certainly worth mentioning that she is employed by an elite Brazilian family in New York, who would presumably expect, even demand, such deferential behavior from a servant.

One Brazilian, a longtime New York resident, pointed out another contrast between the class system in his own country and that in the United States. He is an artist who, to help support himself, cleans and paints apartments in the city. In Brazil, he told me, he could never engage in such menial labor; in fact, his friends and family there think that he earns his living in New York solely from his art, an error, he notes with a wink, from which he has not disabused them. Moreover, when he visits Brazil, his family's housekeeper gets angry when he rinses out his shirts or makes coffee for himself. "Don't you like the way I do things anymore?" she asks. After his years in New York, it bothers him that when he stays with his family in Brazil, he is "not allowed to do anything" for himself.

A CLASS INSULT

One longtime Brazilian resident of New York, a concierge at an upscale hotel, contrasted class-based behavior in Brazil and the United States by recounting the following incident. One day an American hotel guest was very rude to him. He ignored the bad behavior and tried to smooth things over, but when the guest started cursing him and using foul language, the Brazilian concierge became very angry and, in a rising voice, returned the insults in kind before an astonished audience in the lobby. He said his attitude was, Let them fire me but I'm not going to put up with these insults.

The incident ended when the abusive guest left the lobby and went to his room. But in Brazil, the concierge noted pointedly, it would be unheard of for a hotel employee to trade insults with a wealthy hotel guest, whatever the provocation. Had he done so, he not only would have been fired on the spot, but the police would have been called and he might even have been carted off to jail. He ended the story by saying, "What I love most about the United States is that people here can stand up for their rights."

Up the Down Staircase

In the United States identity emerges as a result of what one does. In Brazil, one's social identity is based on what one is, a strand in a web of personal connections, originating in the extended family

—CONRAD P. KOTTAK, "Cultural Contrasts in Prime Time Society"

Over the course of my field research I encountered innumerable individuals from the middle sectors of Brazilian society who had experienced sharp declines in status because of the menial character of their jobs as immigrants in New York City. Examples include a young parking lot attendant with a law degree from a São Paulo university, an engineer from Minas Gerais who drove a radio call cab, a journalist from the same state who worked as a private chauffeur, a baby-sitter who was once employed as a flight attendant for the Brazilian national airline, an accountant from Paraná with a shoe-shining job, a handyman in a Manhattan apartment building who had studied literature at a prestigious university in Rio, and a woman from São Paulo with a degree in psychology who earned a living cleaning houses. And in the New York suburbs, I learned of lawyers, engineers, and agronomists working in construction, as gardeners, house painters, wallpaper hangers, and domestic servants.

Given the Brazilian sensitivity about social class, how do such immigrants adapt to their straitened social position in New York? How do middle-class Brazilian women who once employed domestic servants adjust to being domestic servants themselves? And how do men from the middle sectors of Brazilian society, some with university or professional degrees, deal with shining the shoes of similarly educated American men? How, in the words of anthropologist Katherine Newman, do these Brazilians cope with their "fall from grace?"[9]

Immigrants use various mechanisms to come to terms with their current situation. Seeing their jobs as short term is probably the most important one. Since most Brazilians view their sojourn in New York as temporary, they more willingly take menial jobs that offer little chance of advancement than they would if they envisioned these positions as long term or permanent. Some research suggests that a similar pattern is found among other immigrant groups. Immigrants—or, more accurately, sojourners—generally are more willing to take low-paying, dead-end jobs than Americans because many intend to stay in the United States only long enough to buy property or to bankroll an enterprise back home. Moreover, immigrants, in having made the decision to come to the United States in the first place, already have decided to take whatever work is available there. In other words, unlike most workers, new immigrants who consider their stay temporary are more likely to see their jobs solely as a means to a monetary end.[10]

The social identity of the temporary immigrant, Brazilian or otherwise, is not bound up in his or her job to the same degree as that of the permanent native worker. In the words of economist Michael J. Piore, "The temporary character of the migration flow appears to create a sharp distinction between work, on the one hand, and the social identity of the worker, on the other." If immigrants' identity is primarily derived from their place of origin, they can "treat work abroad in largely instrumental terms, in almost a social vacuum, with little regard to the social component of their job."[11]

A fundamental feature of Brazilian culture enhances the dichotomy between work and personhood and, I believe, helps Brazilian immigrants adapt to their reduced social circumstances in New York. Anthropologist Conrad P. Kottak contrasts the importance of "doing" in the United States and "being" in Brazil. In other words, Americans derive a great deal of their identity from their work, that is, their jobs or professions, while Brazilians derive theirs from social background, especially family ties. American ideology holds that what people achieve in their own right is more important than social origin; thus, an American, Kottak suggests, is more likely to say, "I may be just a plumber, but I am a *very good* plumber." But a Brazilian immigrant in New York is very unlikely to say,

"I may be only a busboy (or maid or shoe shiner) but at least I am a good busboy (or maid or shoe shiner)" since Brazilian identity derives largely from who one is, not from what one does. Brazilian anthropologist Roberto DaMatta neatly encapsulates this duality when he labels the United States a "know-how" society and Brazil a "know-who" society.[12]

Brazilians in New York also adjust more easily to their relatively modest level of creature comforts as immigrants because of the temporary nature of the move itself. This is especially true if they are in New York with a specific monetary goal in mind. People who are saving a sizable portion of their income for the return home view their spartan lifestyle as short term, and therefore more acceptable, or at least more bearable. If one is saving for an improved economic future, it is undoubtedly easier to do one's own housework and forgo the domestic servant who is the sine qua non of the Brazilian middle-class household. Still, for those not planning to return to Brazil any time soon, the adjustment is far more difficult. For example, Elena, a retired nurse, says that when she came to New York, she wanted to live like *gente*, (like a human being), just as she did in Rio, where she had a comfortable apartment in a nice neighborhhood. But when she first arrived in the city, she was forced to live like a *bicha*, (animal), in one tiny room with a shared bathroom down the hall. In time, she again lived like *gente*, once she could afford a small apartment with its own bath in the same building.

Some Brazilians cope with the reality of their lives in the city by concealing the true nature of their employment from friends and relatives back in Brazil. This is especially true of Brazilian women who work as go-go dancers in bars in the New York metropolitan area. Many from *boa famílias* (good families) are loath to let it be known how they earn a living in the city. But there are also busboys whose families in Brazil are told they are restaurant managers, housekeepers who claim to be salespeople in chic New York boutiques, and, as we have seen, an artist who paints apartments to support himself in New York, but whose relatives in Rio think he is painting only canvases, not walls.

Not all immigrants from the middle sectors of Brazilian society make a smooth adjustment to their reduced circumstances in New York through minor deception or otherwise. A few examples will suffice. One woman who had been employed as an executive secretary in Rio de Janeiro and whose father was a lawyer, cleans houses and works as a seamstress in New York. She complained bitterly about her current lifestyle, saying that the house that she rents in Queens "is not fit" for her maid in Brazil. If she had in New York what she had had in Brazil she would be "living in Easthampton, Long Island," a wealthy suburb. Another Brazilian, a mechanical engineer, is also deeply troubled by the downward trajectory of his status in New York. He told me that he "feels like a dog" working for the small moving company that employs him. He finds the work very difficult because he is unaccustomed to doing any kind of hard physical labor. "I live the life of a peasant," he said with self-pity. Likewise, Miguel, a psychologist from Rio, spoke of how humiliated he was when he worked as a delivery truck driver in New Jersey. His boss baited him, calling him "Dr. Michael" and asking him why, if he was so educated, he was working as a truck driver. He used the words "degrading," "humiliating," and "distressing" to describe this experience, and he eventually quit his job.

Brazilian immigrants, of course, are not unique in this social descent. Sociologist Mary Castro has noted the middle-class origins and menial jobs of many Colombian immigrants in New York City: Colombian women with university educations working in the garment industry and other women who had been secretaries and schoolteachers back home employed as domestic servants in New York. But their identity remained the same. Says Castro: "Although they are now blue collar or service workers . . . [they] still see themselves as members of the middle class. Their ideological references are based on this idealized class position."[13]

Some Lateral Pirouettes

Although the primary social trajectory of Brazilian immigrants in New York is downward, there is a small group of well-educated Brazilians who have lived in the city long enough to have moved out of the menial jobs they had when they first immigrated to the United States up to a decade ago. These are lateral pirouettes in the sense that the immigrants in question are now employed in the types of white-collar positions, albeit at better pay, that they likely would have had if they had remained in Brazil. One example is Marta, a chemical engineer from Belo Horizonte, who worked as a maid when she first arrived in New York, and then as a limousine driver, followed by a job selling real estate. Having secured a green card, she is currently looking for work as an engineer. Similarly, Rosalinda, who is from an upper-middle-class family in Rio de Janeiro, was employed as a live-in housekeeper in California and New York. She was able to obtain a green card and is now a junior executive with an international moving concern. Then, there is Geraldo, a university graduate from São Paulo, who held a variety of odd jobs including busing tables and pumping gas before he found a better position first with an electronics firm, and then with a television network. Two final examples are Olivia and Laurenço; both earned graduate degrees in New York while they worked as a housekeeper and a dishwasher, respectively. Olivia now

administers a drug rehabilitation program funded by the city, while Laurenço teaches classes in English as a second language at a local university.

An example of more modest occupational ascent is Anita, a university
graduate in literature from Minas Gerais. When she first came to New
York she worked as a cleaning woman. She is now a reservationist at one
of New York's best-known bistros, a gathering spot for the city's "beautiful people." While not earning a great deal more than she did as a household servant, Anita feels satisfied professionally in her current job because of its opportunities for promotion to a position in restaurant
management.

Despite their university educations, all these immigrants were handi-
capped at some point in the city's job market because they lacked green
cards. Still, their occupational mobility makes them exceptions to the
rule. Because of the obstacles most immigrants face in trying to move up
the employment ladder, getting a better-paying, higher-status job is not
easy even for the well-educated with green cards and a reasonably good
command of English. Antonia's experience illustrates one of the problems. She worked as a domestic servant for a few years after she came to
New York, and then found work at a Portuguese bank in the city. But
Antonia quit that job once she calculated its costs and went back to
housekeeping. Although her bank salary was somewhat higher than her
former wages, once social security, federal, state, and city taxes were deducted, her net income was less than when she was employed off the
books as a servant. Moreover, aside from the taxes withheld, white-collar
jobs, such as those in banks, often pay lower starting salaries—about
$250 a week—than many Brazilians earn working long hours at menial
jobs. Then, too, well-paying, white-collar work is notably scarce in the
midst of a recession, such as the one New York was experiencing in the
late 1980s and early 1990s. Finally, informants often mentioned a typically Brazilian impediment to obtaining a sought-after position. Lacking
job experience, a person needs a *pistolão*, they said, literally, "a big gun,"
a friend or relative who has influence and will use it on one's behalf. Put
simply, a person has to have "connections," which most immigrants lack.

Even rarer than lateral pirouettes are instances of vaults up the social
scale—immigrants from very modest backgrounds in Brazil who have
"made it"; people from relatively poor families who have risen socially or
professionally since coming to the city.[14] Just how unusual such an ascent
is can be gauged from the fact that the same individual was always cited
as the Brazilian rags to riches success story. All the tales focus on Carlinhos, a man from Minas Gerais, who told me that when he left Brazil for
New York two decades ago he was "quite poor." During his first years in
the United States he worked as a dishwasher and a shoe shiner, and then

started driving a call car. He bought his own car, and eventually went into the limousine rental business. Today, he owns a fleet of ten or twelve limousines and employs Brazilian drivers. His clients are mostly Brazilian business executives and diplomats, both permanent residents and visitors to the city. But one of Carlinho's customers—a man who has wide contacts in New York's Brazilian community—told me that this is the only tale of success he can recount. He knows no other "pretty stories of people who started out selling oranges on the street and then made it."

A Question of Color

During the course of researching and writing this book, I gave a number of seminars on my work before various academic audiences. Questions about race invariably were raised: "What percent of Brazilian immigrants in New York are black?" or "What do Brazilians of color think about life in the city?" As noted earlier, the racial makeup of the Brazilian population in New York City is decidedly tipped toward the lighter end of the color scale, making it atypical of Brazil as a whole. Recall that over 80 percent of the Brazilians in my sample were white, 8 percent were of mixed ancestry, and 8 percent were black. Thus, blacks and other people of color comprise about 16 percent of my New York sample, a fraction of the nearly 45 percent reported for the Brazilian population as a whole in the 1980 census. Moreover, the figures in my sample were confirmed both by informants and by my own observations at dozens of large gatherings of Brazilians at street fairs, sports events, concerts, Carnival parties, and the like. Brazilians of color usually comprised 10 percent or less of those present.

The reason for the relative scarcity of dark-skinned immigrants in New York is no mystery to anyone familiar with Brazilian society. Despite Brazil's much-touted image as a "racial paradise," the truth is otherwise.[15] Brazilian racial types are not randomly distributed across social strata, and people of color are overrepresented at the lower echelons of Brazilian society, underrepresented in the middle sectors, and nearly absent among the Brazilian elite.[16] Thus, if Brazilian immigration is largely a middle- and lower-middle-class phenomenon, as it appears to be in New York, then it is not surprising that the immigrant population is lighter-skinned than that of the homeland.

Despite the relative paucity of dark-skinned Brazilians in the Big Apple, a study by my research assistant, Claudia Ehrlich, comparing racial attitudes among Brazilians in New York and São Paulo suggests that white Brazilians actually have *more* interaction with their nonwhite compatriots in the United States than they do with nonwhites in Brazil.[17] This is not the contradiction it first appears to be. Since Brazilians tend to socialize with Brazilians of like social status and since Brazilians in New York, including nonwhites, seem to come mostly from the middle-strata of Brazilian society, middle-class *paulistas*, for example, are more likely to have contact with middle-class nonwhites in New York than they do in São Paulo. Moreover, Ehrlich has reported that this situation, along with the fact that white, middle-class Brazilians are more apt to see blacks in middle-class positions in the United States than in Brazil, can result in an abatement of racist attitudes among white Brazilians. In the words of one of Ehrlich's informants:

> American blacks are different from Brazilian blacks. I think that racial attitudes towards blacks change for all Brazilians who come to the United States. In Brazil you don't see [blacks eating] in restaurants, and here you do. At the beginning it's difficult to accept this idea because we are not accustomed to this. We grew up in a society that has more blacks than whites, but blacks have always lived under very bad conditions in Brazil. What changed was my perception of the Negro race. I respect them for what they've achieved here.[18]

But if many white Brazilians are less bigoted in New York than they were in Brazil, some African-Brazilian immigrants still feel the sting of racism from their compatriots in the city. One man of mixed ancestry from São Paulo says he is experiencing *more* discrimination from Brazilians in New York than he did in Brazil. He is accepted as a musician here, he says, "because this fits their stereotype of people of color," but not as a video technician, a job he has held since coming to the United States. In contrast, Mona, who is light-skinned, with African facial features, says she has been subjected to racism on only one occasion since arriving in New York—from an American, not from a Brazilian. When the woman who employed Mona as a baby-sitter called an American friend to see if the latter wanted to hire Mona to baby-sit, the friend replied that she "didn't want a black taking care of her children." Apart from this instance, Mona says, being "dark" has not been a problem and she "can't complain about Americans in terms of race."

Although Brazilians living in the city sometimes make racially insensitive remarks, far more frequent are comments about how "different" American blacks are from black people in Brazil. White Brazilians contrast what they perceive as the "aggressiveness" of African-Americans with the deferential behavior they are used to and have come to expect from African-Brazilians back home. But what they are actually alluding to, I believe, is not racially based but class-linked behavior. In Brazil people from the lower echelons of society are expected to act with deference towards their purported "social superiors." And, because African-Brazilians are disproportionately found in the lower strata of Brazilian society, Brazilians conflate such behavior with skin color.

RACIAL SELECTION?

Aside from the fact that emigration is tied to social class and non-whites in Brazil are more likely to be from the lower than from the middle sectors of society, some selection against nonwhites also may take place in the issuance of tourist visas by U.S. consular personnel in Brazil. While such selection is impossible to verify, a few Brazilians insist that it occurs. One immigrant told me that when she was waiting to be interviewed for a tourist visa at the U.S. consulate in São Paulo, a man on line with her loudly proclaimed, "Anyone with green eyes can get a tourist visa here"—that is, anyone who is white. A light-skinned woman of mixed ancestry waiting in the same line said she did not expect to have any trouble getting a visa because she "was not black." Meanwhile, two well-dressed black men were denied tourist visas without explanation, seeming to confirm these suspicions.

Still, it is far more likely that visa denial is based on social class rather than on race. Keep in mind that to get a tourist visa to the United States today, one must convince consular officials of one's intention to return to Brazil, an intention that is best demonstrated with a high-paying job, a substantial bank balance, or tangible property, all of which white, middle-class applicants are more likely to have than their poorer, nonwhite compatriots.

What is most notable in regard to race is that it is almost never a spontaneous topic of conversation among Brazilian immigrants in New York. Brazilians are far more likely to talk about other issues that touch on their identity: their invisibility as a distinct ethnic group, their being confused with Hispanics, their lack of community spirit, and the social, economic, and educational backgrounds of other Brazilians in New York. In all of these discussions race is rarely or never mentioned.

Gender Adjustments

Race may not be a common topic of conversation among Brazilians in New York City, but the same cannot be said of gender. Informants were wont to discuss everything from the ratio of males to females in their community, to the differences in the kind of work men and women do in New York, to the problems some married couples face after migrating, to how migration to New York has modified traditional gender roles.

Long-term Brazilian residents of the city agree that men once outnumbered women in the immigrant stream—the most common ratio cited was

70 percent to 30 percent—but that since the mid-1980s, more Brazilian women have been coming to New York. Today, most say, the sex ratio is roughly even, although one woman insists there are still more men than women in the immigrant community. She cites the parties given by her compatriots as evidence. Men outnumber women at the parties, and the hosts are always urging her to "bring her girlfriends along."

Women almost certainly outnumber men in the over-forty age group. Evidence for this comes from a number of quarters. Over the last decade, considerably more women than men in this age cohort have boarded at Dona Dahlia's establishment. Then, too, in my own sample, women in the forty-plus age group somewhat outnumber men. Finally, both informants' statements on the matter and my own casual observation of large numbers of Brazilians in a variety of settings tend to confirm this.

Why is this the case? What is drawing a disproportionate number of middle-aged Brazilian women to the Big Apple? The answer is related to traditional Brazilian gender roles.[19] Often, the first relatives that young Brazilian immigrants invite to New York for a visit are their mothers. These women usually plan on staying a month or two, but some keep delaying the return home. While they are in the city, they may pick up extra money by baby-sitting or doing housecleaning. Others come to New York for a time to care for their grandchildren while both parents are at work; then they simply stay on. Still others do go back to Brazil, only to return to New York after a few months. Whatever the precise scenario, the women eventually find more permanent jobs—most often some form of domestic service—and become immigrants themselves.

The life histories of these women also figure in the equation. Having been housewives since marrying in their early or midtwenties, they usually have grown children. But by the time they visit New York, many are widowed, divorced, separated, or perhaps involved in a less than happy marriage. Most have never held paid employment, having played the traditional role of dependent spouse. Then they visit the Big Apple. There, the occasional stint as a baby-sitter or housecleaner makes them acutely aware of their long financial dependence; for the first time in their lives, these women have money of their own to spend—a lot of money—from the perspective of people used to Brazilian incomes. No wonder they find New York so enticing. In the words of one Brazilian, "They are ready to leave their old lives behind and try something new; they are ready for a taste of liberation and independence."[20]

Some of this newfound independence was much in evidence late one Friday evening at a nightclub in Queens frequented by Brazilians and other newcomers to the city. A group of five Brazilian women who appeared to be in their forties and fifties sat at the bar drinking, smoking, talking among themselves, and apparently having a good time; their peals of laughter could be heard above the 1940s-style swing music played by the house band. The women were occasionally asked to dance by male patrons of the establishment, which caters to a mixed, largely middle-aged clientele of Greeks, Hispanics, Italians, Americans, and Brazilians. What was so memorable about the scene is that it could not have occurred in these women's native land. In Brazil, it would be unthinkable for "respectable" middle-aged women from the middle strata of society to go to a bar or a nightclub "alone," meaning without appropriate male escorts.

There is yet another reason why this country appeals to middle-aged Brazilian women. Although we are accustomed to thinking of the United States as a nation preoccupied with youth and beauty, many Brazilians would argue that this preoccupation is minor compared to the obsession back home. Ana, a forty-six-year-old widowed nurse from Rio de Janeiro, cited this as yet another reason why women her age find the United States a more attractive place to live than Brazil. In her country, "a woman of forty-five or fifty is seen as old; she's only a *vovó* [grandma], and so she's not worth anything." This is why, Ana says, she prefers American men: "They don't think this way as much. Here women are not over the hill once they've hit thirty."

A QUESTION OF FACE

In contrasting the way middle-aged women are perceived in Brazil and the United States, Ana provided me with an example. She said how surprised and pleased she was that a woman her own age was demonstrating the proper use of a face cream in a New York department store. "In Rio," she noted caustically, "a twenty-year-old salesgirl who knows nothing about face creams would be behind the counter."

Old Roles and New

Brazilian women settle in New York for much the same reason that Brazilian men do: for jobs that pay far more than any they could hope to get back home.[21] To be sure, from time to time a Brazilian male would insist that the real reason Brazilian women are flocking to New York is "to find rich American husbands." Looking past this bit of sexist typecasting, however, it is jobs that provide the urban backdrop for a revamping and updating of traditional Brazilian gender roles. Some immigrant women, especially married women, leave dependence behind because of what one immigrant called their "executive power" (*poder executivo*)—their newfound status as breadwinners. They take jobs, and for the first time they earn as much as or sometimes more than their spouses. This, in turn, may have consequences in the domestic realm, most notably on the domestic division of labor.

Brazilians, of course, are not unique in this. Researchers often cite the impact of paid employment on women's status and role within the context of migration. In their book on migration from the Dominican Republic to the United States, Sherri Grasmuck and Patricia Pessar note that since immigrant wages in New York are low, at least in the early years of migration, most Dominican households are unable to keep up the traditional male wage earner/female dependent division of labor. Men's wages are insufficient to support a household, so women start contributing to basic living expenses. Similarly, in her study of Haitian women in New York, Susan Buchanan found that earning money gave immigrant women far greater economic independence. This was especially true for women who had not held jobs in Haiti or whose earnings there had only supplemented their husband's. This reordering of financial responsibilities, in turn, can put a large dent in the timeworn, patriarchal ideology that insists men must be the lone—or at least the primary—breadwinners.[22]

While women's employment can reduce dependence on men and enhance self-confidence, their new financial authority also can lead to greater antagonism between the sexes, particularly among married couples. How such changes can transform the lives and gender relations of real people is illustrated by the following example. Veronica and Claudinho have been married ten years, and have one son. They have lived in New York for two years, and both of them have jobs cleaning apartments. Veronica earns somewhat more than Claudinho, and she buys whatever she wants with her wages—a dining table, a color television set, a videocassette recorder—without consulting her husband, something she could never have done in Brazil because she would not have had the income to do it. Veronica loves to dance, and on weekends she often goes out with friends to discos. Claudinho, who prefers to spend his time listening to his extensive record collection, stays home with their son.

All this is in sharp contrast to their former lifestyle in Brazil. There, Claudinho, then an assistant bank manager, was the sole family breadwinner, and Veronica was a housewife. On weekends Claudinho would go off with his friends to bars and nightclubs or to the beach or a barbecue at someone's house. Veronica stayed home with their young son. She made dinner, and sometimes Claudinho came home to eat it; other times he did not. Now, with her new financial autonomy and the partial reversal of their old roles, Veronica has told Claudinho that he is "paying for his past sins" back home—not showing up for dinner and going out without her. As a result of these role shifts, a great deal of friction was evident between the two, and the couple have since separated.

A number of informants said that this scenario was not at all uncommon and that many marriages broke up after the move to New York. Most credited it to the fact that married women were far more likely to be employed in the United States than in Brazil and that with a job came economic independence and a renegotiation of traditional gender roles. One Brazilian said that he told a close friend who had just arrived in New York "not to let his wife work" if he valued his marriage; he even bet him that they would get divorced if she got a job. Within two months after she went to work, they separated. Grasmuck and Pessar note how ironic it is that for many immigrant women, the achievement of economic parity has led not to more egalitarian households but to the breakup of their marriages.[23]

Other immigrants suggested that Brazilian couples who meet in New York and then marry are less likely to end up separated or divorced than those who were married before coming to the city. The reasoning is that since the woman was already employed when the couple first met, her work and the economic clout that it confers was a given from the start of the relationship. While Brazilian immigration to New York is still too recent to gauge such a pattern, Buchanan's research on Haitian women is suggestive. Informants told her that couples who marry in New York have a better chance of staying together than do couples who were already married when they left Haiti.[24]

The renegotiation of the domestic division of labor is also tied to women's employment and can be a volatile issue that affects the health and longevity of marital and other intimate relationships. A Brazilian woman told me that her boyfriend "never did anything domestic back in Brazil" but has changed his ways since coming to the United States, and a Brazilian man noted his own updated ideology:

> You lose a lot of preconceived notions about the relationship between men and women. Here in the United States, the man participates more in the life of the house, and the woman has much more dialogue with the husband. The man allows [sic] the woman to work out of necessity. A man who helps the woman in domestic chores begins to appreciate what housework is like and he gives it more value.

An American woman married to a Brazilian man provides another twist on coming to terms with altered gender roles. She and her husband, in her words, "have very egalitarian roles in child care and housework." He cares for their baby at least as much as she does, changes diapers, and so on. She cooks, and he does the dishes, as well as the laundry. But this gender flexibility comes to an abrupt halt when her husband's friends from his small hometown in Minas Gerais come to visit. Then she reverts to what she considers the traditional role of a Brazilian wife. She serves the dinner, clears the table, and washes the dishes. Her husband does not help, and she does not ask him to because she "doesn't want him to lose face in front of his old friends." But, she adds with obvious satisfaction, when her husband's more sophisticated friends from São Paulo pay a visit, she does not wait on them, and her husband resumes his new, liberated role.

A MOTHER NOTICES

One Brazilian woman, a schoolteacher, noted with approval the changes in gender roles associated with emigration and cited her own son as a case in point. Calling the United States "the best classroom there is," she said that when her son lived at home before leaving for New York he did nothing for himself; "he didn't lift a finger to help in the house." This, she noted, is typical of the Brazilian male, and she cited her next-door neighbor, a physician, as an example: "He wouldn't so much as get himself a glass of water from the kitchen. He has his wife or the maid fetch it for him."

When her son returned home for a ten-day visit, he was very helpful around the house; he took out the garbage and even did the dishes on occasion. Once when he was sweeping the kitchen and his next-door neighbor, the physician, spotted him, the latter made a snide remark about the "unfortunate results" that living in the United States had on the kinds of domestic chores men were willing to do.

Here, too, research on other immigrant groups in the city suggests some parallels with the Brazilian case. Nancy Foner found that Jamaican men were more likely to "help" their wives with housework and child care in New York than in Jamaica and that many of her informants, both female and male, began questioning "the legitimacy of the traditional divisions of labor that assigns only women to housework." And when Dominican women in New York were asked for an example of better relations between husbands and wives in the United States than in their homeland, they mentioned a more equitable division of household responsibilities. For most of these women, in fact, an "improvement in gender relations had been an unintended outcome of the immigrant experience."[25] I think the majority of Brazilian immigrant women in New York would agree.

Aside from social class and gender as markers of identity in New York's Brazilian community, I have briefly alluded to another salient feature of Brazilian life in the Big Apple: Brazilians' status as members of an invisible minority within the city's kaleidoscopic ethnic mélange. This invisibility stems, in part, from Brazilians immersion in and confusion with the far more numerous Spanish-speaking populations in the city. I now turn to a fuller discussion of the causes and consequences of this cloaked and ambiguous ethnic identity.

CHAPTER ELEVEN

An Invisible Minority

We are a minority within a minority.

—*Brazilian immigrant in New York City*

EARLY IN MY RESEARCH in New York, a Brazilian immigrant who had a green card and was applying for a job with the Bristol Myers Company showed me the employment form she was asked to fill out indicating her race/ethnicity. One category was "Hispanic from Mexico, Central, or South America." She is indeed from South America, yet she steadfastly refused to classify herself as Hispanic. "I simply will not do that," she said vehemently. She went on to recount similar problems: how an American she met insisted that since she was from Brazil, she *must* speak Spanish. In fact, she did speak Spanish, which she had learned while living in Argentina, she told the American, but her native language was Portuguese. He said that he did not believe her because all the Brazilians he knew understood Spanish.

Within this brief vignette are all the elements that make Brazilian identity so problematic in New York City and elsewhere in the United States. Brazilians are confused with Hispanics because most Americans do not know that Brazil is in any way distinct from the rest of Latin America. Americans also do not realize that the term "Hispanic" is a misnomer when applied to Brazilians since in common usage the term refers to Spanish speakers or those of Spanish-speaking descent—and *Brazilians, of course, speak Portuguese.*[1] I emphasize this point because some of the ethnic confusion surrounding Brazilians is attributable to American ignorance. Most Americans, including many educated ones, simply do not know that Brazilians speak Portuguese. They think that Spanish is the language of Brazil and that Portuguese is spoken only in Portugal. As one informant said dejectedly, "Not one American has ever said to me, "Oh, you're from Brazil; then you must speak Portuguese."

Parenthetically, the Portuguese are also touchy about being confused with their Spanish neighbors. When representatives of Portugal, Spain, and nineteen Latin American countries met in Mexico in 1991, the Portuguese government objected to the original rubric for the conference, "the Ibero-American summit." They argued that the name Iberia was associated with Spain and insisted that the meeting be called the Luso-Hispanic-American summit, in deference to Portugal's ancient name: Lusitania.[2]

To summarize Brazilians' jumbled status: they *are* South Americans, and they *are* Latin Americans or Latinos, but they are *not* Hispanics. As a result of this labyrinthine ethnicity, one of the first things that a Brazilian immigrant learns to say when meeting Americans in New York is, "I do *not* speak Spanish." Just as Haitian immigrants to the city do not want to be confused with African-Americans, Brazilian immigrants in the Big Apple are angered when they are identified as Hispanic. That this is a sore point among Brazilians is evident from my informant's vehemence about her ethnic identity. As another Brazilian, who was barely able to contain his frustration, put it: "There are 300 million Portuguese-speakers in the world today, and I find it just incredible that Americans don't know there is a difference between our language and Spanish."

Brazilians in New York tell tales of ethnic confusion with a mixture of exasperation and amusement. "What kind of Spanish" do you speak?" one American demanded of a Brazilian immigrant. And after a Brazilian told an American she met at a cocktail party that she was born in Brazil and did not speak Spanish, the American responded, "Oh, of course, you're from Brazil. That's the country where the upper class speaks Portuguese and the lower class speaks Spanish." Yet another Brazilian enrolled her son, Jorge, in a school in Spanish Harlem. His teachers assumed that he was Hispanic and pronounced his name accordingly; with an initial "h" as in Spanish, rather than the soft initial "g" sound of Portuguese. His mother recounted the battle she had trying to get his teachers to pronounce his name correctly and to convince them that her son did not speak Spanish.[3]

The cultural and linguistic maze that enmeshes Brazilians is made even more complicated by the fact that many Brazilians *do* speak some Spanish, having learned it after they arrived in New York. Some, in fact, speak far better Spanish than English. There are two reasons for this. First, because of the similarity in vocabulary and grammar between Portuguese and Spanish, Brazilians learn Spanish much more easily than they learn English. Also, many of them work in a Spanish-speaking environment in restaurant kitchens and other places where they are surrounded by Spanish-speakers. I was amazed at the number of Brazilians who spoke a minimal amount of English but who had no problem communicating in Spanish. When I was interviewing one Brazilian in her apartment, the doorbell rang, and the visitor turned out to be a Spanish-speaking woman handing out pamphlets for the Jehovah's Witnesses. They had a brief discussion in Spanish, and my Brazilian informant declined to take the literature. This woman speaks almost no English after more than two years in New York but handles Spanish with ease. Parenthetically, her Brazilian husband, who has also learned Spanish since coming to New York, prepared for and received his First Communion in Spanish at a local Hispanic church.

HISPANIC CAMARADERIE

The rampant confusion between Hispanics and Brazilians occasionally works to the advantage of the latter. One Brazilian, a ten-year resident of the United States who picked up fluent Spanish in New York and Miami, believes that his language proficiency got him out of a difficult situation. A Cuban traffic officer in Miami was about to give him a hefty parking fine until he convinced the officer that he was Puerto Rican and thus "practically a compatriot."

Although Brazilians take a certain pride in saying, "No, no, I don't speak Spanish," the language does come in handy on occasion. As one Brazilian immigrant noted, however much his compatriots dislike being confused with Hispanics and however much they prefer American to Hispanic television programs, if there is a story on the news that really interests them, that they *really* want to understand, they will turn to the news program on Channel 41, a Spanish-language station in New York.

Still, Brazilian immigrants' dislike of being confused with Hispanics is very real, and stems from a number of sources. The effort of Brazilians to distinquish themselves linguistically and ethnically from other Latin American groups in the city is partly rooted in cultural pride, in the uniqueness of their "race" (*raça*), as they call it. We can trace this back to Portugal, where as the popular saying goes, "neither good winds nor good marriages come from Spain." This attitude also exists in Brazil, a self-contained nation with a sense of its own distinctiveness—almost isolation—from the rest of South America. Brazilians have long been indifferent to their South American neighbors, dismissing their shared Iberian roots as of no special consequence. As such, Brazilians do not identify very much either with other South Americans or with Hispanics in general, whether in Brazil or in the United States. In the words of Brazilian anthropologist Darcy Ribeiro, "Brazil and Spanish America [are] divided into two worlds, back to back to each other."[4]

Brazilians, moreover, are largely unfamiliar with other Latin American cultures. Wealthy, well-educated Brazilians are far more likely to visit New York or Paris and to learn English or French as a second language than they to visit Buenos Aires or Lima and study Spanish. Spanish is rarely heard in Brazil except for the occasional Argentine tourist, and hardly anyone studies the language in school; Brazilians study English, French, or, less often, German.[5] One Brazilian immigrant told me that it never would have occurred to her to study Spanish in Brazil and that she never appreciated the value of speaking Spanish until she came to New York. Now she is studying Spanish at a local community college.

It is also true that the ethnic category "Hispanic" is unknown to most Brazilian immigrants when they first arrive in New York because it does not exist in Brazil. There, the term "Spanish" refers to people from Spain; those from Spanish-speaking countries in South America are called Bolivians, Ecuadorians, Chileans, and so on, but never Hispanics. But if Brazilian immigrants are not familiar with the term "Hispanic" (*hispano*) when they first come to New York, they quickly learn what it means—and just as quickly learn to insist that it not be applied to them. Most are convinced that they receive better treatment from Americans when they make it clear that they are not Hispanic. In stark terms, Brazilians insist that there is discrimination against Hispanics in this country and that as long as Americans confuse them with Hispanics they, too, bear the brunt of anti-Hispanic prejudice. Thus, while Haitian and Jamaican immigrants in New York reject an African-American identity because it defines a population with limited status and power, Brazilians reject an Hispanic identity for much the same reason. And Brazilians are not the only ones who try to steer clear of the Hispanic label. Because of the perceived prejudice on the part of Americans against Hispanics, even some Hispanics try to disguise their origins. "Mexicans," writes anthropologist Jorge Klor de Alva, "hoping to avoid discrimination presented themselves as Spanish or Latin Americans, and light-skinned Puerto Ricans sometimes tried to pass for "Spanish," "Jewish," or, more commonly, "Italian."[6]

Finally, the effort of Brazilians to disassociate themselves from Hispanics also stems from their own prejudice and elitism. Anti-Hispanic remarks are not uncommon in the Brazilian community in New York. "Americans don't know that Brazilians are different from Hispanics," I was told by one informant, "that Brazilians are very hard workers." Most Brazilians "think of themselves as superior to Hispanics," another explained. "That's why we get angry when we are confused with them." Class elitism is certainly rearing its ugly head here, too. Since the majority of Brazilians in New York are middle and lower-middle class and many are well educated, they resent being confused with the rest of the city's Latin population, most of whom they regard as poorer and less educated than themselves.

But these feelings are by no means universal among Brazilians in the city. I was told, for example, that Hispanics help Brazilians more than most New Yorkers do, and that Hispanics are sympathetic to Brazilians' lack of fluency in English and are patient with Brazilians who speak halting Spanish. Many of these issues were implicit in an argument about ethnic identity that I witnessed between two Brazilians. Marisa became very angry at Rosario when he told her that he gets "furious" when Americans take him for Hispanic. "You are just prejudiced," Marisa said. "Brazilians are discriminating against Hispanics when they say they don't want to be identified with them. They are adopting the same racist attitudes as the dominant culture." But Brazilians "*are* different from Hispanics," Rosario shot back. "We *are* more culturally advanced than they are," a proposition that Marisa heatedly denied as she stomped out of the room.

ALONG THE SAME LINES

"While not eager to cling together as Haitians [read Brazilians], most Haitian [read Brazilian] immigrants were also not eager to accept the type of black [read Hispanic] identity ascribed to them in the United States, since this identity was racially [read linguistically/socially] based and was used to delineate populations with limited access to the productive system, to status, and to power. To accept a black [read Hispanic] identity in the United States would mean accepting the subordinate status of Black Americans [read Hispanic Americans]."

"Jamaicans [in New York] are eager to distinguish themselves from black Americans . . . emphasizing their distinct Jamaican or West Indian character gives them a sense of pride. . . . Setting themselves apart from black Americans, they also believe, brings better treatment from whites."

Sources: Glick-Schiller and Fouron, "'Everywhere We Go, We Are in Danger,'" 336. Foner, "Sex Roles and Sensibilities," 137.

The Secret, Silent Migration

One Brazilian told me that the migration of his compatriots to New York City is "secret" and "silent" because New Yorkers are unaware that it is taking place. This invisibility is due both to ethnic and linguistic confusion on the part of Americans and to the fact that Brazilians—apparently not contributing much to the city's high crime rate—receive little attention in the press.[7] Moreover, there is no existing Brazilian community in New York into which recent immigrants could fit. There is no Brazilian equivalent of Chinatown or Little Italy—no neighborhood with a distinct cultural cast that could give this new ingredient in the city's ethnic stew a soupçon of visibility.

Evidence abounds that Brazilian immigration is "secret" and "silent"—virtually absent from popular consciousness. Coinciding with the opening of the Ellis Island Museum in New York harbor, for example, the local media gave considerable play to what were termed the "new immigrants" in the city's ethnic mix. A one-hour, prime time television special covered various aspects of the new migration, featuring clips of or mentioning recent immigrants from at least fifteen countries. Brazil was not among them. Similarly, in a 1991 cover story about the mélange of ethnic groups in the city in *New York Woman* magazine, thirty-two different nationalities were mentioned, including Argentines, Thais, Cambodians, Guatemalans, Trinidadians, and "40 or 50 Laotian families living in the Bronx." The feature's *sole* mention of Brazilians was in connection to the Portuguese-Spanish Synagogue in Manhattan, the city's oldest congregation, whose origin "can be traced to the arrival of twenty-three Brazilian Jews in 1654."[8]

A MIDSUMMER NIGHT'S NUDITY

A minor flap over a free performance of a Shakespearean play in Central Park is another example of the invisibility of Brazilians to their fellow New Yorkers. When it was announced that *A Midsummer Night's Dream* was going to be presented in Portuguese, there was grumbling in the local press. *Portuguese? Who speaks Portuguese in New York?* The producer responded that while it was true that few people in the city understand Portuguese, the previous summer a play had been presented in Central Park in Japanese and it had drawn quite a large audience.

Putting a quick damper on these complaints, the media then publicized the fact that in the play—to be performed by a Brazilian theater company—some of the female performers would appear topless, a few of the men would wear costumes that were little more than G-strings, and in one scene, the actress who played Titiana would wear nothing at all.

The play, which ran for twelve consecutive nights in a 2,000-seat, open-air theatre in Central Park, was a near-sellout. Commented the producer, "Even though the language might be a problem, nudity is international."

Source: New York Magazine, July 29, 1991, 9.

Although it, too, had numerous articles on recent additions to the city's melting pot, that bastion of coverage, the *New York Times* contained not one word about Brazilian immigration until November 1990. Even then,

11.1 Despite well-attended annual events, such as the Brazilian Independence Day street fair, Brazilians remain an invisible minority in New York City.

the single article to appear did not report on Brazilian immigration to the United States per se or on Brazilians as newcomers to the city. Rather, it was about the town of Governador Valadares in Minas Gerais as an exporter of immigrants and the impact that their remittances had had on the local economy.[9]

Examples of Brazilian invisibility are endless and by no means limited to the American public and the popular media. Even scholars writing books about immigration to the United States, or to New York specifically, ignore Brazilians. Brazilians are notably absent from two books on new immigrants to the city published in the late 1980s. A third book on the topic covers the large number of South Americans residing in Queens by mentioning Colombians, Peruvians, Argentines, and Ecuadorians but not Brazilians. And the only mention of Brazilians in a 1990 book on immigrants in the United States points out how little they have contributed to the immigrant flow in terms of numbers. The figure cited is from the 1980 U.S. census, prior to the mid-1980s influx: 40,000 Brazilians, or 0.3 percent of the foreign-born in the entire United States in that year.[10]

Isn't Geography Taught in American Schools?

How do Brazilians view their ethnic submersion? One clue is a question Brazilian immigrants often ask: "Isn't geography a recognized field of study in the United States?"—a sarcastic jab meant to express disgust at Americans' ignorance about their southern neighbors. As one immigrant put it, "Americans have very little culture when it comes to Latin America." One story about American naiveté that made the rounds of the Brazilian community concerns an American who called the Brazilian consulate seeking tourist information about Buenos Aires; no one could convince her that she had called the wrong place. A member of New York's Brazilian elite related his encounter with some Americans at a dinner party. When the discussion turned to U.S. foreign policy, everyone seemed to know where Nicaragua was. "Not surprising," the man said. "It's so much in the news lately." But when he told them that he was from Brazil, one of the American guests remarked, "Oh Brazil, that's just a little bit below Nicaragua, isn't it?"—geographical benightedness that the Brazilian attributed to the lack of any recent "communist threat" in his country.

Brazilians often regaled me with tales of the inane stereotypes Americans hold about their land. A Brazilian who works as a waiter in Manhattan said that when he told another waiter that he was from São Paulo, his fellow worker said that he had heard that there were "Indians roaming the streets of the city." Another Brazilian remarked that it is very frustrating to socialize with Americans because they are so uninformed about

Brazil. "Do you eat snakes?" Americans ask. "Do you have windows in your houses?" Americans, she said, "think we live in huts. It's disappointing really because I thought Americans were so cultured and they don't even know where Brazil is!"

In late 1990, a dance troupe from Minas Gerais played a limited engagement in a New York theater. The group does both classical ballet and modern dance. However, many Americans, upon hearing that the group was Brazilian, assumed that they were going to see a samba show, with women in scanty costumes and feathers. This, said one informant, is part of the "samba, lambada, string bikini, semi-nude mulatto stereotype" that so many Americans have of Brazil. When she says she is Brazilian, some American men whistle and roll their eyes, while some Hispanic men cry out, "Oh, *mamacita!*"

NEVER UNDERESTIMATE THE IGNORANCE OF AMERICANS
(WHEN IT COMES TO GEOGRAPHY)

One of the reasons Brazilians are invisible in New York City and presumably elsewhere in the country is the ignorance of most Americans about Brazil and things Brazilian. I once overheard an example. Two well-dressed, obviously middle-class women were having a conversation in the sportswear department of the Saks Fifth Avenue department store. One of the women was a tourist from Brazil. She was chatting with the saleswoman who was ringing up her sale. The Brazilian was telling the saleswoman—who was saying how much she loved to travel—that the latter really ought to consider Brazil for her next vacation. The climate was right, it was relatively inexpensive, the food was good, and so on, said the Brazilian, adding that the saleswoman should visit her hometown of São Paulo if she ever came to Brazil.

"São Paulo? That's the capital of Brazil, isn't it?" asked the saleswoman. "No, it is not. It is the largest city in the country like New York is in the United States," replied the Brazilian in a tight but genteel tone. "What's the food like in Brazil? Sort of Spanish, isn't it?" continued the saleswoman. "No," replied the Brazilian visitor with a hint of exasperation, "it is not. In São Paulo, like in New York, we have cuisine from many parts of the world. There are Italian restaurants and Chinese restaurants and French restaurants and. . ." "Really?" said the saleswoman, surprise in her voice, "I thought everything was just sort of Spanish there."

One Brazilian expressed annoyance that even Hispanics in the United States are ignorant about Brazil, citing a Spanish-language periodical that returned the capital of Brazil to Rio de Janeiro—Brasília has been the capital for the last thirty years—and used the word "*carioca*" as a generic term for Brazilians, when, in fact, the term refers only to natives of the city of Rio de Janeiro. "If Americans, who concentrate on their own navels, think that Brazil is in Bolivia, okay," he said. "But when our Mexican, Cuban, Puerto Rican, and other Hispanic friends commit the same assanities . . . why it's pathetic."[11] This was a snide reference to then-President Reagan's gaffe on a trip to Brazil; at a state dinner in his honor, he raised his glass and toasted Bolivia. Rampant ignorance of the South American continent has afflicted both recent Republican administrations. During a stop in Chile on a visit to Latin America, then-Vice President Dan Quayle received a lot of press attention when he told reporters how "sorry he was that he hadn't studied Latin in high school" so that he could communicate with the locals.[12]

Hispanic businesses and the Hispanic media also are confused about how to designate Brazilians and other Portuguese-speakers. For example, in the 1990 "Directory of Hispanic Auto Dealers," published by the periodical *Hispanic Business*, seven dealers are listed who have distinctly Portuguese or Brazilian surnames. Similarly, in the same magazine, the subject of a column on prominent "Hispanic business executives" was a CEO of a Miami bank who was born and raised in Brazil. Finally, in another pubication, *Hispanic*, an article entitled "A Decidedly Hispanic Beat" reviewed the performance of a Brazilian jazz band that played in Miami.

Another interesting case is the state of California, which for purposes of affirmative action, offically classifies Brazilians and other Portuguese-speakers as Hispanics, as does Florida's Dade County. This contrasts with the practice of the U.S. Navy's Office of Civilian Personnel; this office uses the U.S. Civil Service Commission's definition of Hispanics, which specifically excludes Brazilians and Portuguese "unless [they] publicly choose to be covered by the Spanish-speaking program due to professed influence on their lives of Hispanic culture."[13]

Brazilians, of course, are not the only victims of ethnic obtuseness in this country. The American mass media, advertising firms, government agencies, and the non-Hispanic population alike generally do not distinguish among Hispanics from different countries or from different social classes or with different reasons for coming to the United States. The situation is artificially simplified by classifying everyone under the collective rubric "Hispanic," a term with implicit stereotypes about common cultures with common institutions. As a result, useful information on differences among Hispanic groups in this country can be difficult to come by.[14]

CROSSING AMERICA

"Several times, hearing some talk about Brazil, an American would blurt out:

"'Rio de Janeiro!'"

"I never heard anyone refer to Brasília or São Paulo or Juazeiro.

"One might smile, wiggle a little and then add: 'Carnival.' And we'd say:

"'Samba.'

"And he:

"'Bossa Nova.'

"And we:

"'Pelé.'

"And he:

"'Coffee.'

"And that's the way it would end.

"Brazil, a country of continental dimensions with a population of 150 million and many billions of dollars of external debt, is reduced to five or six words to the Americans. Big city Americans, let it be understood."

Source: Novaes and Perdigão, *A Travessia Americana*.

A Case Study in Confusion: Brazilians and the United States Census

The census categories become the language we use to talk about ourselves.

—MARGO J. ANDERSON, *The American Census*

The 1990 U.S. census coincided with my field research on Brazilian immigrants in New York City. This gave me the opportunity to do a case study of how one immigrant population—which includes a sizable number of undocumented individuals—was dealt with in this grand and costly decennial event. I found that the treatment of Brazilians in the collection of census data was a textbook case of ethnic invisibility, symptomatic of the fuzzy thinking about Brazilians in the United States. Nowhere on the census form do the words "Brazil" or "Brazilian" appear, although the form lists nearly every other country in Latin America; individuals from one of the few Latin countries not listed can check the box marked "Yes, other Spanish/Hispanic" and fill in the adjacent blank with their country of origin. This designation was arrived at after considerable thought, according to Jorge del Pinal, chief of ethnic and Hispanic statistics at the Bureau of the Census. The problem was how best to describe the various groups formerly labeled "Spanish-speaking" or "Spanish-surnamed."

Mr. Pinal noted some of the confusion that reigned at the Bureau of the Census: "Not all the people we considered Hispanic spoke Spanish. Not everybody had a Spanish surname."[15] The solution was the "other Spanish/Hispanic" compromise, with Brazilians entirely absent from the equation.

The detailed instructions that accompany the 1990 census form specify that the box marked "other Spanish/Hispanic" should be checked by people of the following origin or ancestry: "Mexican, Mexican-American, Chicano, Puerto Rican, Cuban, Argentinian, Colombian, Costa Rican, Dominican, Ecuadorean, Guatemalan, Honduran, Nicaraguan, Peruvian, Salvadoran, and [those from] other Spanish-speaking countries of the Caribbean or Central or South America, or from Spain."[16] Obviously, since Brazilians speak Portuguese, they cannot use the Hispanic designation as their own.

CENSUS NONSENSE

The muddled identity of Brazilians in the United States is epitomized by the conversation I had when I dialed the toll-free census information hotline to inquire about how Brazilians should list themselves on the census forms.

After I posed the question, the woman who had taken my call put me on hold. After a long wait, presumably for a conversation with her supervisor, she came back on the line and said that Brazilians should check the box marked "Spanish/Hispanic" and then write "Brazilian" in the blank. When I pointed out to her that *Brazilians speak Portuguese, not Spanish*, she again put me on hold. When she came back on the line, she said that Brazilians should check the box marked "No (not Spanish/Hispanic)" and should check the box marked "White." When I told her that there are also nonwhite Brazilians in the United States, she put me on hold for the third time. When she came back on the line, she said that the box "Other Race" should be checked and that "Brazilian" should be written in the blank that followed. When I objected that Brazilians are a *nationality, not a race*, she responded with a sigh of exasperation, told me to have a good day, and hung up.

The conundrum of the census categories was evident in a letter I received from a census field operations supervisor in California, a man of Portuguese descent, who wrote of the "agony" that he observed in individuals, both Hispanics and Portuguese-speakers, trying to fill in the ethnic/racial portion of the census form. He noted that some Portuguese-speaking people wrote in "Portuguese," "Cape Verdean," "Brazilian," or "Azorean" under the Spanish/Hispanic designation, but that most of them used race, usually "white," rather than nationality to identify them-selves.[17] Thus, if the majority of Brazilians classified themselves as "white" and left the Spanish/Hispanic designation blank, their national origin would be lost and an undercount of Brazilians would be assured.

A special half-hour television program aired on "Census Day"—one week before the census forms were supposed to be returned—did nothing to allay this ethnic invisibility. I had been told by a census official that the program would be "directed at Brazilians as well as Hispanics." The pro-gram was entirely in English, although the hosts appeared to be native Spanish-speakers. In the discussion about what the census is and how the forms should be filled out, the terms "Latino" or "Latino community"—which certainly could include Brazilians—were generally used. After all, "Latino" is a more inclusive term than "Hispanic." As sociologist Hector Guadalupe has noted, "Although all Hispanics are Latinos, not all Lati-nos are Hispanic."[18]

Along with emphasizing the confidentiality of the data collected and encouraging undocumented immigrants to complete the forms, the pro-gram stressed the great improvement in the 1990 census over the 1980 census in its recognition of Latinos in the United States. According to the program host, there were only three designations for this popula-tion in the 1980 census forms: "Puerto Rican," "Cuban," and "Mexi-can." But, he noted with obvious pride, in the 1990 forms many addi-tional nationalities were included, and he went on to name all thirteen Latin countries (cited above) listed on the official census form. Unfortu-nately, none of these messages of ethnic pride and inclusion mentioned Brazilians.

At the end of the program, telephone numbers were provided for addi-tional information on filling out census forms. The lines were constantly busy, but I finally managed to get through to the New Jersey number, which was staffed by volunteers from Catholic Social Services in Eliza-beth, a town with a sizable Brazilian population. The volunteer with whom I spoke was the first person I found providing census information who knew that Brazilians speak Portuguese, not Spanish, that they do not consider themselves Hispanic, and that they were therefore unlikely to check the "other Spanish/Hispanic" box on the form. The phone volun-teer also was aware that there was a large Portuguese-speaking popula-tion in his area; he told me that one Portuguese-speaking volunteer was answering the phones.

Still, none of this man's ethnic awareness could compensate for the constraints imposed on Brazilians by the official categories used on the census forms. Although he said that Brazilians should not check "other Spanish/Hispanic" if they "did not think of themselves as Hispanic," they still could write "Brazilian" in the blank next to that designation. When

I asked him how Brazilians were going to be counted as a separate nationality in the census if there were no place on the form for them to identify themselves as such, he sighed and said that the *long form* sent to one in seven U.S. households would pick them up since it had a specific question about country of origin. "The long form, really?" I asked. The problem is that the long form, which asks far more questions than the short form and is estimated to take three times as long to fill out, is unlikely to be seen as user friendly by immigrants with a poor command of English, especially if they are undocumented. If census officials relied entirely on the long form to enumerate Brazilians and other undesignated immigrants, a significant undercount would almost certainly result. And Brazilians are more likely to be undercounted than other immigrant groups since, unlike Asian, African, and other Latin American immigrants, Brazilians have no place to designate themselves as such on the short form if they choose not to check "other Spanish/Hispanic."

As Census Day approached, a couple of Brazilian businessmen, both longtime residents of New York, realized that little or nothing was being done to include their compatriots in the count. They contacted census officials in the New York office to inquire about this and showed them a copy of an article I had published on Brazilian immigrants in the city to "prove" the existence of their community.[19] A Puerto Rican census employee was subsequently assigned to work with the local Brazilian population. I was later told by a census official that before the two-man Brazilian delegation got in touch with them, "we weren't even talking about Brazilians at the Census Bureau."

A conversation with the census officer in charge of the Brazilian count, however, did nothing to allay my feeling that the treatment of Brazilians in the 1990 census—at least in New York—was scandalously inept. The officer assured me that Brazilians were being contacted through ads in Brazilian newspapers and on Spanish-language television stations and that Brazilian census workers were being hired (one hitch: they must have green cards to get the jobs). Incredibly, the officer went on to say that since "Brazilians really are Hispanics anyway," Hispanic census officers were trying to reach out to their "*hermanos brasileños*," their Brazilian brothers. Moreover, he insisted, the only way Brazilians would be counted in the 1990 census would be if they checked the other Spanish/Hispanic category and wrote in "Brazilian" after it. When I told him that I doubted that this would work, he replied that perhaps it was true that Brazilians would be missed in the 1990 census, but that, not to worry, they would surely receive a separate designation in the next census in the year 2000!

The only evidence I ever saw of the supposed census campaign aimed at the Brazilian community—and I looked very hard—was an ad in New

York's Brazilian newspaper and the fliers in Portuguese put out by the Brazilian businessmen mentioned above. The fliers read:

Brasileiros Se Não Nos Contam, Não Existimos

[Brazilians, if they don't count us, we don't exist!]

The fliers advertised temporary positions for census workers, offered help in filling out census forms, and gave a toll-free phone number to call for additional information. The fliers tried to reassure Brazilians that "the census is secret and all the information supplied is confidential. The INS, the IRS, the FBI, military authorities, *even President Bush* won't have access to the data even if your situation in the U.S. is irregular."

What, then, was the result of these efforts? The 1990 census counted 94,023 foreign-born Brazilians living in the United States, with 37,817 living in the Northeast. This is almost certainly a significant undercount (see Chapter One for more realistic estimates). Even the most conservative estimates of the Brazilian population in various regions of the Northeast and in the United States as a whole suggest an undercount ranging from 33 percent to over 80 percent.

Given the weak and problematic effort to include Brazilians in the 1990 census, their tepid response—strikingly reflected in the ridiculously low census figures above—is hardly surprising. Most of the Brazilians I met who were willing to fill out forms were both perplexed and annoyed with the ethnic straitjacket that the census categories provided. They wanted to state their nationality but resented the fact that the only way to do so was to check the "other Spanish/Hispanic" box, and then write in "Brazilian." My Brazilian research assistant argued that her compatriots would have been *far* more likely to participate in the count had they been allowed to specify their ethnicity.

Fear and apathy also played pivotal roles. I was told repeatedly that many undocumented Brazilians were afraid to fill out the forms because they did not believe that census information was really confidential. They were certain it would be turned over to the immigration authorities. As if to confirm this fear, one Brazilian insisted that "all of the data goes right into one great big computer." But other Brazilians suggested that most of their compatriots did not send in the forms not out of fear, but because "they couldn't care less about the census." After all, they said, most Brazilians are in the United States only for the short term and are indifferent to being counted.

Although I have only anecdotal rather than quantitative data on the nonparticipation of Brazilians in the census, the experience of one informant who said that "most Brazilians" he knew did not fill out census forms rings true. A consular employee with wide contacts in the commu-

nity concurred, saying that he thought "relatively few" Brazilians participated in the count. In a conversation I had with four Brazilians, only one
had filled out a census form. One was traveling in Brazil at the time the
forms were distributed, and the other two simply threw them out. One
man in the group estimated that no more than 10 or 20 percent of his
compatriots had participated in the census.

Both the size of the undercount among Brazilians living in New York
City and the rate of undercount among various subgroups of this population—long-term residents, the undocumented, temporary employees of
Brazilian businesses and institutions—are unknown. Still, it seems likely
that the undercount of undocumented individuals in the 1990 census will
be comparable to that of the 1980 census. Analysis of the 1980 census
revealed that somewhere between 20 and 50 percent of the undocumented aliens living permanently in the United States were not counted.[20]
Then, too, looking at the preliminary results from the 1990 census and
seeing the growth in the category "other race," I cannot help but wonder,
Is this the category Brazilians chose for themselves? Is this the rubric
under which the invisible minority is hidden?

One reason many of New York's Brazilians gave for not participating
in the 1990 census is that they are here today, but intend to be gone
tomorrow. But is this the case? Are Brazilians really only sojourners in
this country, temporary visitors who will return home once their nest eggs
reach the requisite size? Or, are they true immigrants comparable to the
many nationalities who came before them, people who will ultimately
decide that their future lies in this country? It is to this question that I now
turn.

CHAPTER TWELVE

Sojourner or Immigrant?

There is the almost universal expression by immigrants of their intention to
return [home].

—DEMETRIOS PAPAPADEMETRIOU AND NICHOLAS DIMARZIO,
Undocumented Aliens in the New York Metropolitan Area

The Brazilian is not an immigrant. The Brazilian's heart is in Brazil. He lives
here, but he buys a house in Brazil to die in.

—*Long-term Brazilian resident of New York City*

ARE BRAZILIAN IMMIGRANTS in New York actually sojourners who
will stay in the city only long enough to save money for some specific goal
and then pack up and return home to Brazil? Or are they true immigrants,
"settlers," to use anthropologist Leo Chavez's term, people who intend to
stay in the United States permanently? Or, then again, will some Brazilians become "commuters," making trips home for varying lengths of
time, but then returning to the United States again and again? The general
feeling in the community can be summed up in the words of one immigrant: "Brazilians come here, they get the money and they run." Other
Brazilians agreed that "95 percent" of their compatriots come to New
York with the idea of returning to Brazil. "Only one in a thousand plans
to stay in the United States permanently," said a longtime Brazilian resident of the city. Dona Dahlia remarked that virtually all the Brazilians
who stayed in her rooming house talked of eventually returning home.
Brazilians are in New York "in body, but not in soul," and "We are here
but our hearts (or heads) are in Brazil," were common refrains. But in my
own sample, feelings were decidedly more mixed: while a clear plurality
(47 percent) planned to return to Brazil, about one-third said they intended to stay in the United States, and the rest, some 21 percent, were
undecided about the future.[1]

These findings reflect the dawning realization that the stated desire of
most immigrants to return home is often more dream than reality. As

Michael J. Piore has pointed out, most migrations to industrial from developing nations are temporary in the beginning. "The typical migrant," writes Piore, "*plans* to spend only a short time in the industrial area; he [*sic*] then expects to return home. *Staying* represents a change of plans." Some studies suggest that many immigrants continue to hold onto the myth of return even after a number of their own deadlines for return have passed. In a review of return migration, anthropologist George Gmelch notes that some immigrant groups cling to an "ideology of return" no matter how long they have been in the host country.[2] In such cases, long-term residents may become self-designated expatriates rather than settlers.

An admittedly extreme example of this from my own research is a Brazilian who arrived in New York in 1956 intending to stay for two years to complete a residency in surgery. When I interviewed him in New York in January 1991, he told me that he still intended to return to Brazil. Another Brazilian predicted that her compatriots would flock home en masse if President Collor's fiscal policies turned the Brazilian economy around. This woman—who has been in New York City for fourteen years and owns a thriving business there—counted herself among the potential returnees, insisting that she, too, would go back to Brazil if the economy improved.

Immigrants' plans to stay in the United States—or return home—are influenced by a host of factors; legal status and the amount of time spent in the United States are two of them. The general rule is that the longer immigrants have lived in this country, the more likely they are to have green cards and the greater the chance that they will remain.[3] Gender is also a factor. Some immigrant women seem reluctant to return home and give up the economic and psychological independence they have achieved through paid employment. According to Sherri Grasmuck and Patricia Pessar, Dominican women "tend to postpone return because they realize that Dominican gender and class ideology, as well as the sexual division of labor in the Dominican economy, militate against wage employment for women of their training and class background." Moreover, in order to delay going home and withdrawing from wage labor, many Dominican women insist on buying expensive durable goods, such as furniture. "This strategy serves both to root the family securely and comfortably in the United States and to deplete the funds needed to relocate."[4]

In my own sample, roughly the same proportion of women and men (49 percent and 46 percent, respectively) said that they planned to return to Brazil, but contrary to the findings on female migrants cited above, a smaller percentage of women than of men (26 percent, compared to 36 percent) said that they intended to remain in this country.[5] I think the reason for the disparity is that the majority of the women in my sample are single; the previous research suggests that it is married women who are most reluctant to return home and resume their traditional domestic lifestyles.

When I asked my informants about their aspirations, the pattern of response was right in line with other research findings. Many New York Brazilians are "target earners," immigrants who, at least initially, are solely motivated by the desire to save money to meet some specific goal in Brazil—buy a house or apartment, start a business, or return to school.[6] Mario is a good example. A young man from Belo Horizonte, Mario worked as a plumber's assistant in New York, for about two years in order to save enough money to study journalism at a university in Brazil. He did, indeed, return home as I was completing my field research. Other target earners are Elena and José, a married couple with a new baby. After two and a half years in New York, they are returning to Brazil to live in the house they bought with the money they saved in the United States Still, they are not certain what the future holds: "If the [economic] crisis is very bad, we'll come back [to New York], but if it's just so-so we'll stay." (As I was completing this book, I was told by a mutual friend that after a six-month stay in Brazil, Elena and José had indeed returned to New York.)

Sometimes the goal of the target earner is very specific. When I met her, Loretta, who came from a modest background in Brazil, had been working as a domestic in New York for five years and was planning her immanent return to Rio. She already had purchased an apartment and telephone there—telephones are limited in Brazil and can cost upwards of $1000—and was making her last payments on a small house intended to produce rental income. Her goal was straightforward: "to better my life in my own country (*melhorar a vida no meu pais*)."

LIVING IN STYLE

An ad for condominium apartments in Brazil in the *Brazilian Times*, a newspaper published in Boston, is meant for the target earner. The ad reads:

BRAZILIANS IN THE UNITED STATES!
Attention!!!

When you return to Brazil, wouldn't you like to live in a three bedroom apartment with a living room, dining room, kitchen, veranda, garage, etc? Then this is your big chance! And an investment that is quaranteed to increase in value! (emphasis added)

In some instances the target changes. One Brazilian told me that he wants to save $50,000 before returning home.[7] His original goal was more modest, but owing to higher costs in Brazil, he now needs more capital to start a business there. Similarly, a part-time building superintendent said his initial intention was to save $10,000 to open an auto parts store in Belo Horizonte. He has long since saved that amount, but remains in New York with a very vague timetable for return. "Brazil has gotten very expensive," he says with a shrug. Or the target can be murky from the start. A limousine driver told me that he intends to go back to Brazil but only when he has "enough money in my pocket." To do what? I asked. "To work for myself," he said. "But I don't know doing what."

In many of these cases, there is a conditional note to the return home: I will go back to Brazil when . . . [fill in the blank]. A conditional return often translates into a delayed return, and the reasons cited for the delay can be rooted in New York or in Brazil. For example, some immigrants say that it has taken longer to achieve their monetary goals because of New York's economic recession. One married couple who came to the United States intending to stay for two years have delayed their return to Brazil for an additional year to give them more time to save money. For much the same reason, another immigrant, who has lived in New York for five years, has put off his departure for the second time and now admits he does not know when he will return home. Other local circumstances can also shape the departure decision. One woman, whose young son is being cared for by her mother in Brazil, has been in New York for two years. She told me that were it not for her son, she would stay in the United States indefinitely, but if she was unable to get a green card by the end of the year—through marriage or some other means—she would return to Brazil.

Also entering into the stay-or-go equation is the very knotty question of economic conditions in Brazil. One shoe shiner said he was planning a visit there to "check out" the situation firsthand. If things are as bad as he has been told, he will come back to the United States and buy a house or an apartment in one of the outer boroughs of New York; the down payment will be the money he had intended to invest in Brazil. Eventually, he would like to have his own shoe repair shop in the city, but all of these plans are contingent on what he finds back home. In a similar case, a woman who works as a baby-sitter and her husband, a private chauffeur, are indefinite about their future because of the dreary economic news from Brazil. They will keep delaying their return, they said, until the situation there improves.

But there were also Brazilian immigrants who told me in no uncertain terms of their plans to remain in the United States permanently. For example, Roberto, a musician, who has been in New York less than a year, has no plans to return to Brazil and wants his wife and children to come to this country. He hopes that when he finds a regular job as a musician, his employer will sponsor him for a green card and his family can join him in the United States Further along in his goal is Edilberto, who has lived in New York for eight years. Now a radio call cabdriver and the proud possessor of a green card secured through the amnesty program, Edilberto started out as a shoe shiner at the World Trade Center. He is married, and his two children were born in the United States. "Brazil?" he says. "It's a nice place for a vacation, but not to live." He has no plans to return home on a permanent basis. Finally, there is Marcela who says she "adores" living in the United States and is "not even Brazilian anymore." She made a point of telling me that she "never reads Brazilian magazines or newspapers" and prefers the *New York Times* and *The New Yorker* to the publications of her homeland.

A LONG WAY TO GO

A most unusual return to Brazil was made by a Brazilian who drives a taxicab in New York City. He hopped on his motorcycle in New York and arrived in Belo Horizonte, the capital of the Brazilian state of Minas Gerais, some seventy-five days later, having made the entire trip overland save for a flight between Panama City and Quito, Ecuador.

How many Brazilians return home for good? How many go back to Brazil intending to stay, only to return to the United States? And how many never return home to live, but only to visit? Unfortunately, it is impossible to say. I can, however, give a very tentative estimate based on my own sample, although it is admittedly incomplete since I was unable to discover the whereabouts of many of those I had interviewed a year to eighteen months earlier. Of the one hundred people in my original sample, I determined the present residence of just over two-thirds of them. Of these, 70 percent are living in New York, 5 percent are living elsewhere in the United States, and one-quarter have returned to Brazil. In sum, roughly three-quarters of the immigrants I was able to trace are still residing in this country. I realize, of course, that many—perhaps most—of those I could not locate have returned home. Moreover, because my initial interviews were only a year to eighteen months earlier, it is possible that many more immigrants will eventually return to Brazil to live. Finally, an indeterminate number of those now living in the United States actually returned to Brazil to live since the time of the interview, but have since remigrated.

Yo-Yo Migration

Many of them made the trip several times, working in America, saving their

money, and then going home again.

—Caption in an exhibit at the Ellis Island Historical Museum

Besides the choices of staying in the United States or returning to Brazil, my data suggest that a third option is common among Brazilian immigrants in New York City. Anthropologist M. Estellie Smith calls it retromigration, and I have labeled it "yo-yo migration"—the remigration to the United States of immigrants who had purportedly returned home "for good."[8] In trying to gauge the frequency of this practice, I asked more than a hundred Brazilian immigrants to estimate how many of their friends, relatives, and acquaintances returned to Brazil presumably permanently and how many of those then remigrated back to the United States.

The consensus was that a somewhat greater number of Brazilian immigrants returned to the United States than remained in Brazil. One longtime observer of New York's Brazilian scene calculated that of those who return to Brazil intending to stay, about half eventually come back to this country. But another old-timer in the city, responding to my question a bit differently, insisted that most Brazilians who come to New York as "economic immigrants" either never go back to Brazil to live or do so for merely a few months or a year or two, only to return to the United States. In other words, most who come to the United States for jobs live here indefinitely. This pattern is so common, she said, that a recurring nightmare of Brazilian immigrants in New York is that they are back in Brazil, trapped because they cannot get a tourist visa to return to the United States.

A Brazilian journalist who has lived in New York for more than two decades told me that although he lacks the figures to prove it, he is convinced that the most common pattern for Brazilian immigrants is to stay in the United States from two to four years—four years is the usual limit—return to Brazil for a year or two, and then remigrate to this country. To be sure, all of this is guesswork; moreover, as another informant pointed out, it may be impossible to answer the question with any degree of accuracy because even those immigrants who returned to Brazil and were never heard from again may well have remigrated to New York or to some other U.S. city without their old friends and acquaintances' being aware of it. Finally, one woman, a non-Brazilian who works for a social service agency and has wide contacts in the Brazilian community, joked about the entire phenomenon: "Irene," Brazilians tell her, "we're leaving.

We can't stand it here anymore. We have such *saudades* [longing] for Brazil." And she replies, "Fine, I'll see you again in a few months," and sure enough many of them return to New York. "Irene, here we are again," they say sheepishly.

What explains yo-yo migration? Why do some immigrants who talk of nothing but going home, return to Brazil and then turn around and start planning their trip back to New York, the "city of suffering," as one Brazilian called it? A major reason is the harsh reality that money saved in the United States does not go very far under conditions of hyperinflation. In a typical scenario, returned migrants use their savings to buy an apartment in Brazil but then cannot get a suitable job, or if they do get work, they find that they cannot make ends meet on Brazilian wages. Thus, while they may have a nice place to live, that is not enough to anchor them permanently to their homeland. Simply put, the lack of decent jobs with reasonably good pay is a major and constant irritant that spurs remigration.

A REAL LUXURY

Sometimes I heard cautionary tales about what happens to migrants who spend their hard-earned money foolishly when they return to Brazil. One such story, perhaps apocryphal, is about a Brazilian immigrant who worked in New York for a few years, lived frugally, and saved a considerable sum of money. He returned to Brazil and spent most of his savings on a luxury sports car.

He quickly went through what little savings remained and, with no job, was forced to return to New York to find work. He is now a waiter in a well-known restaurant in Manhattan. And the car? The man—or so goes the tale—is from a part of Minas Gerais that has relatively few paved roads, and his prized possession remains behind undriven.

Stories of Brazil's (un)welcome mat of economic shock are legion. Nelsinho, who had worked as a shoe shiner and busboy in New York for two years, went home to São Paulo, where he found a white-collar job with a Brazilian airline. While his new job lasted, it paid about one-third of what he had earned in New York, but when the airline cut its work force because of the sagging economy, Nelsinho was laid off. After six months of looking for work commensurate with his educational credentials—he is a university graduate—the only job he found was as a part-time teacher of English, a position that paid the princely sum of just over a dollar an hour. Nearly a year later, he is still unemployed and wrote to me of his desperation to return to the United States. Another example is Manuel, who spent two years in New York working as an office cleaner and dishwasher, and then returned to Belo Horizonte with plans to stay. He remained there only two months, and then came back to New York. "The economic situation was very bad," he told me. "I prefer to work as a cleaner here and have a decent lifestyle than return to Brazil and have to begin all over again." Before coming to the United States, Manuel had worked with gemstones; to get a similar position again, he would have had to start out as a salesperson in a jewelry store at a very low salary— far lower, he noted, than what he had earned at his menial jobs in New York. In somewhat different terms, Alicia, another immigrant, explained the difficulty of returning to Brazil permanently:

> The first thought of most immigrants is to buy an apartment in Brazil, but prices have been skyrocketing, and in Rio a nice condo now costs $60,000. So we have to stay here [in New York] longer in order to save more money. But that's not all. Monthly maintenance payments have also gone up so, not only do you have to have more money to buy the apartment, you also need a regular income to pay the maintenance. And I haven't even mentioned money to eat.

One immigrant encapsulated all these issues by explaining why so many returned migrants fondly recall their days in the "city of suffering":

> They're working full-time in Brazil and maybe earning $200 a month, and they just can't forget that they were earning $300 or $400 *a week* in New York. They are always thinking about that, about how much more they used to earn there. It really bothers them and that's what spurs them to return to the United States.

In other words, my own data, as well as other research, suggest that returnees with education and skills are likely to encounter the same economic barrier that led them to migrate in the first place—the lack of decent jobs that use their skills.[9]

MY HEAD IS SPINNING

"I have been here five months and I've hardly noticed the time pass. As the days went by my doubts [about returning to New York] grew. I marked two return dates. At times I went to sleep thinking about returning to New York and I woke up thinking about staying in Brazil. I told some people I was going back, I told others I was staying. In truth I didn't know myself. My head was spinning day and night. The question that everyone asks me is when I'm going back to New York and this is the question that I ask myself the most."

—Letter from a Brazilian who returned to São Paulo after living in New York for two years

Immigrants who return home with considerable savings to invest also have to contend with burgeoning costs in Brazil. One married couple worked in New York for four years and managed to save $55,000 from their combined wages before returning to Brazil. They started a business, but when their nest egg ran short, the man returned to New York to earn additional money; his wife stayed behind in Brazil, trying to keep the business going. Dona Dahlia also told tales of nightmarish inflation involving former boarders who worked long hours in New York, only to return to Brazil to find that whatever amount they had saved was not enough to start the business of their dreams. This often meant another trip to New York to make up the difference. For example, one man had planned to buy a taxicab in Rio as an investment, but when he went back to Brazil he found that the price had risen sharply; despite three years of scrimping and saving in the United States, his goal was now out of reach.

As these tales suggest, yo-yo migration may involve more than one "permanent" trip home. Despite the distance involved, I met a few Brazilians in New York who had been bouncing back and forth between Brazil and the United States for more than a decade. One example is Flavio, a cabdriver, who has returned to Brazil "for good" three times during the ten years he has been in New York. Twice, he remained in Brazil for more than a year before returning to the Big Apple. During his last stay, he married and returned to the United States with his new wife; he now has an American-born child. Says one of his friends, "Every day, Flavio's going to Brazil to live and six months later—here he comes again." When I interviewed him, Flavio insisted that he was planning to return home "to try again." The last I heard, he had indeed gone back to Brazil "permanently," but as his friend told me, Flavio plans to visit the United States once a year so that his green card will not lapse. After all, who knows when he might need it again.[10]

And Flavio is not alone. Over the course of my research, I was told of Brazilians who had returned to Brazil to live, two, three, even four times, only to remigrate to the United States. In the words of political scientist Wayne Cornelius, these yo-yo migrants come closer to "commuting" than to "immigrating." Some returnees become "shuttle migrants," or "cultural commuters," who move back and forth between home and host country and are never fully satisfied with either one. Some studies suggest that some of these migrants are disillusioned and unhappy upon returning home and that homesickness in the host country is replaced by discontent with conditions in the homeland; a sort of "reverse culture shock" sets in.[11]

This is certainly true of many Brazilians who remigrate to the United States. Although their primary complaints center around their homeland's lack of jobs, low wages, and hyperinflation, some also deprecate

Brazil's "inefficiency," "uncertainty," "red tape," and "corruption." I was repeatedly told that once Brazilians have lived in New York for three or four years, they find it difficult to readapt to life back home. Even seemingly minor things can irk the returnee. One woman told me of her son's disgust with the electric showers in common use in Brazil. "They give so little hot water," he complained to her. "How can you stand to take a shower with that thing? I just can't live like that anymore."

IF YOU ASK A SILLY QUESTION

One Brazilian who returned home wrote to me about the inane questions he was asked about life in the United States and his tongue-in-cheek replies:

"Didn't you forget how to speak Portuguese?"

"I forgot nearly everything and I'm going to have to go back to school to relearn it."

"Don't Americans speak Portuguese?"

"Yes, they speak Portuguese but they prefer to speak English except for one anthropologist friend."

"How long has it been since you've eaten rice and beans?"

"It's been more than two years. I don't even remember what they taste like anymore."

Routes Home, Temporary and Otherwise

Going home to Brazil for good and then deciding to return to the United States is easier said than done. In fact, in the absence of a green card, any type of remigration can be problematic since the difficulty of getting a tourist visa can stymie the best laid plans of even the most determined yo-yo migrant. One Brazilian, who has lived in New York for years, recounted myriad tales of friends who returned to Brazil with the idea of staying permanently, and then changed their minds, only to find themselves unable to get visas to come back to this country. One returnee was so anxious to come back to the United States that he paid $4,000 for the documents—false income tax returns and business ownership papers—necessary to obtain a tourist visa.

Equally awash with obstacles is the path home for undocumented Brazilians who live in the United States and want to go back to Brazil just for a visit. Several examples illustrate the problems migrants face and how they deal with them. Renato, an undocumented immigrant from Rio de Janeiro, planned to visit his family there over Christmas, and then return to New York. How could he do that, I asked—wasn't he afraid of not getting a tourist visa to come back to this country? No, he said, he would have no problem because his four-year tourist visa was still valid. But tourist visas are good for a maximum stay in the United States of six consecutive months, and by this time, Renato had been living in the United States for nearly two years. In other words, he was a visa over-stayer. He explained the simple solution to this dilemma: he would return to Brazil at Christmas, and when he went through immigration control, he would give a "gratuity" to an immigration agent to stamp his passport with a much earlier return date, making it appear as though he spent only a month or two in the United States. Then, when he went through U.S. immigration control upon his reentry, he would simply be a returning tourist, and no one would suspect his past history as a visa overstayer. Renato remarked in recounting his plans, "With money anything is possible."

And the story continues. Renato did, indeed, return to Brazil and wrote to tell me that the "stamp trick" had worked well. When going through Brazilian immigration control, he said nothing until an immigration agent casually mentioned that for $100 he could stamp Renato's passport with whatever date he wanted. He witnessed the same offer being made to several others.

When I first met Norman, another Brazilian immigrant, he had been living in the United States for quite some time but had managed to remain technically within the limits of his tourist visa. How did he do it? When the six-month maximum stay permitted on the visa was almost up, Nor-man would leave the United States and take an inexpensive package tour to Mexico or the Bahamas for four or five days. When he returned to the United States, his passport would be restamped, allowing him an addi-tional six-month stay. Norman said that since his four-year tourist visa was about to expire, he was planning to return to Brazil and apply for a new one. He believed he would have no trouble getting it because the multiple entry and exit stamps in his passport would "prove" that he was a tourist, not a visa overstayer.

Then, there is the disappearing-passport gambit, in which the pass-ports of immigrants whose visas are about to expire are "lost" or "sto-len." A trip to the Brazilian consulate for a replacement, combined with the passport holder's claim to have "just arrived in the United States," results in a new passport that notably lacks a visa with a date of entry stamped in it. According to officials of the Brazilian consulate, some peo-ple have "lost" their passports four or five times. Since consular personnel are now on to this ruse, they have been cracking down and refusing to issue new passports in suspect cases. Instead, those seeking to return to Brazil receive travel authorization after presenting their plane tickets and identification to consular officers. But on at least a few occasions, the ploy still worked. I encountered a woman who had been in the United States for more than four years and still possessed a valid tourist visa. Three times, she had managed to tell a convincing enough tale of a stolen passport to get a new one.

Where Do They Go from Here?

The distinction between a migrant and a settler is not easily drawn;

the distinction appears to be one of degree, not of kind.

—LEO CHAVEZ, ESTEVAN FLORES, AND MARTA LOPEZ-GARCIA,

"Here Today, Gone Tomorrow?"

On March 15, 1990, Fernando Collor de Mello was inaugurated as President of Brazil; he immediately announced a sweeping package of economic reforms, whose primary goal was to combat inflation. Part of the package tried to dampen consumer spending by freezing savings accounts of over $1,000 for eighteen months. Brazilians living in New York were of two minds about the plan's impact on continued emigration from their country. Some suggested that since many people would be barred from withdrawing their savings to pay for plane tickets, fewer Brazilians would be able to go abroad. But others insisted that since the entire reform package put a greater financial squeeze on the Brazilian middle class, it might actually spur emigration. A high-ranking official of the U.S. consulate in São Paulo told me that the emigrant outflow had not abated since the announcement of the Collor package. People whose savings were frozen and who had little cash on hand could still buy plane tickets on credit from tourist agencies and readily pay off the debt when they got jobs in the United States. He said wealthier people with money stashed in banks abroad were also leaving, to "wait out" Brazil's current economic storm.

The Collor plan was announced while I was doing my research on Brazilian immigrants in New York City; with Brazilians seeming to arrive daily, I could not see that it had done much to stem the exodus. One informant noted that seven of his friends had come to New York after the plan went into effect; having lost their jobs as a result of the economic crisis in Brazil, all used unemployment insurance to pay for the trip. He predicted that as more Brazilians were thrown out of work because of the Collor package, they, too, would finance the trip to the United States with their unemployment insurance —assuming, of course, that they could get tourist visas.[12]

Whatever the immediate effect of the Collor plan on emigration, its failure to revive the Brazilian economy surely will have a far greater impact over the long term on the numbers of Brazilians going abroad to live. Virtually everyone agrees that the economic reform package has been an utter failure, and inflation is again out of control. In 1990, inflation was even higher—1,795 percent—than in 1989, the year before the economic reform package was instituted, and by late 1992 it was still running at 1,500 percent annually. Moreover, prices had shot up 13,000 percent since the plan was put into effect, and real per capita income had dropped by 7 percent. In what is now being called "the sharpest recession in a decade," 265,000 workers in the city of São Paulo lost their jobs in 1990 and another 46,000 were thrown out of work in the first three weeks of 1991. In that year, real GDP was lower than it was in 1986, and economists predicted that the two-year-old recession would last at least through 1993. Finally, things do not look much brighter for the more distant future; various studies suggest high levels of unemployment and underemployment in Brazil at least through the year 2000.[13]

What about the other side of the coin: the economic downturn in the New York economy? What has it done to the flow of immigrants from Brazil? During the late 1980s and early 1990s, New York was in the midst of a serious recession. Unemployment in the city had climbed to over 10 percent by May 1992, and newspaper headlines screamed of massive layoffs—5,000 people at Chase Manhattan Bank and thousands more at now-defunct Pan Am, to cite just two examples.[14] While these and similar companies are unlikely to employ Brazilians or other recent immigrants—other than perhaps as office cleaners—their cutbacks have a trickle-down effect that is felt by immigrants. Restaurants hire fewer dishwashers and busboys as business slows down, people without jobs are not wont to employ housekeepers and baby-sitters, and even tips for shoe shiners are less generous.

Still, the actual impact of these economic conditions on Brazilians, or other immigrants for that matter, is hard to gauge since it involves three separate, albeit closely related, issues: (1) the employment picture for immigrants already living in New York; (2) the decision to stay in this country or return to Brazil; and (3) the magnitude of the continued immigrant flow to the United States. The first question is deceptively simple: is it more difficult for Brazilian immigrants in the city to find jobs, and is their unemployment rate higher than before the recession? My data on this question are mixed. Over the course of my research, I personally met or was told about two or three dozen Brazilians who were out of work and looking for jobs. Those working in construction seemed to be particularly hard-hit, although evidence of a decline in restaurant work was less clear. Moreover, some Brazilians were underemployed; with only part-time work, they had long sought additional hours. Veronica, for example,

cleans apartments four days a week and spent months looking for another employer to fill out her work schedule. But some evidence contra-
dicts this gloomy employment picture. A woman who runs a social service program used by many Brazilian immigrants told me that she rarely
had to help Brazilians with food donations because "they all have jobs
and don't need that kind of assistance."

There is also a confounding factor here. For undocumented immigrants unable to find jobs—and many Brazilians are undocumented—it is
difficult to separate the recession's role in their futile quest for work from
that of IRCA, which penalizes employers for hiring undocumented workers. In other words, are there simply fewer jobs to be had, or do immigrants without green cards have a harder time convincing employers to
hire them?[15]

The second issue is the effect that the New York recession has had on
immigrants' decisions to return to Brazil. Many Brazilians did indeed
leave the United States while I was doing research, but their numbers and
motivation are illusive. Nearly everyone I interviewed agreed that it had
become harder for Brazilian immigrants to find work, and many cited the
increasingly anemic job market as the "push" that had sent their compatriots packing. Mario, a part-time handyman from Rio de Janeiro,
claimed to know seven or eight immigrants who had returned to Brazil
because they could not find work. His cousin, Clemente, confirmed this,
adding that by the end of 1991, the recession had made the job pickings
so slim that he, too, knew many Brazilians who had headed home, including some who had lived in New York for several years and had green
cards. "What good are documents, if you can't find a job?" he shrugged.
And Bento, a friend of Mario and Clemente, explained why, despite the
ongoing economic crisis in Brazil, many of his compatriots were leaving
the United States: "If you can't get work in either place, it's better to live
in your own country."

Previous research suggests, however, that "push" factors, such as a
recessionary economy and dwindling job market in the host country, are
less decisive in immigrants' decisions to return home than "pull" factors,
such as the continued presence of close family members there. This was
the conclusion of anthropologist George Gmelch in his review of studies
of return migration; he found that "push" factors had "surprisingly little
effect" on the decision to return home. Once networks of friends and
relatives are in place in the host country, migrants often stay put. They do
not automatically or immediately respond to diminished economic opportunities in their adopted land, to lowered earnings, for example, or a
tighter job market.[16]

Even more surprising is the finding that a weak economy does not necessarily staunch the stream of new migrants into the host country. Here,
too, previous studies show that economic recession and increased jobless-

ness in the host nation do not always put a damper on immigrant flow. This is counterintuitive and requires an explanation. Alejandro Portes and Robert Bach have suggested that the function of international migration is not just to supplement the native labor force, but to weaken its organizational base, to sap its ability to unionize and demand higher wages and better working conditions. This is why, they argue, over time a positive correlation exists between unemployment levels and immigrant flows, negating the orthodox perspective that immigration merely "supplements" the domestic labor force.[17]

But is this true of Brazilian immigrants? Are they still arriving in New York despite the city's severe economic squeeze? Once again, although the evidence is mixed, the answer is an emphatic yes. The city's murky job picture notwithstanding, Brazilian immigrants are still coming to the Big Apple. The migratory stream continues—at least for the time being—despite changed economic circumstances. But what is much less certain is the degree to which New York's weaker job market has cut down on the size of the stream. Here, immigrants themselves disagree. Many members of New York's Brazilian community were convinced that the city's economic downturn and resulting unemployment had severely cut the size of Brazilian immigration to New York. Three men from Governador Valadares told me that they used to receive news virtually every week of Brazilians arriving in the city, but that beginning in mid- or late 1990, the number of arrivals was down to a trickle and they "rarely hear about newcomers anymore." Dona Dahlia noted the change in late 1989. The tide of immigrants from Brazil had diminished substantially, she said, and it is true that by 1990, she had fewer guests staying at her rooming house than in earlier years.

While word of the unfavorable job situation in New York has certainly filtered back to prospective migrants in Brazil, some Brazilians in the city, Dona Dahlia among them, attributed the lower numbers not to the troubled New York economy but to the difficulty that many would-be immigrants have in securing U.S. tourist visas. The Governador Valadares natives suggested that fewer people were arriving from their hometown because of the imposition of a tourist visa requirement by Mexico, a fairly common route to the United States for *valadarenses* unable to get U.S. tourist visas. And most informants agreed that, employment difficulties aside, far more Brazilians would be emigrating to this country were it not for their problems in obtaining tourist visas.

Whether limited visas or limited job opportunities were most responsible for the purported decline in Brazilian immigration to New York is impossible to say. I use the word "purported" because other Brazilians question whether the number of immigrants from their homeland has in fact declined to any considerable extent. My Brazilian research assistant, for example, believes that in the late 1980s and early 1990s, as many of her compatriots were arriving in New York because of the dire economic situation in Brazil as were leaving New York because they could not find work there. One member of the local Brazilian elite, who has lived in the city since 1984, says he sees no letup in Brazilian immigration; in the words of a Baptist preacher who ministers to the local Brazilian community and denies a decline in numbers, "They're still coming, they're still coming."

Finally, my own experience also belies the suggestion that Brazilian migration to the Big Apple is drying up. While researching and writing this book between 1990 and 1992—a supposed low point in the Brazilian immigration stream—I encountered a great many Brazilian "greenhorns," immigrants who had just arrived in the United States. I even met a few classic visa denials waiting to happen, such as a young unmarried man from a lower-middle-class background in Minas Gerais who said he had had "no problem" getting a tourist visa in early 1990 and had entered the United States legally via Kennedy Airport, rather than being forced to use the clandestine Mexican route.

New York businesses that cater to Brazilian immigrants report no decline in activity that might indicate a significant lull in the number of new arrivals. In fact, some data suggest the opposite. Between 1989 and 1990, for example, the number of subscribers to Brazilian newspapers in the New York metropolitan area rose from 1,500 to 3,800, and the owner of a store whose clientele is almost exclusively Brazilian reported in 1990 that her business was up about 30 percent over the previous year.[18]

Reports coming out of Brazil also contradict the suggestion that because of the United States recession, fewer Brazilians are attracted to New York and other U.S. cities. The Brazilian newspaper *Folha de São Paulo*, for example, reported in 1990 that the number of tourist visas issued to Brazilians by the American consulate in São Paulo had continued to increase. Between October 1988 and September 1989, nearly 96,000 visas were issued, a figure that rose to over 110,000 visas for the same period the following year. These, numbers, in turn, are reflected in the figures for Brazil as a whole. According to the INS, in 1989, a total of 272,000 tourist visas were issued to Brazilians, an increase of 17 percent over the previous year, and in 1990, 300,000 were issued, a further jump of nearly 10 percent. Finally, Brazilian Federal Police statistics reflect this unexpected upsurge in "tourism." The number of passports issued to Brazilians for foreign travel also increased, going from an average of 1,000 a day in 1989 to an average of 1,500 a day in 1990.[19]

While no one knows what percentage of Brazilians coming to this country on tourist visas are actually immigrants with plans to stay on and look for work, it does seem rather odd that tourist visa applications were rising at a time of severe economic crisis in Brazil, a crisis that drew the financial vise ever tighter around the country's middle class. All of this suggests that far from winding down, Brazilian immigration to New York and other U.S. cities has continued apace.

From Sojourners to Settlers

The philosophy of life of the Brazilian immigrant . . . has undergone change.

Four, five or six years ago the Brazilian led a life of disciplined work without

leisure. He needed to return home as soon as possible. At that time there were

no social groups or socializing. Today, the situation is different. Because of

the continuing unstable conditions in Brazil, our immigrants are strengthen-

ing their roots in this land.

—*Brazilian Voice* (Boston)

As the 1990 newspaper editorial quoted above suggests, Brazilians who have been in the United States for some time have noted a recent shift in their compatriots' behavior. A Baptist minister told me that the majority of Brazilians in his congregation are now "putting down roots in the United States" When he first came to the city four years earlier, most of his parishioners were working solely to save money to return to Brazil. Now, he estimates, 70 to 80 percent of the Brazilians in his congregation intend to remain in this country at least for the foreseeable future. A shoe shiner, a relative old-timer with wide contacts in the Brazilian community, agreed:

> Their thinking has changed. Before many Brazilians stayed for a year or two, saved money and left. They lived in poor conditions so they could save every penny. But since things in Brazil have gotten worse, people are more oriented to staying here longer. And they want to live better. They want a better apartment or they want a car. Sure, there are still Brazilians who stay a short time and go back to Brazil with their savings, but there are fewer of them now.

Even if I had not been told of this shift, it would have become evident to me from visiting the homes of several Brazilians. Their behavior made it clear: "we are planning long-term futures in the United States," they seemed to be saying, in deeds, if not in words. José is a good example. He had spent a great deal of time and effort renovating his rent-controlled apartment on Manhattan's Lower East Side, installing a private bathroom, building kitchen cabinets, and generally making the apartment more livable, an effort that would seem futile were he planning to pack his bags anytime soon. Other immigrants acted similarly. They invested in furniture or wall-to-wall carpeting, items that are meant to improve the quality of life in New York and are not easily transported back home.

This sea change among immigrants has been noted by others. Michael J. Piore has described the gradual process of starting to think more about life in the host country and less about returning home.[20] As the new orientation takes hold, immigrants become less willing to put in long hours of work at dead-end jobs. They become more reluctant to put in overtime or continue to hold down a second job. Rather than devoting nearly every waking minute to work, they spend more time at home, and the crowded conditions of sharing an apartment with other immigrants begin to grate. Perhaps, they decide, having fewer roommates is worth the higher cost in rent. Working shorter hours, they earn less money, but they spend more of it on leisure; they go out to eat, they go to the movies or to a concert. Since they are saving less money for the future and the return home, their original monetary goal remains illusive, and they stay on in the host country for another year and yet another. As more and more immigrants go through this process, a community of sojourners is transformed into a community of settlers.

This scenario will likely hold for Brazilians as they become a permanent ingredient in New York's vibrant ethnic medley. Having been sojourners, many will turn settlers. They will become true transnationals. They will continue to live in the United States, but they will not abandon Brazil; they will not stop thinking of themselves as Brazilians or stop going home on visits to see family and friends; they may even retire in their native land. But like so many immigrants to these shores before them, Brazilians will see their lives and future as intimately tied to the fortunes and future of their adopted home.

NOTES

PREFACE

1. I take this phrase from a 1991 photo essay on international immigrants by Judith Miller ("Strangers at the Gate") published in the *New York Times Magazine*.
2. Portes and Bach, *Latin Journey*, p. 7.
3. Rimer, "New Immigrant Group Displays Its Enterprise."
4. This analysis is based on the work of economist Michael J. Piore. See Piore, *Birds of Passage* and "The Shifting Grounds for Migration."
5. For a transnational perspective on migration, see Glick-Schiller, Basch, and Blanc-Szanton, eds., *Towards a Transnational Perspective on Migration*, and Sassen, *The Mobility of Labor and Capital*.
6. Sanjek, "Urban Anthropology in the 1980s."
7. Two novels in Portuguese have been published by Brazilians who lived and worked in New York, *Moreno Como Vocês*, by Sonia Nolasco Ferreira, and *Stella Manhattan*, by Silviano Santiago. These appear to be romans à clef. Another Brazilian also privately published her memoirs about her experience as an immigrant in New York (Guimarães, *Febre Brasil em Nova Iorque*). There is also an article comparing kinship among Brazilians in New York and São Paulo (Barrow, "Generations of Persistence"). Except for Brazilian newspaper and magazine articles, a lone article in the *New York Times* (Brooke, "Town That Uncle Sam Built, You Might Say") and a handful of other reports in the *Boston Globe*, the *Cape Cod Times*, and the *Miami Herald* appear to be the entire corpus of publications about Brazilians in the United States. After my research was well under way, a study of Brazilians in Framingham, Massachusetts, appeared: José Bicalho's *Yes, Eu Sou Brazuca*. It was published privately in Governador Valadares in Minas Gerais and is not widely available.
8. Staub, *Yeminis in New York*; Kim, *New Urban Immigrants*; Shokeid, *Children of Circumstances*; Fisher, *The Indians of New York City*; Wong, *Chinatown*; Laguerre, *American Odyssey*; Altamirano, *Los Que Se Fueron*; Georges, *The Making of a Transnational Community*; Grasmuck and Pessar, *Between Two Islands*; Foner, *Jamaica's Migrants*.
9. Cornelius, "Interviewing Undocumented Immigrants"; Chavez, "Households, Migration and Labor Market Participation"; Biernacki and Waldorf, "Snowball Sampling"; Bernard, *Research Methods in Cultural Anthropology*.
10. Bertaux and Kohli, "The Life Story Approach."

CHAPTER ONE: THE NEW VOYAGERS

My thanks to Dr. Roger Sanjek of Queens College–CUNY for suggesting the subhead "Up the Down Staircase," after the book of the same title.

1. Skidmore, "The Results of the Brazilian Presidential Election."

2. *Folha de São Paulo*, March 18, 1990; *Veja*, "Os Brasileiros Vão à Luta: Bye-bye, Brasil"; *Veja*, "O Povo da Diáspora." Other major articles on the "Brazilian diaspora" include a 1991 cover story in *Veja* ("Invasão à Brasileira") and a piece about my own research in *Isto É* (Freitas, "Invasão Brazuca").

3. Goza and Simonik, "Who Are the Brazilian Americans?" About two-thirds of the Brazilians counted in the 1980 census had arrived in the United States after 1965.

4. Brooke, "Brazil Freezes All Wages and Prices"; *Folha de São Paulo*, "Cresce o Numero de Brasileiros Que Não Querem Mas Ser Brasileiros"; Brooke, "Brazil's Fresh Young President Has Grown Old Fast"; Brooke, "As Collor Completes First Year, Brazilians Write Off Their Highest Hopes."

5. Malan, "The Brazilian Economy"; Riding, "Bourgeois Dreams of the Heady Days"; Cohen, "Brazil's Price Spiral Nears Hyperinflation"; Brooke, "A New Assault on Brazil's Woes," C16.

6. Baer and Beckerman, "The Decline and Fall of Brazil's Cruzado." See also Riding, "Unfamiliar Feelings of Pessimism Overtake Brazil's Politics and Economy"; *Veja*, "O Povo da Diáspora."

7. The town of Scarsdale not only has one of the highest per capita incomes in the United States, but in 1991 the average price of a home there was $585,000 (Handelman, "The Japanning of Scarsdale").

8. I cannot confirm these impressions since my field research on Brazilians was limited to New York City. However, a paper by Diana Brown, "Faith, Curing and Ethnic Identity: Brazilian Umbanda in Newark's Ironbound," on Brazilians in Newark and a monograph by José Bicalho, *Yes, Eu Sou Brazuca*, on the Brazilian community in Framingham, suggest a more homogeneous, working-class Brazilian population than that which resides in New York City.

9. Grant, *New Immigrants and Ethnicity*; Bogen, *Immigration in New York City*; Kessner and Caroli, *Today's Immigrants*, 23.

10. Brooke, "Town That Uncle Sam Built, You Might Say"; *Jornal do Brasil*, "Governador 'Valadólares' Faz 20 Prédios de 12 Andares"; *O Globo*, "Valadares com um Pé em Nova York"; Margolis, "An American in Governador Valadares."

11. Coleman, "Quietly, Community of Brazilians Forms." A series on Brazilian immigrants in the *Cape Cod Times* estimated that 3,000 Brazilians live on Cape Cod (Miller, "Money Tree Image Lures Poor Brazilians to U.S." and "Lambada Night: 'I Just Feel Like I'm Home'").

12. U.S. INS, *1991 Statistical Yearbook*.

13. The 20 percent figure for Brazilian visa overstayers seems reasonable in light of the figures for other immigrant groups. For example, the U.S. consulate in Lima cited an overstay estimate of 22 percent for Peruvians on tourist visas in the United States (Altamirano, *Los Que Se Fueron*). Warren's "Annual Estimates of Non-Migrant Overstays in the U.S." estimates on visa overstayers by nationality seem unreasonably low. He suggests only a 1 percent rate of visa overstays for Brazilians in 1988. Also, the number of Brazilians coming to the United States on nonimmigrant visas of all kinds has risen dramatically. By 1991, Brazilians ranked seventh worldwide in the number of nonimmigrant visas issued to them by the U.S. government (U.S. INS, *1991 Statistical Yearbook*).

14. *Folha de São Paulo*, March 18, 1990, C1; *Veja*, "Invasão Brasileira." A figure of 400,000 for the United States as a whole is conservative if there are 300,000 to 350,000 *undocumented* Brazilians in this country, as one estimate suggests (Braga, "Casuísmo no Lugar de Lei Que Não 'Pegou,'"). Another relevant datum is the number of Portuguese-speakers in the United States. A study done for Portuguese-language programming on an educational television station in Rhode Island estimated that about 3.5 million Portuguese-speakers live in this country. The majority are from Portugal, although the breakdown of people from Brazil, Portugal, the Azores, and other Portuguese-speaking areas is unknown. Additional data on the size of the Brazilian population in the United States is found in a series of magazine articles. Articles in *Veja* in 1991 estimated that between 30,000 and 50,000 Brazilians live in Florida and about 20,000 live in California (*Veja*, "A Febre dos Negócios na Flórida"; *Veja*, "Nova Terra Prometida"; *Veja*, "O Povo da Diáspora"; and *Veja*, "Invasão à Brasileira"). In its August 1991 cover story on the "Brazilian diaspora," *Veja* calculated that by 1991 about 630,000 Brazilians were living abroad and that the number leaving was increasing by 20 percent annually. In sum, all evidence suggests that the 1990 census figure of 94,023 people of Brazilian birth in the U.S. population is a gross undercount. This is discussed in Chapter 11.

15. Bogen, *Immigration in New York City*; Foner, *New Immigrants in New York City*; Reimers, *Still the Golden Door*.

16. *New York Magazine*, September 10, 1990, 80.

17. *Webster's Seventh New Collegiate Dictionary* defines "Hispanic" as "of or relating to the people, speech or culture of Spain, Spain and Portugal, or Latin America." However, colloquial usage of the term in the United States always refers to Spanish-speakers.

18. Sassen-Koob, "Changing Composition and Labor Market Location of Hispanic Immigrants in New York City"; Freedman, "The Labor Market for Immigrants in New York City"; Marshall, "New Immigrants in New York's Economy"; Sassen-Koob, "New York City: Economic Restructuring and Immigration."

19. Sassen-Koob, "New York City's Informal Economy"; Waldinger, "Immigration and Industrial Change in the New York City Apparel Industry"; Waldinger, *Through the Eye of the Needle*.

20. I am greatly indebted to Sassen-Koob's (1985, 1986, 1989) research and analysis for the discussion of the restructuring of New York's economy. Sassen, *The Mobility of Labor and Capital*, 145.

21. Sassen-Koob, "New York City: Economic Restructuring and Immigration," 302–303. Since this is a discussion of the long-term economic restructuring of New York, I am purposely ignoring the 1991–1992 recession and the concomitant loss of some high-paying managerial and executive positions in the city.

22. Piore, *Birds of Passage*. Contrary to popular belief, the willingness of immigrants to work at low-wage, dead-end jobs does not seem to lower the earnings or increase the unemployment of native-born Americans, including American minorities. See Portes and Rumbaut, *Immigrant America*; Bean, Lowell, and Taylor, "Undocumented Migration to the United States"; and Bailey, *Immigrant and Native Workers*.

23. Mydans, "Immigrants Face a Threat to Amnesty"; Suro, "1986 Amnesty Law Is Seen as Failing to Slow Alien Tide." One example of confusion is that amnesty applications must be made in two stages—filing for amnesty and applying for permanent residence—but many undocumented immigrants were unaware of the second requirement and missed the filing deadline for this phase of the program. There is also evidence that IRCA may have led to bias in hiring (Bishop, "California Says Law on Aliens Spurs Job Bias"). For general evaluations of IRCA, see Bean, Vernez, and Keely, *Opening and Closing the Doors*, and Bean, Edmonston, and Passel, *Undocumented Migration to the United States*.

24. Johnston, "Border Crossings Near Old Record"; Stevenson, "Study Finds Mild Gain in Drive on Illegal Aliens"; Suro, "1986 Amnesty Law Is Seen as Failing to Slow Alien Tide"; Golden, "Mexicans Head North Despite Job Rules"; Kilborn, "Law Failed to Stem Illegal Immigration, Panel Says"; Smith, "Mexican Migration from South Central Mexico and Los Angeles to New York City."

25. Suro, "1986 Amnesty Law Is Seen as Failing to Slow Alien Tide."

26. Suro, "Traffic in Fake Documents Is Blamed as Illegal Immigration Rises Anew"; Stevenson, "U.S. Work Barrier to Illegal Aliens Doesn't Stop Them." Since IRCA was passed, there have been large seizures of expertly produced fake documents that illegal aliens were using to "prove" their legality to employers. In one raid in southern Texas, a laser scanning device had produced nearly perfect copies of a number of different kinds of documents, including social security cards (Suro, "Traffic in Fake Documents Is Blamed as Illegal Immigration Rises Anew"; Suro, "Boom in Fake Identity Cards for Aliens").

27. Chavez, Flores, and Lopez-Garza, "Here Today, Gone Tomorrow?" 203. See also Suro, "1986 Amnesty Law Is Seen as Failing to Slow Alien Tide," and Howe, "New Policy Aids Families of Aliens," for the unanticipated consequences and problems stemming from the amnesty program.

28. DaMatta, quoted in Scheper-Hughes, *Death without Weeping*, 473.

29. U.S. INS, *1990 Statistical Yearbook*, 94–95. There is considerable evidence of fraud in the SAW program. For example, the number of SAW applicants in California is believed to be three or four times the number of foreign-born farm workers, both legal and illegal, in that state (Woodrow and Passel, "Post-IRCA Undocumented Immigration to the United States").

30. Although this indicates a rather high proportion of undocumented individuals in New York's Brazilian community, it is low compared to those of some other Brazilian populations in the United States. For example, a study of Brazilians in Framingham, Mass., reported that nearly all of them were undocumented (Bicalho, *Yes, Eu Sou Brazuca*). The ratio for Brazilians in New York is also lower than that for Peruvians in the United States, at least two-thirds of whom are thought to be undocumented (Altamirano, *Los Que Se Fueron*).

31. Simcox, "Illegal Immigration: Counting the Shadow Population"; Passel and Woodrow, "Geographic Distribution of Undocumented Immigrants."

32. Simcox, "Illegal Immigration; Counting the Shadow Population"; Bogen, *Immigration in New York City*; Edmonston, Passel, and Bean, "Perceptions and Estimates of Undocumented Migration to the United States"; Woodrow and Passel, "Post-IRCA Undocumented Immigration to the United States," 39.

33. Papademetriou and DiMarzio, *Undocumented Aliens in the New York Metropolitan Area*.

CHAPTER TWO: BYE-BYE, BRAZIL

1. Mr. James Halmo of the Consular Section of the U.S. Department of State graciously provided me with the statistics on visa denials. Concern about visa denials and other issues relating to U.S. immigration has become of such interest to many Brazilians that a book, *How to Emigrate to the United States*, by two American lawyers, Martha S. Siegal and Laurence A. Canter, has been translated into Portuguese (*Veja*, "Cartão Vermelho de Saída").

2. There is no doubt that people from Minas Gerais are overrepresented among Brazilians in the United States. Virtually all accounts of *brazucas* in the Brazilian media mention this. Forty-one percent of my own sample are *mineiros*, as were 87 percent of Bicalho's (*Yes, Eu Sou Brazuca*). Finally, Brazilians in New York, and presumably elsewhere, continually comment on how many of their compatriots are *mineiros*.

3. *Folha de São Paulo*, "Para Agências de Viagens, a Recusa Chega a 30% dos Pedidos de Minas"; *Folha de São Paulo*, "Consulado dos EUA no Rio Nega Visto a Mineiros"; *Veja*, "Um Atalho na Fila."

4. *Folha de São Paulo*, "Consulado dos EUA no Rio Nega Visto a Mineiros."

5. *Folha de São Paulo*, "Sociólogo Vê Exportação de Mão-de-Obra."

6. *Veja*, "Um Atalho na Fila." See, e.g., Christian, "For U.S. Visa, Peruvians Try Lots of Ruses."

7. *Veja*, "Um Atalho na Fila."

8. Garrison and Weiss, "Dominican Family Networks and United States Immigration Policy"; Hendricks, "The Phenomenon of Migrant Illegality"; Georges, *The Making of a Transnational Community*; Grasmuck and Pessar, *Between Two Islands*.

9. Clines, "As Shadowy Figures Slip In, U.S. Faces Queries on Aliens"; Simcox, "Illegal Immigration: Counting the Shadow Population"; Reimers, *Still the Golden Door*. Many people are amazed to learn that the U.S. government has no administrative records system for tracking the emigration of foreign-born individuals from the United States.

10. A woman who worked for Varig, the Brazilian national airline, at Kennedy Airport for three years estimated that over that period, on average, one Brazilian national per flight was apprehended by INS agents while going through immigration.

11. Januzzi, "Terra do Tio Sam, Um Sonho Clandestino Que Pode Virar Pesadelo."

12. Ibid.

13. Bicalho, *Yes, Eu Sou Brazuca*.

14. Georges, *The Making of a Transnational Community*. On the increasing danger of entering the United States clandestinely via Mexico, see Mydans, "Border Near San Diego Is Home to More Violence." A Minas Gerais newspaper reported in April 1991 that a Brazilian from that state had been killed while trying to cross the U.S.-Mexican border.

15. Rohter, "Soft Underbelly: Sneaking Mexicans (and Others) into U.S. Is Big Business"; Suro, "1986 Amnesty Law Is Seen as Failing to Slow Alien Tide."

16. Ibid.

17. French, "Caribbean Exodus: U.S. Is Magnet"; Rohter, "Dominicans Find a Back Door to New York in Puerto Rico."

18. Georges, *The Making of a Transnational Community*. This can also be a very perilous route. In April 1991 there were media reports that four or five Dominicans drowned when a boat carrying some sixty or seventy would-be immigrants capsized on its way to Puerto Rico. There also have been reports that Brazilians on their way to the United States have been detained in Puerto Rico (*Brazilian Times*, "Brasileiros Detidos em San Juan, Porto Rico, Denunciam Guia").

19. *Veja*, "Viagem Perdida"; *Veja*, "Fim Melancólico"; *Manchete*, "Clandestinos."

20. The $2,000 minimum assumes entry to the United States by plane. As we have seen, the cost of the trip via Mexico is considerably more, often as much as $5,000. I was told about immigrants from humble backgrounds, particularly *mineiros*, who sold everything to raise money to come to the United States through Mexico, a route of last resort for those unable to get visas.

21. Many Brazilian employers prefer giving their employees severance pay to providing the job security to which the employees are entitled after having worked for the same company for a specified number of years.

CHAPTER THREE: FIRST DAYS

1. Papademetriou and DiMarzio, *Undocumented Aliens in the New York Metropolitan Area*, 76. The percentages do not add up to 100 because three people in my sample accompanied their employers to the United States. All three were women under contract to work as live-in housekeeper/nannies. Another three women, who had similar contracts with families, traveled to the United States by themselves.

2. In Brazil, breakfast is included in the price of a hotel room.

3. Piore, *Birds of Passage*. For a graphic account of the stark conditions under which new Chinese immigrants to New York live, see Kinkead, "A Reporter at Large," and for similar living conditions in New York for new immigrants in general, see Rimer, "Crammed into Tiny, Illegal Rooms, Tenants at the Margins of Survival."

4. Once again, the percentages do not add up to 100 because at the time they were interviewed, five people in the sample either lived at Dona Dahlia's boarding house or were live-in household servants and thus are not included here.

5. Kottak, "Cultural Contrasts in Prime Time Society," 83; DaMatta, cited in ibid.

6. This contrasts with Bicalho's Brazilian subjects in Framingham, Mass., more than 70 percent of whom lived in *puleiros* with five or more people in residence (Bicalho, *Yes Eu Sou Brazuca*).

7. Piore, *Birds of Passage*.

8. Grasmuck and Pessar, *Between Two Islands*, 92.

9. Skidmore, "Whatever Happened to Latin America?"; Malan, "The Brazilian Economy"; Brooke, "Brazil's Plans for Economy Drawing Fire"; Nash,

"Amid Latin Growth, Brazil Falters"; Kamm, "Daily Inflation Struggle Obsesses Brazil."

10. Another example of paltry Brazilian wages: a full-time university faculty member with a Ph.D and twenty years' experience was earning $920 a month in 1991 (Hart, "New Education Minister in Brazil Faces a Campus Crisis over Faculty Strike").

11. Brooke, "Economy of Brazil Still Ails."

12. Brooke, "Free-Trade Perils a Free-Trade Zone in Brazil."

13. De Moura Castro, "What Is Happening in Brazilian Education?"; Faria, "Changes in the Composition of Employment and the Structure of Occupations"; Piore, *Birds of Passage*, 138. Educated Japanese-Brazilians, including lawyers and dentists, have been taking menial jobs in Japan for much the same reason: lack of opportunities in Brazil (Jones, "Latin-Japanese Workers Feel Cool Welcome").

14. Cardoso, "Inflation and Distribution in Brazil: The Recent Experience."

15. Brooke, "As Collor Completes First Year, Brazilians Write Off Their Highest Hopes"; Brooke, "Brazilians' Belt Tightening: Anguish and Relief." By 1991, inflation in Brazil had returned with a vengeance, and the currency was losing its value at the rate of 1 percent a day (Brooke, "In Brazil, Pessimism Starts to Keep Pace with Inflation").

CHAPTER FOUR: WHO ARE THEY?

1. In an M.A. thesis on English acquisition and acculturation among Brazilians in New York City, Luis Guerra also came up with an evenly split sex ratio in the nonrandom sample of one hundred Brazilians that he used in his study (Guerra, "Acculturation and English Proficiency among Brazilians in New York"). Bicalho's Brazilian sample in Framingham, Mass., was more heavily male: 66 percent were men, and 33 percent were women (Bicalho, *Yes, Eu Sou Brazuca*). A very similar ratio was reported for another new immigrant group in New York, Paraguayans: 64 percent male and 35 percent female (Caballero, "Los Paraguayankis en la Mira"). Approximately 73 percent of Brazil's population are Roman Catholic.

2. See Wood and Carvalho, *The Demography of Inequality in Brazil*, on racial categories in the Brazilian census. One person in my sample was a Japanese-Brazilian. I am including a mixed-ancestry racial category to approximate the more complex system of racial categorization used in Brazil. Brazilians commonly employ many different color terms, ranging from light to dark, not the simple dualistic white/nonwhite system used in the United States. On Brazilian racial categories, see Harris, *Patterns of Race in the Americas*, and Degler, *Neither Black nor White*.

3. *Veja*, "Brazucas de Boston."

4. Hoffman, "Poverty and Property in Brazil."

5. Home ownership per se is a poor indicator of economic well-being in Brazil; in 1982, 62 percent of those in the lowest income category said they owned their dwellings, and data on the actual value of the dwellings are not available. Car

ownership is a far better indicator. In 1980, just under 23 percent of Brazilian households owned a car (Hoffman, "Poverty and Property in Brazil").

6. Hart, "Brazil's Universities Come to the Aid of Deteriorating Public Schools." Argentine immigrants in the United States also are singularly well educated compared to their compatriots back home. See Marshall, "Emigration of Argentines to the United States."

7. There have been reports of capital flight from Brazil as the economic situation there worsened. On capital flight to Florida, see *Veja*, "A Febre dos Negócios na Flórida"; *Veja*, "Nova Terra Prometida"; *Veja*, "Invasão à Brasileira"; Reveron, "A Little Piece of Brazil Grows in Miami" and Pinder, "Foreigners Find a Place in the Sun." There are also reports of a "brain drain," as Brazilian scientists and researchers have taken jobs abroad. See *Veja*, "A Fuga dos Cérebros"; and Kamm, "Brazil's Swelling Wave of Emigration Reflects Gloom about Nation's Future."

8. Piore, *Birds of Passage*; Georges, *The Making of a Transnational Community*, 87; Pessar, "The Role of Households in International Migration and the Case for the U.S.-Bound Migration from the Dominican Republic." Georges notes that 77 percent of the migrants to New York from the Dominican town she studied came from households with moderate to large-sized landholdings (Georges, "Gender, Class, and Migration in the Dominican Republic").

9. Portes and Rumbaut, *Immigrant America*; Papademetriou and DiMarzio, *Undocumented Aliens in the New York Metropolitan Area*.

10. There have also been reports of middle-class Peruvians migrating to the United States (Riding, "Starting Over, the Ex-Peruvian Way"; Altamirano, *Los Que Se Fueron*). Recent immigration from the Dominican Republic also has been largely middle class. See Grasmuck and Pessar, *Between Two Islands*.

11. There was a small community of perhaps 2,500 working-class Brazilians living in Newark in the 1960s and early 1970s (Brown, "Faith, Curing and Ethnic Identity.")

12. Bicalho, *Yes, Eu Sou Brazuca*.

13. Cornelius and Portes, cited in Suro, "Your Tired, Your Poor, Your Masses Yearning to Be with Relatives." For a capsule history of the contacts between Governador Valadares and the United States, see Margolis, "An American in Governador Valadares."

14. Piazarollo and Instante Cia. Oba Estamos Vivo, "O Último A Sair Apague A Luz."

15. Bicalho, *Yes, Eu Sou Brazuca; Veja*, "Brazucas de Boston." In Guerra's nonrandom sample of Brazilians in New York, 27 percent had a primary school education, 36 percent had gone to secondary school, and 37 percent had gone to university. The proportion with only an elementary education seems high, and I have no explanation for the discrepancy between his figures and my own (Guerra, "Acculturation and English Proficiency among Brazilians in New York").

16. When I visited Governador Valadares in July 1990, I was told by about three dozen people, including a number of local officials, that Boston is the most common destination for immigrants from the area, followed by Newark and Danbury, and to a lesser extent, southern Florida. Relatively few *valadarenses* head for New York. This is also partially confirmed by Bicalho's (*Yes, Eu Sou*

Brazuca) study of Brazilians in Framingham, Mass., the overwhelming majority of whom were from the Governador Valadares–Rio Doce Valley area; by a report in the magazine *Veja* ("De Olho na América"), and by a series on Brazilian immigrants in the *Cape Cod Times* that suggests that most of the 3,000 Brazilians on Cape Cod come from Governador Valadares and nearby towns (Miller, "Money Tree Image Lures Poor Brazilians to U.S.").

17. This figure exactly matches the percentage of urban residents cited in a study of undocumented immigrants in the New York metropolitan area. Papademetriou and DiMarzio, *Undocumented Aliens in the New York Metropolitan Area*. The figures cited here refer to where people lived at the time they left Brazil. Their place of birth is more variable; 44 percent were born in Minas Gerais, 24 percent in Rio de Janeiro, 13 percent in São Paulo, 14 percent in one of the northeastern states, and 5 percent in the southernmost region of Brazil.

18. Bicalho, *Yes, Eu Sou Brazuca*.

19. The impact of these remittances are impossible to gauge, but some data I gathered while in Governador Valadares are instructive. The largest remittance agency in town takes in up to $1 million a month, and an ex-mayor suggested that remittances for the whole town total about $2.5 million a month. See Margolis, "An American in Governador Valadares." A much higher estimate was given by unnamed city officials, who suggested that as much as $15 million a month is sent back to Valadares. See Miller, "Money Tree Image Lures Poor Brazilians to U.S."

20. Massey, "Economic Development and International Migration in Comparative Perspective"; Feldman-Bianco, "Multiple Layers of Space and Time," 145.

21. Papademetriou and DiMarzio, *Undocumented Aliens in the New York Metropolitan Area*.

22. Garrison and Weiss, "Dominican Family Networks and United States Immigration Policy," 270.

23. Massey, "Economic Development and International Migration in Comparative Perspective," 397.

24. Garrison and Weiss, "Dominican Family Networks and United States Immigration Policy," 272.

25. Ibid.

26. Chavez, "Households, Migration and Settlement," 19.

CHAPTER FIVE: MAKING A LIVING

1. Piore, *Birds of Passage*; Papademetriou and DiMarzio, *Undocumented Aliens in the New York Metropolitan Area*; Portes and Bach, *Latin Journey*. As Portes and Bach note, "[W]omen and blacks, previously available as pliant sources of labor, have increasingly refused to accept these jobs at those wages" (p. 19).

2. See, e.g., Borjas, *Friends or Strangers*.

3. Passell, "So Much for Assumptions about Immigrants and Jobs."

4. Borjas, *Friends or Strangers*; Passell, "So Much for Assumptions about Immigrants and Jobs," E4. See also Castro, "Latinos Nos EUA." For an analysis of

the role of immigrant and native-born workers in the restaurant industry in New York City, see Bailey, *Immigrant and Native Workers*. Undocumented workers do the "dirty work" that natives do not want in other countries as well. See, e.g., Riding, "Welcome or No, Foreigners Do Spain's Dirty Work."

5. See Portes and Bach, *Latin Journey*, ch. 5. On ethnic employment enclaves in New York City, see Lorch, "Ethnic Niches Creating Jobs That Fuel Immigrant Growth."

6. The immigrants in my New York sample have somewhat more diverse employment patterns than those reported for other Brazilian immigrants. For example, Guerra reports that in his nonrandom Queens sample of one hundred Brazilians, over 70 percent of the women were working in domestic service, and 78 percent of the men were employed in four job categories: drivers, shoe shiners, restaurant workers, and construction workers. In contrast, 54 percent of the men in my sample worked in those four categories. Brazilian immigrants in Framingham and Boston are also heavily employed in restaurants and as domestic servants, but hotel work, primarily in porter and chambermaid positions, is also an important source of employment there (Guerra, "Acculturation and English Proficiency among Brazilians in New York"; Bicalho, *Yes, Eu Sou Brazuca*).

7. Papademetriou and DiMarzio (*Undocumented Aliens in the New York Metropolitan Area*) also report that about two-thirds of the undocumented immigrants in their New York study said that they had found their jobs through friends and relatives. See also Houstoun, "Aliens in Irregular Status in the United States."

8. Papademetriou and DiMarzio, *Undocumented Aliens in the New York Metropolitan Area*; Smith, "Mexican Migration from South-Central Mexico and Los Angeles to New York."

9. A far higher proportion—over half—of Bicalho's Framingham, Mass., informants were working at more than one job (Bicalho, *Yes, Eu Sou Brazuca*).

10. Simon and DeLey, "Undocumented Mexican Women." Fifty-five percent of the Mexicans worked in factories, and only 11 percent worked as domestic servants. Papademetriou and DiMarzio, *Undocumented Aliens in the New York Metropolitan Area*.

11. Quoted in Seper, "1986 Amnesty Law Cited in Immigration Increase."

12. Stevenson, "Fight is Intensified on Fake Documents for Aliens."

13. Quoted in Seper, "1986 Amnesty Law Cited in Immigration Increase."

14. In mid-1991 the INS was reportedly planning to step up enforcement of sanctions against employers hiring illegal aliens. See Pear, "Wide Attack on Hiring of Illegal Aliens."

CHAPTER SIX: FROM MISTRESS TO SERVANT

1. On the increase in female labor force participation and changing domestic responsibilities, see Margolis, *Mothers and Such*, ch. 6.

2. Mydans, "More Mexicans Come to U.S. to Stay." On immigrants and domestic service see Sassen-Koob, "New York City's Informal Economy"; Colen, "Housekeeping for the Green Card"; Castro, "Work versus Life: Colombian Women in New York"; Simon and DeLey, "Undocumented Mexican Women";

Haines, "Vietnamese Refugee Women in the U.S. Labor Force"; and Rieff, *Los Angeles: Capital of the Third World*, ch. 5.

3. On the nature of housework, see Margolis, *Mothers and Such*, chs. 4 and 5.

4. Colen, "Housekeeping for the Green Card," 104; Foner, "Sex Roles and Sensibilities." See also Rollins, "Ideology and Servitude."

5. It is possible that today it is not only lower-class Brazilian women who take such positions. With the ongoing economic crisis in Brazil, "positions wanted" ads have been appearing in Brazilian newspapers for women seeking work as domestic servants with families going abroad. For example, in early 1992, the following ad appeared in the *Folha de São Paulo*: "Two girls are available for work abroad as domestic servants or baby-cite [*sic*]."

6. I was told that about forty Hasidic families in the Borough Park area have some connection to Brazil, but not all employ Brazilian women as domestic servants.

7. Foner, "Sex Roles and Sensibilities." Colen also found that most of the women she studied stopped living in once they got the green card. If they continue in domestic service, they typically shift to day child care or home care. With green card in hand, wages usually increase and they are better able to have a say about working conditions and responsibilities (Colen, "Housekeeping for the Green Card").

8. Not only are they paid off the books, but the 1986 Immigration Reform and Control Act seems to have had little effect on the employment of undocumented domestic servants in general. This is probably because there have been very few cases of employers of domestic servants being fined under the provisions of the law, although there have been increased reports of employer abuses of domestic workers since IRCA went into effect (Colen, "Housekeeping for the Green Card"). See also Lewin, "A Law That's Often Ignored for Domestic Workers."

9. In this category I am including the two or three men in my sample (and about the same number of women) who held jobs as home care attendants for elderly people. Their pay ranged from $200 to $400 a week, also usually off the books. About the same number of men had jobs cleaning offices. Then, too, a number of Brazilian men living in the New York suburbs of Long Island and Westchester are employed as gardeners. I was told that in Port Chester in Westchester County, there is a street on which Brazilians and Mexicans line up every day waiting to be hired for short-term gardening jobs.

10. Foner, "Sex Roles and Sensibilities." Other studies of women who held mostly professional and white-collar jobs in their countries of origin but had to take service and blue-collar jobs in the United States include Stafford, "Haitian Immigrant Women"; Haines, "Vietnamese Refugee Women in the U.S. Labor Force"; and Prieto, "Cuban Women and Work in the United States."

11. Colen, "Housekeeping for the Green Card."

12. Ibid., 99.

13. For a similar finding see, Bailey, *Immigrant and Native Workers*.

14. Ibid.

15. O'Neill, "Recession and Guilt Pare Dining Trade and Menus."

16. Freedman, "The Labor Market for Immigrants in New York City."

17. Many students of Brazilian culture have discussed the stigma attached to

manual labor in that country; it is said to have deep historical roots. See, e.g., Freyre, *The Masters and the Slaves*; and Wagley, *Introduction to Brazil*.

18. These figures mesh with those cited in an article on street vendors in the *New York Times*. According to the article, a typical seller earns $40 a day in cash, and each sidewalk bookstand grosses $250 to $300 a day (Levine, "On the Sidewalks, Business Is Booming").

19. Evidence suggests that desirable pushcart spaces are "owned," and one report claims they can be sold for as much as $9,000 (Valla, "O 'Abacaxi' da Pequena 'Mafia' Invisível").

20. In his study of Mexican flower vendors in New York City, Robert Smith also found that some of his informants prefer street selling to other types of work because they do not have to "tolerate being ordered around" (Smith, "Mexican Immigrant Women in New York City's Informal Economy").

21. Freedman, "The Labor Market for Immigrants in New York City."

22. Miami appears to be more of a hotbed of Brazilian entrepreneurial activity than New York (*Veja*, "Invasão à Brasileira").

23. Along these same lines, I met a few Brazilian men who washed cars for about $30 a day plus around $10 in tips. Car washing is usually a first job for Brazilian men, one that they hold for a few weeks at most until they can find something that pays more.

24. Rimer, "For Flier Distributors, Peskiness Can Be a Virtue."

CHAPTER SEVEN: SHOE SHINE "BOYS" AND "GO-GO" GIRLS

1. For example, I gave an interview about my research on Brazilians in New York to the Brazilian newspaper *O Estado de São Paulo*. The headline read: "Go-Go Dancers and Shoe Shiners in the Majority" (Decol, "Dançarinas e Engraxates São Maioria"). There also have been at least two features about New York–area go-go dancers on Brazilian television.

2. There are a handful of "freelance" shoe shiners in Manhattan who work on the sidewalks outside busy train and bus stations. My impression is that most of these independents are African Americans.

3. I am purposely using the term "man" here. Although informants said that they had heard of a few female shoe shiners in the Wall Street area, I was never able to confirm this. However, a friend visiting Washington, D.C., told me about a Brazilian couple who shined shoes together in the lobby of the posh hotel in which he was staying.

4. Some of these positions are much sought after, as evidenced by the fact that some Brazilians have sold their jobs in these shops to other Brazilians. For example, in a busy shop near the Pan Am Building, noted for the generosity of its clientele, a shoe shining chair has been known to change hands for $300 to $400.

5. A number of informants told me that there are also Brazilian men who work as go-go dancers. They said that some work in bars with female audiences and others work in gay clubs in Manhattan or at private parties, for which they may be paid as much as $1,000. I cannot confirm this since I never met a Brazilian man

who worked as a "go-go boy." In another twist on these two stereotypical Brazilian jobs, the *New York Times* reports that there are now topless women in some go-go dancing establishments who shine shoes! (Ravo, " 'Quality' Topless Clubs Go for the Crowd in Pin Stripes").

6. According to a report in *Veja*, about 80 percent of the dancers in the Newark area are Brazilian, but less than 40 percent of go-gos in Manhattan are Brazilian because bar owners there insist that all the dancers speak English (Sekles, "Dólares a Go-Go").

7. *Folha de São Paulo*, "Mineiros e Portugueses Disputam a 'Baixada Fluminense' dos EUA." I was told that Boston also is home to a large number of Brazilian go-go dancers.

8. Dines, "GO-GOS: Os (As) Brasileiros (as) Entram na Dança do Dólor."

9. Some Brazilian women work as barmaids and receive about $25 from the house in addition to tips. On a good night, when they make $150 or $200, their earnings compare favorably with those of the dancers. The dancers themselves will occasionally agree to dance at a private bachelor party, for which they earn about $600 for the evening.

10. Similar reports come from Newark. A 1991 article on go-go dancers in that city notes the decline in earnings. Where some dancers once made up to $1,500 a week, they are now earning $600 to $800. But, "I can still make as much as $300 a night," one dancer said, "if all of my fans show up" (*Folha de São Paulo*, "Lana, 'Go-go' em Newark, Queria Falar Inglês"). Because of the precipitous decline in earnings, some go-gos have stopped dancing entirely and have found other work. Some import string bikinis for sale to still-active dancers, while others sew go-go outfits themselves and sell them for up to $100 a piece.

11. Quoted in Dines, "GO-GOS: Os (As) Brasileiros (as) Entram na Dança do Dólor."

12. For an ethnographic account of female go-go dancers, see Lewin, *Naked Is the Best Disguise*; for a discussion of male go-go dancers, see Margolis and Arnold, "Turning the Tables?"

13. The restaurant industry, in fact, is the single most important source of employment for all immigrants in New York. In 1980, when immigrants comprised 25 percent of the city's population, they accounted for 54 percent of all restaurant workers. Bailey, *Immigrant and Native Workers*.

14. Portes and Bach, *Latin Journey*. For a discussion of ethnic economic niches, see Barth, "Ecological Relationships of Ethnic Groups in Swat, North Pakistan."

CHAPTER EIGHT: LIFE AND LEISURE IN THE BIG APPLE

"Tia Mimi" is translated from the Portuguese and reprinted with permission courtesy of Lucinho Bizidão. The lyrics in Portuguese are as follows: "Olha a Tia Mimi, olha a Tia Mimi / Não saio de casa que ela ti leva embora daqui / Vou fazer iqual urso polar / Eu vou preparar minha hibernação / Cinco litros de cachaça / Não saia de casa nessa confusão / Estou longe de minha terra / E sempre fugindo da imigração / Como eu existem milhares / Querendo sair dessa situação / Olha a Tia Mimi, olha a Tia Mimi . . . / Mas eu 'tou sem dinheiro no bolso / E aqui me conhecem como um ilegal / Estão andando atras dessa gente / E com esse negocio a coisa vai mal / Se me pegam eu perco o emprego / Vão ter que me dar casa e comida / Aí o negocio melhora / E eu nunca mais vou sair dessa vida / Olha a Tia Mimi, olha a Tia Mimi. . . ." I thank J. T. Milanich for his help with the translation.

1. For a discussion of the importance of family ties in Brazil even in urban settings, see Miller, "The Function of Middle-Class Extended Family Networks in Brazilian Urban Society."

2. Gonzalez, "Mexican Migrants Crowd New York," 13. The reasoning behind the Koch administration's ruling was that with so many undocumented immigrants in the city, it would be harmful if they avoided city agencies, such as the police, for fear of being reported to immigration authorities. For further discussion of what it is like to live in the United States as an undocumented immigrant, see Chavez, *Shadowed Lives*, ch. 9.

3. A number of Brazilians in New York City say they prefer to go to Brazilian and Portuguese restaurants in the Ironbound District of Newark because they are much less costly than those in Manhattan.

4. Another distinctly Brazilian specialty found in New York is *capoeira*, a martial arts–like dance that originated during slave times in northeastern Brazil. *Capoeira* classes are offered in Manhattan and Brooklyn, but I was told that more Americans than Brazilians take the classes.

5. A percussion (*batucada*) group with both Brazilian and American members marched in the 1990 ticker tape parade that honored Nelson Mandela upon the occasion of his first visit to New York.

6. The street fair, originally intended as an annual event, was called off in 1990. It resumed under new sponsorship in 1991.

7. For a discussion of carnival as a quintessentially Brazilian celebration, see Parker, *Bodies, Pleasures and Passions*, ch. 6.

8. Another television show, "Sounds Brazilian," is a weekly program of Brazilian music and videos aired on the city-owned television station. However, it is in English and is not primarily aimed at Brazilians, but at people who like Brazilian music.

9. The Brazilians in Bicalho's study in Framingham, Mass., were even more isolated from American society. Over two-thirds said that they had no American friends at all, and of those that had American friends, 60 percent said that they never went out with them socially (Bicalho, *Yes, Eu Sou Brazuca*).

10. Guerra, "Acculturation and English Proficiency among Brazilians in New York." Hendricks, in a study of Dominicans in New York City, found that illegal immigrants from that country made no effort to acculturate to life in the city because of the tentativeness of their sojourn. Their goal was to make money and return home. Fear of the immigration authorities also kept them apart from American society (Hendricks, "The Phenomenon of Migrant Illegality: The Case of Dominicans in New York").

11. See, e.g., Papademetriou and DiMarzio, *Undocumented Aliens in the New York Metropolitan Area.*

CHAPTER NINE: LITTLE BRAZIL: IS IT A COMMUNITY?

1. Kottak, *Prime Time Society*, 166.

2. In this, as in a number of other ways, Brazilians bear a striking resemblance to Israelis in New York City, who also exhibit a paucity of community spirit and organization. Like Brazilians, Israelis see themselves as sojourners, not settlers, and hence are reluctant to invest in community building. See, Shokeid, *Children of Circumstances*, ch. 3.

3. On ethnic economic enclaves, see Portes, "Modes of Structural Incorporation and Present Theories of Migration"; Wilson and Portes, "Ethnic Enclaves"; and Bonacich and Modell, *The Economic Basis of Ethnic Solidarity*.

4. Kim, *New Urban Immigrants*; Staub, *Yemenis in New York*. See also Basch, "The Vincentians and Grenadians."

5. Shokeid, *Children of Circumstances*, 44, 53, 54.

6. Piore, *Birds of Passage*, 55.

7. Distrust within the Brazilian immigrant community apparently is not limited to New York. In an article about Brazilians in Boston in the weekly news magazine *Veja*, one immigrant is quoted as saying that Brazilians "only think of taking jobs from each other. . . . As soon as I arrived I was advised not to have Brazilian friends." And in an article on Brazilians in Framingham, Mass., similar sentiments were expressed: "[T]he worst enemy of the Brazilian in the U.S. is other Brazilians" (*Veja*, "Brazucas de Boston"; see also Fonseca, "Brasileiros em Massachusetts").

8. Here, too, there is a striking Israeli parallel. When Israelis meet in New York, Shokeid was told, they greet each other with the question: "How much do you earn?" (Shokeid, *Children of Circumstances*, 69).

9. Of interest is that toward the end of my research, this same employer began hiring Hispanic immigrants—almost certainly undocumented—for some jobs in her establishment. She was the only Brazilian business owner I encountered who employed immigrants from other ethnic groups. For a discussion of immigrant businesses' hiring outside of their own ethnicity, see Smith, "Mexican Migration from South-Central Mexico and Los Angeles to New York."

10. The diatribes against compatriots are reminiscent of attitudes of Israeli immigrants desribed by Shokeid. He met very few Israelis in New York City who did not view other Israelis in the city "in derogatory or derisive terms." Nevertheless, as in the case of the Brazilians, their social life revolved around their compatriots (Shokeid, *Children of Circumstances*, 56).

11. The ideology was originally said to be characteristic of peasant populations, particularly in highland Latin America, and was first labeled by anthropologist George Foster, in "The Image of Limited Good," published in the *American Anthropologist* in 1965.

12. These community cleavages were also evident at a luncheon at the Plaza Hotel honoring the visit of the Brazilian president, Fernando Collor de Mello, to New York. Members of New York's Brazilian elite were well represented, but only one Little Brazil merchant was among the hundreds of Brazilians present.

13. Here, too, Brazilians bear a marked resemblance to their Israeli counterparts in New York, who also have strained relations with the staff of the Israeli consulate and other official government representatives in the city. See Shokeid, *Children of Circumstances*, ch. 3.

14. DaMatta, "Brazil: A Changing Nation and a Changeless Society?" 100. Brazilians direct the same sort of complaints at some of their country's other consulates in the United States, as is evident from letters to the editor critical of the Los Angeles and Miami consulates in *News from Brazil*, a monthly newsletter published in Los Angeles.

15. A charitable effort sponsored by the Brazilian elite in New York City is the Brazilian Children's Fund of Memorial Sloan-Kettering Cancer Center, which gives assistance to Brazilian families with children being treated at the center. The initial impetus for the group was a Brazilian physician who specializes in pediatric oncology and is affiliated with Sloan-Kettering.

16. In late 1991, *El Diario*/La Prensa, the Spanish-language newspaper with the largest circulation in New York City, began publishing a weekly insert in Portuguese intended for the Brazilian community.

17. Parenthetically, one member of the Brazilian elite lamented these representations of Brazilian culture. "They are not the best quality," he said. "If you are going to show samba schools and carnival parades to the American public they should be the most artistic forms of these institutions with the very best best costumes, the best dancers and so on."

18. Yinger, *Religion, Society and the Individual*; Williams, *America's Religions*; Roof and McKinney, *American Mainline Religion*.

19. The Universal Church has received widespread criticism in the Brazilian press as a cultlike organization whose main concern is its own financial success, primarily achieved through the monetary contributions of its converts.

20. The church is aiming its ministry at New York's large Hispanic population. It has a nightly half-hour program on one of the city's Spanish-language television stations.

21. In Brazil, Kardecism has been called "predominately a religion of the white educated sectors." Further, "its rituals celebrate class values related to education and culture and act to discourage the participation of those who lack them" (Brown, *Umbanda*, 17, 24).

22. Diana Brown, an anthropologist and student of spiritist practices in Brazil attended the Queens session with me. She pointed out that it was much less formal and the speeches were far less "pompous" than those she had witnessed in Brazil. There, the discussions are usually dominated by older men, while in the Queens group, the women were at least as active as the men.

23. On Umbanda, see Brown, *Umbanda*.

CHAPTER TEN: CLASS PICTURES

1. This figure is from Instituto Brasileiro de Opinião Pública e Estatística (IBOPE), the Brazilian Statistical Public Opinion Institute, cited in Kottak, *Prime Time Society*. This datum, however, does not indicate the highly unequal

distribution of income in Brazil, which is better gauged from the following statistic: in 1976 the top 1 percent of the Brazilian population had a larger slice of the total national income than did the bottom 50 percent (Hewlett, *The Cruel Dilemmas of Development*). For a masterful discussion of traditional Brazilian social classes and class relations, see Scheper-Hughes, *Death without Weeping*. On social class and social mobility, see Pastore, *Inequality and Social Mobility in Brazil*.

2. In Brazil, only a small percentage of the population is university educated. *Academe*, "From Political to Economic Siege in Brazil." Today, some 75 percent of Brazil's university students attend private institutions. Paradoxically, Catholic and tuition-free federal universities mostly educate the country's elite. Federal universities, in fact, receive about 60 percent of the nation's entire budget for public education although only about 500,000 students attend them, nearly all of whom are well-to-do. Less well-off students from inferior public high schools often do not score high enough on university entrance exams to be admitted to a free public university and are more likely to pay tuition to attend a private one. Also important in the distribution of university students by social class is the fact that public universities usually do not offer night classes, while private institutions do. Students from less privileged backgrounds who have to hold jobs to support themselves while attending university may have no choice but to go to private institutions with night classes. Wealthier students who are supported by their parents are more likely to have the luxury of full-time study in day classes. On the growth of private institutions of higher learning in Brazil, see De Moura Castro, "What Is Happening in Brazilian Education?" See also *The Economist*, "Drunk, Not Sick."

3. It is impossible to know how many Brazilian immigrants remit money home or what its total value is. Still, in 1988, the owner of the largest Brazilian remittance agency in New York, which then had nine branches in the United States, told me that about 6,000 Brazilians sent a total of some $3.5 million a month to Brazil through his agency; remittances averaged $700 apiece. One can assume these amounts have increased because by 1992 this agency had five additional branches. In an article in the Brazilian weekly news magazine *Veja*, the owner of another remittance agency with branches in a number of U.S. cities is quoted as saying that his agency sends $7 million a month to Brazil (*Veja*, "Brazucas de Boston"). Even if accurate, these figures are only part of the picture because many immigrants send money home only when they know someone traveling to Brazil who can take it to their relatives. This saves remittance agency fees, but, of course, it also results in less regular payments since it depends on when friends or relatives are traveling to Brazil.

4. There are two other groups of Brazilians in the city, the size of which is unknown. The first group comprises Brazilians married to Americans, who have largely lost touch with the resident Brazilian community. Nearly all of their friends are Americans, and they do not seem so much to avoid or disdain the new Brazilian immigrants as to have little knowledge of or contact with them. The second group, a generally transient one, comprises Brazilian students attending one of the city's universities.

5. DaMatta, *Carnivals, Rogues, and Heroes*, 140–141.

6. The traditional Brazilian disdain for manual labor, sometimes called "the gentleman's complex," comes into play here since most of the jobs held by recent immigrants do involve physical labor. See Freyre, *The Masters and the Slaves*; and Wagley, *Introduction to Brazil*.

7. Quoted in Vilella, "Uma Sociedade Anonima."

8. For a description of interclass behavior, see De Azevedo, *Cultura e Situação Racial no Brasil*.

9. Newman, *Falling from Grace*. See also Margolis, "From Mistress to Servant."

10. Bogen, *Immmigration in New York City*; Piore, *Birds of Passage*; Sassen-Koob, "Changing Composition and Labor Market Location of Hispanic Immigrants in New York City." Staub notes that Yemeni immigrants with low status and grueling jobs in New York City "draw strength from their ideology of return" (*Yemenis in New York*, 85).

11. Piore, *Birds of Passage*, 54; Papadametriou and DiMarzio, *Undocumented Aliens in the New York Metropolitan Area*, 81.

12. Kottak, "Cultural Contrasts in Prime Time Society"; DaMatta, "Brazil: A Changing Nation and a Changeless Society?" 96.

13. Castro, "Work versus Life: Colombian Women in New York," 242. Moving farther afield, there are also cases of downward mobility among illegal Chinese immigrants in New York City. Chinese engineers who work in factories are something akin to indentured servants. Having paid up to $30,000 to be smuggled into the United States, it takes them years to pay off the debt at very low wages (Hays, "Immigrants Strain Chinatown's Resources").

14. Here, I am not referring to the lower-class Brazilian women who were brought to the United States as live-in housekeepers and who have vastly improved their standard of living while still working as domestic servants.

15. Freyre, *The Masters and the Slaves*. See Skidmore, *Black into White*, on the ideology of racial democracy in Brazil.

16. Hasenbalg, "Race and Socioeconomic Inequalities in Brazil." See Wood and Carvalho, *The Demography of Inequality in Brazil*, on the relationship between race and infant mortality.

17. Ehrlich, "Beyond Black and White"; Ehrlich, "Stereotypes of Racial Conflict."

18. Ehrlich, "Beyond Black and White," 62.

19. For a discussion and analysis of gender roles in Brazil, see Patai, *Brazilian Women Speak*. See also Margolis, "Women in International Migration." For a discussion of women in international migration, see Simon and Brettell, *International Migration: The Female Experience*. On women as immigrants in the United States, see Gabaccia, *Seeking Common Ground*.

20. This is similar to Foner's findings for Jamaican women in New York. The women she interviewed talked of the "independence" and "financial control" that migration had brought them. Foner, "Sex Roles and Sensibilities," 143.

21. Studies have shown that women are just as likely as men to migrate for economic reasons. For example, a study of undocumented Mexican women in California found that 70 percent had migrated for economic reasons (Simon and DeLey, "Undocumented Mexican Women").

22. Grasmuck and Pessar, *Between Two Islands*; Buchanan, "Haitian Women in New York City." Pessar notes that another consequence of this new division of labor is that because of the measure of economic independence they have gained in New York, women who work outside the home are often very reluctant to return to their home country (Pessar, "When the Birds of Passage Want to Roost").

23. Of the fifty-five women in their sample, eighteen were divorced or separated after they came to New York, and fourteen of these indicated that it was the battle over domestic authority that led to the breakup (Grasmuck and Pessar, *Between Two Islands*).

24. Buchanan, "Haitian Women in New York City."

25. Foner, "Sex Roles and Sensibilities," 152; Grasmuck and Pessar, *Between Two Islands*, 155.

CHAPTER ELEVEN: AN INVISIBLE MINORITY

1. Colloquial usage of the term "Hispanic" in the United States almost always refers to Spanish-speakers or their descendants.

2. Riding, "Bedfellows with Spain, Lisbon Won't Cuddle."

3. Ethnic confusion about Brazilians in the United States is nothing new. One Brazilian who has lived in this country for many years says that when she went to register her daughter at an elementary school in New York City in the late 1940s, only two categories appeared on the enrollment form; she was told that she must identify herself as either "white" or "Puerto Rican."

4. The popular saying is quoted in Riding, "Bedfellows with Spain, Lisbon Won't Cuddle. Ribeiro's comment is quoted in Riding, "Aloof Giant, Brazil Warms to Neighbors."

5. Although Spanish is generally not taught in Brazilian schools, the exception is in public schools in southernmost Brazil, where Spanish, not English, is the foreign language of choice. The reason is the presence of large numbers of tourists from Argentina, Uruguay, and Chile in this part of Brazil. See Holston, ". . . in Southern Brazil."

6. Klor de Alva, "Telling Hispanics Apart," 114. Some people from Spanish-speaking countries dislike the designation Hispanic and prefer being called Dominican, Colombian, and so on. They complain that they lose their national distinctiveness when labeled Hispanic. The term is often used for political ends, since it combines disparate groups of people, who may have little in common other than language, into a more potent political force (Klor de Alva, "Telling Hispanics Apart"). See also Safa, "Migration and Identity."

7. When a Brazilian immigrant living in Newark was arrested and charged with murder, the case became a cause célèbre in Brazil and was widely covered in the media there. But the case—the man was tried and acquitted—was ignored by the New York press (Ribeiro, "Brazilians, Uma Minoria Étnica Descoberto Por Uma Suspeita").

8. Brenner, "The New New York," 78.

9. Brooke, "Town That Uncle Sam Built, You Might Say." The *New York*

Times ran articles on emigration from Peru, Argentina, and Paraguay to the United States even though the number of immigrants from Argentina and Paraguay combined almost certainly does not equal the number from Brazil (Riding, "Starting Over, the Ex-Peruvian Way"; Riding, "Caraguatay Journal: People Leave and the Dollars Arrive"). In 1991 the paper carried a story on Japanese-Brazilian emigration to Japan (Weisman, "In Japan, Bias Is an Obstacle Even for the Ethnic Japanese").

10. Bogen, *Immigration in New York City*; Foner, *New Immigrants in New York City*; Reimers, *Still the Golden Door*; Portes and Rumbaut, *Immigrant America*. The only book I found on immigrants in New York that even mentions Brazilians is a travel guide to the city's ethnic groups and ethnic restaurants (Leeds, *Ethnic New York*).

11. Quoted in *News from Brazil*, "Lost Angels," 15.

12. Americans are not the only ones who know little about Brazil. Brazilians of Japanese descent who have gone to Japan seeking high-paying jobs report that the Japanese are equally ignorant of their homeland. "The people over here think Brazilians are living in Brazil like wild Indians," complained a Japanese-Brazilian immigrant to a *New York Times* reporter (quoted in Weisman, "In Japan, Bias Is an Obstacle Even for the Ethnic Japanese"). Brazil is not the only country about which Americans know very little. Immigrants from many countries complain about Americans' ignorance about their homelands. Senegalese in New York, for example, criticized Americans' lack of knowledge of Africa: "They don't know that there are 'modern things' there, cars and high rise buildings." "When Americans see me," said one Senagalese woman, "they think I live in the trees with the animals" (quoted in Fleisher, "Visions of Dallas.")

13. United States Navy Affirmative Action Guidelines.

14. Klor de Alva, "Telling Hispanics Apart."

15. Quoted in Gonzalez, "What's the Problem with 'Hispanic'? Just Ask a 'Latino,' " 6.

16. This is the precise wording in the instruction sheet that accompanied the short form of the 1990 U.S. census. The Questionaire Reference Book used by census workers also shows the state of confusion regarding Brazilians and other Portuguese-speakers. While Portuguese and Azorians are to be listed as "white" under the census's racial designation, Brazilians and Cape Verdians are to be listed as "other race," even though, of course, many Brazilians are white.

17. Initial results from the 1990 census show that in many states the category "other" has increased considerably over the 1980 census, and that the number of people identifying themselves as "other" went from 6.75 million in 1980 to 9.8 million in 1990, an increase of 45 percent nationally (Atkins, "When Life Simply Isn't Black or White"). Census officials expect that most people in this category will eventually be classified as "white." According to a report in the *New York Times*, "The people who assigned themselves to the "other race" category on census forms will be assigned to recognized categories by statistical means." Census officials say most of these people are of Hispanic origin, but their cultures have established different racial categories since so many are of mixed Spanish, Indian, and African descent. Faced with the unfamiliar census categories, they are likely

to check "other" (Barringer, "Census Shows Profound Change in Racial Make-up of the Nation," B8).

18. All of the program's graphs, however, on the size and distribution of the target audience in the United States were labeled "Hispanic," rather than "Latino." Guadalupe, "Take Your Pick."

19. Margolis, "A New Ingredient in the Melting Pot."

20. Woodrow and Passel, "Post-IRCA Undocumented Immigration to the United States"; Durand and Massey, "Mexican Migration to the United States." Preliminary evidence also suggests a similar rate of undercount of the undocumented in the 1990 census. For example, it has been suggested that for every Mexican counted in New York, three were not. Thus, a recorded population of 61,000 translates into more than 200,000 Mexicans (Millman, "New Mex City").

CHAPTER TWELVE: SOJOURNER OR IMMIGRANT?

1. Chavez, "Settlers and Sojourners." In his study, Guerra found a higher rate of planned return to Brazil—63 percent, with the remaining 37 percent of respondents saying that they intended to stay in the United States. The absence of an "uncertain" category in his study might account for the discrepancy between his figures and my own (Guerra, "Acculturation and English Proficiency among Brazilians in New York").

2. Piore, *Birds of Passage*, 50. See also Papapademetriou and DiMarzio, *Undocumented Aliens in the New York Metropolitan Area*; Castro, "Work Versus Life"; Gmelch, "Return Migration."

3. On the decision to stay or return home, see Papapademetriou and DiMarzio, *Undocumented Aliens in the New York Metropolitan Area*; Bean, Edmonston, and Passel, introduction to *Undocumented Migration to the United States*; Chavez, "Outside the Imagined Community"; Bohning, *Studies in International Labour Migration*. Georges found in her study of Dominican migrants that nearly all viewed their sojourn in the United States as temporary, including one who had lived there for thirty years (Georges, *The Making of a Transnational Community*).

4. Grasmuck and Pessar, *Between Two Islands*, 156. Grasmuck and Pessar also note that many women who returned to the Dominican Republic expressed dissatisfaction with traditional gender roles, missed paid employment, and resented renewed economic dependence on their husbands. See also Reimers, *Still the Golden Door*; Bernard and Comitas, "Greek Return Migration"; and Bernard and Ashton-Vouyoucalos, "Return Migration to Greece."

5. In Guerra's study, 73 percent of the men, compared to 53 percent of the women, planned to return to Brazil, but, here again, an "undecided" category was absent (Guerra, "Acculturation and English Proficiency among Brazilians in New York").

6. Portes and Bach, *Latin Journey*, 8. Guerra reports that buying a house and/or car in Brazil was the most common objective of the immigrants in his sample

and that most planned to save the target amount in two years (Guerra, "Acculturation and English Proficiency among Brazilians in New York").

7. According to an immigrant couple, "You really can't do anything in Brazil" with much under $50,000 in savings. They gave the following breakdown: $20,000 for an apartment, $5,000 to furnish it, $13,000 for a car, and $20,000 or $25,000 to invest in a small business.

8. M. Estellie Smith, personal communication. Smith points out that this is a common pattern among Portuguese immigrants in the United States. It also has a long history. According to a caption in an Ellis Island Museum exhibit, "It is estimated that as many as one-third of the immigrants traveled back and forth, some finally staying in the old country, others settling in the U.S."

9. See, e.g., Bray, "Economic Development."

10. One related arrangement may become more common in the future. I encountered a few Brazilians, mostly natives of Governador Valadares, who had moved to the United States permanently, but who still owned houses or apartments in Brazil, which they rented out. They returned home to see friends and relatives or for vacation every year or two.

11. Cornelius's comment is cited in Grant, *New Immigrants and Ethnicity*. On "reverse culture shock," see Gmelch, "Return Migration," 146; Bernard and Ashton-Vouyoucalos, "Return Migration to Greece," 36.

12. The Collor freeze on savings accounts may have affected tourism to some extent. A woman who owns a New York boutique that caters to Brazilian tourists said that since the Collor package, her business has suffered because there are fewer of them.

13. Brooke, "As Collor Completes First Year, Brazilians Write Off Their Highest Hopes"; *The Economist*, "Drunk, Not Sick"; Brooke, "Brazilians Fret Over New Leader"; Wood and Carvalho, *The Demography of Inequality in Brazil*. In mid-1992 Brazil was also thrown into a political crisis, as President Collor, accused of accepting millions of dollars in bribes, funneled through his former campaign finance chief, was impeached and eventually resigned from the presidency, but was then tried before the Brazilian senate and found quilty. See *Veja*, "O Jardim do Marajá da Dinda"; Brooke, "Looting Brazil"; and Nash, "Brazil Leader Quits as His Trial Starts in Senate."

14. On the New York recession, see Finder, "All Walks of Life Now Converge in New York City's Jobless Lines."

15. For a report on IRCA and the recession's impact on immigrants in the New York metropolitan area, see Mitchell, "Wary Recruits."

16. Gmelch, "Return Migration," 140. See also Bleier, "Impact of Venuzuela's Recession on Return Migration to Colombia."

17. Portes and Bach, *Latin Journey*. They continue: "[I]mmigrants are used to undercut domestic workers who are themselves weak and frequently unorganized. . . . Competitive labor, most of it non-white, is pitted against the new workers and is frequently displaced by them" (p. 20).

18. Paolozzi, "NY Tem Lojas Brasileiras."

19. Lucena, "Aumenta Exôdo Para Japão e Estados Unidos"; U.S. INS, *1990 Statistical Yearbook*; Lucena, "Aumenta Exôdo Para Japão e Estados Unidos."

20. Piore, *Birds of Passage*. However, for Brazilians a community of immigrants does not become a community of citizens. Very few Brazilians seem to become American citizens. I met only four or five immigrants who had taken out citizenship papers over the course of twenty months of field research. Informants suggest that this may be because according to Brazilian law, Brazilians who become citizens of another country lose their Brazilian citizenship, something most Brazilians are very reluctant to do.

abraço—hug, embrace
a senhora—formal third person singular, "you"
babá—nanny, nursemaid
bacalhau—codfish
bahiano—a native of the northeastern state of Bahia
batucada—African-Brazilian percussion music
bicha—animal
bizidão—slang, busy
boa família—good family
boite—nightclub
brazuca—a Brazilian immigrant in the United States
buraco—a card game
cachaça—Brazilian distilled cane alcohol
café de manha—breakfast
caipirinha—a potent drink made of Brazilian cane alcohol, sugar, and limes
Candomblé—an African-Brazilian religion, primarily practiced in the Brazilian
   state of Bahia
capoeira—a Brazilian martial arts–like dance
carioca—a native of the city of Rio de Janeiro
churrasco a rodizio—a Brazilian barbecue in which waiters pass from table to
   table with large skewers of grilled meats
crente—literally, "believer"; Protestant
cucas—short for *cucarachas*, Spanish for "roaches"; a perjorative term for
   Hispanics
dançarina—go-go dancer
dar um jeito—to cut through red tape, to achieve an end through minor chicanery
decoração de lixo—"garbage decor"
despachante—literally, "dispatcher"; an expediter who cuts through red tape to
   get a document or reach another desired end
dicha—dishwasher
dula—dollar; see also *verdinhas*
fantasma—apparition, ghost
farinha—manioc flour, a Brazilian staple
farofa—toasted manioc flour
favelado—a resident of a *favela* (shantytown)
fazendeiro—large landowner, cattle rancher
fazendo uma farra—carousing
fazer América—to migrate to the United States
feijão—black beans, a Brazilian staple

feijoada—the Brazilian national dish, consisting of assorted meats cooked in black beans and various accompaniments

fio dental—literally, "dental floss"; a Brazilian string bikini

frango à passarinho—literally, "chicken in the style of a little bird"; small pieces of chicken fried in garlic

fulano de tal—so-and-so

fumaça—literally, "smoke"; a perfunctory shoe shine given to poor tippers.

fundo de garantia—severance pay

futebol—soccer

Gal Costa—name of a popular singer; Brazilian slang for a green card

gaucho—a native of the southern state of Rio Grande do Sul

gente—people, folks

gente fina—fine, upscale people

gente baixa—low-class people

graças a Deus—thank God

guaraná—a Brazilian soft drink

hispano—Hispanic

ingraxate—shoe shiner

kibe—a fried Brazilian snack of Lebanese origin

mal educado—poorly educated, ill mannered

mineiro—a native of the state of Minas Gerais

morar dentro—to live in as a household servant

orelinhas—literally, "little ears"; earmuffs

pasteis—a Brazilian fast food consisting of savoury pastries filled with meat, shrimp, or olives

pastelaria—a Brazilian-style fast food restaurant that specializes in *pasteis*

paulista—a native of the city of São Paulo

pensão—rooming house, boarding house

pistolão—literally, "big gun," an influential backer, usually a relative or friend

pobres—poor people

poder executivo—literally, "executive power"; monetary clout

puleiro—literally, "chicken coop"; crowded living quarters that house new immigrants

raça—race

salgadinhos—Brazilian savoury snacks

saudades—homesickness, longing for something

Silvio Santos—name of a Brazilian television personality; Brazilian slang for a social security card

um social—a social security card

socorro—help, aid

solteiro(a)—unmarried man (woman)

tanga—a Brazilian string (thong) bikini

Tia Mimi—literally, "Aunt Mimi"; Brazilian slang for the U.S. Immigration and Naturalization Service (INS).

umbandista—a practitioner of Umbanda, a Brazilian religion that blends Spiritism, folk Catholicism, and African-Brazilian beliefs and rituals *um, dois, tres*—literally, "one, two, three"; a perfunctory shoe shine given to customers who tip poorly

valadarense—a native of Governador Valadares, in Minas Gerais

verdinhas—literally, "little green ones"; dollars; see also *dula*

vovó—grandma

REFERENCES

Academe
1990 "From Political to Economic Siege in Brazil." *Bulletin of the American Association of University Professors*, May–June, pp. 27–30.

Altamirano, Teofilo
1990 *Los Que Se Fueron: Peruanos en los Estados Unidos*. Lima: Pontífica Universidad Catolica del Peru.

Anderson, Margo J.
1988 *The American Census: A Social History*. New Haven: Yale University Press.

Atkins, Elizabeth
1991 "When Life Simply Isn't Black or White." *New York Times*, June 5, pp. C1, C7.

Baer, Werner, and Paul Beckerman
1989 "The Decline and Fall of Brazil's Cruzado." *Latin American Research Review* 24(1): 35–64.

Bailey, Thomas R.
1987 *Immigrant and Native Workers: Contrasts and Competition*. Boulder, Colo.: Westview Press.

Barringer, Felicity
1991 "Census Shows Profound Change in Racial Makeup of the Nation." *New York Times*, March 11, pp. A1, B8.

Barrow, Anita
1988 "Generations of Persistence: Kinship amidst Urban Poverty in São Paulo and New York." *Urban Anthropology* 17(2–3): 193–228.

Barth, Fredrik
1974 "Ecological Relationships of Ethnic Groups in Swat, North Pakistan." In *Man in Adaptation: The Cultural Present*, Yehudi Cohen, ed. 2d ed., Chicago: Aldine, pp. 378–385.

Basch, Linda
1987 "The Vincentians and Grenadians: The Role of Voluntary Associations in Immigrant Adaptation to New York City." In *New Immigrants in New York City*, Nancy Foner, ed. New York: Columbia University Press, pp. 159–193.

Bean, Frank D., Barry Edmonston, and Jeffrey S. Passel, eds.
1990 *Undocumented Migration to the United States: IRCA and the Experience of the 1980's*. Santa Monica, Calif., and Washington, D.C.: Rand Corporation and Urban Institute.

Bean, Frank D., Lindsey Lowell, and Lowell J. Taylor
1987 "Undocumented Migration to the United States: Perceptions and Evidence." *Population and Development Review* 13:671–690.

Bean, Frank D., George Vernez, and Charles B. Keely
    1989   *Opening and Closing the Doors: Evaluating Immigration Reform and Control.* Santa Monica, Calif.: Rand Corporation and Urban Institute.
Bernard, H. Russell
    1988   *Research Methods in Cultural Anthropology.* Newbury Park, Calif.: Sage.
Bernard, H. Russell, and Sandy Ashton-Vouyoucalos
    1976   "Return Migration to Greece." *Journal of the Steward Anthropological Society* 8(1): 31–52.
Bernard, H. Russell, and Lambros Comitas
    1978   "Greek Return Migration." *Current Anthropology* 19(3): 658–659.
Bertaux, Daniel, and Martin Kohli
    1984   "The Life Story Approach: A Continental View." *Annual Review of Sociology* 10:215–237.
Bicalho, José Vitor
    1989   *Yes, Eu Sou Brazuca.* Governador Valadares, Minas Gerais: FUNSEC.
Biernacki, R., and D. Waldorf
    1981   "Snowball Sampling." *Sociological Methods and Research* 10:141–163.
Bishop, Katherine
    1990   "California Says Law on Aliens Spurs Job Bias." *New York Times*, January 12, pp. 1, 10.
Bleier, Elisabeth Ungar
    1988   "Impact of Venuzuela's Recession on Return Migration to Colombia: The Case of the Principal Urban Sending Area." In *When Borders Don't Divide: Labor Migration and Refugee Movements in the Americas*, Patricia R. Pessar, ed. New York: Center for Migration Studies, pp. 73–95.
Bogen, Elizabeth
    1987   *Immigration in New York City.* New York: Praeger.
Bohning, W. R.
    1984   *Studies in International Labour Migration.* London: Macmillan.
Bonacich, Edna, and John Modell
    1980   *The Economic Basis of Ethnic Solidarity: Small Business in the Japanese-American Community.* Berkeley: University of California Press.
Borjas, George
    1990   *Friends or Strangers: The Impact of Immigrants on the U.S. Economy.* New York: Basic Books.
Braga, Teodomiro
    1991   "Casuísmo no Lugar de Lei Que Não 'Pegou,'" *Jornal do Brasil*, August 11, p. 23.
Bray, David
    1984   "Economic Development: The Middle Class and International Migration in the Dominican Republic. *International Migration Review* 18(2): 217–236.

Brazilian Times
  1990   "Brasileiros Detidos em San Juan, Porto Rico, Denunciam Guia." May 25, pp. 1, 21.
Brenner, Leslie
  1991   "The New New York." *New York Woman*, April, pp. 68–81.
Brooke, James
  1990   "A Rising Sun Beckons, to Highly Paid Drudgery." *New York Times*, February 23, p. A4.
  1990   "A New Assault on Brazil's Woes." *New York Times*, March 15, pp. C1, C16.
  1990   "Brazilians' Belt Tightening: Anguish and Relief." *New York Times*, May 23, pp. A1, C9.
  1990   "Town That Uncle Sam Built, You Might Say." *New York Times*, November 30, p. 8.
  1990   "Economy of Brazil Still Ails." *New York Times*, December 3, pp. C1, C5.
  1990   "Free-Trade Perils a Free-Trade Zone in Brazil." *New York Times*, December 17, p. D10.
  1991   "Brazil Freezes All Wages and Prices."*New York Times*, February 1, p. 3.
  1991   "As Collor Completes First Year, Brazilians Write Off Their Highest Hopes." *New York Times*, March 14, p. 3.
  1991   "Brazil's Plans for Economy Drawing Fire." *New York Times*, May 6, pp. C1, C8.
  1991   "Brazil's Fresh Young President Has Grown Old Fast." *New York Times*, October 20, p. C4.
  1991   "In Brazil, Pessimism Starts to Keep Pace with Inflation Rate." *New York Times*, December 1, p. 11.
  1992   "Venuzuela's Policy for Brazil's Gold Miners: Bullets." *New York Times*, February 16, p. 9.
  1992   "High Wages Lure Brazilians to 'Bright Lights of France.'" *International Herald Tribune*, July 6, pp. 1, 6.
  1992   "Jobs Lure Japanese-Brazilians to Old World." *New York Times*, August 13, pp. 1, 7.
  1992   "Looting Brazil." *New York Times Magazine*, November 8, pp. 30–33, 42, 45, 70–71.
  1992   "Brazilians Fret over New Leader." *New York Times*, November 22, p. 12.
Brown, Diana
  1986   *Umbanda: Religion and Politics in Urban Brazil.* Ann Arbor, Mich.: UMI Research Press.
  n.d   "Faith, Curing and Ethnic Identity: Brazilian Umbanda in Newark's Ironbound." Unpublished manuscript.
Buchanan, Susan H.
  1979   "Haitian Women in New York City." *Migration Today* 7(4): 19–25, 39.

Caballero, J. Walberto
    1989   "Los Paraguayankis en la Mira." *ABC Revista*, November 26, pp. 4–5.
Cardoso, Eliana
    1992   "Inflation and Distribution in Brazil: The Recent Experience." Paper presented at the Columbia University Brazil Seminar, New York, February 20.
Castro, Mary Garcia
    1985   "Work versus Life: Colombian Women in New York." In *Women and Change in Latin America*, June Nash and Helen Safa, eds. South Hadley, Mass.: Bergin & Garvey, pp. 231–259.
    1991   "Latinos Nos EUA—Unindo Ámericas, Fazendo a Ámerica de la ou Perdendo A Nossa Ámerica?" *Travessia*, September–December, pp. 14–20.
Chavez, Leo R.
    1985   "Households, Migration and Labor Market Participation: The Adaptation of Mexicans to Life in the United States." *Urban Anthropology* 14(4): 301–346.
    1988   "Settlers and Sojourners: The Case of Mexicans in the United States." *Human Organization* 47 (2): 95–107.
    1989   "Households, Migration and Settlement: A Comparison of Undocumented Mexicans and Central Americans in the United States." Paper presented at the 88th annual meeting of the American Anthropological Association, Washington, D.C.
    1991   "Outside the Imagined Community: Undocumented Settlers and Experiences of Incorporation." *American Ethnologist* 18(2): 257–278.
    1992   *Shadowed Lives: Undocumented Immigrants in American Society.* New York: Harcourt Brace Jovanovich.
Chavez, Leo R., Estevan T. Flores, and Marta Lopez-Garza
    1989   "Here Today, Gone Tomorrow? Undocumented Settlers and Immigration Reform." *Human Organization* 49:193–205.
Christian, Shirley
    1990   "For U.S. Visa, Peruvians Try Lots of Ruses." *New York Times*, August 8, p. 7.
Clines, Francis X.
    1993   "As Shadowy Figures Slip In, U.S. Faces Queries on Aliens." *New York Times*, March 12, pp. A1, B5.
Cohen, Roger
    1988   "Brazil's Price Spiral Nears Hyperinflation." *Wall Street Journal*, December 8, pp. 1, 19.
Coleman, Sandy
    1990   "Quietly, Community of Brazilians Forms." *Boston Globe*, October 8, p. 10.
Colen, Shellee
    1990   "'Housekeeping' for the Green Card: West Indian Household Workers, the State, and Stratified Reproduction in New York." In *At Work in Homes: Household Workers in World Perspective*, Roger Sanjek and

Shellee Colen, eds. AES Monograph Series. Washington, D.C.: AES, pp. 89–118.

Cornelius, Wayne A.
1982 "Interviewing Undocumented Immigrants: Methodological Reflections Based on Fieldwork in Mexico and the U.S." *International Migration Review* 16(2): 378–411.

DaMatta, Roberto
1990 "Brazil: A Changing Nation and a Changeless Society? Further Notes on the Nature of the Brazilian Dilemma." In *Looking through the Kaleidoscope: Essays in Honor of Charles Wagley*. Florida Journal of Anthropology Special Publication no. 6, pp. 93–102.
1991 *Carnivals, Rogues, and Heroes, An Interpretation of the Brazilian Dilemma*. John Drury, trans. Notre Dame, Ind.: University of Notre Dame Press.

De Azevedo, Thales
1966 *Cultura e Situação Racial no Brasil*. Rio de Janeiro: Civilização Brasileira.

Decol, René
1991 "Dançarinas e Engraxates São Maioria." *O Estado de São Paulo*, June 12, p. 1.

Degler, Carl N.
1970 *Neither Black nor White: Slavery and Race Relations in Brazil and the United States*. New York: Macmillan.

De Moura Castro, Cláudio
1989 "What Is Happening in Brazilian Education?" In *Social Change in Brazil, 1945–1985*, Edmar L. Bacha and Herbert S. Klein, eds. Albuquerque: University of New Mexico Press, pp. 263–309.

Dines, Debora
1989 "GO-GOS: Os (As) Brasileiros (As) Entram na Dança do Dólor." *Ele Ela* 21(August): 88–92.

Durand, Jorge, and Douglas S. Massey
1992 "Mexican Migration to the United States: A Critical Review." *Latin American Research Review* 27(2): 3–42.

The Economist
1991 "Drunk, Not Sick: A Survey of Brazil." December 7.

Edmonston, Barry, Jeffrey S. Passel, and Frank D. Bean
1990 "Perceptions and Estimates of Undocumented Migration to the United States." In *Undocumented Migration to the United States: IRCA and the Experience of the 1980's*, Frank D. Bean, Barry Edmonston, and Jeffrey S. Passel, eds. Santa Monica, Calif., and Washington, D.C.: Rand Corporation and Urban Institute, pp. 11–31.

Ehrlich, Claudia
1989 "Beyond Black and White: A Perspective on Racial Attitudes of Paulistas in São Paulo and New York." Senior Project, Division of Social Studies, Bard College, Annandale-on-Hudson, N.Y.
1990 "Stereotypes of Racial Conflict." *Link Magazine* (November): 8–9.

Faria, Vilmar
  1989   "Changes in the Composition of Employment and the Structure of Oc-
          cupations." In *Social Change in Brazil, 1945–1985*, Edmar L. Bacha
          and Herbert S. Klein, eds. Albuquerque: University of New Mexico
          Press, pp. 141–170.
Feldman-Bianco, Bela
  1992   "Multiple Layers of Time and Space: The Construction of Class, Eth-
          nicity and Nationalism among Portuguese Immigrants." In *Towards a
          Transnational Perspective on Migration: Race, Class, Ethnicity and Na-
          tionalism Reconsidered*, Nina Glick-Schiller, Linda Basch, and Cristina
          Blanc-Szanton, eds. Annals of the New York Academy of Sciences
          645:145–174.
Ferreira, Sonia Nolasco
  1984   *Moreno Como Vocês.* Rio de Janeiro: Editora Record.
Finder, Alan
  1991   "All Walks of Life Now Converge in New York City's Jobless Lines."
          New York Times, April 20, pp. 1, 27.
Fisher, Maxine
  1980   *The Indians of New York City: A Study of Immigrants from India.*
          Columbia, Mo.: South Asia Books.
Fleisher, Michael L.
  1991   "Visions of Dallas: A Study of Senegalese Immigration to the United
          States." Unpublished honors thesis, Department of Anthropology, Uni-
          versity of Michigan.
Folha de São Paulo
  1989   "Consulado dos EUA no Rio Nega Visto a Mineiros." July 23, p. 4.
  1989   "Para Agências de Viagens, a Recusa Chega a 30% dos Pedidos de
          Minas." July 23, p. 4.
  1989   "Busca de Dólares Ja Atraiu 18% dos Habitantes da Cidade de Re-
          splendor." July 23.
  1989   "Sociólogo Vê Exportação de Mão-de-Obra." July 23.
  1990   "Cresce o Numero de Brasileiros Que Não Querem Mas Ser Brasi-
          leiros." March 18, p. C1.
  1990   "Estudo Mostra Como Vivem 90 Mil Brasileiros em Boston." June 19,
          p. C5.
  1991   "Mineiros e Portugueses Disputam a 'Baixada Fluminense' dos EUA."
          June 10, p. D1.
  1991   "Lana, 'Go-go' em Newark, Queria Falar Inglês." June 10, p. D3.
Foner, Nancy
  1983   *Jamaica's Migrants: A Comparative Analysis of the New York and Lon-
          don Experience.* New York: Center for Latin American and Caribbean
          Studies, New York University.
  1986   "Sex Roles and Sensibilities: Jamaican Women in New York and Lon-
          don." In *International Migration: The Female Experience*, Rita J.
          Simon and Caroline B. Brettell, eds. Totowa, N.J.: Rowman & Al-
          lanheld, pp. 133–151.

Foner, Nancy, ed.
    1987   *New Immigrants in New York City*. New York: Columbia University Press.

Fonseca, Danilo
    1991   "Brasileiros em Massachusetts." *A Gazeta*, October 14.

Foster, George
    1965   "Peasant Society and the Image of Limited Good." *American Anthropologist* 67:293–315.

Freedman, Marcia
    1983   "The Labor Market for Immigrants in New York City." *New York Affairs* 7:94–110.

Freitas, Osmar, Jr.
    1991   "Invasão Brazuca." *Isto É Senhor*, July 24, pp. 36–37.

French, Howard W.
    1992   "Caribbean Exodus: U.S. Is Magnet." *New York Times*, May 6, pp. 1, 12.

Freyre, Gilberto
    1964   *The Masters and the Slaves*. Rev. and abridged 2d ed., New York: Borzoi.

Gabaccia, Donna, ed.
    1992   *Seeking Common Ground: Multidisciplinary Studies of Immigrant Women in the United States*. Westport, Conn.: Praeger.

Garrison, Vivian, and Carol I. Weiss
    1979   "Dominican Family Networks and United States Immigration Policy: A Case Study." *International Migration Review* 13(2): 264–283.

Georges, Eugenia
    1990   *The Making of a Transnational Community: Migration, Development and Culture Change in the Dominican Republic*. New York: Columbia University Press.
    1992   "Gender, Class and Migration in the Dominican Republic: Women's Experiences in a Transnational Community." In *Towards a Transnational Perspective on Migration: Race, Class, Ethnicity and Nationalism Reconsidered*, Nina Glick-Schiller, Linda Basch, and Cristina Blanc-Szanton, eds. Annals of the New York Academy of Sciences 645:81–99.

Glick-Schiller, Nina, and Georges Fouron
    1990   " 'Everywhere We Go, We Are in Danger': Ti Manno and the Emergence of a Haitian Transnational Identity." *American Ethnologist* 17(2): 329–347.

Glick-Schiller, Nina, Linda Basch, and Cristina Blanc-Szanton, eds.
    1992   *Towards a Transnational Perspective on Migration: Race, Class, Ethnicity, and Nationalism Reconsidered*. Annals of the New York Academy of Sciences 645.

Gmelch, George
    1980   "Return Migration." *Annual Review of Anthropology* 9: 135–159. Palo Alto, Calif.: Annual Reviews.

Golden, Tim
  1991   "Mexicans Head North Despite Job Rules." *New York Times*, December 13, pp. 1, 28.
Gonzalez, David
  1991   "Mexican Migrants Crowd New York." *New York Times*, May 19, p. 13.
  1992   "What's the Problem with 'Hispanic'? Just Ask a 'Latino.'" *New York Times*, November 15, sec. 4, p. 6.
Goza, Franklin, and Patricia Simonik
  1992   "Who Are the Brazilian-Americans?" *The Brasilians*, no. 218 (June): 6.
Grant, Geraldine
  1981   *New Immigrants and Ethnicity: A Preliminary Research Report on Immigrants in Queens*. New York: Queens College Ethnic Studies Project.
Grasmuck, Sherri, and Patricia R. Pessar
  1992   *Between Two Islands: Dominican International Migration*. Berkeley: University of California Press.
Guadalupe, Hector Velez
  1992   "Take Your Pick." Letter to the Editor. *New York Times*, November 18, p. 16.
Guerra, Luis
  1990   "Acculturation and English Proficiency among Brazilians in New York." M.A. thesis, Hunter College–CUNY.
Guimarães, Norma
  1990   *Febre Brasil em Nova Iorque*. Belo Horizonte: Editora O Lutador.
Haines, David
  1986   "Vietnamese Refugee Women in the U.S. Labor Force: Continuity or Change?" In *International Migration: The Female Experience*, Rita J. Simon and Caroline B. Brettell, eds. Totowa, N.J.: Rowman & Allanheld, pp. 62–75.
Handelman, David
  1991   "The Japanning of Scarsdale." *New York Magazine*, April 29, pp. 40–45.
Harris, Marvin
  1964   *Patterns of Race in the Americas*. New York: Walker.
Hart, Daniela
  1991   "New Education Minister in Brazil Faces a Campus Crisis over Faculty Strike." *Chronicle of Higher Education*, September 18, pp. A43, A46.
  1992   "Brazil's Universities Come to the Aid of Deteriorating Public Schools." *Chronicle of Higher Education*, May 13, pp. A39–40.
Hasenbalg, Carlos A.
  1985   "Race and Socioeconomic Inequalities in Brazil." In *Race, Class and Power in Brazil*, Pierre-Michael Fontaine, ed. Los Angeles: University of California Press, pp. 25–41.
Hays, Constance L.
  1990   "Immigrants Strain Chinatown's Resources." *New York Times*, May 30, pp. B1, B4.

Hendricks, Glenn L.
  1975   "The Phenomenon of Migrant Illegality: The Case of Dominicans in
         New York." In *Adaptation of Migrants from the Caribbean in the Eu-
         ropean and American Metropolis*, Humphrey E. Lamur and John D.
         Speckmann, eds. Amsterdam: University of Amsterdam, pp. 130–142.
Hewlett, Sylvia Ann
  1980   *The Cruel Dilemmas of Development: Twentieth-Century Brazil*. New
         York: Basic Books.
Hoffman, Helga
  1989   "Poverty and Property in Brazil: What Is Changing?" In *Social Change
         in Brazil, 1945–1985*, Edmar L. Bacha and Herbert S. Klein, eds. Al-
         buquerque: University of New Mexico Press, pp. 197–231.
Holston, Mark
  1992   ". . . In Southern Brazil." *Américas* 44(1): 35–41.
Houstoun, Marion F.
  1983   "Aliens in Irregular Status in the United States: A Review of their Num-
         bers, Characteristics, and Role in the U.S. Labor Market." *Interna-
         tional Migration* 21(3): 372–414.
Howe, Marvine
  1990   "New Policy Aids Families of Aliens." *New York Times*, March 5, p.
         11.
Januzzi, Dea
  1990   "Terra do Tio Sam, Um Sonho Clandestino Que Pode Virar Pesadelo."
         O Estado de Minas, June 17, p. 16.
Johnston, David
  1992   "Border Crossings Near Old Record; U.S. to Crack Down." *New York
         Times*, February 9, pp. 1, 13.
Jones, Clayton
  1992   "Latin-Japanese Workers Feel Cool Welcome." *Christian Science Mon-
         itor*, February 27, p. 4.
Jornal do Brasil
  1989   "Governador 'Valadólares' Faz 20 Prédios de 12 Andares." July 16, p.
         8.
Kamm, Thomas
  1990   "Daily Inflation Struggle Obsesses Brazil." *Wall Street Journal*, January
         8, p. 1.
  1991   "Brazil's Swelling Wave of Emigration Reflects Gloom about Nation's
         Future." *Wall Street Journal*, October 1, p. 16.
Kepp, Michael
  1992   "Japanese-Brazilians Find Cold Cash in Ancestral Home." *Times of the
         Americas*, February 5, p. 3.
Kessner, Thomas, and Betty Boyd Caroli
  1981   *Today's Immigrants: Their Stories*. New York: Oxford University
         Press.
Kilborn, Peter T.
  1993   "Law Failed to Stem Illegal Immigration, Panel Says." *New York
         Times*, February 11, p. 16.

Kim, Illsoo
  1981   *New Urban Immigrants: The Korean Community in New York*. Princeton, N.J.: Princeton University Press.
Kinkead, Gwen
  1991   "A Reporter at Large. Chinatown—Part 1." *The New Yorker*, June 10, pp. 45–83.
Klor de Alva, J. Jorge
  1988   "Telling Hispanics Apart: Latino Sociocultural Diversity." In *The Hispanic Experience in the United States*, Edna Acosta-Belén and Barbara J. Sjostrom, eds. New York: Praeger, pp. 107–136.
Kottak, Conrad Phillip
  1990   *Prime Time Society: An Anthropological Analysis of Television and Culture*. Belmont, Calif.: Wadsworth.
  1990   "Cultural Contrasts in Prime Time Society: Brazil and the United States. In *Looking through the Kaleidoscope: Essays in Honor of Charles Wagley*. Florida Journal of Anthropology Special Publication no. 6, pp. 81–89.
Laguerre, Michel
  1984   *American Odyssey: Haitians in New York*. Ithaca, N.Y.: Cornell University Press.
Leeds, Mark
  1991   *Ethnic New York: A Complete Guide to the Many Faces and Cultures of New York*. Lincolnwood, Ill.: Passport Books.
Levine, Richard
  1990   "On the Sidewalks, Business Is Booming." *New York Times*, September 24, pp. B1, B3.
Lewin, Lauri
  1984   *Naked Is the Best Disguise*. New York: Morrow.
Lewin, Tamar
  1993   "A Law That's Often Ignored for Domestic Workers." *New York Times*, January 15, p. B8.
Lorch, Donatella
  1992   "Ethnic Niches Creating Jobs That Fuel Immigrant Growth." *New York Times*, January 12, pp. 1, 14.
Lucena, Rodolfo
  1990   "Aumenta Exôdo Para Japão e Estados Unidos." *Folha de São Paulo*, November 4, p. C3.
Malan, Pedro
  1990   "The Brazilian Economy: The Last Six Months and the Next Few Years." Paper presented at the Columbia University Brazil Seminar, New York, September 13.
Manchete
  1988   "Clandestinos." Vol. 1898. September 3.
Margolis, Maxine L.
  1984   *Mothers and Such: Views of American Women and Why They Changed*. Berkeley: University of California Press.

1989   "A New Ingredient in the Melting Pot: Brazilians in New York City."
        City and Society 3(2): 179–187.

1990   "An American in Governador Valadares." *The Brasilians*, no. 18 (September): 4.

1990   "From Mistress to Servant: Downward Mobility among Brazilians in
        New York City." *Urban Anthropology* 19(3): 215–231.

1992   "Women in International Migration: The Case of Brazilians in
        New York City." Conference Paper no. 66. Columbia University–New
        York University Consortium for Latin American and Caribbean
        Studies.

Margolis, Maxine L., and Marigene Arnold
    1992   "Turning the Tables? Male Strippers and the Gender Hierarchy in
            America." In *Sex and Gender Hierarchies*, Barbara D. Miller, ed. New
            York: Cambridge University Press, pp. 334–350.

Marshall, Adriana
    1987   "New Immigrants in New York's Economy." In *New Immigrants in
            New York City*, Nancy Foner, ed. New York: Columbia University
            Press, pp. 79–101.

    1988   "Emigration of Argentines to the United States." In *When Borders
            Don't Divide: Labor Migration and Refugee Movements in the Americas*, Patricia R. Pessar, ed. New York: Center for Migration Studies, pp.
            129–141.

Massey, Douglas S.
    1988   "Economic Development and International Migration in Comparative
            Perspective." *Population and Development Review* 14(3): 383–411.

Michaels, Julia
    1992   "*Dekasegi* Drawn by Promise of Jobs." *Christian Science Monitor*, February 27, p. 5.

Miller, Charlotte I.
    1979   "The Function of Middle-Class Extended Family Networks in Brazilian
            Urban Society." In *Brazil: Anthropological Perspectives*, Maxine L.
            Margolis and William E. Carter, eds. New York: Columbia University
            Press. pp. 305–316.

Miller, Judith
    1991   "Strangers at the Gate." *New York Times Magazine*, September 25, pp.
            32–37, 49, 80–81.

Miller, Richard
    1991   "Money Tree Image Lures Poor Brazilians to U.S." *Cape Cod Times*,
            July 28, pp. 1, 8.

    1991   "Lambada Night: 'I Just Feel Like I'm Home.'" *Cape Cod Times*, July
            29, pp. 1, 10.

Millman, Joel
    1992   "New Mex City." *New York Magazine*, September 7, pp. 36–43.

Mitchell, Alison
    1992   "Wary Recruits: Immigrants Vie for Day Jobs." *New York Times*, May
            26, pp. 1, B7.

Mydans, Seth
  1989 "Immigrants Face a Threat to Amnesty." *New York Times*, August 1, p. 1.
  1991 "More Mexicans Come to U.S. to Stay." *New York Times*, January 21, p. 14.
  1991 "Border Near San Diego Is Home to More Violence." *New York Times*, April 9, p. 20.
Nash, Nathaniel C.
  1991 "Amid Latin Growth, Brazil Falters." *New York Times*, September 28, pp. 17, 29.
  1992 "Brazil Leader Quits as His Trial Starts in Senate." *New York Times*, December 30, pp. 1, 8.
Newman, Katherine S.
  1989 *Falling from Grace: The Experience of Downward Mobility in the American Middle Class*. New York: Vintage Press.
News from Brazil
  1990 "Lost Angels." No. 41 (December). Los Angeles.
Novaes, Carlos Eduardo, and Paulo Perdigão
  1984 *A Travessia Americana*. São Paulo: Editora Atica.
O Globo
  1988 "Valadares com um Pé em Nova York." May 22, p. 12.
O'Neill, Molly
  1991 "Recession and Guilt Pare Dining Trade and Menus." *New York Times*, March 31, pp. 1, 20.
Paolozzi, Vitor
  1990 "NY Tem Lojas Brasileiras." *Folha de São Paulo*, November 4, p. C3.
Papademetriou, Demetrios G., and Nicholas DiMarzio
  1986 *Undocumented Aliens in the New York Metropolitan Area*. New York: Center for Migration Studies.
Parker, Richard G.
  1991 *Bodies, Pleasures and Passions: Sexual Culture in Contemporary Brazil*. Boston: Beacon Press.
Passel, Jeffrey S., and Karen A. Woodrow
  1984 "Geographic Distribution of Undocumented Immigrants: Estimates of Undocumented Aliens Counted in the 1980 Census by State." *International Migration Review* 18: 62–71.
Passell, Peter
  1990 "So Much for Assumptions about Immigrants and Jobs." *New York Times*, April 15, p. E4.
Pastore, José
  1982 *Inequality and Social Mobility in Brazil*. Madison: University of Wisconsin Press.
Patai, Daphne
  1988 *Brazilian Women Speak: Contemporary Life Stories*. New Brunswick, N.J.: Rutgers University Press.

Pear, Robert
  1991   "Wide Attack on Hiring of Illegal Aliens." *New York Times*, August 7,
         p. 8.
Pessar, Patricia R.
  1982   "The Role of Households in International Migration and the Case for
         U.S.-Bound Migration from the Dominican Republic." *International
         Migration Review* 16: 342–364.
  1985   "When the Birds of Passage Want to Roost: An Exploration of the Role
         of Gender in Dominican Settlement in the U.S." In *Women and Change
         in Latin America*, June Nash and Helen I. Safa, eds. South Hadley,
         Mass.: Bergin & Harvey, pp. 273–294.
Piazarollo, Silvio, and Instante Cia. Oba Estamos Vivos
  1989   "O Último A Sair Apague A Luz." Unpublished play, Governador Vala-
         dares, Minas Gerais.
Pinder, Jeanne B.
  1993   "Foreigners Find a Place in the Sun." New York Times, July 2, pp. D1,
         D5.
Piore, Michael J.
  1979   *Birds of Passage: Migrant Labor and Industrial Societies*. New York:
         Cambridge University Press.
  1986   "The Shifting Grounds for Migration." *Annals of the American Acad-
         emy of Political and Social Science* 485:23–33.
Portes, Alejandro
  1981   "Modes of Structural Incorporation and Present Theories of Migra-
         tion." In *Global Trends in Migration*, Mary M. Kritz, Charles B. Keely,
         and Silvano M. Tomasi, eds. Staten Island, N.Y.: Center for Migration
         Studies Press, pp. 179–298.
Portes, Alejandro, and Robert L. Bach
  1985   *Latin Journey: Cuban and Mexican Immigrants in the United States*.
         Berkeley: University of California Press.
Portes, Alejandro, and Rubén G. Rumbaut
  1990   *Immigrant America: A Portrait*. Berkeley: University of California
         Press.
Prieto, Yolanda
  1986   "Cuban Women and Work in the United States: A New Jersey Case
         Study." In *International Migration: The Female Experience*, Rita J.
         Simon and Caroline B. Brettell, eds. Totowa, N.J.: Rowman & Al-
         lanheld, pp. 95–112.
Ravo, Nick
  1992   " 'Quality' Topless Clubs Go for the Crowd in Pin Stripes." *New York
         Times*, April 15, pp. B1, B4.
Reimers, David
  1985   *Still the Golden Door*. New York: Columbia University Press.
Reveron, Derek
  1991   "A Little Piece of Brazil Grows in Miami." *Miami Herald*, May 6,
         p. 14.

Ribeiro, Gustavo Lins
    1991   "Brazilians, Uma Minoria Étnica Descoberta Por Uma Suspeita," *Correio Braziliense*, June 23.

Riding, Alan
    1988   "Caraguatay Journal: People Leave and the Dollars Arrive." *New York Times*, February 20, p. 5.
    1988   "Bourgeois Dreams of the Heady Days." *New York Times*, June 16, p. 6.
    1988   "Unfamiliar Feelings of Pessimism Overtake Brazil's Politics and Economy." *New York Times*, November 10, p. 8.
    1989   "Starting Over, the Ex-Peruvian Way." *New York Times*, January 21, p. 21.
    1989   "Aloof Giant, Brazil Warms to Neighbors." *New York Times*, February 21, p. 15.
    1992   "Bedfellows with Spain, Lisbon Won't Cuddle," *New York Times*, June 14, p. 13.
    1993   "Welcome or No, Foreigners Do Spain's Dirty Work." *New York Times*, February 17, p. 6.

Rieff, David
    1991   *Los Angeles: Capital of the Third World*. New York: Simon and Schuster.

Rimer, Sara
    1991   "New Immigrant Group Displays Its Enterprise." *New York Times*, September 16, p. 16.
    1992   "Crammed into Tiny, Illegal Rooms, Tenants at the Margins of Survival." *New York Times*, March 23, p. 7.
    1992   "For Flier Distributors, Peskiness Can Be a Virtue." *New York Times*, May 3, p. 22.

Rohter, Larry
    1989   "Soft Underbelly: Sneaking Mexicans (and Others) into U.S. Is Big Business." *New York Times*, June 20, p. 8.
    1992   "Dominicans Find a Back Door to New York in Puerto Rico." *New York Times*, December 13, p. 16.

Rollins, Judith
    1990   "Ideology and Servitude." In *At Work in Homes: Household Workers in World Perspective*, Roger Sanjek and Shellee Colen, eds. AES Monograph Series. Washington, D.C.: AES, pp. 74–88.

Roof, Wade Clark, and William McKinney
    1987   *American Mainline Religion: Its Changing Shape and Future*. New Brunswick, N.J.: Rutgers University Press.

Safa, Helen I.
    1988   "Migration and Identity: A Comparison of Puerto Rican and Cuban Migrants in the United States." In *The Hispanic Experience in the United States*, Edna Acosta-Belén and Barbara J. Sjostrom, eds. New York: Praeger, pp. 137–150.

Sanjek, Roger
    1990   "Urban Anthropology in the 1980s: A World View." *Annual Reviews of Anthropology* 19:151–186.

Santiago, Silviano
  1985   *Stella Manhattan*. Rio de Janeiro: Editora Nova Fronteira.
Sassen-Koob, Saskia
  1985   "Changing Composition and Labor Market Location of Hispanic Immigrants in New York City, 1960–1980." In *Hispanics in the U.S. Economy*, George Borjas and Marta Tienda, eds. New York: Academic Press, pp. 299–322.
  1986   "New York City: Economic Restructuring and Immigration." *Development and Change* 17:85–119.
  1989   "New York City's Informal Economy." In *The Informal Economy: Studies in Advanced and Less Developed Countries*, A. Portes, M. Castells, and L. Benton, eds. Baltimore: Johns Hopkins University Press, pp. 60–77.
Sassen, Saskia
  1988   *The Mobility of Labor and Capital*. New York: Cambridge University Press.
Scheper-Hughes, Nancy
  1992   *Death without Weeping: The Violence of Everyday Life in Brazil*. Berkeley: University of California Press.
Sekles, Flavia
  1992   "Dólares à Go-Go." *Veja*, September 9, pp. 68–71.
Seper, Jerry
  1992   "1986 Amnesty Law Cited in Immigration Increase." *Washington Times*, June 10, p. 7.
Shokeid, Moshe
  1988   *Children of Circumstances: Israeli Immigrants in New York*. Ithaca, N.Y.: Cornell University Press.
Simcox, David E.
  1986   "Illegal Immigration; Counting the Shadow Population." In *U.S. Immigration in the 1980s: Reappraisal and Reform*, David E. Simcox, ed. Boulder, Colo.: Westview Press, pp. 23–30.
Simon, Rita J., and Caroline B. Brettell, eds.
  1986   *International Migration: The Female Experience*. Totowa, N.J.: Rowman & Allanheld.
Simon, Rita J., and Margo Corona DeLey
  1986   "Undocumented Mexican Women: Their Work and Personal Experiences." In *International Migration: The Female Experience*, Rita J. Simon and Caroline B. Brettell, eds. Totowa, N.J.: Rowman & Allanheld, pp. 113–132.
Skidmore, Thomas E.
  1974   *Black into White*. New York: Oxford University Press.
  1990   "The Results of the Brazilian Presidential Election." ISIS: The Monthly Newsletter and Calendar of Events for the Brown University Community, January–February.
  1990   "Whatever Happened to Latin America?" Lecture delivered at Brown University, October 20.

Smith, Robert
    1991   "Mexican Migration from South-Central Mexico and Los Angeles to
            New York: The Formation of Mexican Labor Market Niches and Social
            Space in New York City." Paper presented at the meetings of the Latin
            American Studies Association, Washington, D.C.
    1992   "Mexican Immigrant Women in New York City's Informal Economy."
            Conference Paper no. 69. Columbia University–New York University
            Consortium for Latin American and Caribbean Studies.
Sontag, Deborah
    1993   "Increasingly, 2-Career Family Means Illegal Immigrant Help." *New
            York Times*, January 24, pp. 1, 32.
Stafford, Susan Buchanan
    1984   "Haitian Immigrant Women: A Cultural Perspective." *Anthropologica*
            26(2): 171–189.
    1987   "The Haitians: The Cultural Meaning of Race and Ethnicity." In *New
            Immigrants in New York City*, Nancy Foner, ed. New York: Columbia
            University Press, pp. 131–158.
Staub, Shalom
    1989   *Yemenis in New York*. Philadelphia: Balch Institute Press.
Stevenson, Richard W.
    1989   "U.S. Work Barrier to Illegal Aliens Doesn't Stop Them." *New York
            Times*, October 9, pp. 1, 13.
    1990   "Study Finds Mild Gain in Drive on Illegal Aliens." *New York Times*,
            April 21, p. 24.
    1990   "Fight Is Intensified on Fake Documents for Aliens." *New York Times*,
            August 4, p. 8.
Suro, Roberto
    1989   "1986 Amnesty Law Is Seen as Failing to Slow Alien Tide." *New York
            Times*, June 18, p. 1.
    1990   "Traffic in Fake Documents Is Blamed as Illegal Immigration Rises
            Anew." *New York Times*, November 26, p. 9.
    1991   "Your Tired, Your Poor, Your Masses Yearning to Be with Relatives."
            New York Times, January 6, p. C4.
    1992   "Boom in Fake Identity Cards for Aliens." *New York Times*, February
            19, p. 18.
United States Department of Commerce
    1990   *Census, Population, Housing*. CPH-L-90. Washington, D.C.: Bureau of
            the Census.
United States Immigration and Naturalization Service
    1985   *1984 Statistical Yearbook*. Washington, D.C.: U.S. Government Print-
            ing Office.
    1986   *1985 Statistical Yearbook*. Washington, D.C.: U.S. Government Print-
            ing Office.
    1987   *1986 Statistical Yearbook*. Washington, D.C.: U.S. Government Print-
            ing Office.
    1988   *1987 Statistical Yearbook*. Washington, D.C.: U.S. Government Print-
            ing Office.

1989   *1988 Statistical Yearbook.* Washington, D.C.: U.S. Government Printing Office.

1990   *1989 Statistical Yearbook.* Washington, D.C.: U.S. Government Printing Office.

1991   *1990 Statistical Yearbook.* Washington, D.C.: U.S. Government Printing Office.

1992   *1991 Statistical Yearbook.* Washington, D.C.: U.S. Government Printing Office.

Valla, Franz
1991   "O 'Abacaxi' da Pequena 'Máfia' Invisivel." *Folha do Brasil,* October 1, p. 5.

Veja
1988   "Os Brasileiros Vão à Luta: Bye-bye, Brasil." March 16, pp. 38–46.

1988   "Viagem Perdida." August 17, p. 49.

1988   "Fim Melancólico." August 24, pp. 38–39.

1990   "Um Atalho na Fila." May 9, pp. 48–49.

1990   "Brazucas de Boston." May 30, pp. 13–15.

1991   "A Febre dos Negócios na Flórida." January 2, pp. 50–55.

1991   "Nova Terra Prometida." January 2, pp. 56–58.

1991   "Cartão Vermelho de Saída." April 24, p. 73.

1991   "O Povo da Diáspora." August 7, pp. 36–41.

1991   "A Fuga dos Cérebros." August 7, p. 41.

1991   "De Olho na América." August 7, pp. 42–43.

1991   "Invasão à Brasileira." December 4, pp. 80–87.

1992   "O Jardim do Marajá da Dinda." September 9, pp. 16–25.

Vilella, Heloisa
1990   "Uma Sociedade Anonima." *Link Magazine,* November 9, pp. 12–16.

Wagley, Charles
1968   *The Latin American Tradition.* New York: Columbia University Press.

1971   *Introduction to Brazil.* 2d ed., New York: Columbia University Press.

Waldinger, Roger
1985   "Immigration and Industrial Change in the New York City Apparel Industry." In *Hispanics in the U.S. Economy,* George Borjas and Marta Tienda, eds. New York: Academic Press, pp. 323–349.

1986   *Through the Eye of the Needle: Immigrants and Enterprise in New York's Garment Trade.* New York: New York University Press.

Warren, Robert
1990   "Annual Estimates of Nonimmigrant Overstays in the United States: 1985–1988." In *Undocumented Migration to the United States: IRCA and the Experience of the 1980's,* Frank D. Bean, Barry Edmonston, and Jeffrey S. Passel, eds. Santa Monica, Calif., and Washington, D.C.: Rand Corporation and Urban Institute, pp. 77–110.

Weisman, Steven R.
1991   "In Japan, Bias Is an Obstacle Even for the Ethnic Japanese." *New York Times,* November 13, pp. 1, 8.

Williams, Peter H.
1990   *America's Religions: Traditions and Cultures.* New York: Macmillan.

Wilson, Kenneth L., and Alejandro Portes
   1980   "Ethnic Enclaves: A Comparison of the Cuban and Black Experiences
           in Miami." *American Journal of Sociology* 88(2): 295–319.
Wong, Bernard
   1982   *Chinatown: Economic Adaptation and Ethnic Identity of the Chinese.*
           New York: Holt, Rinehart.
Wood, Charles, and José Alberto Magno de Carvalho
   1988   *The Demography of Inequality in Brazil.* New York: Cambridge Uni-
           versity Press.
Woodrow, Karen A., and Jeffrey S. Passel
   1990   "Post-IRCA Undocumented Immigration to the United States: An As-
           sessment Based on the June 1988 CPS." In *Undocumented Migration to
           the United States: IRCA and the Experience of the 1980's*, Frank D.
           Bean, Barry Edmonston, and Jeffrey S. Passel, eds. Santa Monica,
           Calif., and Washington, D.C.: Rand Corporation and Urban Institute,
           pp. 33–75.
Yinger, J. Milton
   1957   *Religion, Society and the Individual.* New York: Macmillan.
Yoshida, Ernesto K.
   1990   "Brasileiros 'Dekassequis' Sofrem Mas Querem a Familia no Japão."
           Folha de São Paulo, March 25, p. C3.